We Must Take Charge

Our Schools and Our Future

Chester E. Finn, Jr.

The Free Press
A Division of Macmillan, Inc.
NEW YORK

Maxwell Macmillan Canada
TORONTO

Maxwell Macmillan International
NEW YORK   OXFORD   SINGAPORE   SYDNEY

The Free Press
A Division of Macmillan, Inc.
866 Third Avenue, New York, N. Y. 10022

Maxwell Macmillan Canada, Inc.
1200 Eglinton Avenue East
Suite 200
Don Mills, Ontario M3C 3N1

Macmillan, Inc. is part of the Maxwell Communication Group of Companies.

First Free Press Paperback Edition 1993

Printed in the United States of America

printing number

1 2 3 4 5 6 7 8 9 10

Library of Congress Cataloging-in-Publication Data

Finn, Chester E.
    We must take charge: our schools and our future/Chester E. Finn, Jr.
        p.   cm.
    Includes bibliographical references (p.   ) and index.
    ISBN 0–02–910276–6
    1. Educational change—United States.   2. Education—United States—Aims and objectives.   3. Educational planning—United States.   I. Title.
LA217.2.F56   1991
370'.973—dc20   91–6526

The author and the publisher gratefully acknowledge permission to reprint excerpts from the following material:

Bruce Babbitt, "Babbitt: Shared Culture Is Vital," *Education Week*, January 25, 1989, sect. A.

Robert J. Barnet, "Reflections," *The New Yorker*, July 16, 1990, p. 48.

John Bishop, "The Productivity Consequences of What Is Learned in High School," unpublished paper presented at Allied Social Science Meeting, New York, December 28, 1988, pp. 29–30.

H. Dickson Corbett and Bruce L. Wilson, "Unintended and Unwelcome: The Local Impact of State Testing," unpublished paper presented at the Annual Meeting of the American Educational Research Association, Boston, April 16, 1990, pp. 6–7.

Mihaly Csikszentmihalyi, "Literacy and Intrinsic Motivation." Reprinted by permission of *Daedalus*, Journal of the American Academy of Arts and Sciences, "Literacy in America," Spring 1990, vol. 199/2: 123, 131.

Jaime Escalante and Jack Dirmann, "The Jaime Escalante Math Program," *Journal of Negro Education*, Summer 1990, pp. 415–418.

Chester E. Finn, Jr., "A Nation Still at Risk," *Commentary*, May 1989, by permission of Commentary Magazine.

Chester E. Finn, Jr., "Narcissus Goes to School," *Commentary*, June 1990, by permission of Commentary Magazine.

Chester E. Finn, Jr., "Ten Tentative Truths," unpublished paper presented at a Conference of the Center of the American Experiment, St. Paul, MN, April 4, 1990.

Chester E. Finn, Jr., "The Political Process of Education Reform," unpublished paper written for the National Governors' Association, April 25, 1990.

Susan Fuhrman, "Legislatures and Educational Policy," unpublished paper presented at the Eagleton Institute of Politics Symposium, Williamsburg, VA, April 27–29, 1990, p. 26.

B. Honig, *Last Chance for Our Children*, pp. 4–5, 56–58, 76–77. © 1987 by Louis Honig. Reprinted with permission of Addison-Wesley Publishing Co., Inc., Reading, MA.

Barbara Kahn, "Beliefs and Achievement: A Study of Black, White and Hispanic Children," *Child Development*, vol. 60, no. 2 (1990): 520.

Jane Kramer, "Letter from Germany," *The New Yorker*, June 18, 1990. Reprinted by permission; © 1990 Jane Kramer. Originally in The New Yorker.

Daniel P. Moynihan, "Towards a Post-Industrial Social Policy," *The Public Interest*, Summer 1989, pp. 16–27.

Ferdinand Protzman, "A Worry in West Germany: Indolence in East Germany," *The New York Times*, April 4, 1990. Copyright © 1990 by The New York Times. Reprinted by permission.

Harold Stevenson, "The Asian Advantage: The Case of Mathematics," *American Educator*, Summer 1987, p. 30.

Roberto Suro, "Cavazos Criticizes Hispanic Parents on Schooling," *The New York Times*, April 11, 1990. Copyright © 1990 by The New York Times. Reprinted by permission.

Tommy Tomlinson, "Class Size and Public Policy: Politics and Panaceas," *Educational Policy*, September 1989, pp. 262–264.

Fred Whitehead, Letter to Connie Moritz, April 18, 1989.

For those great American teachers who beat the odds,
and the children whose lives they touch

Contents

PART III
Taking Charge: Revolutionizing Education from the Outside In   235

Acknowledgments

When Diane Ravitch and I launched the Educational Excellence Network almost a decade ago, we resolved to speak the truth about American education. In books, articles, speeches, conferences and seminars, as well as in the Network's monthly *News & Views*, we have striven to honor that commitment.

In the same spirit, this book is as honest as I can make it, notwithstanding that candor in this field is often unpopular and sometimes painful. These pages are the product of a quarter century's observation and participation in the enterprise of American education and—as will be evident—of mounting discontent with it and upwelling impatience at the fecklessness of our efforts to set it right.

Since leaving the U.S. Department of Education in late 1988, I have tried, initially in articles and addresses, to examine what has gone awry and why our "reforms" are accomplishing so little. Peter J. Dougherty, senior editor at The Free Press, heard one of those talks and suggested that perhaps a book lurked therein. Diane Ravitch nudged me in the same direction. So did my wife, Renu Virmani, whose professional field of cardio-vascular pathology is about as far distant as one can get but whose instincts about education (and about me) are keen indeed.

The small but terrific staff of the Educational Excellence Network kept the ship on course while I hunkered down in the hold with my laptop. Deputy director John P. Crisp, Jr. was a splendid helmsman during those months of heavy weather—as he has been before and since. Andrew Forsaith added to his regular duties the burden of serving as my chief research aide and, in his tireless, quiet way, proved indispensable to this project. Summer intern Mary C. Greenfield, a student at Barnard College, also pitched into the unromantic labors of a research assistant with rare perspicacity and dedication.

Network research associates Matthew Gandal and Theodor Rebarber lent a hand with the book, too, while lightening my load by carrying out their other assignments with independence and alacrity. Joyce Wilson, as always, was a cheerful and efficient bridge between the Network office and the world outside. Mary Ellen Hanssen kept my work-life organized, shielded my writing time, and did heroic service on the word processor, while channelling a small flood of articles about late-breaking developments that bore on the book. To all of them, I owe a great debt.

Peter Dougherty was more than early catalyst. He proved himself a wise counsellor, discerning (and speedy) editor and reliable ally as well. Two long-time colleagues and friends also agreed to read the manuscript in draft: Mitchell B. Pearlstein, a fellow alumnus of the Education Department, now president of the Minneapolis-based Center of the American Experiment; and Diane S. Ravitch, who manages to be my partner, mentor, confidant, advisor and occasional co-author, all the while maintaining an extraordinary schedule of her own and keeping intact a wry sense of humor that is all too scarce in this solemn and sometimes sanctimonious field. The rituals of book acknowledgments oblige me to note that neither Peter, Mitch nor Diane is to be blamed for any mistakes made herein, but they deserve much credit for any good this volume may do.

I have borrowed and adapted ideas and data from many sources and have tried conscientiously to record these in the footnotes. Special mention must be made, though, of professors Harold W. Stevenson of the University of Michigan and John H. Bishop of Cornell University, whose inspired research and keen insights were indispensable to me, especially in the preparation of chapters 6 and 7.

In the domain of public policies bearing on education, I am indebted to more people than I can name. I want, however, to single out Lamar Alexander and Bill Bennett, both of whom have repeatedly provided me with extraordinary first-hand experience, as well as with their counsel, their friendship and the examples of their courage.

The Free Press has been terrific throughout. In addition to Peter Dougherty, I have especially benefitted from the efforts of Eileen DeWald, Jim Connor, Suzanne Herz, ace copy-editor Sue Llewellyn and, of course, Erwin A. Glikes.

Vanderbilt University has been a congenial home for the Educational Excellence Network as well as for a professor whose views sometimes put him at odds with much of his profession. I am particularly grateful to Chancellor Joe B. Wyatt and Vice Chancellor Jeff R. Carr, as well as to Clifford S. Russell and his associates at the Vanderbilt Institute for Public Policy Studies, under whose organizational roof the Network comfortably dwells.

The Network's 1600 members help to underwrite it, as do contributors, sponsors and friends too numerous to list. But there wouldn't even be an Excellence Network without "core" support provided by the Lynde and Harry Bradley Foundation, the John M. Olin Foundation and the Smith-Richardson Foundation, philanthropic organizations whose virtues include a keen interest in the improvement of American education, unswerving devotion to the truth, and respect for the risky, old-fashioned enterprise of book-writing.

That Renu, Arti and Aloke have been through this before didn't make it much easier when "Dad's book" pressed against the pleasures and regimens of family life and, some weeks, practically removed Dad from sight. Rather than griping, however, they rooted for me, as well as freeing many hours by quietly hefting my parts of the household duties as well as their own. Never has an author had a more supportive and loving family.

In the back of my mind throughout this undertaking, as well as in a photograph on the shelf before my eyes, has been the image of my late mother, Phyllis Kessel Finn, who exemplified better than anyone I have known the character, temperament and values we yearn for all young Americans to acquire en route to adulthood, as well as the intellectual qualities we associate with a good education. If this book moves even a few adults to lead a few more girls and boys in those directions, it will do further honor to her memory.

December 1990

Introduction
Reform Is Not Enough

If a nation expects to be ignorant and free, in a state of civilization, it expects what never was and never will be.
—Thomas Jefferson, 1816

The wide-body aircraft I boarded in Minneapolis that spring afternoon in 1990 was going on to Frankfurt after a stop in Boston. I intended to review my notes for the talk I was to give that evening near Copley Square, but some of those who had boarded for the long haul to Germany were already starting to party.

The quartet in the row behind me was hard to ignore, boisterous Yuppies downing Bloody Marys and regaling one another with plans for the good times they would have tooling around the Continent in the Mercedes they had reserved for their vacation. As I eavesdropped, this exchange ensued:

"Does it get earlier or later as we fly west?"

"I dunno. I never crossed the Pacific Ocean before."

One of their pals eventually got things more or less straightened out, but it was evident that at least two of these cheerful, prosperous "thirty-somethings" had clambered onto the Frankfurt flight without the remotest notion of which direction they were headed or what ocean lay between them and the nearest autobahn.

Such ignorance caused them no apparent discomfort. These obviously weren't things they needed to know to get through their European sojourn, much less their lives. Multiply their condition by tens of millions of people, however, and apply it to the forty-eight or fifty weeks a year most Americans aren't on vacation, and it causes grave malfunctions throughout the society. Eventually it causes individual hardship as well.

This book is about ignorance, about discomfort, and about education. I want it to alarm you, to rouse you to anger at our children's empty-headedness and the costs it levies on them and us. I hope that when you put this volume down, you will want to take action, beginning with the assertion of control over a system that to all intents and purposes now runs itself—and is fast running itself into the ground, carrying our future along with it. Despite all the talk of reform, despite the investment of tens of billions of extra dollars, public education in the United States is still a failure: It is to our society what the Soviet economy is to theirs.

The shortcomings of American education do not stem from malevolence—I've yet to meet a teacher or principal who wants anything but the best for children—or from some perverse love of ignorance. Rather, so far as I can tell, they arise from the maintenance of archaic practices (such as the abbreviated school year typical of an agrarian society), dysfunctional customs (such as the insistence that teachers be paid uniformly regardless of performance), and cumbersome governance arrangements (such as entrusting decisions to fifteen thousand local school boards at a time when the entire nation is imperiled) and from strongly held but sadly mistaken ideas and beliefs (such as the view that boosting a child's self-esteem is more important than ensuring that he or she acquires intellectual skills and knowledge).

Mindful that the sincere pursuit of a wrong conviction can do more damage than half-hearted devotion to a sound one, I contend that many of the ideas that animate American education are flawed and that carrying them out more efficiently won't improve—and could well worsen—our plight.

Because dubious notions thrive within the education profession, I mistrust reform schemes that seek to enhance only its power. This book is partly about power, to be sure, but most of the empowering we need has to do with parents, voters, and taxpayers; with community leaders and state officials; with businessmen and neighborhood associations; with grandparents, employers, working people, and ordinary citizens. It has to do with people like yourself—people who may not have realized the gravity of the problem, who didn't think it applied to them, or who never supposed they had a right to meddle in educational affairs.

We *all* have the right to meddle here, to turn ourselves into informed, demanding, persnickety consumers of perhaps the single most valuable product of any society. The Europe-bound Yuppies on my flight, let's remember, would never settle for an ill-fitted suit, an overcooked salmon fillet, an out-of-tune car, or a shortage of hot water in the showers of their health club. They would make a fuss until the problem was solved. Yet they, and millions of other young Americans, have been nurtured on a diet of educational junk food. They bought an educational car that turned out to be a lemon. It is time we see it for what it is—and send it back to be fixed, however fundamental the reconstruction that's required. It is time, above all, to know that we have the right to do this—the right, the power, and the obligation.

If this sounds like another plea for "civilian control" of education, I mean it to. In fact, it's more like a call to arms. But that's just the beginning; mistaken ideas and harmful practices dwell outside the schools, too. We also have to gird ourselves for other changes: in our beliefs about how we are doing, in some of our cultural assumptions and institutional habits, perhaps above all in our sense of who is responsible for what.

Nor is this ambitious agenda confined to the troubled precincts of the inner cities. The passengers on that Frankfurt flight hailed from the great American middle class. Tens of thousands of schools in quiet towns and verdant suburbs are not doing half so well as their clients and proprietors suppose. Our average graduates, despite reasonably stable and comfortable surroundings, are sadly underprepared for the world they will inhabit.

Yet they and their parents may not know that. Family by family and school by school, most Americans think their own education is okay, even as they concede that the system as a whole is wanting. This schizophrenia may be the most pernicious problem of all.

That the nation is "at risk" is no news—we've been inundated for almost a decade by solemn declarations of this fact. Of late we've even heard it at international summit meetings and bilateral trade negotiations. Normally reticent Japanese officials, for example, have told their U.S. counterparts that if we really want to reduce our huge trade deficit with Tokyo, we're going to have to do something about our education system.[1] A panel of economists, including Nobel laureates Paul Samuelson and Milton Friedman, asked recently by Robert MacNeil if our confrontation with Iraq would pose an economic problem for the United States, downplayed the implications of this massive military action and instead described the education system as our real problem.

Perhaps we've heard it too often and are becoming inured. When you live with a problem long enough, you start to take it for granted. The comedian Buddy Hackett says that until he moved out of his mother's house at the age of twenty-one he didn't realize there was such a thing as not having heartburn. It's difficult, after so many glum commentaries on American education, to believe it need not be this way. Yet, as I try to show in the chapters that follow, it could be very different. It doesn't always have to cause pain behind the breastbone.

We could live instead in a land where every young adult meets a high standard of skills and knowledge. Where we conduct our affairs on the basis of shared information and understanding. Where parents know how well their children and schools are doing. Where policy-makers decide what the goals are, expert educators select effective ways to reach them, and families choose the schools that work best for their daughters and sons. Where everyone engaged in education is accountable for the results—and rewarded accordingly. Where schools are good at what they do and aren't expected to do things they're not good at. Where teaching promotes reason, which oils the wheels of our democracy and fosters both stability and civility.

We could live in such a land. In these pages we will visit it—after negotiating the minefields and jungles that today keep us out. If we get a grip on our ideas about education and put better ones into practice, someday we will dwell there. When we do, societal heartburn will diminish along with individual discomfort.

A friend from New York recently recalled his first visit to Paris:

As I was roaming around the neighborhoods one Sunday evening, something struck me as odd. Little kids, eight and nine years old, were outdoors playing without the hawklike supervision we parents train on kids in New York. I was incredulous. Where were the drug dealers? The sex criminals? The drive-by gunmen? At first I was afraid for these little French kids, until I realized they were not threatened as they would have been in Manhattan. This was French society speaking, with its norms and values, its mores and customs. It occurred to me that *all* Parisians were the beneficiaries of the civility which kept these city streets safe.

All Americans, too, would benefit from an education system that produced informed citizens. (The streets would probably be safer also.) Education isn't just a service we obtain for our own daughters and sons and grandchildren. It is a public good, after defense perhaps our most important form of common provision and, in a sense, itself a defense against the ills that plague us at home. It has incalculable influence on the quality of our social relationships, the vitality of our culture, the strength of our economy, the comfort we feel in our communities and the wisdom of our government decisions. The better our education system, the better our public and private lives become. But reciprocity is called for. Institutions like schools don't just work for us. We have to struggle for them—and sometimes *with* them. We have to invest money, to be sure, but we also owe them our attention, our energy, and some of our passion. To be part of any society is to be engaged with its mechanisms of teaching and learning. To ensure the soundness of those mechanisms is to take a giant step toward realizing the society we dream of inhabiting. To take charge of education, therefore, is to take charge of our future—to look it in the eye without blinking.

I

❦

A Nation Still At Risk

After two centuries of progress, we are stagnant. . . . No modern nation can long afford to allow so many of its sons and daughters to emerge into adulthood ignorant and unskilled. The status quo is a guarantee of mediocrity, social decay and national decline.
—President George Bush, Charlottesville, Virginia, September 28, 1989

On the NBC television news one evening in late August 1990, Tom Brokaw interviewed a U.S. marine, perspiring in the Arabian desert where he had been sent as part of the American response to Iraq's invasion of Kuwait. What had he known about Saudi Arabia before getting there, the anchorman asked. "I never even knew it existed," the young serviceman replied with a grin.

Less than a year earlier, as totalitarian regimes crumbled in Eastern Europe, the *Washington Post* recounted the frustration of American high school teachers who were striving to impress on their students the significance of these events. Not many youngsters were interested; few found them noteworthy; fewer still possessed the background knowledge against which to interpret them. "They don't understand what communism is in the first place," observed one California teacher. "So when you say it's the death of communism, they don't know what you're talking about." In an honors government class in Texas, a pupil asked, "What is this talk of satellites? I'm confused. Are we talking about satellite dishes or what?"[1]

Like the Yuppies en route to Germany, neither the sweating marine near the Persian Gulf nor the muddled students in our classrooms were perceptibly bothered by the gaps in their knowledge. They were as affable and easygoing as most of their age-mates, with the pleasant personalities, helpful dispositions, and laid-back temperaments that often impress foreign visitors to our schools. Nor was anything wrong with their brains. People are born ignorant, but not stupid. These young people, like their peers in other lands, have the capacity to absorb, retain, and use great gobs of information. But theirs is an underutilized capacity. Their batteries have not been fully charged. Nobody has obliged them to learn much, and clearly they have not chosen to do so on their own. After eighteen or twenty years, mostly spent in school, there is much that they should know.

As the last decade of the millennium began, American education was choking on the mediocrity of which George Bush spoke in Charlottesville. For years we had been striving to improve it, and by the time he and the governors organized their education "summit" in late 1989, we were spending 29 percent more "real" dollars per pupil in our public schools than we had when he was first elected vice president. Yet we had little to show for this infusion of attention, energy, and money. Test scores were essentially flat. Graduation rates were up only a bit. The gauges that the National Commission on Excellence in Education considered when declaring us a "nation at risk" in 1983 had barely moved.

We cannot yet know whether the United States will whip itself into better shape during the 1990s. The stern regimen we need to set ourselves reaches far beyond the schools, and we may not have the self-discipline and stamina to stick with it. Even recognizing how flabby we've become has taken too long.

Yet the first step toward solving a problem is to acknowledge and define it. And it was in the 1980s, history will surely record, that Americans came to see that our education system was not serving the nation satisfactorily. It was also in the eighties that we changed the criteria by which such judgments are made.

For as long as anyone could remember, we had gauged the quality of schools by their facilities and resources, their programs and activities, the credentials of their teachers, the honors courses they offered, and the number of books on their library shelves. A good school was one with impressive plans, ample resources, an enthusiastic staff, and a lot going on. A good education was what happened to children in such a school.

That began to change as we came to see the miserly dividends we received from our investments. We keep boosting the resources, yet the children do not learn more. Indeed, by many measures they learn less. We observed that no reliable link joins inputs to outcomes. And we admitted that only outcomes truly matter.

Not a harmonious or uniform shift, it was messy and uneven

and is still incomplete. Yet nothing could be more basic than to transform what we mean by *educated* from a calculus of effort to an insistence on result.[2]

Former New York school administrator Sy Fliegel offers a homey example of this revolution in the statement: "I taught my son to swim, but every time he gets in the water he sinks to the bottom." Traditional concepts of education permitted us to get by with this. It was enough to say "I taught it," meaning one had made a reasonable attempt to impart knowledge and skills to one's pupils. It wasn't necessary to prove that they had actually learned anything.

Today we want evidence of learning, not just of teaching. We look at outcomes. Unsatisfactory results were what led the Excellence Commission in 1983 to exclaim that we were threatened by a "rising tide of mediocrity." Unsatisfactory results were what Bush and the governors still criticized in 1989 and 1990.

In part 1 we explore that profound transformation in emphasis and examine the efforts we have made thus far to set matters right. We also consider changes in the zeitgeist that have made this undertaking far harder; review some of the persistent evidence that, judged by its outcomes, American education remains woefully inadequate; and witness the radicalism that had begun to fertilize the reform movement by 1990, as we saw how meager was the yield from our plantings thus far.

1

♏

Asleep at the Wheel
A Society Loses Its Mind

Large proportions, perhaps more than half, of our elementary, middle-, and high-school students are unable to demonstrate competency in challenging subject matter in English, mathematics, science, history, and geography. Further, even fewer appear to be able to use their minds well.

—National Assessment of Educational Progress, September 1990

We stand today at one of history's intersections, where the well-marked path our education system followed for many years crosses half-blazed trails that lead into the future. Some of these veer off in sharply divergent directions; others hold to more familiar headings. Momentous choices await, and at the intersection we find much milling about and confused activity unaccompanied by any evidence of progress. As we pause to get our bearings, readying ourselves for the big decisions we face, it is helpful to review the major landmarks along the routes we have already traveled and the paths we chose at earlier crossroads. After all, they are what brought us to our present situation.

THE AGE OF ACCESS

From World War II until the late 1970s, the primary dynamic of American education was a crusade to expand access for the entire population. This effort had five major elements:

First we set out to provide everyone with secondary as well as primary schooling. Despite the swarms of children pouring into American classrooms from the postwar baby boom, state compulsory attendance laws were amended to require everyone to go to school for more years than we had judged sufficient in the 1930s and 1940s. Though statutes vary, the most common pattern now is one in which mandatory schooling starts at six and continues until at least sixteen (in some jurisdictions, seventeen or even eighteen). Thirty-seven states also require that kindergarten be offered, and in eleven of these the children—usually five-year-olds—are obliged to attend. Publicly provided education for four-year-olds is spreading too.

Nowhere is high-school completion obligatory, but it is available to all at no cost. So thoroughly have our norms changed that, where once we lauded the graduate for uncommon pluck, today we view as aberrant those who leave school without completing the full twelve grades.

Second, we built the largest and most accessible college and university system in the world. Hard on the heels of universal secondary education, Americans embraced the proposition that everyone wanting higher education should be able to obtain that too. Though college is rarely free, hundreds of state-subsidized institutions charge modest tuitions, and financial aid programs offer further help to needy students. Admission—somewhere—is assured.

Third, we strove to remove racial and ethnic barriers throughout the education system. The essential step was the Supreme Court's 1954 ruling that public schools could no longer be segregated. Since then, myriad policies and programs have been adopted, and court decisions rendered, in an effort to purge discrimination and inequality from our schools and colleges.

Fourth, we developed many extra services for children from deprived circumstances: before entering school (for example, the well-known Head Start program), within the schools, at the college level, even in graduate and professional schools. These typically deploy additional resources and services to strengthen the performance of such youngsters. The watershed year was 1965, when the federal government launched several large compensatory education programs that endure today.

Fifth, we widened educational opportunities for handicapped children and sought also to end discrimination on the basis of physical and mental disability. We did much the same for immigrant youngsters and others whose native language is not English and who may therefore need special help to make satisfactory progress.

Although we won unconditional victory on none of these fronts, and obstacles remain, widening and paving the paths of access to school and college was the premier mission of American education for more than three decades. Its political foundation comprised the prevailing "liberal consensus" that ruled the education profession, the powerful moral imperative of the civil rights movement, the inherent disposition toward equality of an increasingly activist federal judiciary, a sense of the limitlessness of the "Great Society" to be created by an energized federal government, sustained economic prosperity, a strong belief in American preeminence on the world scene, and the confidence that no meaningful distinction existed between more and better education.[1]

A brief challenge to the prevailing ethos arose in the 1950s, first from the pens and tongues of such commentators as Arthur Bestor, Robert Maynard Hutchins, Jacques Barzun, and Admiral Hyman Rickover, who wrote critical books and articles and founded a new organization, the Council for Basic Education, out of the conviction that greater attention must be given to the content of academic learning in American schools. "On almost every count," Bestor wrote in 1953, in words that remain apt almost four decades later,

> there is general dissatisfaction with the results of the twelve years of education currently provided by most of our public schools.
> . . . Businessmen are dismayed at the deficiencies in reading, writing, arithmetic and general knowledge displayed by the high school and college graduates they employ. Parents are alarmed at the educational handicaps under which their children are obliged to labor as they enter upon the serious business of life.[2]

These educational "essentialists," as some have termed them, gained influential allies after the Soviet Union launched its first *Sputnik* space satellite in 1957. Among the anxieties triggered by that feat was the fear that American education had become inferior, especially in math, science, and technology. This prompted a number of federal programs designed to improve school curricula and teacher preparation, which had several lasting effects. They persuaded many Americans that the country's well-being is linked to the quality of its education system; they legitimized federal efforts to boost that system's performance; and they identified curricular content as one lever to manipulate. Yet these changes of the late 1950s had little chance to deflect the egalitarian thrust of American education. Indeed, they had barely commenced when we "discovered" poverty and embarked on a major campaign to devise strategies to overcome its effects, perhaps one day even to eradicate it.

The War on Poverty and the loosely related goal of racial desegrega-
tion dominated reform efforts through the 1960s. By the end of that
decade, however, two small seeds had been planted that would
later germinate into tall policy trees. First, at the behest of U.S. Education Commissioner Francis Keppel, the eminent psychologist Ralph
Tyler, and a few other farsighted individuals, the federal government
decided to start—and, after many compromises, won the assent of
the education community to implement—a "national assessment"
program by which reliable data on actual learning levels could be
gathered. "Economic reports existed on family needs," Keppel wrote
in 1966,

> but no data existed to supply similar facts on the quality and
> condition of what children learned. The nation could find out
> about school buildings or discover how many years children stay
> in school; it had no satisfactory way of assessing whether the
> time spent in school was effective.[3]

The new assessment scheme would begin to fill that void. Instead
of construing education quality in terms of services provided and
classroom days endured, we would ascertain what our children
had actually kept in their heads.

Second, in 1966 the U.S. Office of Education quietly published
what would in time be seen as a blockbuster study by James S.
Coleman and his associates. Its title was *Equality of Educational
Opportunity*, and it dealt mainly with the prevailing "equity" issues
of the day. Among its many findings, however, was a profound challenge to the conventional wisdom: Coleman reported that student
achievement did *not* vary from school to school in close relation to
the resources present in those schools.[4] The implication, of course,
was that boosting school inputs did not reliably lead to stronger
education outcomes, at least when the latter are defined in terms
of pupil learning. The insight was portentous.[5] At the time, however,
it drew only a fraction of the attention it deserved, in large measure
because federal officials who sensed its power and shunned controversy accompanied the bulky technical report with a summary that
masked its key findings.

Though there was no widespread anxiety about the learning
achievements of middle-class children, the education community—
inspired by the likes of Paul Goodman, Ivan Illich, and John Holt—
grew restive about what was going on in its schools and colleges.
During the 1960s and 1970s, many educators concluded that these
were stodgy, old-fashioned places, rigid and unresponsive to student

needs. Such anxieties were deepened by the protests that swept U.S. campuses between 1968 and 1973 and by the countercultural crusade of the intelligentsia. It was a time, wrote the late Lawrence A. Cremin, "of upheaval, innovation and radical reform at all levels of American education."[6]

There ensued many efforts, often underwritten by the federal government or private foundations, to renew, liberalize, and "humanize" the education system in a thousand different ways. These ranged from metric education to alternative schools, from values-clarification curricula to pass-fail courses, from community control to the Women's Educational Equity Act, from the "new math" to countless attempts to introduce modern technology into the schools. Their dominant goals, however, remained the five "access" objectives described above, now tinged with romanticism and accompanied by the music of Woodstock and the scent of teargas.

Save for New York City's ill-fated 1969 decentralization plan, the reforms of the sixties and seventies brought no fundamental alterations in the structure or political control of the education system. The schools and those who led and taught in them grew no more accountable for the quality of the education they delivered. The prevailing ideologies of the era scorned accountability and quality alike.

DAWN OF THE EXCELLENCE MOVEMENT

In the mid-1970s, America's national confidence wavered. Vietnam, Watergate, oil embargoes, energy shortages, economic stagnation, the decline of smokestack industries, the surging success of Asian and European rivals, domestic problems of crime, violence, and drug addiction—these and other symptoms were associated with what President Jimmy Carter termed our national "malaise."

On the education front, the College Board disclosed in 1975 that the average score on its celebrated Scholastic Aptitude Test had been falling for the previous eleven years. "More than any other single factor," historian Diane Ravitch recounts, "the public's concern about the score declines touched off loud calls for instruction in 'the basics' of reading, writing, and arithmetic."[7] Data from international achievement tests also indicated that American youngsters lagged behind those of other lands in such core subjects as math and science. Colleges reported weak academic preparation among many freshmen. In too many instances these were minority youngsters, often the products of desegregated schools yet somehow still poorly educated.

Businessmen grumbled about inadequate skills and sloppy thinking among those they were hiring, sometimes even about their inability to recruit enough suitable employees, occasionally followed by a corporate decision to export skilled work to other lands. The same problem emerged in the public sector, perhaps most vividly in the armed forces, now dependent on volunteers.

The media spotlighted young people with high-school diplomas who could barely read and write. Adult illiteracy had long been a national concern, but now we sensed that the schools themselves might be stocking the ranks of poorly skilled citizens, that passing grades did not necessarily translate into satisfactory levels of actual learning.

Hence the cry that America needed to point its education system "back to the basics," that our efforts to change it were proving counterproductive, that we had our priorities askew. By the late 1970s one could detect the stirrings of a new and very different sort of school reform movement—one focused on results. It did not yet have a name, but in time it would become known as the "excellence movement"—after the commission whose 1983 report became its manifesto.

Its first substantial appearance in the policy domain was a spate of state laws obliging high-school students to pass new tests before they could receive their diplomas. By 1983, Ravitch reports, thirty-eight legislatures had ordered their public schools to "administer minimum competency tests in the basic skills."[8] Though the exams were embarrassingly easy, with passing levels set far below students' nominal grade levels, these policies sent momentous signals. For a legislature to levy such a requirement was to intrude directly into the setting of criteria by which pupils are judged, a province long entrusted to professional educators. This not only indicates flagging confidence in the standards devised by those professionals. It also adopts a performance gauge for the education system that consists of cognitive learning outcomes rather than resources, effort, or time. To make someone pass such a test as a condition of graduation or promotion is equivalent to saying, "We don't care how much schooling you had, how much money was spent on it, or how many years you devoted to it; if you can't demonstrate the ability to read, write, and cipher, we don't consider you sufficiently 'educated' to deserve a diploma." Thus did the tenuous link Coleman had found between school inputs and student achievement begin to emerge from the precincts of social science into the real world of public policy.

A NATION AT RISK

In April 1983, the National Commission on Excellence in Education delivered its famous report to the nation, informing us that the weakness of our schools menaced our well-being as a country:

> If an unfriendly foreign power had attempted to impose on America the mediocre educational performance that exists today, we might well have viewed it as an act of war. As it stands, we have allowed this to happen to ourselves. . . . We have, in effect, been committing an act of unthinking, unilateral educational disarmament.

This panel of educators and citizens had been appointed by Education Secretary T. H. Bell to examine and report back on the condition of the education system. It might have been like a thousand other commissions, laboring in obscurity for a year and a half, enjoying a day of modest celebrity when releasing its report, then disappearing forever. Instead, to everyone's surprise, the verdict of the Excellence Commission turned out to be an era-defining event, marking a fundamental shift in the dominant priorities of the previous thirty-five years. Yet the actual report was as much a symbol as a cause of this shift. By the time it was delivered, several other studies and analyses had been published and a number were under way. Within eighteen months there would be dozens. "All," Cremin noted, "in one way or another re-sounded the themes of *A Nation at Risk*—the need for emphasis on a new set of basics, the need for a more intensive school experience for all young people, and the need for a better trained teaching profession in the nation's schools."[9]

Several governors had already begun to agitate for education reform in their states. Individual critics were also writing about the need for more attention to the quality of what was learned. By way of personal example, I warned in 1980 that education's dominant "liberal consensus" was in jeopardy because of its "pronounced lack of interest in the issues of quality."[10] The next year, I pointed out to readers of *Life* magazine that "literacy is in decline in one state after another. . . . Young people are graduated from high school unfamiliar with the rudiments of American history and unacquainted with concepts fundamental to the common heritage of Western man." And in 1981, still two years before *A Nation at Risk*, Ravitch and I founded the Educational Excellence Network to foster the exchange of information among like-minded educators and lend moral support to those whose criticisms of the status quo and heterodox notions about how to change it made them feel like outcasts within the profession.[11]

The commission thus drilled into a reservoir of dissatisfaction that had been accumulating for some time and that by 1983 had built up considerable pressure. Its report released what the oil industry calls a "gusher," as that concern and dissatisfaction spewed forth. Some of it had leaked through crevices already, and much more was to follow.

The commission legitimized "quality" and "excellence" as mainstream education priorities, and it joined the fate of the nation to its explanation of what was awry. But if the American public had not been ready to believe these things and to move education in the direction they implied, the commission's report would likely have had no more impact than the exhortations of other such panels.

THE PRESENT CONDITION

Reformers carrying the banner of the excellence movement have made valiant efforts during the past decade to upgrade educational performance. Nearly all of these have been well-intentioned, hard fought, and compatible with the diagnoses rendered by innumerable studies, experts, panels, and task forces.

The problem is that they do not seem to have done much good, at least when gauged in terms of student learning. The average pupil continues to emerge from the typical school in possession of mediocre skills and skimpy knowledge. Most of the trend lines are flat. The patient is in more-or-less stable condition but still gravely ill.

Some commentators use stronger language. "Mountains of evidence," writes television personality Steve Allen,

> establish that the American people are suffering from a new and perhaps unprecedented form of mental incapacitation for which I have coined the word "dumbth." . . . [W]e are now, in a broad statistical sense, also guilty of a form of stupidity that, although also an ancient human problem, now threatens to swamp our efforts to conduct the affairs of an at least generally rational society.[12]

Consider some of the bleak evidence Allen refers to, data derived from the National Assessment of Educational Progress (NAEP) and similar barometers:

• Just 5 percent of seventeen-year-old high-school students in 1988 could read well enough to understand and use information found in technical materials, literary essays, historical documents, and college-level texts. Contending with this book, for example, demands reading skills at a level of sophistication possessed by barely one in twenty of today's senior high-school students. And that proportion, the data show, has declined—modestly but steadily—since 1971.

• As for writing, the authors of the most recent (1988) NAEP report on student performance found that the "vast majority of high-school juniors still could not write a persuasive paper that was judged adequate to influence others or move them to action."[13]

• Barely 6 percent of eleventh-graders in 1986 could solve multistep math problems and use basic algebra. That means 94 percent of them could *not* answer questions at this level of difficulty: "Christine borrowed $850 for one year from the Friendly Finance Company. If she paid 12% simple interest on the loan, what was the total amount she repaid?"[14]

• Only 7 percent of seventeen-year-olds could infer relationships and draw conclusions from detailed scientific knowledge in 1986. Here is an example of the kind of question that these few students are able to answer correctly: "A female white rabbit and a male black rabbit mate and have a large number of baby rabbits. About half of the baby rabbits are black, and the other half are white. If black fur is the dominant color in rabbits, how can the appearance of white baby rabbits best be explained?" (The correct answer, among four choices given, is: "The male rabbit has one gene for black fur and one gene for white fur.")[15]

• Sixty percent of eleventh-graders in 1986 did not know why *The Federalist* papers were written; three-quarters could not say when Lincoln was president; just one in five knew what Reconstruction was.[16]

• Asked on the 1988 assessment of U.S. history to write a mini-essay discussing whether contemporary presidents wield greater power than George Washington possessed, just 10 percent of twelfth-graders supplied solid responses.[17]

• A related exercise on the 1988 civics assessment invited high-school seniors to name the current president and then to describe his primary responsibilities in a short essay. Nearly all of them correctly identified Ronald Reagan—one has to wonder about the 6 percent who didn't—but on the essay portion not quite one student in five could furnish a "thoughtful response with a mix of specific examples and discussion."[18]

• On a survey given to high-school students in the spring of 1988 by the Joint Council on Economic Education, 55 percent failed a question asking what causes a "government budget deficit"; two-thirds did not know what "profits" mean.[19]

• Presented with a blank map of Europe and asked to identify certain countries, young American adults (ages eighteen to twenty-four) supplied the correct answer fewer than one time in four. Twenty-six percent spotted Greece, 37 percent France, just 10 percent Yugoslavia. Given a map of the United States, fewer than half found New York and only one in four properly labeled Massachusetts.[20]

Such examples are so familiar nowadays, and so depressing, that we're tempted not to pay them much heed. Why make ourselves miserable? We're also inclined to suppose they apply to people on the other side of town, not to our children or neighbors. In fact, they are but the tip of an iceberg of ignorance, a mountain of "dumbth"—and they signal the emergence from schools all around us of young adults akin to those who sat behind me on the plane from Minneapolis and are perspiring on the Saudi sands. Note, too, that most of the reports from which these data are drawn describe young people who have stayed in school and will soon graduate, boys and girls commonly deemed to be "succeeding" in our education system. They have served their time in the classroom, to be sure, but they have not learned much. In many cases they didn't even sit through courses designed to impart the knowledge and skills that we later rue their not having acquired. Only 16 percent of 1987 graduates, for example, had taken the package of high-school courses that the Excellence Commission recommended as a minimum for all young Americans.[21]

COLLEGE AND BEYOND

In an age when so many high-school graduates are poorly educated, yet when nearly 60 percent of them head straight into college (and more stroll through the ivy gates later), we cannot be surprised that institutions of higher education find themselves enrolling ill-prepared students. There is no uniform standard of college readiness, nor are there good national data on the matter, but those who have looked closely at today's matriculants see huge shortcomings. American Federation of Teachers president Albert Shanker estimates: "Ninety-five percent of the kids who go to college in the United

States would not be admitted to college anywhere else in the world."[22] Three-quarters of the university professors queried in a 1989 Carnegie Foundation survey reported that their students lacked basic skills. Almost seven in ten said that their institution "spends too much time and money teaching students what they should have learned in high school."[23] Said one liberal arts professor: "I do feel sorry for these young students in the 1980s, as I feel that the majority of them are grossly underprepared for coping with college-level academic study."[24]

It's not surprising that remedial and "developmental" programs have burgeoned on campus. By 1988 virtually all institutions of higher education (including 89 percent of four-year colleges) offered such instruction.[25] When the Southern Regional Education Board (SREB) surveyed its members in 1986, 60 percent of responding institutions reported that at least 30 percent of their entering freshmen needed academic assistance; on almost three campuses in ten, the majority of freshmen arrived in that condition.[26]

New Jersey has for some years administered a basic skills test to students entering its state colleges and universities. One purpose is to assist institutions in matching students with needed remedial courses. On the round of tests given in the autumn of 1989, just 24 percent of all freshmen "appeared proficient" in verbal skills, 31 percent in math computation, and 14 percent in elementary algebra. All the rest—keep in mind that these are now college students—either "lacked proficiency" or were proficient only in part of the subject.

The standards were none too exacting, either. To be judged proficient in verbal skills, for example, meant being able to "comprehend a relatively mature idea and develop it in standard English." Even more dismaying, despite nearly a decade of energetic school reform efforts in New Jersey, the skill levels of recent high-school graduates entering the state colleges show scant change. Math proficiency rose a bit between 1980 and 1989, but verbal prowess fell slightly.[27]

Those who attend college wind up with stronger skills and knowledge than those who don't—but not by much. In 1985 the National Assessment program gauged literacy levels among young (twenty- to twenty-five-year-old) adults. Within that population it's possible to isolate those with substantial postsecondary education. When Audrey Pendleton of the U.S. Department of Education performed such an analysis, here is what she found:

> More than half of college upperclassmen and college graduates were *unable* to perform at the 350 level of the scales [emphasis

hers]. . . . Tasks characteristic of this level include stating in writing an argument made in a lengthy newspaper column, using a bus schedule to select the appropriate bus for given departures and arrivals, and calculating the amount of a tip in a restaurant given the percentage of the bill. While these tasks are at the upper levels of the literacy scales, the knowledge and skills required to complete them would generally not be considered college level. It is unclear whether the ability to perform these basic tasks is a prerequisite to higher-level skills needed in college. If they are, then it is questionable whether many college students have the foundation needed to pursue college-level studies.[28]

Do not be lulled by the flat prose of a government report. These are young adults with at least two years of college under their belts, and many have graduated. Yet not even half of them can function intellectually at the level described by Pendleton.

Another body of evidence comes from the National Endowment for the Humanities, which retained Gallup in 1989 to survey the history and literature knowledge of college seniors. Here, in the words of Endowment Chairman Lynne V. Cheney, is what they found:

> [Twenty-five] percent of the nation's college seniors [were] unable to locate Columbus's voyage within the correct half-century. About the same percentage could not distinguish Churchill's words from Stalin's, or Karl Marx's thoughts from the ideas of the U.S. Constitution. More than 40 percent could not identify when the Civil War occurred. Most could not identify Magna Carta, the Missouri Compromise, or Reconstruction. Most could not link major works by Plato, Dante, Shakespeare, and Milton with their authors. To the majority of college seniors, Jane Austen's *Pride and Prejudice*, Dostoyevsky's *Crime and Punishment*, and Martin Luther King, Jr.'s "Letter from the Birmingham Jail" were clearly unfamiliar.[29]

On a smaller scale, in 1989 the pathology department chairman at Wake Forest University devised a 250-question exam based on E. D. Hirsch's *Dictionary of Cultural Literacy*. These were short "free-response" answers, not multiple-choice items. Students were asked to "specifically identify each term with a short answer" or definition. Included were such terms as *George Eliot, bas-relief, hypothalamus, Luftwaffe, Gang of Four, capital gain, Mount Saint Helens, photoelectric effect,* and *Sanskrit*. The test was administered to 450 medical, law, and business students at Wake Forest.

Nobody supposed they would recognize all these terms. But even I was stunned by the results reported by Dr. Robert Prichard and his colleagues. The overall average correct score was 24.7 percent. Business students fared worst, with an average of 17.2. Law students were in the middle at 24.1. The medical students led, but with a meager 28.4 percent.

To my knowledge this particular study has been repeated on just one other campus. A colleague of Prichard's at the University of Kansas arranged to test 128 first-year medical students at that institution. They fared even worse than did the Wake Forest students, earning an average score of 13.8 percent correct.

This is not the place to rehash the old argument about what higher education should teach. Surely college ought to transport one's intellect well beyond factual knowledge and cultural literacy. But it's hard to add a second story to a house that lacks a solid foundation.

BEYOND OUR BORDERS

Looking overseas for points of reference, we find even greater reason for dismay, particularly at a time when we're concerned with world-wide economic competition. Though international education assessment efforts are irregular, every few years we somehow come into possession of data from another one. The most recent of these studies, reported by the Educational Testing Service (ETS) in early 1989, compared the performance of thirteen-year-olds in mathematics and science in five countries and four Canadian provinces. Our youngsters placed dead last in math. In science American girls and boys were tied (with Ireland and two Canadian provinces) for the bottom position. Korea led in both subjects. The United States was also bested in both by England, Spain, and two other Canadian provinces. Note that practically all thirteen-year-old children in these industrial nations are still enrolled in school. In this age group, the lackluster performance of American youngsters cannot be explained away by asserting that we have a universal system while other countries educate only their elites.

Math and science are the subjects most easily examined across national and linguistic boundaries, but once in a while we obtain comparative results in other fields. In the spring of 1988, for example, Gallup was engaged by the National Geographic Society to administer a test of "basic geographic literacy" to adults in the United States and eight other lands. On simple "map fact" questions (identifying fourteen countries and two bodies of water), Americans scored in the third of four tiers of countries, meaning we were tied with the United Kingdom, a bit ahead of Italy and Mexico, but well behind Sweden, West Germany, Japan, France, and Canada. Far more disturbing, when the population was partitioned by age, our older adults fared moderately well on the geography test, but Americans between the ages of eighteen and twenty-four had the lowest scores of all. "The United States," Gallup reported, "is the only one of the nine countries whose youngest respondents did not do better than the oldest. . . . Thus, while other countries that did not do well overall . . . seem to be making strides in the right direction, the U.S. seems to be heading the opposite way—all by itself."[30]

Nor is the world a static place in which nations can count on maintaining their relative positions. Our competitors in Asia and Europe are striving to improve their education systems, too. At a time when many young Americans are barely literate in English, European business leaders are urging their schools to ensure that all youngsters learn at least three languages.[31] Education reform is under way in Japan and the United Kingdom, as well as the newly democratizing countries of Eastern and Central Europe. The Soviet Union, too, is striving to revitalize its education system. Few countries are standing pat, and the performance gaps we have been struggling to narrow could instead widen.

"Competitiveness begins in the classroom," says John L. Clendenin, head of the BellSouth Corporation and (in 1989) chairman of the U.S. Chamber of Commerce, "because, quite simply, the technologies driving our economy today require more educated workers." Yet his is just one of many American companies that have been experiencing difficulty finding qualified employees. Motorola reports that four-fifths of the candidates it screens fail an entry-level test at the levels of seventh-grade English and fifth-grade math. In 1988 New York Telephone received 117,000 applications for jobs, but only 2,100 of these passed the company's employment exam.[32]

Such anecdotes and tales of woe have grown so familiar that we tend not to pause over them long enough to realize that they are actually examples of a worsening alignment between the personnel needs of a changing economy and the typical products of our schools. A new study by Arnold H. Packer for the Hudson Institute finds a widening gap between the literacy level of the average American young adult and the level needed to handle new jobs. He offers the "conservative estimate" that twenty-five million workers must upgrade their skills during the 1990s if the nation's employment needs are to be met and productivity gains made. Too many of today's young people, Packer says, "are qualified for such jobs as helpers and laborers or service workers, while a healthy economy requires more marketing and salespersons and technicians."[33]

When they cannot find a sufficiency of trained personnel among the products of U.S. schools and colleges, employers look across the sea for highly skilled workers. Sometimes they export the jobs; sometimes they import the employees. The mismatch between our manpower needs and the performance of our education system thus affects even our immigration policies. The immigration law passed in 1990, for example, almost triples (to 140,000 a year) the quota for skilled professionals and practically eliminates the bureaucratic barriers to some 40,000 "priority workers" annually, people described as "international superstars, your basic Einsteins," by a Labor Department official. "We are where we are today," notes the director of risk management at the National Association of Manufacturers, "because the American educational system has failed us."[34]

Education is not only about jobs and economic competitiveness, to be sure. "The narrow, technocratic view ignores the equally important role that education plays in glueing a democracy together," writes former New Jersey governor Tom Kean. "A democratic government depends on a citizenry that not only can read and write, but has some common body of knowledge and experience, some sense of its own history."[35] We send our children to school and college to acquire knowledge and skills, habits and values, that will enrich their lives in a hundred different ways. Some have to do with earning a living, some with citizenship, some with becoming a parent and neighbor, others with personal fulfillment and the uses of leisure.

Education is not just our personal possession either. After generations of argument among economists as to whether it is a "public" or "private" good, the only acceptable answer is that it is both. Individuals benefit in myriad ways from acquiring an education. But the larger society has a bona fide interest in it, too. Educating the next generation is how any nation secures its future. In 1991, however, even as the United States remains generally prosperous and optimistic, it is hard to point to any significant indicators in the education domain that give us grounds for satisfaction with our present performance or serenity about our future. Stated more bluntly, the country is gradually losing its mind, and that means we're all in big trouble.

2

☞

Schooling in a No-Fault Culture

Refusing to accept responsibility for one's own actions is a low grade form of lying.
—Columnist Meg Greenfield, May 1990

School consumes a surprisingly small portion of American children's lives. The young person who diligently attends class six hours a day, 180 days a year, from kindergarten through twelfth grade, will, upon reaching her eighteenth birthday, have spent just 9 percent of her hours on earth under the schoolhouse roof. Omit kindergarten and it shrinks to 8.2 percent. Add preschool and it swells to 9.6 percent.

What is the leverage of the 9 percent, especially in situations where the other 91 percent works at cross-purposes? How much should we expect schools to accomplish?

Quite a bit but not too much, are the seemingly contradictory answers, both of them often ignored.

AN OLD AND LIMITED INSTITUTION

The public school of 1991 is still, by and large, an institution designed in the nineteenth century to serve only part of the population and to do that within a framework of complementary influences. We sometimes forget how good it is—or was—at this mission, while also overlooking how much the mission has changed.

Securely lodged in the framework it was designed for, the school has demonstrated the capacity to manage its distinctive portion of

20

Callslip Request   1/6/2017 1:44:09 PM

Item Location: stx
Call Number: 370.973 F514
Enumeration:
Copy Number: 1
Chronology:
Year:
Item Barcode:

3 4 7 1 1 0 0 1 3 0 9 5 1 9

Title: We must take charge : our schools and
     our future / Chester E. Finn, Jr.
Author: Finn, Chester E., 1944-

Patron Name: Guillermo Antonio Hurtado
             Reyes
Patron Group: UBLong
Patron Barcode:

S T U 8 5 1 2 6 3 5 7 6

Reason if item is not available:
__At Bindery: Seeking next available
__Item Charged Out: Seeking next available,
__Damaged: Seeking next available
__Local Circulation Only: Seeking next availab
__Missing/Not on Shelf: Seeking next available
__Noncirculation item: Seeking next available

Reassignment History:
None

Patron comment:

Request date: 1/3/2017 05:15 PM
Request number: 55876

5 5 8 7 6

Pick Up Location if Local Request:

the tasks of socialization and cultural transmission. This has consisted mainly of "cognitive learning," educators' jargon for the intellectual skills and academic knowledge that constitute the chief contribution of effective schools to the development of young people. School is where you learn algebra, literature, and chemistry; where you train your intellect, hone your analytic powers, and discover how to express yourself effectively. That isn't all there is to education, of course, but it's the singular province of the institution we call school.

When family, church, neighborhood, and peer group all do their parts, too, especially when they are joined by a hundred other agents and agencies of childhood—pediatrician and Little League; Y and recreation center; scouts, piano teacher and Sunday school; museum, library, and summer camp—when all these pieces are fitted into the mosaic of child development, the school's resources are more or less sufficient to complete the picture.

For a long time these roles and missions worked in reasonable harmony in the lives of most youngsters. The typical American school was part of an interlocking set of institutions and relationships that anchored a fairly stable community. Today's public school is still suited to such a society, to the little towns on the prairie, the manicured lawns and curving roads of the bedroom suburb, even the homogeneous ethnic neighborhoods of the metropolis. It fitted snugly into a way of life in which sidewalks were safe, a parent was waiting at home in the afternoon, the neighbors could be counted on to keep an eye on everyone's children, morals and ethics were served up with the family dinner, and the church or synagogue attended to your soul at least once a week.

Some American communities still function that way today, and in these we commonly find that schools are deemed "successful." To be sure, even *their* pupils do not learn enough for the 1990s, but generally they learn as much as the school requires, and school and community appear comfortable with one another, like old married couples grown accustomed to each other's strengths and frailties. Where there is conflict, it most often arises when the mounting cost of schooling collides with the dwindling proportion of the local population that still has school-age children.

Many of our communities have changed dramatically, however. The security and predictability with which they once enveloped schools have been swamped by dislocations in families, churches, neighborhoods, work lives, personal mores, and leisure-time pursuits. Social mobility, mass immigration, and other demographic shifts have erased more of the familiar environment to which schools were well adapted and for which their 9 percent was about right. Ethnic fragmentation and cultural divisiveness have eroded still more. Technology and instant communications have transformed almost every aspect of our lives *except* what happens in schools—institutions that in most respects still look and act as they did fifty years ago. The modern plagues—drugs, AIDS, suicide, child abuse, television addiction, teen pregnancy—have borne down on the education system, too, both directly (through immediate impact on students, teachers, and parents) and indirectly (for example, by creating pressures for curricular changes meant to immunize youngsters against them).

TODAY'S NONCOGNITIVE CHALLENGES

Buttressed by families and backstopped by all those other institutions, schools can have considerable success in introducing a child to the geography of exotic places, the glories of the written and spoken language, the history of civilizations, the mysteries of biology, the elegance of mathematics, and a hundred other wonders of the academic and intellectual worlds. Our best schools still cram a great deal of learning into their 9 percent.

But the school is hard pressed to support its part of the burden unless its environs are safe and tranquil, its pupil population remains fairly stable, and others pitch in to aid children who are ill, disturbed, handicapped, or otherwise in need of help beyond the teachers' know-how and the principal's resources. When out-of-school conditions are hostile, when other agencies don't carry their share of the responsibility, when a child's tangled problems exceed their capabilities, especially where his home situation is itself destructive— the limits of the 9 percent are fast reached. If a youngster turns up at the schoolhouse door hungry, sick, upset, tired, or frightened, it is hard to teach her to multiply and divide. When a six-year-old arrives in first grade without a basic vocabulary, lacking self-control, unaccustomed to books, hypnotized by television, and ignorant of the rudiments of group behavior, the school's leverage seems puny indeed. When a teenager lands in high school with a drug or alcohol habit, a baby of her own, a record of lawless behavior, a part-time job that runs well into the evening, or a gang membership that fills the wee hours with fighting and frivolity, it's not likely that a lot of book reports are going to get written or French verbs conjugated.

The education system is not helpless against such odds. Anyone acquainted with the stories of great teachers, crusading principals, and outstanding schools knows how much they can accomplish with youngsters, even when the children bear heavy loads and the world beyond the parking lot is chaotic and hostile. To recall a single inspiring example, the film *Stand and Deliver* dramatizes the extraordinary success that Jaime Escalante has had in bringing his low-income Hispanic students from the barrios of East Los Angeles up to a level of math proficiency that has enabled many to pass the advanced placement calculus test, gain entry (and often scholarships) to college, and thereby tranform their lives. Reality proves feasibility; that it has been done demonstrates that it *can* be done. Observe, though, that Escalante, like most uncommonly effective educators, enlarges the school's portion of his students' lives well beyond 9 percent and, when necessary, leaps the schoolhouse wall and engages himself directly with other elements of those lives. He does not restrict his efforts or limit his influence to a single class period a day.[1]

Entire schools sometimes behave similarly, extending their reach into the communities beyond their doors and their influence deep into the lives of students. We scarcely even notice when private schools do this, so accustomed are we to thinking of them as agents of moral, physical, and spiritual formation and as close collaborators with parents. When new private schools open, especially in tough neighborhoods, their founders and leaders take for granted that they will not pause for long at the 9 percent marker. The Corporate/Community School in Chicago's Lawndale section, for example, is open from seven to seven throughout the year. "Teachers assume responsibility for their pupils' physical and emotional welfare outside school," reports Ellen Graham of the *Wall Street Journal:*

> If a child needs housing, heat, glasses or a hearing aid, nurse Phyllis Pelt cuts red tape with the network of social agencies that the school has carefully cultivated. Mornings may find Mrs. Pelt conferring with a teacher about helping a parent discipline without hitting, conducting a stress-relief workshop for mothers, or telephoning a parent who can't get a child to school. . . . Teachers visit students' homes, stressing the need for all the adults in a child's life to support schooling. Although public schools in the area typically get only a handful of parents to turn out for meetings, attendance here averages 85%.[2]

When public schools do likewise, we are more apt to take special notice, usually lavishing much-deserved praise on teachers and principal for superhuman efforts in "battling the odds," "end-running the regulations," or "out-foxing the union contract." There are certainly dozens and probably hundreds of such public schools in the United States today, many of them located in harsh neighborhoods. These schools nevertheless achieve solid results not only because they run a strong academic program but also because they push back the boundaries of time and role, enmeshing themselves with the lives of their children, families, and communities; procuring the requisite services from other agencies when possible; digging into their own human resources when necessary. I have seen some of these schools myself. Former Secretary of Education William J. Bennett visited many more. Here is what he says about them:

> Among them have been good schools in the poorest areas of Dallas, Cleveland, Chicago, Washington, D.C., Boston, Phoenix and New York. These are schools that give their students what a good school must: a respect for and interest in learning and the habits and motivation necessary for success and achievement. Few students drop out of these schools. Most perform at or above grade level in reading and math; many go on to college. In these schools, children's family circumstances and their parents' lack of income or education do not hold them back.
>
> The success of such schools is not a miracle. It is not a mystery. It is accomplished through the inspired effort of committed adults who adhere strictly to certain bedrock principles and sternly refuse to succumb to defeatism.[3]

From Edison Primary in Dayton to William Lloyd Garrison in the Bronx, from Hine in the District of Columbia to Garfield in Phoenix, from Chambers Elementary in East Cleveland to Charles Rice in Dallas, from A. Philip Randolph in Harlem to Carrizozo High in New Mexico and Alexander Dumas on Chicago's South Side, one observes public schools that succeed despite their unpromising environments.[4]

WHY SOME SCHOOLS SUCCEED

The schools that overcome the heavy odds turn out to share important characteristics. Whether public or private, they are orderly and safe places, refuges from a tumultuous environment. They have high standards and expectations for all their students. That means they must stay focused on lofty academic goals without ignoring other lessons that children also need to learn. In Syracuse University professor Gerald Grant's phrase, they are "neither morally neutral factories for increasing cognitive output nor witless producers of obedient 'well-adjusted' youngsters."[5] They have a crackerjack principal who takes no guff from anyone, who infuses the entire staff with team spirit, a strong sense of purpose, and an ethos of achievement and sound character, and who labors practically around the clock and calendar to do whatever needs doing.[6] They nearly always have after-school programs, often including tutoring to reinforce academic accomplishment, and they either sponsor or help the students arrange summer activities, too, lest the long break between June and September erode cognitive gains and tempt children into trouble. They engage parents in a hundred ways in the education of their children and the work of the school. In short, they do not confine themselves to what happens in the classroom, and they pay as little heed to the 9 percent limit as they do to the rules of the bureaucracy downtown.

That such schools exist is once again proof that they *can* exist, even within the toils of vast urban systems. No single development would do more to revitalize American education and give a needed boost to the "underclass" than to create about twenty thousand more of them tomorrow. Yet we have constructed a public education system in which it is all but inevitable that such schools will remain rarities. The qualities that enable them to flourish, while consistent with common sense and sound management theory, violate standard practice, union contracts, and the organizational inertia that becalms so many school systems.

THE LIMITS OF SCHOOLING

Boosting cognitive learning by pushing back the 9 percent limit and reaching outside the schoolhouse door is one thing. Handing schools a fistful of responsibilities they cannot cope with well is quite another. Yet Americans have a nearly overwhelming impulse to turn to the education system to solve the other domestic problems we face. The temptation is obvious: Schools are the only institutions susceptible to public policy that everybody passes through—and at an impressionable age. Nonetheless, we would be well advised not to let our rapture about the accomplishments of unusual schools blind us to the limits of what formal education can do.

Each generation seemingly has to learn this afresh. In the 1920s and 1930s, "progressive" educators like George S. Counts challenged the schools to humanize industrial civilization.[7] In the 1950s we looked to them to end racial discrimination and prejudice. In the 1960s architects of the "Great Society" believed that education could eliminate poverty. In the 1970s we asked schools to liberate the spirit, reduce the threat of nuclear war, and offset the effects of physical handicaps. In the 1980s, among many other assignments, we wanted them to end drug abuse and youth suicide, diminish stress, increase self-esteem, lower the incidence of AIDS, eliminate pregnancy among young teens, and make children conscious of the environment.

Effective though they can be in the province of cognitive learning, even good schools are not powerful-enough instruments to accomplish all these other worthy objectives. Schools cannot repair a broken family, prevent abuse in the home, or make an addict quit a habit. They cannot redistribute income, cure mental illness, or restore peace to communities torn by gunfire. They may assist modestly, usually by cooperating with other agencies and organizations and by going about their work in ways that "model" for students the behavior favored by civil society. But their greatest contribution by far is to produce a next generation sufficiently educated to make informed and wise decisions about how to arrange its affairs. Their singular strength, in short, continues to be in the cognitive domain.

This limitation must be kept in mind when seeking solutions to problems that arise elsewhere. It is a fine thing for the school to provide surcease from violence and to furnish such help as it can to children dealing with multiple woes. It is another matter altogether to expect schools to right the underlying wrongs. Yet in a shifting and sometimes fearful world, they have been asked to shoulder responsibilities that go far beyond their historic mission and present-day capabilities. Educators nearly always consent to these additional assignments, out of a sense of duty or the sincere belief that they can help. Certainly most would like to. These are compassionate men and women, glad to do what they can to assist a needy child. But they usually try to cram the extra duties into the same 9 percent that is barely sufficient for the limited purposes of cognitive learning even when other community supports are present.

THE TIME FACTOR

The school's leverage is further weakened by the facts that it is no longer the principal focus of American children's lives and that academic matters do not occupy enough of those lives. This is a middle-class as much as an inner-city phenomenon. Today some youngsters spend more time watching television than they do in class. Twenty-seven percent of fourth-graders in 1988, for example, devoted six or more hours per day to television (Sixty-nine percent watched at least three hours a day.) School seldom lasts that long, and it only owns five days a week whereas its rival possesses seven.[8]

Virtually all children cede a larger portion of their waking hours to the "tube" than to homework. The average eighth-grader in 1988 spent twenty-one hours a week on television, five and a half hours on homework, and less than two hours on nonschool reading. Thirteen-year-olds in the United States were glued to the TV set for more of the day than their peers in other countries.[9] Our youngsters also lagged behind those of Spain, Ireland, Britain, and South Korea in time devoted to homework.[10] American twelfth-graders, not surprisingly, are assigned more homework than are their younger brothers and sisters, but one in five reports doing none, and only one in ten devotes more than two hours a day to this school-related activity—while half watch television for at least that long.[11]

For high school students, part-time jobs also vie with the classroom. The Bureau of Labor Statistics (BLS) reports that more than 42 percent of 16–24 year olds who were enrolled in high school in 1987 were also in the workforce, and the actual rate may be far higher. Using 1980 data, two reputable scholars contend that three quarters of 16 and 17-year-old boys and 68 percent of girls held jobs while in school that year, and there is no reason to suppose that more recent patterns are very different.[12] This is no marginal pursuit for these young workers, either. In February 1990, according to BLS figures, the average jobholder in the 16–17-year-old age group worked 17.1 hours a week.[13] Among 1989 high school seniors, almost one in three worked in excess of twenty hours a week during the school year.[14] Some of these youthful wage-earners contribute to the family food and housing budget, but many work chiefly to buy cars, fancy clothes, and other non-essentials.

Though adolescents seem to think their lives are infinitely elastic (so that more of one thing need not mean less of another), in fact, youngsters who spend lots of time working are less apt to do well in their studies. On almost every subject tested by the National Assessment, high-school students who work more than fifteen hours a week know less than their peers. A 1990 study by the New Hampshire Department of Employment Security found high-school grades in the Granite State declining as the hours worked per week rose above ten.[15]

"I get tired more than I used to," twelfth-grader Robert Pimentel told a *Boston Globe* reporter. "Sometimes, right around 11 o'clock, I'll start dozing off in my classes." This is not surprising, considering that he was working in a fast-food restaurant from six to eleven-thirty four evenings a week and all day on Saturday besides.[16] Pressed by her (supermarket) employer to devote full eight-hour shifts to her job in New York, seventeen-year-old Latysha Place yielded. "I would come in after school at 2:30," she admitted to a *Newsweek* reporter, "and work until 11. By the time I got home, I really didn't do my homework. I did what I had to do to get by."[17]

A heavy commitment to jobs and other nonacademic activities. Gobs of television. Not much homework. One of the shortest school years in the industrial world, and among the shorter days as well— that is education in the United States today. It's different in most other places. In Japan, for example, "being a student is . . . a full-time job," notes Deborah Fallows, an American mother whose children spent several years in a suburban Yokohama school:

> Students go to school six days a week. The only long vacation lasts six weeks during the summer, and even then there is assigned summer homework.
>
> The days can be long. On regular school days, classes were followed by "club" meetings or sports. After a quick supper with mom, many students joined their schoolmates again for evening *juku*, or cram school, to do remedial work, review regular class lessons or prepare for exams. After all this came the night's homework.[18]

Time is not the only variable, to be sure.[19] It can be squandered and abused. Sitting in geography class for additional hours is not the same as learning more geography. But there is a sturdy old adage about education (and many other pursuits), which holds that the amount accomplished varies in rough proportion to the time and effort invested. "It does not take a wise man to understand that if Americans go to school 180 days per year while the rest of the industrial world is in school 220 to 250 days per year," Lester C. Thurow noted in 1990, "Americans won't learn as much."[20] If we want markedly higher levels of educational achievement, our young people and their parents are going to have to alter their behavior patterns in ways they surely do not wish to.

The Excellence Commission urged that "significantly more time" be devoted to the pursuit of academic knowledge. Specific recommendations included more homework, better classroom management, and "strong consideration" of a seven-hour school day and a 200- or even 220-day school year.[21]

These suggestions were not likely to be popular, the commission undoubtedly realized. But its purpose was not punishment. More time on academics is another way of saying that the 9 percent boundary needs to be pushed back, that learning has to occupy a larger chunk of the lives of young Americans.

Changes in our society and economy would press in this direction even if we were generally content with the performance of our schools. The "information explosion" of the late twentieth century is fast expanding the knowledge base and hiking the intellectual skills one must acquire in order to function satisfactorily in most contemporary settings. The transformation of the American economy from smokestack industry to services, information, and high technology is putting a greater premium on agile and inventive minds than on the brawny bodies and simple skills of yesterday.[22] Civic life keeps growing more complex, too. Abortion, euthanasia, and a host of vexing economic trade-offs and foreign-policy puzzles demand informed and clear-headed judgment, the more so when wily manipulators of opinion strive to skew our decisions. Nine percent is puny by comparison.

The traditional 180-day school year and six-hour day pose serious child-care problems for many families, too. Youngsters are no longer needed to help bring in the crops during summer months, and many a family has no adult at home to mind them through those long vacations or after school each day. The "latchkey child" may or may not be well educated, and certainly there are many other sources of child care besides schools. But we should be getting greater mileage out of these institutions, especially when they are also our principal bulwark against "dumbth."

Yet the Excellence Commission's recommendations concerning time have been the most widely ignored and resisted of all. Though several states added extra minutes to their school days or inserted an additional class period (often by whittling down the others!), and some have adopted minimum homework norms, few youngsters are spending more of their lives on academic pursuits in 1991 than did so in 1983.

Judging from survey data, the American public is almost evenly divided in its attitude toward students devoting more time to cognitive learning.[23] There is certainly no consensus that longer school days and years are needed. In late 1990, for example, Fairfax County, Virginia Superintendent Robert Spillane proposed adding a couple of hours a week to the schedule by eliminating that school system's two decades' old practice of dismissing the children on Mondays right after lunch. When vigorous objections were voiced by the teachers' union and some parent groups, Spillane's own school board turned thumbs down on his recommendation. Los Angeles has been the scene of intense controversy merely for using its school buildings year round, a move designed to ease overcrowding and make more efficient use of costly facilities, not to hike the number of days that pupils attend. Just changing the calendar is vexatious enough. In 1983 Polk County, North Carolina, actually extended its school year by a month, but the community soon revolted. Test scores rose during the two years that this innovation lasted, yet public unhappiness at the change in established practice was more influential. In short order a new school board was elected, the superintendent who had proposed the change fled to a job in another state, and the old calendar was reinstated. "Educationally, it was a real success," is the rueful conclusion of the unappreciated former superintendent, but "politically it was a failure."[24]

THE NO-FAULT SOCIETY

Formal education is plainly going to have to change in fundamental ways if it is to serve the nation well in the twenty-first century, and so is the public's willingness to endure—even demand—those changes. Yet that is no reason to throw up our hands, glibly excusing our lackluster educational performance by claiming that "forces beyond our control" are making it practically impossible for schools to function at all or for children to learn much in them.

Almost every time I talk with educators, someone seeks to assign primary responsibility for weak academic achievement to heedless parents, decaying families, changes in the ethnic or socioeconomic composition of the students, drugs and alcohol, violence on television, bad role models in the neighborhood, and so forth. Nobody has yet mentioned sunspots, but almost every other imaginable non-school influence has been suggested.

I generally respond by recalling Lester Maddox, the infamous ax-handle-wielding, segregation-minded former governor of Georgia. When asked how he proposed to improve the sorry condition of the state prison system, Maddox replied: "There's not a lot more we can do unless we start getting a better class of prisoner."[25]

He had part of a valid point, to be sure. Prisons would obviously be more tractable and tranquil places if only nice people were incarcerated in them. Their rehabilitation rates would probably be up, recidivism down. Yet those questioning Maddox should not have been satisfied by his rejoinder. For a public official in his position to suggest that we can shrug our shoulders, that there is no more to be done until some improvement takes place in the condition of those entering the prison walls—well, one might as usefully respond to drought by praying for rain or to arthritis by donning a copper bracelet.

I can think of no institution that would not have an easier time producing satisfactory results if those with whom it deals were not so sorely afflicted. Hospitals would have a terrific cure rate if nobody presented maladies more serious than hangnails and head colds. Defense attorneys would win many more acquittals if all their clients were innocent.

And schools would enjoy greater success if every child were ready and eager to learn, had supportive parents and no serious personal problems, and the neighborhood were peaceful and other community institutions available and active. In the same vein, we know that the school faces a far harder task when other influences undermine and contradict its lessons. We will surely need to devise means of boosting its leverage, and these are likely to include increasing the fraction of their lives that children spend under its influence. Yet it little avails us as educators to cast about for scapegoats, to yearn for a better class of students, to blame forces beyond our control, or to insist that society's other shortcomings be set right before we can begin to do our part. The challenge of the 1990s is to wrestle our education system into such a shape that it *can* do its part, meeting the cognitive learning needs of a modern society as well as those of its individual students, even when other conditions are unhealthy.

Its shape will have to change considerably, and changing it will doubtless bring discomfort. We are talking, after all, of whipping our sluggish couch potato of an education system into one resembling Jane Fonda or Arnold Schwarzenegger. Many of its longtime assumptions and standard practices will need to be replaced. Above all, we will need to hold our schools—all of them—responsible and accountable for the results achieved within their assigned domain. This means properly defining the limits of that domain and not overpromising what schools can deliver outside it. And it means holding others responsible for doing their parts in their respective realms.

If such phrases seem quaint or dated, it is because while we transform a nineteenth-century institution into one suited to the twenty-first, we would also do well to save some of the beliefs and attitudes about human behavior that characterized the earlier culture. *Responsibility* is a term too often scorned today, living as we do in a society that is quick to say people and institutions are "at risk" but that scrupulously refrains from suggesting anyone is ever "at fault." We readily assert that a person or group is a victim of malign forces or circumstances beyond its control. Yet we are allergic to holding people and institutions accountable for the consequences of their actions. We dismiss that way of thinking as "blaming the victim," a morally callous thing to do.

Certainly it is not a politically prudent thing to do. Observe the storm that broke around former Education Secretary Lauro Cavazos in early 1990 when he dared to suggest that Hispanic parents should shoulder more responsibility for the educational achievement and behavior of their children. As reported by the *New York Times:*

> Mr. Cavazos, a sixth-generation Texan who is of Mexican descent, leveled his criticism at Hispanic parents. Hispanic cultures long placed a high value on education, he said, but "somewhere along the line we lost that. . . . I think in part we Hispanics have not acknowledged that problem. . . . I think that's been one of our problems in America today. We really have not cared that youngsters have dropped out of school. . . . We must have a commitment from Hispanics, from Hispanic parents especially, that their children will be educated. That is the first vital step."[26]

Leaders of Hispanic groups did not thank the secretary for saying something true and important about the education of children. Rather, they hastened to denounce him for not saying the politically correct thing, which, in the words of former San Antonio mayor Henry Cisneros, is that Hispanic parents are amply committed to education but "confront the reality of unequally financed school systems, the reality of low-paying jobs and language barriers."[27] Added Gloria Rodriguez, director of a parent-child program in Texas: "He's wrong to say the families are at fault, when society is at fault for not supporting families that are overwhelmed by economic problems." "How can you blame the victim?" New York Congressman Jose Serrano asked rhetorically.[28]

That a Hispanic cabinet member was in trouble with Hispanic leaders for remarks about Hispanic parents lent piquancy to the situation but, in truth, any public official who had laid substantial blame on any minority group or at-risk population would have provoked a similar response.[29] In our no-fault society, it is acceptable to be a victim but not to be held responsible for one's own situation or for that of one's children. Something closer to the preferred explanation was offered a few weeks earlier by a community group named ASPIRA, whose leaders, reported the *Philadelphia Inquirer,* "decried the high Hispanic dropout rate in the Philadelphia public schools and declared it a failure of the system, not of the students." "We have a system that is no longer functioning," explained City Councilman Angel L. Ortiz. "When we see such high numbers, we're looking at a system that has failed the kids."[30]

Had one taken the matter up with teachers and administrators in the Philadelphia public schools, some would doubtless have echoed Cavazos, attributing the excessive Hispanic dropout rate to parents and peer group. And they would have had a point, as do community leaders who charge the education system with serving their children poorly. Both are partly correct—but just partly.

Our tendency to lay the entire problem at someone else's doorstep is by no means confined to minority groups or impoverished neighborhoods. Teachers in middle-class suburbs also complain that when they voice criticisms to parents about the behavior or academic progress of children, the parents are apt to react by denying the problem, castigating the child for it, or denouncing teacher and school for not having solved it. The last thing the parents want is to share the responsibility. Yet when the same teachers are criticized for the paltry knowledge and weak skills of their students, they are likely to utter some variant of the Maddox explanation. They don't want to be held to account either.

Nobody does. Yet we're quick to engage a lawyer to bring suit against someone we'd like to hold responsible for any imaginable mishap or failure, even to demand immense sums in compensation for damages. We've turned the liability and malpractice fields into gold mines for attorneys and busy markets for insurance companies. We have taken to heart the notion that others are accountable for their actions. But practically never in contemporary discussions of American social policy does anyone assign responsibility for anything to himself or his own institutions. Somebody else is at fault for what happens to us; we are not at fault for what we do to ourselves. We're victims of circumstances beyond our control or perhaps just bad luck. How can we expect our children to mature into responsible citizens in a society in which community "leaders" get away with "explanations" akin to the comment of a three-year-old staring at his mother's shattered vase: "Uh-oh. It broke."

A stunning instance of this mind-set was expressed at the 1990 convention of the American Psychological Association (APA), where a senior scholar solemnly informed his peers that the increasing mayhem and homicide among adolescents was attributable (at least in part) to reductions in the federal Food Stamp program.[31]

But we may have had enough of such explanations. When the 1990 SAT results—showing that the stunted verbal aptitudes of our high-school students had further deteriorated—came out, even so softhearted an observer as *Washington Post* columnist Richard Cohen erupted. "I am for humiliating, embarrassing, mocking—you name it—the dummies who have scored so low on these tests," he sizzled. "I'm sick of explanations that take everything into account but the values and mentality of students and their parents."[32]

A few months earlier, Meg Greenfield declared in her *Newsweek* column that adults ought to stop behaving like three-year-olds: "The assumption of responsibility for one's own conduct, after all, is another way of describing the basic act of growing up. It means facing up to the consequences of what you do and thus inevitably incurs both costs and pain. But those who are unwilling to make this transaction forfeit dignity and self-respect, not to mention the respect of others."[33] Not to mention the quality of education for their—and everyone else's—children.

3

⚜

Band-Aids for Battle Wounds
Reforms of the 1980s

*A single courageous state may, if its citizens choose, serve
as a laboratory [and] try novel social and economic
experiments without risk to the rest of the country.*
—Justice Louis D. Brandeis, 1932

The excellence movement made many attempts to reform American schools during the eighties, but its results, as we've seen, have been meager. The limited leverage of formal education, confined to so small a portion of children's lives, partly explains why learning levels have not risen. Our habit of ascribing inadequacies to forces beyond our control suggests a further explanation. The unrealistic noncognitive demands we have nailed onto the framework of formal education inflame our sense of frustration. Yet none of these reasons suffices, especially when we also know that some schools work near-miracles with their students.

In part 2, we will examine some deeper reasons for the epidemic of "dumbth," reasons embedded in the basic structure of the education system and its enveloping culture. First, though, we must get better acquainted with the major efforts already undertaken in the name of school reform. They did not accomplish what we hoped, but they surely kept us busy—and cost a bundle. We're dealing with a very sick patient in the early nineties, and it's prudent to take the full case history before venturing new therapies.

MOTIVES AND MONEY

Underlying virtually all the elementary-secondary innovations of the 1980s was the conviction that standards had slipped, expectations had eroded, and the system as a whole had grown sluggish and inefficient.

These were—and are—essentially true beliefs, useful as far as they go. That they do not go far enough meant the campaigns waged under their banners were fated to prove inadequate. In organizing those campaigns, however, we overturned assumptions, changed a number of established practices, and altered some hoary decision-making patterns.

We also spent a great deal more money on education—a truth resisted by many professionals, not least because it undermines their comfortable beliefs about the social values and political priorities of the era.

In the school year 1979–80, which ended a few weeks before Ronald Reagan first won his party's nomination for the presidency, the average expenditure per pupil in American public schools was $2,491. Ten years later, during the first complete school year of the Bush administration, the average outlay per student was $5,284, or about $121,000 per classroom.[1] That represents a 111 percent rise in current dollars; converted to constant (1988–89) dollars, the increase during the decade came to 28.7 percent. This came on top of real increases of 26.8 percent in the 1970s and 57.7 percent in the 1960s.

A bit of the per-pupil expenditure rise of the eighties can be ascribed to slight shrinkage in public school enrollments—a net decline of 3.3 percent across the decade.[2] But the lion's share can be explained only in terms of bona fide spending increases, primarily in the form of greater state and local education outlays.

These were not uniform, to be sure. Illinois boosted its spending for public education just 49 percent between 1980 and 1989, not quite keeping pace with inflation, while Georgia expanded its school outlays by 166 percent. Localities were subject to even greater variation. For the nation as a whole, though, the 29 percent real-dollar figure is accurate. Perhaps it was not enough. Conceivably it was too much. I know nobody, however, who claims that the output of American public education rose by anything approaching 29 percent during the eighties.

Most of the additional moneys, of course, went into salaries of school employees, always the largest single item in education budgets. Yet the teachers' share of the school dollar has actually been declining for years: from fifty-one cents in 1970 to forty cents in 1989.[3] The salaries of public school teachers have nevertheless been rising—another fact that many in the profession tend not to mention.

The real increase in the average teacher's salary during the 1980s was 27 percent. When the decade opened, the typical U.S. public school teacher was paid $15,970. When it closed, the figure was $31,278, almost twice as much.[4] In few other fields did earnings double during this period. Had the teachers' share of the school budget held steady, the improvement would have been still greater. Again, one may feel that the rise was insufficient, and certainly it was unevenly spread around the map, but one cannot credibly assert that the primary explanation for the weak results of the reforms of the 1980s is fiscal parsimony, budgetary retrenchment, or neglect of teachers. It was a period in which we pumped more into our education system than ever before.

STATE AND NATION

Although the Excellence Commission was unmistakably a creature of the federal government, its diagnosis and recommendations barely alluded to Washington. Instead it spoke of the education of the "nation." This distinction is crucial for purposes of understanding the reform efforts that followed, and in some cases anticipated, *A Nation at Risk.*

Though the federal government plays a small and mostly peripheral role in American education, it had catalyzed many of the changes of the 1950s, 1960s, and 1970s. Indeed, within the field the view was widely held that states and localities were responsible for operating the basic system, but Uncle Sam should be expected to instigate and pay for innovations and experiments.

This apportioning changed dramatically in the 1980s, for several reasons. The old assumptions were thoroughly entangled with the goals of access and equality that had propelled education reform for so long. It was not unimaginable that a major shift in priorities would be accompanied by different roles for the major actors. Moreover, the Reagan administration made plain its belief that states should henceforth bear greater responsibility—and Washington proportionately less—in such social policy domains as education. Part of Ronald Reagan's highly successful 1980 campaign strategy was a promise to abolish the newly created federal Department of Education. Though this did not in fact occur, the symbolism could not have been more stark.

Public anxiety about education quality—visible by 1983 in one poll and survey after another—also meant that elected officials at the state and local levels sensed a new political imperative. Here is how New Jersey's Tom Kean recalls it:

> By 1981, when I ran for governor, disillusionment with the schools was widespread. . . . Teachers complained that the state cared more about paperwork than about children, and many parents . . . felt strongly that their children were not getting as good an education as they themselves had received. That startled me. Our country had made great progress politically, economically, and technologically. The suggestion that education, the underpinning of all of the improvement, had gone backward really made me wonder how long the advance in other areas could continue. I was not alone. Governors in other states were hearing the same complaints.[5]

Kean and his fellow state officials throughout the nation were constitutionally and legally responsible for schooling. Though their predecessors had long since delegated most policy and management duties to specialized boards and experts, an uneasy electorate would not be appeased. Education was by now the largest single item in the budget of every state government, a sponge soaking up vast sums of local revenue as well. By 1986–87, elementary-secondary education accounted for about 25 percent of all state and local spending. (Higher education absorbed an additional 9 percent.)[6] It was reasonable to ask whether sufficient return was being earned on this immense public investment. Certainly it was unreasonable to forswear involvement with the policy direction of so consequential a recipient of the taxpayer's dollars at a time when many voters were disgruntled about both taxes and education.

The tie between the quality of schooling and the vitality of the economy was taken seriously. How strong that link really is will forever be debated by scholars. But there is no denying that in the minds of much of the public, the views of business leaders, the commentaries of editorial writers and columnists, and the prophecies of those scanning the future, improvements in American economic competitiveness hinge on higher-quality "human capital," which in turn depends on a more rigorous and effective education system. It wasn't happenstance, we began to suspect in the 1980s, that the Japanese, Germans, and Koreans were so productive, energetic, disciplined, and successful. Surely it had something to do with how hard their children work in school and how much they learn there. "Never," Kean wrote in 1988, "has the link between education and the economy been clearer or more compelling."[7]

Better education held out the possibility not just of remedying shortcomings but also of gaining advantage, not only for the whole country but perhaps even for one's own region or state. By strengthening school standards and student performance, one might entice more of those vibrant new industries, those high-tech elements of the emerging service economy, those mobile but persnickety corporations, and those tempting foreign investments.

This opportunity was first grasped by civic and business leaders in the Southeast. States such as North and South Carolina, Tennessee, Florida, Arkansas, and Mississippi began to buzz with talk of an economic renaissance via improved education. Living in Nashville in the early 1980s, I cannot count the number of times I heard Governor Lamar Alexander argue for education reform by declaring: "Better schools mean better jobs for Tennesseans, young and old." Variants of that statement were uttered by his counterparts in half a dozen states, often joined by influential legislators, and melded into a chorus by that remarkable Atlanta-based organization, the Southern Regional Education Board.

Some reform activists were Republicans, some Democrats. It was uncharacteristically nonpartisan. And in short order it was no longer confined to the South. Kean in New Jersey and Rudy Perpich in Minnesota began to voice similar sentiments. California's new superintendent of public instruction was elected in 1982 on a platform of improving the quality of education in our most populous state. Industry groups in many communities addressed themselves to the same issue, as did such national voices of the business community as the Committee for Economic Development.

From the education profession, too, flowed a stream of books, studies, and reports with such well-regarded authors as Theodore Sizer, John Goodlad, Mortimer Adler, and Ernest Boyer. Though their explanations and recommendations varied, none disputed the basic message of the Excellence Commission: American youngsters were leaving school with insufficient skills and meager knowledge; the country was weakened by this situation; and setting matters right was going to require basic alterations in long-established ideas and practices.

Meanwhile, the bleak data kept piling up. The annual release of college admissions test scores became a major media event—and the news was not getting brighter. The SAT decline had lasted from 1965 to 1980, and only a few of those lost "points" were being retrieved.

The federally sponsored NAEP reported achievement scores every two years and, as these results were rendered more intelligible during the 1980s, they became even more alarming. It was abundantly clear that huge proportions of American students were not rising above the most modest levels of reading, writing, math and science proficiency. And when Secretary Bell inaugurated the Education Department's infamous "wall chart" in 1984, intended as an unvarnished display board of national and state-level educational performance, we began to see figures on the condition of learning in individual states, arrayed in a format that made it possible to compare them with one another and to track their progress (or its absence) over time. Bell's successors turned the wall chart into an annual event and, though there were legitimate complaints about some of its data and interpretations, its contents were always front-page news.

Some analysts have attempted to sort the excellence movement of the 1980s into several waves or periods. I use a simpler approach in the remainder of this chapter, describing four large characteristics of the reform effort as a whole, then illustrating them with ten particular changes that were undertaken.

GENERAL FEATURES OF EDUCATION REFORM, 1980s-STYLE

PREOCCUPATION WITH COGNITIVE LEARNING OUTCOMES

The excellence movement was not naive about student learning. For that to be the end product of any education system, obviously a system with certain resources and capabilities must first be in place. But input enhancement and resource augmentation were now seen as means to stronger cognitive learning, a sea change from earlier efforts to change American education. Because of their emphasis on ends, the reformers of the 1980s were remarkably open minded about means, willing to try almost anything that might yield the desired result.

STATE-CENTERED

Dozens of local educators eventually embraced the goals of the excellence movement, and by decade's end some notable examples of school reform had been initiated in communities as far-flung as Chicago, San Diego, Miami, and Chelsea, Massachusetts. Yet historians will view the 1980s as a period in which American education became markedly less local in its policy direction and governance. Though the structures did not change, local decisions receded in importance as states came to the fore, prodding, pulling, tempting, pleading, and sometimes simply commanding schools, teachers, principals, and children to change their ways. The states had always held in reserve the authority to behave this way but had rarely exercised it. Instead, for as long as anyone could remember, most states had been cautious, bureaucratic, and incrementalist in the field of education, leaving bold ideas and striking initiatives to the federal government and innovation-prone municipalities.

The excellence movement changed that. Not everywhere, to be sure, but viewed as a group there is no gainsaying the growing leadership role of the states, their newfound willingness to trample on local prerogative, or their boldness in changing long-established practices and overturning cherished assumptions.

LAY-LED

A structural change at least as momentous was the shift of leadership and influence from the education profession and its specialized governance structures to the laity, especially to elected leaders of the general-purpose government. Americans have long believed that war is too important to be left to soldiers and have crafted careful arrangements to ensure civilian control of the military. Few outside the medical profession think any longer that health policy should be made only by doctors. A kindred attitude overtook education during the 1980s. It was clear that the traditional managers of the system, for all they had done to extend services and foster access, had also permitted mediocrity to take root and spread. So long as they were insulated from political influence, they would likely continue marching to their own drummers—and mediocrity would persist as well. One tactic for changing that situation was to make the system more directly subject to political guidance and public accountability.

What is more, as governors, legislators, and mayors started to move into policy domains heretofore entrusted to experts and specialized governing boards, no lightning bolts struck them down. The doctrine that politicians ought not to meddle with schools turned out to be more legend than sacred principle. And as the years passed, more than a few such politicians found education reform to be a potent issue with the voters and saw that their ideas and actions vis-à-vis the schools could be grounds for winning—or losing—elections.

Governors (and, in some communities, mayors) evolved into de facto school superintendents, and state legislatures behaved like giant boards of education. Though they still did not select principals or hire teachers, run schools or award diplomas, they injected themselves into matters of curriculum and school organization, the norms by which students and teachers are judged, the principles by which licenses and diplomas are awarded, the criteria by which employees are compensated, the prerequisites for moving from one level of education to the next, the indicators by which progress is gauged, the protocols by which students and schools are matched, and much more.

TOP-DOWN VERSUS BOTTOM-UP

Many changes wrought by the excellence movement took the form of laws, regulations, and mandates applicable to everyone. This is one way in which the reforms of the eighties flew in the face of conventional education wisdom. They tended to standardize and homogenize, partly out of a sense of evenhandedness and equity but mostly because the policy tools available to laymen are blunt instruments, particularly when operating on the large scale and considerable remoteness of the state capitol.

If the reform tactics of the laity inclined toward the simple, uniform, universal, and abrupt, the kinds that sprang from the profession— and the decade saw lots of these, too—emphasized handcrafted, school-specific changes, the sort that are almost certain to be slow, gradual, and uneven. Attempts to harmonize these very different approaches yielded some of the notable policy dynamics of the period—and many of the confusions we have inherited in the 1990s.

SPECIFIC STRATEGIES

Ten types of school reform typified the excellence movement of the 1980s. To my knowledge no jurisdiction attempted all of them, but I mention none that was not actually tried somewhere.

1. *Standards for students.* Inasmuch as boosting student learning was the supreme goal of reformers, it is no surprise that some sought the straightest path to that destination: explicitly requiring boys and girls to meet higher achievement norms. If one recalls the "minimum competency exams" adopted earlier by many states, this was also the strategy with the most precedent.

One popular version of this strategy remained achievement tests that youngsters must pass as a condition for receiving their diplomas. Another—echoing the Excellence Commission—was the expansion of the number of academic courses that high-school students had to take before graduating. All but five states boosted their graduation requirements between 1980 and 1990. Still another approach was the construction of "promotional gates," imposing performance standards as a condition for moving to the next grade. A somewhat different approach did not directly require students to do anything but made something they prized hinge on their ability to meet a prescribed standard. Thus several states and localities adopted "no pass, no play" rules, under which students could play on school athletic teams (and, sometimes, participate in other activities) only if they maintained a certain grade-point average or passed all their courses.

2. *Standards for teachers.* If student standards could be raised via mandatory examinations, why not fashion a similar approach for their instructors? The imposition of a test for teachers was an appealing outcome-based form of quality control for the profession.

And so, where just ten states had required teachers to take competency tests in 1980, by decade's end forty-four of them obliged new teachers to pass written exams before being certified. Many jurisdictions have chosen the same test, called the National Teachers' Examination, but individual states fix their own cutoff points, usually in an arbitrary way that owes more to political than educational considerations. (How many classrooms need teachers this year? How many minority candidates can be allowed to fall below the cutoff?)

There was little resistance, save sometimes in colleges of education, to the idea of an entry-level exam for new teachers, at least so long as the passing mark was not set too high. The explosive issue was forcing *veteran* instructors to take a test—or in fact to meet any other new standard.

To policymakers it seemed straightforward: Any classroom practitioner so underskilled or ignorant as to fail a basic literacy test ought not to be inflicted on students. Yet state teachers' unions were adamantly opposed. Most of their members already held tenured jobs. There was no way they could go along with jeopardizing the assurance of permanent employment. Besides—they and others asked—how much of what you really want to know about a teacher's abilities can be determined by a paper-and-pencil exam? In the end just three states (Georgia, Arkansas, and Texas) obliged all teachers to take a written test, and this was accompanied by so much acrimony, so many chances to retake the test, and, finally, by passing scores pegged to such humble levels of actual attainment, that it is unlikely this form of standard setting will be widely used in the near future. Former Texas Governor Mark White, generally esteemed by educators and laymen for the far-reaching school reforms undertaken in the Lone Star State during his tenure, lost his 1986 reelection bid in no small part because of the furious opposition elicited by the teacher-testing program.

Observing the political cost of testing classroom veterans, other states and localities chose instead to adopt more complex evaluations that teachers may undergo en route to higher levels of rank, status, and pay. All teacher-appraisal schemes are fraught with controversy, at least among those affected, but policymakers have been able to prevail with the voluntary kind so long as they do not lead to grief for those who fail but to benefits for those who pass.

3. *Changes in teacher recruitment, education, and licensure.* Teacher training, a prime suspect in the search for perpetrators of the nation's educational decay, seemed something that ought to be easy to change. Teacher-education programs number only in the hundreds, after all, and they derive their legitimacy and leverage from state laws. Oversimplifying a bit, states confer licenses on individuals, without which they may not teach in the public schools, and historically the main prerequisite for such a license has been completion of a university-run teacher-education program approved by the state. If students do not know enough because their teachers did not teach them enough, why not beef up the norms for becoming a teacher? One enduring bit of folk wisdom about American education, it must be understood, is that courses given by teacher-education programs are near worthless in their own right and consume so much of future teachers' college schedules that they have little time left in which to master the subjects they will one day be teaching. It does not take long in freewheeling discussions of how to repair American schools for someone to suggest abolishing all colleges of education. "The willingness to endure four years in a typical school of education," asserts Boston University President (and 1990 Massachusetts gubernatorial candidate) John Silber, "often constitutes an effective negative intelligence test."[8] Few institutions are so widely despised.

Reform strategies under this heading can be sorted into four types. First, efforts to attract able people, especially minority-group members, into the teaching profession by creating high-status programs, special scholarships, forgivable loans, and other inducements and concessions—all this in addition to the general teacher-salary escalation of the decade.

Second, efforts to elevate the intellectual standards of teacher-education programs, either by raising their entrance criteria, hiking their exit requirements, or mandating changes in their curricula and practices.[9]

Third, efforts to beef up the subject-matter knowledge of future teachers by boosting their liberal arts requirements, imposing ceilings on the education credits they can earn, or—an initiative taken by a cluster of institutions styling themselves the "Holmes Group"—shifting all "professional" courses to the postgraduate level, leaving the undergraduate years to the arts and sciences. A collateral benefit of that strategy is that it makes teachers look more like other professionals by equipping them all with graduate degrees. A matching drawback is that it raises the time and dollar costs of becoming a teacher.

Fourth, and boldest, by 1990 forty-eight states had opened alternate paths into teaching, so that prospective instructors no longer all had to complete a university-based preservice teacher-training program before gaining responsibility for a classroom and receiving a paycheck. Such programs have particular appeal for midcareer people with liberal arts degrees who, during their college days, had not planned to become teachers—hence had not taken any "methods" courses—but who later concluded that they would like to try teaching, provided that the opportunity cost of entry was not too stiff.[10]

4. *Curriculum change.* No aspect of American education is in greater disarray, yet no decision about education is more basic than what children will study. If they are not learning enough history or geography, for example, overhaul the social studies curriculum to pay greater heed to those fields. If few can write adequately, infuse more writing instruction and practice throughout the school program. If math classes are not yielding sufficient "higher-order problem-solving skills," change the curriculum to place less emphasis on basic computation drill and more on intellectually challenging activities.

This approach to education reform had many advocates during the 1980s, conspicuously including William J. Bennett and E. D. Hirsch. They had logic and common sense on their side. Dry as it sounds, revising the curriculum means rethinking exactly what students should learn. Harmonized with textbook selection, teacher preparation, and student testing, this may well be the soundest approach to education reform. It is now being tried in a number of localities and states—with particular finesse in California where Bill Honig, the smart and dynamic superintendent of public instruction, has chosen it as his primary strategy for improvement.

Curriculum revision may, however, also be the approach least suited to the mandates of lay policymakers. It is complex, tedious, and technical. Few education issues generate greater political friction than decisions about what children should learn in school. Every tension within the polity, argument about the culture and division in the population descends upon the operating room whenever the curriculum undergoes surgery. So do innumerable fads and fears. The textbook guidelines that Honig inherited in California, for example, banned pictures of children eating ice-cream cones, a prohibition inserted at the behest of nutrition-advocacy groups. The businessman or legislator seized by a simple notion—"children in this state should learn more geography" (or science, literature, whatever)—can scarcely imagine the fracas that will erupt as people seek to put flesh on the bones of his idea. Nor can he imagine how resented he will be by an education profession that dislikes lay "meddling" in curricular matters.

5. *Testing and assessment.* As an education reform strategy, testing comes under the broad heading of "accountability" mechanisms, ways of furnishing parents, policymakers, and educators with accurate information about the efficacy of their efforts. Such information affords a way of tracking progress over time. It is also a powerful tool since what is measured is what gets attention. What is tested usually turns out to be what is taught, what is studied, and what is learned. But accountability via testing is not a trouble-free solution. No single test is perfectly suited to all needs. High-stakes testing— when palpable consequences are linked to results—boosts the temptation to cheat. Nor does better information per se lead to better products; for outcomes to improve, other changes must be made on the basis of what the information shows. This is what accountability is all about, but those working in an enterprise seldom wish to have their results held up to public scrutiny. Much less do they want their own terms of employment to be affected by those results.

Yet testing and assessment are among the easiest reforms to mandate. They are relatively inexpensive. Laymen think they understand them, believe them to be objectively fair, and also see them as a legitimate basis for giving professionals greater autonomy with respect to school processes. Tennessee's Alexander spoke for many lay reformers when he wrote, in the introduction to *Time for Results*, the 1986 manifesto of the National Governors' Association that was perhaps the second most influential of the decade's education reform reports, that "the Governors are ready for some old-fashioned horse-trading. We'll regulate less, if schools and school districts will produce better results."[11]

6. *Incentives and rewards.* Better data on learning outcomes are not sufficient. People also have to be motivated to alter those outcomes. Accordingly, rewards for success and interventions in response to failure proliferated during the 1980s. Prominent examples of the former include prizes, recognition programs, and bonuses or awards for students, teachers, principals, and entire schools that are deemed uncommonly successful. A couple of states offered the unusual incentive of "deregulation": Schools achieving specific performance levels would thereafter be spared from having to fulfill certain procedural requirements.

With its entrenched ethos of equity and marked distaste for comparisons, the education system turns skittish when individuals or schools are singled out, even for rewards. Far greater anxiety is roused when failure triggers unpleasant actions. Hence the battle lines practically drew themselves as officials in several jurisdictions proposed "education bankruptcy" procedures by which the state empowered itself to intervene in the management of local school systems that produce poor results. Nine states now have such laws on their books, usually after fierce legislative tussles. The most dramatic instance of this form of accountability in action was New Jersey's decision in 1988 to dismiss the Jersey City school board and superintendent and directly manage that troubled urban system for a period of time. We cannot be certain that state education agencies, themselves often sluggish and bureaucratized, will do a better job—though in situations like Jersey City's it is hard to imagine them doing worse. The point, rather, is that a number of local educators (and board members) now understand that they are no longer accountable only to themselves and their Creator, that their performance is being monitored by state officials who now possess the authority, should their performance be unsatisfactory, to intervene directly, even to boot them from their posts.

7. *Business and university partnerships.* Unique among the reform strategies of the 1980s, this one did not depend on elected officials or public policy to authorize, catalyze, or pay for it. Individual companies, corporate chieftains, and the myriad "roundtables," "chambers,"

and "alliances" into which American business has clustered itself for purposes of civic betterment and political action, in many cases opted to participate directly in the school reform effort. So did a number of university presidents and institutions of higher education. In 1988 the U.S. Department of Education tallied 140,000 school-business partnership projects in operation.[12] These typically consisted of corporations donating or loaning resources, both human and material, to the schools; making facilities available for instructional purposes; furnishing technical assistance to school officials; offering incentives and rewards to teachers and students; and occasionally guaranteeing jobs, college entry, or financial aid for successful high-school graduates.

For the most part, these were add-on programs that augmented what the schools were doing, rather than permanently altering the norms and priorities of the education system. As businessmen came to see more clearly by decade's end that their generosity induced gratitude but little real improvement in student learning, some of them inclined toward more direct action in the political and policy spheres—and we also began to spot signs of a backlash among educators who welcomed largesse but not interference and who doubted the honorable motives of the business community.[13]

8. *School restructuring.* By 1990 the term *restructuring* was as widely used—and subject to as many interpretations—as *excellence* had been a few years earlier. It came in a hundred varieties. All, however, entail reallocating roles and responsibilities, power relationships, and decision-making arrangements within individual schools and systems. The theoretical foundation (insofar as something so amorphous can be said to have one) of school restructuring closely resembles the principles of organizational success that found much favor in the corporate world during the same period. Typical strategies include devolution to the building level of decisions previously made centrally, and more collegial relationships among staff members.

Reform via restructuring is notable because it has been the approach favored by change-minded educators themselves, the only one indigenous to their profession (even if key elements were borrowed from business and other fields), and the one entailing the least lay initiative and leadership.[14] This is the sole education reform genre of the eighties whose leading figures were educators: such people as Sizer, Adler, Shanker, Don Moore, Joseph Fernandez, Adam Urbanski, Mark Tucker, and Tom Payzant. Gradually, however, influential lay reformers, including state governors and business leaders, also took the vows of school restructuring. Especially significant was the conversion of the National Governors' Association to this faith.[15]

9. *Making more schools "effective."* Even before the excellence movement gained momentum, such scholars as Ronald Edmonds, Michael Rutter, Marshall Smith, and Stewart Purkey had sought to answer the question of why some schools are more successful than others at imparting cognitive skills and knowledge to their students. While they found no patented formulas or magic potions, they did spotlight some features commonly encountered in strong schools but seldom visible in weak ones.

As we saw in chapter 2, these include a clear sense of institutional mission shared by teachers and principal; high expectations for all students; a well-developed team spirit on the part of everyone working in the school; a safe and orderly atmosphere congenial to learning; and adroit leadership of the instructional process, ordinarily by a principal who views his or her role as that of an educational executive rather than a building manager.[16]

The research was solid and persuasive, at least with regard to elementary schools. It hewed to experience as well as common sense. And it provided a tempting menu for policymakers and reformers. If the features of effective schools could be spelled out, and if the country's education crisis could be defined as having too few such schools, the path to improvement seemed obvious: Devise straightforward means of causing the less effective schools to acquire the characteristics of the more effective.

A number of states and localities followed this path. There was only one big problem: As noted earlier, the attributes that distinguish the very best schools tend to be homegrown, idiosyncratic, defiant of bureaucracy, and generally immune to efforts to mandate them into existence. Laws and regulations cannot substitute for—or themselves create—the commitment and shared values that must be embodied in the soul of the school. Nor can they guarantee the presence of extraordinary people in every school. If the principal is weak, if teachers work in virtual isolation from one another, if there is fundamental disagreement among the staff over goals and expectations, and if teachers and students stumble over each other racing for the door at 2:45 every afternoon, then that school is not likely to become more effective merely because state or local officials order it to do so.

Yet—because tailoring such reforms to thousands of individual situations proved too daunting an undertaking for even the most intrepid public officials—the result was a series of programs designed to put certain pieces of the "effective schools" research into common practice. One example is the proliferation of "principals' academies" and "leadership institutes" at the local, state, and national levels, meant to turn more school principals into dynamic executives, in part by acquainting them with the pertinent research findings. This is a sound plan so far as it goes, and many of the programs have been excellent.[17] But there are about 83,000 public (and 27,000 private) school principals in the country, many of them set in their ways. Revitalizing this throng is a far larger task than was actually undertaken. But even when such projects have an immediate effect, in terms of overall school effectiveness it is like supplying a single ingredient in a complex recipe. The frustration for reformers trying to turn research into policy and practice is that the recipe is the sort that starts: "First, you engage the services of a great chef, and then you renovate your kitchen." What they wanted was something more along the lines of a muffin mix.

10. *Parent choice.* Empowering parents to select their child's school is an education-improvement strategy in three ways: first, because proponents believe that youngsters learn more when enrolled in schools they want to attend and parents have some stake in; second, because we assume that, given the opportunity, individuals will flee bad learning environments and gravitate toward better ones; and, third, because accountability via the "marketplace" is believed to have a salubrious effect on schools, rewarding good ones with more students, esteem, and resources while giving unpopular ones potent incentives to change (or be changed) so as to attract more "customers."

Counterarguments have been made to each of these claims, but during the 1980s the provision of choice within public education emerged as a significant school-reform strategy. It appealed to some liberals because it offered poor and minority youngsters a route out of inferior, racially homogeneous inner-city schools—and perhaps a roundabout means of improving those schools as well. It drew many conservatives to its marketplace features and its affirmation of parental primacy. Elected officials liked it because it was bold and sweeping, hugely popular (at least in concept) with the public, and capable of being inaugurated with the stroke of a pen.[18] A number of scholars found ample basis in research for making schools more responsive to their customers.[19] And some practitioners welcomed this approach, too, both as a means of quality improvement and because of its compatibility with—some would say inseparability from—school restructuring. They reasoned that as a decentralized, building-managed education system begins to supply more varied and distinctive offerings to children who already differ in their needs and interests, youngsters and schools should be matched with one another on the basis of their individual strengths and preferences.[20]

By 1990 nine states had enacted laws providing, in effect, that children could attend public school anywhere in the state. Magnet-school programs also flourished in many cities and some suburbs. "Schools within schools" were appearing, as were "alternative" schools of many kinds. Some communities turned all their schools into schools of choice.[21] Academic specialty schools were operating, too, sometimes on a statewide basis, often for gifted students. Half a dozen states even established residential high schools for talented youngsters from throughout the state, some with a heavy emphasis on math and science. And various special arrangements were made for former dropouts to enroll in schools different from those they had left, for advanced students to take university courses while still in high school, and so forth.

With only the rarest exceptions, however, such as severely handi-capped children, these options were confined to public institutions operated directly by government. Individuals might still select private schools if they could afford to, but they got no public-policy aid or succor. Indeed, it was the discovery that an array of choices might be provided *within* public education, and that these were attractive to disadvantaged and minority families as well as to the prosperous and white, that dislodged the constitutional and political logjam in which most discussions of educational choice had previously been stuck.

That, in any case, was the situation during the eighties. By 1990 it appeared to be undergoing a dramatic change—an important in-stance of the radicalization of education reform, to which we turn next. Even in its public-only version, however, widening acceptance of choice betokened an historic development: The United States is slowly sloughing off the old assumptions that children are inter-changeable, that parents may be ignored, and that students can therefore be assigned arbitrarily to schools, with these distributions usually made on the basis of geographic residence (and sometimes race). Instead American education is evolving into a cafeteria of op-tions from which one may select the offerings that one savors for oneself or one's children.

4

❦

Educational Perestroika

*Blow up the current public education system. The system
doesn't work. No more tinkering at the margins. We need
to create fundamentally new learning environments. . . .
Traditional approaches simply won't work anymore.*
—Louis V. Gerstner, Jr., chief executive officer, RJR Nabisco, March 23, 1990

S ome of the bandages applied to our ailing schools in the 1980s
may yet heal superficial wounds. Many were not put in place
until late in the decade, and public education systems are ponderous
creatures at best, well endowed with inertia and slow to change.
Children still take eighteen years to reach their eighteenth birthdays,
and twelve or thirteen of these are still ordinarily spent in school.
A youngster graduating in 1990 would have been nearing the end
of fifth grade when the Excellence Commission reported. If those
first half dozen years of school had been disastrous, any reforms
that followed would have limited impact. Children entering the system after changes were made would obviously derive greater benefit
(or harm) from them.

Yet by decade's end, more and more educators, business leaders,
and policymakers were confessing that their efforts to cure American
schools seemed wholly inadequate to the challenge at hand. Like
the Soviet economy in the age of Gorbachev, no single alteration
did much good. Sometimes, as with bread shortages in Moscow
amid record wheat harvests, conditions perversely worsened, as if
the system were taking revenge on those fiddling with it. Occasional
progress was gauged in millimeters. For every star that twinkled,
vast stretches of sky remained dark.

"Sweeping, fundamental changes in our education system must
be made," said the National Governors' Association in early 1990,
notwithstanding five years of heavy lifting by that organization.[1] "The

public schools don't work worth a damn," said a Los Angeles businessman in mid-1989. "Band-Aids won't work anymore. We need a total restructuring."[2] A group of Harvard Business School students whose summer assignment in 1989 was an appraisal of the schools reported: "We began this project with a general sense of civic responsibility. We leave with the conviction that our nation's competitiveness and future standard of living are at stake."[3] "There is a growing sense of frustration that the reform efforts haven't worked and that more radical steps are needed," notes California attorney Virgil Roberts, head of the Los Angeles Educational Partnership.[4] "My game plan is to change the system—the massive, obsolete, ineffectual system," announced a Chicago executive.[5]

Nor was this sense of frustration and nascent revolution confined to inner-city schools and poor youngsters. "Even very middle class districts—some of the most advantaged kids who ever walked the face of the earth . . . ," complained the AFT's Albert Shanker in March 1990, "are not doing very well. . . . On any world standard, these kids would be considered academic failures rather than academic successes. For the most part, we're kidding ourselves."[6]

After evaluating state education reforms of the 1980s, William Firestone, Susan Fuhrman, and Michael Kirst of Rutgers University's Center for Policy Research in Education, concluded that

> More state activity aimed at improving public education took place
> in the 1980s than ever before. . . . But the reforms met with only
> modest success in achieving their goals. It is true that high school
> curricula are more academically oriented, standards for entering
> the teaching profession are more selective and teacher salaries
> are higher. But doubts still linger about the rigor and challenge
> of the new academic courses, the impact of these courses on at-
> risk students, and the adequacy of indicators to correctly measure
> the progress reform is making.[7]

Some educators saw silver linings. In California, for example, state superintendent Bill Honig said in mid-1990 that the state is "making steady and significant gains in getting more students groomed for college."[8] He pointed out that "from 1983 to 1988, 12th-grade test scores improved one whole grade equivalent in mathematics and one-half grade in reading. For three-quarters of a million junior-high-school students, the gains were even more impressive."[9]

By 1990, it is not unfair to note, Honig had acquired a sizable stake in the reforms under way in California, where he had led the education system for almost eight years, had labored tirelessly and imaginatively to upgrade it, and was campaigning for a third term. He did have some progress to trumpet, and he was surely due much credit for redirecting goals and priorities. He had, after all, moved into a grim situation in 1983. California, the nation's legendary trend-setter, had in the 1970s blazed a trail to educational mediocrity. As Honig recalled in his excellent book, *Last Chance for Our Children:*

> The Scholastic Aptitude Test verbal scores of college-bound seniors dropped by an average of 19 points nationwide in the seventies, but in California they plummeted by 27. Graduation requirements were weakened around the country in that same period, but in California the legislature reduced them to a single (symptomatically non-academic) demand—two years of physical education. A typical California student's school life, from kindergarten through high school graduation, was 72,000 minutes shorter than his or her national counterpart's—the equivalent of more than a year of instruction skipped. Whatever category one looked at—the amount of homework assigned, the reliance on vacuous textbooks, the booming enrollment in such dubious courses as Marriage Simulation, Gourmet Cuisine, or Baja Whalewatch—the California system had become a virtual caricature of the nation's schools in its lack of purpose, discipline, and standards.[10]

Education in California had nowhere to go but up and, after all his hard labor to raise it, Bill Honig was justified in emphasizing such evidence of elevation as he could find. Yet other indicators showed that not nearly so much had been accomplished as the situation demanded. "California businesses are finding that the ma-jority of the applicants for entry level positions cannot pass minimum verbal and math skill requirements," reported the state's Business Roundtable in late 1990. The organization acknowledged that "incre-mental improvement" was visible in the recent past but said this "will fail to close the gap."[11]

After several years of gains on the California Assessment Program, the scores of third- and sixth-graders were flat—even down a bit—by decade's end. On the state's eighth-grade writing test, just 43 percent of students were performing "adequately" in 1989.[12] While the proportion of high-school graduates fulfilling course prerequisites for the University of California had risen to 31 percent by 1989, 69 percent of the state's graduates still were not mastering those courses—a less-exacting array than the Excellence Commission had urged for everyone.[13]

A team of scholars who have been monitoring education in the

Golden State concluded in 1990 that "the academic performance of California's students is close to the national average, neither dramatically below nor reassuringly above it," and that, while state test results have "shown a generally upward trend over the past decade . . . the pattern is a halting and uneven one across grades, subjects and years."[14]

Honig himself all but admitted that he was trying to boost educators' morale by depicting the glass as half full. "I'm not saying everything is fine," he explained after Secretary Cavazos unveiled the latest edition of the Wall Chart in May 1990, "but if you throw cold water on people if they've tried, that's a terrible way to lead. People do more if they see results."[15]

Some other jurisdictions that had held to a steady reform course in the eighties averred that they, too, could see progress. Summarizing changes made during the Kean era in New Jersey, that state's Department of Education claimed: "We are turning the tide against mediocrity in New Jersey schools."[16] Certainly no jurisdiction had made more imaginative and plucky changes in its public education system during these years. Yet we have seen how ill-prepared for college are most of the graduates of New Jersey's schools. And with Governor Jim Florio undoing some of Kean's strongest accomplishments, the curves are not likely to slope upward in the next few years.[17]

In South Carolina, where a comprehensive Education Improvement Act was enacted in 1983, an evaluation six years later by a business panel monitoring progress under the reform legislation reported gains in "all eight outcomes targeted for improvement" and boasted that in seven of these "the state's public schools met or exceeded the original targets."[18]

South Carolina's education system, like those of California and New Jersey, was surely getting better, and accountability measures built into the 1983 act meant that citizens and policymakers had greater information about its performance. Yet in 1989 just two-thirds of the Palmetto State's tenth-graders passed the basic skills "exit test" the first time around.[19] On tests given in the elementary grades, only 62 percent of eighth-graders in 1988 met state standards in both reading and math.[20] There were documented (if scattered) allegations of cheating on these exams by children and teachers. And the state's long-time commissioner of education lost his bid for re-election in 1990.

My purpose is not to deprecate the progress in these three states. To the contrary, theirs were among the boldest, most vigorous, and most comprehensive education reform efforts of the eighties, and I have deep respect and affection for their leaders. The point, rather, is that the kinds of gains that even they have been able to bring off thus far have indeed been "modest," that many other jurisdictions can display nothing comparable, and that in some we see evidence of continuing (or renewed) erosion.

The average SAT verbal score fell again in 1990. Miami-Dade Community College, the largest in the nation, reported that 60 percent of students entering from the Dade County public schools were deficient in basic skills and had to take remedial courses, a proportion that had not changed in the past five years. Georgia reported that nearly one-fifth of those earning the state's relatively demanding "college prep" diplomas nevertheless required remedial help after arriving on state college campuses.[21]

In Georgia's elementary schools in 1990, after several years of slow but steady improvement, scores on both state and national achievement tests were flat in six of eight grades. Boston students were reading worse in nine of twelve grades, the first such decline after four years of slight gains. In the District of Columbia, elementary pupils deteriorated in reading, math, and language arts. New York City reported unchanged reading and math results, except in the ninth and tenth grades, where reading scores fell. In Dallas, too, after several years of improvement, 1990 brought either level or faltering results in every grade tested.

SOME HAPPIER NEWS

Not all is gloomy, however. Three encouraging trends are visible in the elementary-secondary domain for the nation as a whole.

First, on the dropout front, the U.S. Department of Education reported in 1989 that despite much talk to the contrary, "In fact dropout rates have been declining over the past ten years."[22]

School dropout-and-completion data are messy and confusing. Still, we have made gains on this front, even though some measures showed that these began before 1980 and hence could not have been caused by the reforms of the past decade. It is particularly noteworthy that recent efforts to boost school standards have not dampened completion rates, even for minority youngsters. To the contrary. What federal number crunchers call the "status dropout rate" for blacks aged sixteen to twenty-four was 28 percent in 1970 and 19 percent in 1980; by 1988 it had declined to 15 percent, only a bit worse than the 13 percent recorded for whites that year.[23]

Second, while few young Americans attain the higher plateaus of cognitive learning, we have strong evidence that the country has successfully made it "back to the basics." National Assessment data show that in reading and math, practically every student who stays in school reaches the "rudimentary" level of achievement and all but a handful make it to the (slightly higher) "basic" level in those two key skills. Ninety-seven percent of seventeen-year-olds attending school in 1986 could also "understand simple scientific principles." Writing was in worse shape, but even in this vexed domain, on the exercises with which students had the greatest success (informative and analytic rather than persuasive or imaginative writing), as many as 90 percent of eleventh-graders were at least minimally proficient in 1988. As with the dropout data, however, much of this progress had occurred before the Excellence Commission reported.

Third, achievement gaps between minority and white students have narrowed. The average black proficiency level on the 1975 NAEP reading test had trailed the average white score by 53 points at age seventeen; by 1988 that divide had shrunk to 20 points. For Hispanic students, the corresponding gaps were 41 and 24 points.[24]

The differences that remain, especially at the middle and higher levels of attainment, are anything but trifling. Whereas 46 percent of white seventeen-year-olds could read at or above NAEP's "adept" level in 1988, for example, this was true of just 26 percent of blacks and 24 percent of Hispanics. Still, the gains of the past few years are impressive. As recently as 1980, only 7 percent of black students were reading that well.

College-entrance test results show a similar pattern. The average black student's SAT score in 1989 was 51 points higher than in 1976. For Mexican-American students, the gain was 30 points. That still left immense gaps—200 and 126 points, respectively—between these minority medians and the score of the average white student, but they were narrower than the 244- and 149-point chasms of the earlier year.[25] The American College Testing Program has reported a similar trend.

RADICAL ALTERNATIVES

Had the starting point been acceptable, such signs of improvement could be taken as evidence that by decade's end we were beginning to realize the hopes of the Excellence Commission and earn some returns on our education investment. But we had begun too far down, our gains were too small and patchy, and plenty of evidence pointed the other way. "Stagnation at a relatively low level appears to describe the level of performance of American students" was the overall conclusion of the U.S. Education Department in 1990.[26] Comparing the U.S. education excellence movement to perestroika in the USSR, Peter Brimelow of *Forbes* magazine concluded in mid-1990 that it "looks pretty much like the Soviet original: For all the talk of reform, qualitative and quantitative collapse and overhead proliferation are proceeding uninterruptedly." A "more radical approach" is indicated, he said.[27]

Even as Brimelow wrote, that is precisely what could be spotted emerging in a number of places. Whereas the dominant reform strategy of the 1980s was to levy greater demands on the existing school system and raise standards for its students and teachers, in effect trying to force greater harvests from the old fields, some of today's most determined tillers of the education soil are carving new farmlands out of the wilderness. A few are actually making nonincremental changes in fundamental assumptions, ingrained relationships, long-established policies, and power allocations. These seem to me to qualify as the "radical" approaches that Brimelow urged. In the rest of this chapter, we look at four such reforms—and pay a brief visit to England as well.

CHICAGO

In 1988 the people of Chicago, Illinois, in effect declared war on their own school system, which William J. Bennett had branded the nation's worst. Violent schools; wretched achievement scores; a stodgy, selfish teachers' union; a vast, inefficient, and immobile bureaucracy—the community had endured these blights for too long. In 1986 Mayor Harold Washington invited a cross-section of the city's leadership to participate in an education "summit" but, recalls one key player, G. Alfred Hess, Jr.:

> The first year of the Education Summit was built upon the false premise that the school system would be willing to take steps to reform itself. . . . [S]ummit sponsored negotiations between the business community and the school system failed during the summer of 1987. They foundered on the general superintendent's demand for $83 million in additional support before the system would agree to any significant effort to improve its schools.[28]

When teachers went out on a nineteen-day strike in September 1987, it was the last straw. The community grew livid. The "summit" reconvened and this time, Hess reports, "the fears and desires of system administrators and union representatives were largely ignored."[29] An extraordinary alliance began to form, spanning State Street tycoons and housing-project dwellers on the South Side, transcending most of Chicago's myriad ethnic and political divisions, and incorporating nearly all of the city's numerous civic betterment organizations and philanthropies.

There was nothing to be gained, the reformers quickly understood, from tinkering with the system or asking those who had run it into the gutter to please change their ways. A full-scale power shift was indicated, unseating the traditional proprietors of public education and putting new decision makers in charge, with different rules to follow, different incentives and rewards, and different constituencies to which to be accountable. Moreover, this shift had to be locked in via legislation.

A specific plan was needed, and one happened to be available, already well formed in the minds of people like Hess and Don Moore, who had spent years analyzing the shortcomings of the old system, examining alternatives, and sketching different ways of organizing Chicago's schools.

Their plan—which, with modifications, was embraced by the reform coalition and adopted by legislature and governor in late 1988—called for wholesale decentralization of most education decision making to the building level and for the preponderance of authority in the new structure to be vested in laymen rather than professionals, especially in the parents of children attending a particular school. The new "local school councils" elected in October 1989 have the authority to set school improvement priorities, manage a portion of the budget, and, most important, hire and fire the principals.

Nowhere else in urban America has building-level decentralization been wedded to lay control. One has to turn to tiny villages in the countryside to find this combination, and even there one cannot count on finding parents in the driver's seat.

One year into actual implementation of Chicago's massive reform scheme, no catastrophes are visible but neither are daring improvements. The structures mandated by the legislation are in place, yet many of the new councils started slowly, few were seized by visions of boldly different approaches to teaching and learning, and some were consumed with interpersonal tussles and micropolitics.[30] Aggrieved principals turned to the judiciary with a challenge to the constitutionality of the entire reform act and won a partial—and probably short-lived—victory in late 1990 when the Illinois Supreme Court held that the means by which the local councils were elected (allowing only parents to vote for parent members, teachers for teacher members and so forth) violated the "one person, one vote" principle. This means the legislature must act once again to revamp the electoral arrangements and restore the legitimacy of the structural reforms. Meanwhile, racial and ethnic tensions—never far below the surface in Chicago—have reared their heads in a few schools with respect to curriculum, language issues, and principal selection. The *Chicago Tribune*'s education editor termed the first year "a bitter-sweet mixture of success, confusion and even tumult" and predicted that the second would be characterized by "growing pains as school officials, reformers, councils and teachers struggle to find their footing in a system that has never before been tried."[31]

The history of urban school decentralization in twentieth-century America is not, on the whole, a happy or reassuring tale. Yet Chicago's intrepid venture is unlike anything tried to date, and a good deal more time must pass before its success can be appraised.[32] For now, its significance lies in the insistence of the people of that sprawling city on replacing—not just reforming—their public school system.

CHELSEA

Far to the east, the city fathers of Chelsea, Massachusetts, were as disheartened by the condition of their 3,300 pupils and six schools as Chicagoans were with their giant education system. Half a century earlier, Chelsea had been one of the lighthouse districts of New England, but the community had fallen on hard times. Now among the poorest municipalities in Massachusetts, it has high unemployment, soaring rates of teenage pregnancy, a 52 percent school dropout rate, low test scores, and a large proportion of impoverished new immigrants among its 25,000 residents.

The city itself had neither the resources nor the imagination to work a wholesale change in its schools but, here, as in Chicago, people sensed that a top-to-bottom overhaul was needed.

Meanwhile Boston University's controversial and dynamic president, John Silber, had repeatedly volunteered BU to effect dramatic improvement in Boston's much-troubled public schools if that city would place the university in charge of its education system.

Boston spurned Silber's invitation, but Chelsea decided to venture it. The former chairman of the city's school committee had been quietly talking with Silber since 1985. BU had also conducted a state-mandated study of the Chelsea schools that proclaimed them to be "in crisis," their performance "abysmal."[33] And so, in July 1988, the school committee agreed in principle to let the university run the Chelsea schools.

Silber promptly consented, having hired the talented Peter Greer, a former Portland, Maine, school superintendent and senior official at the U.S. Education Department, as dean of BU's school of education.

Silber also pledged the university to raise $20 million in outside funds to help underwrite needed changes in Chelsea, promising that within five years these would produce 90 percent school attendance, a dropout rate reduced to 35 percent, and third-grade test scores boosted by 20 percent. Among the changes to be made along the way would be preschool (complete with nutrition and health care) for all toddlers in Chelsea, adult literacy programs, parent-education schemes, and higher teacher salaries.

Though it was a seductive package, the teachers' union nevertheless was up in arms, insisting that the proposed "takeover" by BU would serve both to "privatize" a public education system and to threaten numerous teacher rights and prerogatives. Lawsuits were filed; minority groups were roused, and much noise was made in the statehouse where, as in Illinois, legislative approval was needed before the city could inaugurate the changes it sought. In Massachusetts, this presented no small dilemma for then Governor Michael Dukakis, whose 1988 campaign for the presidency depended on such political assets as the perception that he was a stronger champion of public education (and labor unions) than any Republican. And, in fact, it was mid-1989 before the legislature passed the enabling bill, which Dukakis signed after adding a layer of state oversight to the arrangement.

A ten-year management contract between BU and the Chelsea school committee was quickly negotiated and, when school opened in 1989, Greer and his team were in charge. They moved rapidly to hire a dynamic new superintendent and to make other initial shifts. Though Chelsea has retained oversight of most BU decisions, as well as the right to terminate the arrangement any time it likes, the fact is that, for the first time in memory, a private university is now in charge of a public school system. Major decisions about budget, curriculum, personnel, and management are being made by Silber, Greer, and the people they hire.

At the start of the second year of Chelsea's striking school reform strategy, the eventual outcome is as unknowable as Chicago's. Money is short; local politics are pervasive; a number of promised components remain on the drawing board. In his "first annual report" on the venture, Dean Greer listed both shortcomings and accomplishments—notably including a hard-bargained new contract with the teachers' union that provides for performance-based pay. Though it was far too early to describe any results, Greer insisted that "Chelsea is moving forward."[34]

KENTUCKY

Our first two examples of radical education reforms had local origins. The third involves the entire state of Kentucky where, in June 1989, the state supreme court declared the whole school system to be unconstitutional.

A number of state courts elsewhere have invalidated school financing formulas on the grounds that they inequitably distribute money. The Kentucky court said this, but that was just the beginning. The judges then considered educational outcomes and, finding them inferior to those of other states, declared all laws and statutes pertaining to the existing school system to be null and void.

The court in effect commanded the governor and legislature to start from scratch and construct a new public education system for the Bluegrass State. After a period of confusion, the empaneling of committees, and the retaining of consultants, by February 1990—barely half a year after the court decision—a plan was developed. In late March it was enacted into law.

Chiefly the work of David Hornbeck, former Maryland state school superintendent and one of a handful of valorous and wise contemporary education policy architects, the Kentucky plan has some striking features: Instead of regulating textbooks, curricular materials, time allocations, and other school inputs and processes, the state will establish student learning goals, including performance standards for each subject and grade. Meeting these will be primarily the responsibility of individual schools, which gain substantial autonomy under the plan, but the state is to operate a system of rewards and interventions keyed to schools' performance vis-à-vis outcome goals. The rewards for success are substantial. The sanctions—if poorly performing schools do not improve—include dismissing teachers, closing schools, and giving families their choice of other schools.

Grade levels were also abolished in Kentucky's primary schools; an alternative certification program for teachers was authorized; a number of provisions were designed to minimize patronage and nepotism; and the state education structure was totally revamped, with an appointed (rather than elected) commissioner and a separate "accountability" office reporting directly to the legislature.

The price tag for all this was considerable. The legislature increased several taxes, for a total boost in state spending of $1.3 billion, and devised a new formula to distribute the money more equitably.

The prelude to the final vote in Frankfort had both high and low moments. The House majority leader, his voice breaking, made an impassioned plea to his colleagues to support this legislation for the benefit of children who "all too often start out behind in life and all they do is just get farther behind." Meanwhile the press reported that legislative leaders "dangled certain construction projects in front of reluctant House members until their votes were secured."[35]

Kentucky school reformers deferred some key issues, notably specification of academic performance standards and creation of a new assessment system by which pupil progress can be satisfactorily monitored—and rewards and sanctions administered. These are central, of course; until they are in place, the state's shiny new education car has no engine. Innumerable other issues are bound to arise as the plan is put into operation and, as in Chicago and Chelsea, we won't know for some time whether it will yield more learning for young Kentuckians. But on paper this plan represents the greatest advance toward a public education system designed around student outcomes and institutional accountability that I've seen on American shores.

PRIVATE SCHOOL CHOICE

As the public school choice movement gathered steam in the 1980s, it seemed that private schools had been forgotten. By decade's end, not even the Reagan administration was still pressing for government aid to their students, and George Bush began his term of office by making clear that he was interested only in public school choice. Congress avoided private education like typhus. When it couldn't sidestep the issue, such as when debating which institutions might provide federally financed child care, tempers flared and old wounds opened. Even the Supreme Court appeared hostile, notably in its 1985 *Aguilar* v. *Felton* decision striking down the most widely used mechanisms for delivering federal aid to disadvantaged students attending church-affiliated private schools.

Though some private school groups, faced once again with declining enrollments, pushed for inclusion in various federal programs and proposals, nobody in power in Washington gave them even the time of day. Hence when reporters asked my opinion, though my heart said students attending private schools should get whatever students in public schools get, and my mind knew that private schools are generally more effective and economical, my political antennae led me to say that this was a hopeless cause, at least for the foreseeable future, and that we should focus instead on the very winnable campaign for public school choice.

It seems that I was wearing inside-the-beltway blinders and therefore not observing clearly. While discussions of federal policy remained constipated, there was renewed activity in the states. The most dramatic example occurred early in 1990 in Wisconsin where, of a sudden, the legislature enacted a bill introduced by Representative Annette ("Polly") Williams, a black Democrat from inner-city Milwaukee and a political radical. The new program, also supported by conservative Republican Governor Tommy Thompson, provides for up to one thousand low-income Milwaukee youngsters to be assisted to attend private schools at public expense. It is, to all intents and purposes, a voucher program, albeit a rather cramped one. Its political energy came from Ms. Williams's conclusion, shared by many in Milwaukee's black community (which supplies 70 percent of the city's public school students), that children are receiving a wretched education from the public schools and that rectifying that situation is more important than preserving the system's monopoly.

The most divisive constitutional issue was sidestepped by limiting eligibility to secular private schools, but neither that severe constraint nor the tiny number of students allowed to participate made the measure palatable to the state education commissioner, various civil rights groups, the PTA, and the teachers' unions.

They quickly set out (via regulation) to make participation so complex that neither parents nor private schools would be able to navigate the shoals and (via lawsuit) to find some constitutional basis to prevent the program even from starting. State Superintendent Herbert Grover, an elected Democrat, was thus in the interesting position of seeking to block a program enacted by the legislature and signed by the governor. He was hardly bashful, though, bitterly declaring that Williams and her allies "want to tear apart the public school system."[36]

The U.S. Department of Education—which seized this occasion to declare that the Bush administration never meant to rule out private school choice—found no grounds in federal law for interfering. Nor did the first judge to scrutinize the program find any constitutional violation. After school had already opened in 1990, however, with several hundred low-income Milwaukee youngsters newly enrolled in private schools at state expense, a state appellate court ruled that the Wisconsin legislature had blundered procedurally by enacting the program as a rider on an appropriations measure. The supreme court has not yet ruled on the matter, but Williams and Thompson may need to bring the measure back through the legislature once again—if mounting hostility by Grover and his allies has not foreclosed that possibility. However, the fact that a blue ribbon education advisory panel appointed by the governor recently recommended expanding the voucher plan may be a sign that political support for it is growing. Meanwhile, Williams has become a much-sought speaker on the school choice lecture-and-conference circuit. She had accomplished something practically nobody thought possible. Throngs wanted to hear her story.

As election day 1990 neared, it began to look as if Wisconsin might not be unique. On the Oregon ballot was a voter-sponsored initiative to provide both interdistrict public school choice for the state's children *and* a tuition tax credit of up to $2,500 apiece for those selecting private schools or being taught at home.[37] The Oregon measure did not distinguish between secular and church-related schools, and we can be sure that, if and when such an initiative succeeds, a challenge will follow in the federal courts on grounds that it violates the "establishment clause" of the First Amendment. But with the changing composition of the U.S. Supreme Court, and with some respected constitutional scholars convinced that the justices have woven a tangled web of inconsistent doctrine in this area that violates the intent of the Founding Fathers, it is still possible that a program like this one would pass muster.[38]

However the courts may one day rule, the significant development in Oregon was political: As in Milwaukee, impatience with public education is mounting, as is popular support for giving people who choose private schools some help in paying their costs. Petitions to place the initiative onto the state ballot were signed by 127,000 people, many more than were needed for it to qualify. Though it eventually lost by a sizable margin, due at least partly to an intense and well-financed lobbying campaign by the teacher unions and other opponents, it remains noteworthy that a third of the voters cast their ballots in favor of so sweeping a change in the education ground rules.

We do not know, of course, whether these developments in Wisconsin and Oregon will turn out to be mere sneezes amid a chorus of public school choice or outriders of a popular movement to include nongovernment schools as a matter of course. In many other countries public aid to private schools is taken for granted. In the United States, however, it has been perhaps the most contentious of all education policy issues except for those related to race. Even reopening the possibility of assisting private school students betokens a major shift in the terms of debate.

Unlike Chelsea, Chicago, and Kentucky, where we cannot be sure that learning outcomes will improve in consequence of their sweeping school reforms, we have ample evidence that students attending private schools *do* learn more than their classmates in public institutions—and that some of this margin is due to what happens in the schools themselves, not to differing family backgrounds, income levels, or the like.[39] We have serious scholars forecasting that choice schemes confined to public schools are doomed to produce mediocre results.[40] And it is common knowledge that private schools cost less per pupil, on average, than those run by government. In many respects, therefore, inviting these institutions into the public policy tent is a wise move. Perhaps it is becoming an inevitable one.

A RADICAL PUBLIC?

Anything involving private education instantly brings out the long knives of the public school establishment. But change itself is threatening; and the more radical the reform, the more representatives of the profession seem to resemble hard-line Soviet bureaucrats contemplating a market economy. Even Albert Shanker, who has undergone a personal transformation from militant strike leader into one of the nation's foremost education statesmen, terms the changes in Chicago and Chelsea "desperate remedies" and warns his colleagues that they portend the demise of public education.[41] While Shanker shrewdly employs that argument to prod his peers into initiating bolder reforms of their own—and has himself suggested some highly original models—elsewhere in the sprawling profession there is a palpable tendency to circle the wagons and dig in the heels. Kentucky's sweeping innovations, for example, were enacted despite the misgivings of a dozen education groups, and even before they went into operation, disgruntled lobbyists were back in the statehouse trying to have certain provisions rolled back or modified. The Kentucky Education Association was also in court suing over the reform law's ban on teacher participation in school board elections.

Outside the profession, however, we see widening receptivity among business leaders, elected officials, and other elites to revolutionary changes in the ground rules. Tom Kean, who became president of Drew University after his eight-year stint as New Jersey's governor, says: "It's becoming apparent that the very organization of the school is a problem. . . . You can't tinker at the edges. You have to go to the center."[42] This is precisely what's proposed in John Chubb and Terry Moe's powerful plea for wholesale rebuilding of education's political and organizational foundations. (It's also what part 3 of this book is about.)

The general public is of two minds, however, about big education changes. Ironically enough, most people seem reasonably content with their own and their children's situations. Hence relatively few avail themselves of school choice plans where these have been enacted. And when policymakers disrupt long-established practices, such as the September-to-June school year, the popular backlash can be strong. Yet whenever they are asked on surveys, most people place the decrepitude of the nation's education system near the top of their lists of societal problems. It ranked first among domestic concerns cited by voters in 1990 election day exit polls. Most people also voice scant confidence in the capacity of the education system to solve its own problems, and welcome thoroughgoing changes in its traditional assumptions.

The annual Gallup education poll has several times asked respondents whether they favor the idea of a national high-school graduation examination. By 1988 the proportion endorsing such a drastic departure from customary practice had risen to 73 percent—up from 50 percent in 1958 and 65 percent as recently as 1984. In 1989 Gallup also asked whether people favor requiring schools "to conform to national achievement standards and goals," "to use a standardized national curriculum," and to use "standardized national testing programs to measure the academic achievement of students." To these, the responses were overwhelmingly positive: 70, 69, and 77 percent, respectively, for the public at large, with parents even more favorably disposed.

Gallup also inquired when youngsters should be allowed to decide for themselves to leave school. Here the feedback was just as startling. Only 13 percent said the decision point should come upon attaining a "minimum age," though that is standard practice in every state. Thirty-eight percent said children ought not be allowed to drop out until they "have met certain standards of knowledge and skill," and 45 percent would oblige them to attend until they graduate from high school.[44]

We can never be certain that people who respond one way when queried by a pollster will feel the same when the proposed change is actually made and they are inconvenienced by it. Still, few assumptions run deeper into the subsoil of American schooling than the idea of "local control." Few ideas have been so widely deemed beyond the pale of public acceptability as a national curriculum. And few practices are more firmly rooted than the framing of compulsory school-attendance laws in terms of chronological age rather than educational attainment. Yet unless the American public is fibbing to itself, all three of these (and many other well-watered doctrines) now seem to be dispensable habits rather than strongly held principles. As Ernest Boyer, head of the Carnegie Foundation for the Advancement of Teaching and former U.S. Commissioner of Education, said in a newspaper interview in early 1990:

> That's an historic transition we're facing. I think for the first time America is more preoccupied with national results than local school control. . . . Today, Hondas and Toyotas and Japanese VCRs have us really worried about the national competitiveness, and that's more important than whether we have local governance. The question is whether the school system is performing nationally. . . . All of this suggests there has been a sea change in the way Americans think about education.[44]

No doubt these fast-changing public attitudes and growing receptivity to radical change were on the minds of the governors and president when they convened in Charlottesville in September 1989 for their education "summit." At this historic gathering, the chief executives of the nation and the fifty states agreed to produce, for the first time in our history, a set of education goals for the entire country. They also vowed to construct measures and indicators by which to track movement toward these goals and to issue annual progress reports.

This dramatic undertaking, like the nonincremental reforms noted earlier, is in its embryonic stages. Time is needed before we can gauge its results. Establishing goals was a bold step, yet—like planning a luscious banquet menu but having neither kitchen nor cook to execute it—goals alone have little impact. Still, there is considerable popular support for this initiative. Here, once again, the American public says it welcomes changes in the education ground rules that would have been deemed unthinkable not long ago. Just as the 1989 Gallup survey indicated strong support for the idea of national goals, the 1990 poll revealed that more than three-quarters of respondents assigned high or very high priority to all six of the goals that Bush and the governors embraced. More than two-thirds even said that a political candidate's support for each goal would substantially influence their decision to vote for him or her. People were markedly less sanguine, however, about our prospects for attaining these goals by the year 2000. Perhaps they could not yet visualize a kitchen capable of serving up so grand a feast.[45]

ACROSS THE SEA

The chief cook and bottle washer of the 1980s in Great Britain also devoted herself to the education menu, and the procession of new dishes emerging from Margaret Thatcher's kitchen was as remarkable as anything to be tasted in the United States. Her Conservative government was every bit as unhappy with British education as the Excellence Commission was with ours, and it promised during the 1987 election campaign to clean up the mess. Though England's top schools (many of them private) have been celebrated for centuries for the high-quality instruction they provide to the upper classes, most young men and women in the United Kingdom were getting a thoroughly mediocre education—and not much of that, inasmuch as almost two-thirds of them terminated the process at age sixteen. The British economy was faltering, too, and with the empire gone and European economic unification on the horizon, it was time to take drastic action.

This effort, of course, proved swifter and simpler in a nation with a parliamentary structure and where decisions made in Whitehall serve as ground rules for schools throughout the land. After lively debate, some compromises, but never any real hesitation, just a year after the election Parliament put the final touches to the most sweeping education reforms since 1944.[46]

Thatcher's education revolution was grounded in two principles that at first appear slightly contradictory.[47] On the one hand, a comprehensive national curriculum and assessment system were imposed on what had long been a highly decentralized structure. Considerable thought has gone into the content of this curriculum, which spans ten subjects and eleven years of schooling, and into the assessment design, which will examine each child at ages seven, eleven, fourteen, and sixteen to see whether they are learning what the curriculum says they should.

On the other hand, and at the same time, most decisions about school management were decentralized down to the building level, effectively bypassing the local governments that formerly ran the schools. Parents gained the right to choose the schools their children will attend. Parents also comprise the majority of each school's "governors" (a building-level school board akin to Chicago's "local school councils"), and those bodies have authority over budget, personnel, and many policies.

The package is complicated, of course, by many variations and special arrangements, and a number of difficult issues remain to be resolved. Predictably, most education groups in Britain were stunned by—and opposed to—virtually the entire set of reforms. The Labour party resisted certain elements, and there has even been grumbling from Conservatives who don't like the way the national curriculum has been shaping up. But nothing broke the Thatcher government's iron determination to move far beyond perestroika-type reforms and instead rewrite the ground rules by which the system operates and authority is allocated within it. Never did anyone suppose that consensus had to be reached before radical reform could occur, or that all those affected had to give their blessing. The vital ingredient, of course, was the prime minister's steadfast insistence that the country establish clear goals for what its children should learn, construct valid means of seeing whether they've learned it, and hold the institutions to account for their results—in part by enabling the parent marketplace to reward schools that do well and to forsake those in which children do not learn.

Some menu. Some chef.

II

American Education Is to Education What the Soviet Economy Is to Economy

We have met the enemy, and he is us.

—Pogo

One morning in mid-1990, the letters editor of the *Miami Herald* was opening some of the 250 or so communications the newspaper receives from readers in the average week. Most are a page or two in length; some run four or five. But she had never seen anything like the letter that arrived that day from Jaroslav Piskacek, a *Herald* reader living in Miami Beach.

It was 221 pages long, handwritten, in an inch-wide ring binder.

Mr. Piskacek, who had spent five months composing it, was well aware that the newspaper wouldn't run the full text. This was no crank missive, though. Piskacek is a native of Czechoslovakia with twenty-three years of school- and college-teaching experience in three countries. A U.S. citizen since 1973, he is fluent in six languages and has traveled in sixty-five lands. What prompted his extraordinary letter to the *Herald* (which in turn prompted a column by the publisher) was Piskacek's burning desire to call attention to what he termed "the worst educational system that I have ever seen," to document his allegation with a lot of evidence, and to urge that something drastic be done. "We should be realistic enough," he

71

wrote, "to face the fact that our American education has been mismanaged nearly as badly as the Soviet economy had been mismanaged during the 72 years of communist rule." If the situation is to be turned around, he concluded, a total overhaul is indicated. "Let's hope that our leading educators will not waste . . . time by taking unproductive half-measures."[1]

The similarities between American public education and the Soviet economic system have been noted frequently of late. Each is a huge monopoly, run by the state according to bureaucratic and political imperatives, with little or no incentive for improved productivity, efficiency, or quality. Neither has worked satisfactorily, but each is highly resistant to change. Each has been through a time of reform: perestroika in the Soviet Union, the excellence movement in American schools. In neither case, however, have the reforms thus far had the desired effect. The Soviets cannot get enough bread into the shops. The Americans cannot get enough knowledge and skills into the heads.

Perestroika, it's now clear, did not change the Soviet economy sufficiently to alter outcomes. The interesting question is whether it was really meant to. Yuri Afanasyev, rector of the Historical Archives Institute in Moscow, explains that it was never intended to produce fundamental change. "To the accompaniment of talk about perestroika, markets, and so on," he wrote in the *New Republic* in September 1990, "the Party demonstrated once again that in essence it is fighting to preserve the system of power relations that formed over the last seventy years." Viewed in that light, he observes, perestroika "has succeeded handsomely. It was conceived as a way of restructuring society without changing its foundations."[2]

Much the same conclusion, I think, can be reached with respect to the excellence movement of the 1980s. It was the education system playing at reforming itself. It was designed to restructure without fundamentally altering the system of power relations, hence it was doomed to accomplish very little.

The more radical measures we began to see at decade's end, the kind that replace the old ground rules with new ones, may yield a bigger harvest. But they haven't yet been planted in many fields, and they're not rooted very deeply.

The roots of mediocrity, by contrast, run deep in our cultural subsoil, into the basic sources of information by which Americans appraise the performance of their local schools and their children's education, and into the entrenched habits, attitudes, and practices of many institutions besides public education. That multifaceted problem is more than the excellence movement was up to handling, however imaginative and sincere its efforts at improvement. More is involved than changing the schools; more is needed than perestroika.

In this section we examine a half dozen of what I take to be the deeper causes of educational mediocrity in the United States and of the resistances we encounter—both inside and outside the formal education system—when we contemplate efforts at reform. Many of these, the reader will observe, relate to problems the excellence movement never even got near and in some cases has barely acknowledged.

Two such problems are paramount. First, though public dissatisfaction with the education system continues to mount, it is not yet the sort of discontent that leads people to impose new demands on themselves, their children, and their own schools. We are, in that sense, continuing to allow this to happen to ourselves.

Second, the mechanisms by which American education, like the Soviet economy, is organized and run have barely changed, notwithstanding almost a decade of agitation. The structures, constraints, ideas, power relationships, and governing arrangements of public education remain grossly out of sync with the goals and values of authentic reform. The game is still being played by its old rules. In that important sense, we are not yet in charge of our own schools—or our future.

5

⚕

"How About a Marshall Plan for the Schools?"
and Other Talk-Show Explanations of Educational Meltdown

Simplicity is the most deceitful mistress that ever betrayed man.

—Henry Adams, 1907

We all fancy ourselves education experts, if only because we have all gone through the experience of schooling and most of us know children going through it today. Unlike, say, neurosurgery, jetliner safety, or anti-inflation strategies, education is a field in which we instinctively feel that success ought to be attainable through the pursuit of common sense and folk wisdom. It should not demand arcane, specialized knowledge. The thousands of members of the American Educational Research Association (AERA) will doubtless continue to hold their teeming conclaves at which scholarly presentations are made on every obscure issue imaginable. Yet education is also a domain in which research is widely ignored and occasionally mocked, not one in which scholars are honored and newscasters breathlessly report their latest findings in language accessible to the laity, as often happens with medical and scientific research.

There is great merit in applying commonsense principles to education, reason to be wary of much that is labeled research, and ample cause to resist the profession's tendency to shroud the whole enterprise in complexity. This is a field in which expertise often mingles with ideology and, when applied, yields folly. But if we err when we over-refine education issues, it is equally tempting to oversimplify them. Many Americans are quick to indict a single villain, to hinge everything on a unique variable, and especially to link the improvement they seek to one distinctive change—a magic reform carpet on which they hope we will be transported to the land of learning.

I've come to think of these as "talk-show" explanations because that is the venue in which I most often encounter them. Sooner or later in any discussion of educational decay and how to arrest it, the show's genial host or a listener who is moved to phone in can be counted on to use a phrase like, "But doesn't it all depend on . . .?" or, "Do you agree that the situation won't improve until we . . .?" or, "Isn't the real problem . . .?"

Most of the dozens of responses hold at least a grain of truth. Seldom do I hear an explanation or remedy that deserves to be dismissed out of hand, even when one can detect a trace of idiosyncratic personal experience or self-interest in it. The impulse to clarify and simplify, to cut through the Gordian knot in which American education is snarled, seems to me entirely praiseworthy; so does the pragmatic quest for straightforward, manageable solutions. But no single explanation is sufficient unto itself in this domain, no one villain deserves all the blame, nor have I yet spotted any "silver bullet" in the education policy arsenal, awaiting a sharp-eyed marksman to eliminate all our problems with a single well-placed shot.

In this chapter we take up fifteen of the most commonly encountered talk-show explanations. My purpose in briefly examining each is both to note the plausible insight the explanation rests on and to suggest why it does not suffice as a guide to action.

• *Won't more money solve the problem?* This familiar query has many subtler variants, several of which we'll consider in turn. The three responses to the generic question are, first, that we have been spending tons more money on education in recent years, yet we have little by way of improved results to show for it. Since the mid-1950s, real per-pupil expenditure has tripled. It has doubled since the mid-1960s, when, by most indicators, the qualitative decline began. As we have seen, it rose 29 percent during the 1980s and is rising another 4 percent in 1990–91, to

$5,638 per student, far more than is spent by countries whose school results are superior to ours.

However, second, much solid analysis has shown that there is no reliable relationship between school spending levels and pupil achievement.[1] It is the fragility of that link, of course, that explains today's well-warranted obsession with learning outcomes instead of education-system inputs. Having stipulated that it is results we must monitor, we cannot logically revert to spending levels as the answer to our outcome woes.

Third, large portions of our education investment are supporting the expansion of just about everything *except* pupil instruction. This is evident when one compares the $130,000 that we're now spending each year for the twenty-three children in the average public school classroom with the $33,300 average salary paid to the teacher in that classroom. Even if we make generous allowance for fringe benefits, it's still clear that two-thirds of the outlay-per-classroom is going elsewhere. This rough-and-ready estimate corresponds to a more sophisticated analysis of New York City's high-school spending conducted by Fordham University professor Bruce Cooper and his associates. They concluded in 1990 that:

> Out of the $6107 per student allocated to education by the City of New York, only 32% reaches the classroom. About 51% of the funds are "lost" prior to reaching the school, to cover the "overhead" of school system management, but another 17% or so is converted from "teacher lines" to administrative, support, and supervision within the school by the principal.[2]

More dollars lavished on the existing education system, in short, cannot be counted on even to reach the classroom, let alone to make a palpable difference in how much students learn there. I recognize that some of the changes we need to make in American education will likely require added resources (I'll be suggesting some costly strategies of my own in part 3), but surely we should first agree on what the changes will be, then calculate the price tag—and perhaps offset it with economies elsewhere in the system—rather than demand additional funds "up front" for more of the same.

• *Don't we have to pay teachers more?* Since professional salaries are the largest item in school budgets, the proposition that we must pay teachers more is a first cousin of the suggestion that we need to spend more on education. Instinctively, however, it is more appealing, as it associates the extra money with a specific, understandable, and meritorious use.

The fact is that teacher earnings have risen a lot in recent years—this being where much of the overall spending increase has gone. As we saw in chapter 3, the average salary paid to U.S. public school teachers rose 27 percent during the 1980s after adjusting for inflation. Bear in mind, too, that the average teaching work year lasts 180 days, three-quarters of the 240-day year worked by the typical American with a full-time job. Compensated at the same daily rate for a forty-eight-week year, the average public school teacher would be earning about $44,400 in 1990–91.

Though teachers continue to receive lower salaries than members of most other professions, the relationship of their pay to earnings in many fields has been improving. During the eighties, the average incomes of attorneys, professors, and engineers, for example, rose (in constant dollars) by 18, 18, and 14 percent respectively.

Unfair though it is, U.S. women still generally earn less than men, and most teachers are women. Compared to other professional women, teacher wages are not out of line. Emily Feistritzer notes, for example, that in 1985 the average earnings of American women aged thirty-five to forty-four, with four or more years of college, who worked full-time and year-round, were $24,604. For female schoolteachers in the same age bracket, the average salary that year (for a nine- or ten-month contract) was $24,016. And this was before the teacher pay boosts of the past half decade.[3]

It is worth noting that most teachers are married, many of them to individuals (often other teachers) with incomes of their own, and that many teachers also have summer earnings or other income in addition to their basic teaching salary. Hence the average family income of teachers in recent years has been roughly twice their stated salary. It was $47,421 for public school teachers in 1986, placing them close to the family income threshold of the top fifth of the population, which that year was $50,370.[4]

That is not exactly subsistence income, and it helps explain why, despite much talk about stinted salaries, many school systems are now inundated with qualified applicants for nearly every teaching slot they seek to fill. Nor are salaries and working conditions driving hordes of people out of teaching. In stark contrast to the conventional wisdom on this issue, actual turnover rates among public school teachers are quite low. Between 1986–87 and 1987–88, the most recent period for which federal data are available, just 4.1 percent of public school teachers—about one in twenty-five—left the profession. (In private schools, the attrition rate was 8.7 percent.) Among those who did, fewer than one-quarter went into different occupations or were unemployed and seeking work. The rest retired, went back to college, started a family, or took a leave of absence.[5]

Simply stated, it appears that only about 1 percent of public school teachers actually "left teaching" that year in the sense that the phrase is commonly used—that is, in order to take up another line of work. And it seems unlikely that this rate will soar in the near future. Feistritzer's 1990 survey asked teachers what they expect to be doing five years hence. Though only 62 percent plan to continue teaching where they are, just 7 percent anticipate being employed in a field other than education—and that's 7 percent spread across half a decade. I do not suggest that the huge numbers of teachers who stay in the classroom from one year to the next are all outstanding, that they're all content with their lot, or that we're doing all we could to attract, nurture, and retain more good ones. But it does seem to me that the Chicken Littles of the education profession are spreading falsehood when they allege that wretched wages are driving teachers out of education en masse.[6]

Let us also note—and be grateful—that teachers are not motivated exclusively by financial considerations. While it's true that one cannot feed a family on noble intentions, it's probably also significant that when schoolteachers are asked what drew them to this line of work and is holding them there today, the "desire to work with young people" is by far the most often-cited reason, given by nearly four out of five. Next in importance (in 1990) were "value or significance of education in society," "interest in subject-matter field," "job security," and "long summer vacation." Then came pay.[7]

Teacher salaries will continue rising, and well they should. (The National Center for Education Statistics estimates that they gained another 2 percent in "real dollars" from 1989–90 to 1990–91.)[8] Like any other field, this one must compete for talent in the marketplace, and it cannot count on appealing entirely to selfless impulses or—as it once could—on privileged access to the services of talented women and minority-group members with few professional alternatives.

Yet if teaching is to be paid according to the vicissitudes of the marketplace, we must follow that reasoning all the way: We should expect to pay teachers in shortage or high-demand fields more than we pay instructors in overstocked ones. We should pay excellent teachers more than mediocre ones and average teachers more than weak ones. And we should pay teachers willing to work in trying or hazardous conditions more than we pay those who teach in comfortable surroundings. ("Combat pay," it is sometimes called.) An outstanding physics teacher who works a 240-day year in a tough high school should earn far more than a fair-to-middling English teacher who works 180 days in a tranquil suburban setting. These are commonsensical distinctions, taken for granted in most labor marketplaces, including higher education, and easily understood by any talk-show host. Yet in the public schools today we customarily honor none of them. Teaching remains the only profession in which we pretend that everyone is exactly alike and compensate them accordingly. No wonder the pay is not as good as many teachers deserve.

• *Wouldn't smaller classes make a big difference?* The single most durable myth in education is the belief that students would learn more if teachers did not have to handle so many of them. This is also a classic example of a commonsense insight about education that turns out to be mostly wrong. And, of course, it is another version of the "spend more" and "spend more on teachers" arguments, inasmuch as the only way to operate smaller classes for the same total enrollment is to employ more people to teach them.

The allure of smaller classes as an education-reform strategy is easy to understand. "Teachers swear by" the idea, reports Tommy M. Tomlinson, one of its most rigorous analysts:

> Parents prefer them. . . . It seems obvious that children would learn more in smaller classes. They would get more personal attention; teachers could assign more homework and grade more tests and essays; creativity, innovation, and higher-order thinking could be encouraged; drop-outs and other disinterested students would be restored for learning [sic]; and teachers would not go home exhausted every night. It is an old and compelling litany, but one that regrettably rests more on faith than on fact.[9]

Class size, it turns out, has been shrinking throughout the entire period of educational deterioration. The median number of pupils in U.S. elementary classrooms was thirty in 1961, twenty-four in 1986. Corresponding figures at the secondary level are twenty-seven and twenty-two. Just 22 percent of high-school classes had more than thirty pupils in 1986, while 39 percent had fewer than twenty. Teachers' total student loads have lightened, too: In public secondary schools, the median number of pupils per teacher per day was 130 in 1966, 105 in 1986.[10]

That educational outcomes faltered while class size dwindled proves nothing, but it scarcely strengthens the claim that smaller works better; nor does systematic research into the matter, of which there has been a great deal. As Tomlinson summarizes it:

> From any standpoint, smaller classes are not a cost-efficient approach to school improvement. Indeed, viewed in total context, they are counterproductive: because they force less qualified teachers into the schools, do not improve instructional skill, cost a great deal of money (especially in times of teacher and classroom shortages), and when examined under ordinary and likely conditions of schooling, they provide only trivial and transient benefits for student achievement.[11]

Others who have examined the evidence reach similar conclusions. Robert Slavin finds no "evidence of genuinely significant achievement gains" in the early grades until and unless class size is reduced below five students—essentially a tutorial situation.[12] Glen E. Robinson concludes: "Research does not support the expectation that smaller classes will of themselves result in greater academic gains for students." "Systemwide class-size reduction would have little effect on student performance," Allan Odden observes, "and even if it did, would cost too much money."[13]

There may be other persuasive reasons to reduce class sizes and instructor workloads still further than they already have been. Improved teacher morale, for example, is worth something, and experience has shown it to be associated with smaller classes. Contented parents may be desirable, too. As a strategy for boosting student achievement, however, reduction of class size is more costly and less effective than other measures that can be undertaken.

• *If the nation is at risk, the national government should take heroic steps to fix the situation.* Debates about the proper federal role in education are old and threadbare. The most important—and enduring—fact about Washington's involvement with elementary-secondary schooling is how limited it is. In fiscal terms, Uncle

Sam now supplies between six and seven cents of the public school dollar. At its all-time peak in 1979, the federal share was just shy of ten cents. The education-budget battles that rage along the Potomac each year can be viewed as contests between the six-percenters and the nine-percenters. Though billions of federal dollars are at stake, as a proportion of total school spending the range extends from miniscule to very modest.

From time to time the National Education Association (NEA) and others have agitated for Washington to supply a much greater share. For a while the NEA pressed for school funding to become one-third federal, one-third state, and one-third local. Yet in this era of immense deficits that are all but certain to remain the dominant fiscal reality "inside the beltway" throughout the 1990s, I do not know anyone who forecasts a nonincremental increase in federal education support. Even the NEA now expects Washington's deficit fighting efforts to "exert a continuing downward pressure on the federal government's share of public school finances."[14]

Uncle Sam can be helpful in other ways: fostering innovation, paying for high-visibility pilot projects, subsidizing the schooling of needy populations, preaching from the "bully pulpit," and providing some of that impalpable commodity known as "national leadership," which is needed more than ever now that we have national goals toward which to strive. In only two domains of schooling, however, is Washington pre-eminent: the protection of individual civil rights and the production of research, information, and statistical data. With trivial exceptions, the federal government employs no teachers, confers no diplomas, selects no textbooks, and establishes no graduation requirements. Education is thus altogether different from Social Security, national defense, water quality, space exploration, and other realms in which Uncle Sam does most of the heavy lifting. That is why we should be wary of cries for him to treat school reform as some kind of a "moon shot" or to mount a "Marshall Plan" to reconstruct it. He does not occupy center stage in this drama. The most we should reasonably expect of him is an Academy Award–level performance in a supporting role, neither upstaging the stars nor giving them grounds to think they need not do their best. I don't suppose this view will persuade everyone. But I believe it would be a mistake to impute to Washington major responsibility for improving something over which Washington has no control and little leverage.

• *Start children in school earlier.* Advocates of more early-childhood education are often supporters of a larger federal role as well, mainly because the best-known and most-loved early childhood program, Head Start, is a federal undertaking. Now twenty-five years old, it generates immense enthusiasm and little opposition, and its growth over the next few years seems virtually assured.

Even Head Start's admirers, however, concede that most of the lasting good it does consists of improving the health, nutrition, and noncognitive development of disadvantaged children, and sometimes of strengthening the links between their families and other agencies and social services. Its effects on academic achievement, alas, are transitory, generally vanishing within the first few grades of regular school. "In the long run," reported a major research synthesis prepared for the federal government in 1985, "cognitive and socioemotional test scores of former Head Start students do not remain superior to those of disadvantaged children who did not attend Head Start."[15]

Though that conclusion is more an indictment of regular schooling than it is a criticism of Head Start, it must caution us against the assumption that exposing all children, or even all disadvantaged children, to programs such as Head Start before kindergarten will yield higher levels of cognitive skills and knowledge when they reach sixth or tenth grade. As Ron Haskins of the House Ways and Means Committee staff summarized the existing knowledge base in *American Psychologist* in 1989: "The considerable research literature on preschool education will not support the claim that a program of national scope would yield lasting impacts on children's school performance nor substantial returns on the investment of public dollars."[16]

Other careful scholars reach similar conclusions. Natriello, McDill, and Pallas, for example, write:

> In reflecting on the results from a host of evaluations of both national and local preschool programs over the past quarter of a century, our most important conclusion is that the most carefully conceptualized and rigorously designed, implemented, and assessed of these efforts have decreased the educational deficiencies of disadvantaged children in the short term. However, the compensatory education movement has yet to document an appreciable cognitive impact that carries through well into the elementary years.[17]

William J. Bennett has warned against the "fallacy of the fourteen egg omelet": if the chef has a terrible recipe, is an inept cook, and is accustomed to dishing up twelve- or thirteen-egg omelets that few customers will eat, simply adding another egg or two to the mixture is unlikely to yield a tastier result. If the education system is doing a mediocre job of educating youngsters who are in its grip for twelve or thirteen years, adding a year or two to the front end of that experience, and doing so in the same institutions and on the same terms, is not likely to produce much gain. It can even do harm, especially if a very young child is rushed too early into formal learning.[18] Conversely, Bennett notes, first-rate schools are able to make large differences in the lives of children who do not enter their doors until the age of five, six, or even seven.

I welcome early childhood programs as part of an overall reform strategy. Particularly for disadvantaged youngsters, the society should strive through its institutional arrangements to furnish more of the "school readiness" attributes we traditionally looked to family and community to supply. Only a grinch would object to providing young children with medical and dental care, food and clothing, caring and responsible adults, and social settings in which they can learn how to relate properly to others. For working parents and their progeny, satisfactory day-care arrangements are also important. My caution is narrower, albeit just as serious: We have no solid grounds for supposing that making all children start school at the age of five or four, or even three, would of itself produce high-school graduates who are better supplied with cognitive skills and knowledge.

• *Isn't it true that most youngsters are getting an adequate education today and that the real problem is pretty much confined to big cities and "at-risk" populations?* A particularly mischievous illusion because it feeds into the vexing inclination of many middle-class Americans to suppose that their own immediate situation is satisfactory, this view is, quite simply, wrong.

Although one can point to some splendid schools and successful pupils, the number of high-achieving American youngsters is woefully small. While most students today acquire basic skills and rudimentary knowledge, the great majority never ascend beyond that low plateau. Arnold Packer's study of the "skills gap" finds, for example, that barely one-fifth of young American adults have literacy levels in the upper domain where he expects to find two-thirds of the new jobs that will be created between 1985 and 2000.[19]

The proportion of seventeen-year-olds reading at the highest ("advanced") level on the national assessment tests actually shrank between 1971 and 1988. A similar pattern is visible in the upper tiers of the math and science assessments, as well as on most of the NAEP writing exercises.

While there has been a laudable rise in the number of high-school students taking honors courses and advanced placement exams, we must not look only at the rates of increase and fail to see how small the absolute numbers remain. Only seven out of every hundred twelfth-graders in 1989 took *any* AP tests; they averaged 1.6 tests each; and roughly a third of them scored below the 3 that is generally deemed satisfactory.[20] We could conclude with some justice that American education is presently doing a creditable job with a very small fraction of its population. But that is exactly the opposite of the "talk-show" statement we have been considering.

• *Is the situation really any worse today than ten, twenty, or fifty years ago?* The implication of this question, of course, is that if we cannot demonstrate real deterioration in educational performance, we shouldn't make such a fuss over the loss of something that never was, or at least was never so terrific.

This argument is seductive, albeit backward-looking. It fosters such commentaries as an op-ed column in the *New York Times* in February 1990, entitled "Johnny Couldn't Read in 1905, Either," quoting a principal from that long-ago year who reported that it had often been his experience, "when a pupil has reached the seventh or eighth year, to find that he or she doesn't know how to write a sentence without making a mistake in grammar."[21] We can also find a report on Albany's schools, written before the Civil War, that complained of "low, vulgar, obscene, intemperate, ignorar.t, profane and utterly incompetent teachers."[22]

That we were discontented with the condition of our education system in earlier times seems to me cold comfort in the 1990s. Comparing ourselves with yesterday is far less important than relating our present performance to our needs and hopes for tomorrow. If we aren't doing well enough to assure ourselves and our children—all of them, not just the most fortunate—a secure, prosperous, well-governed, law-abiding, culturally vibrant, and civically vital society in the years ahead, does it really matter whether we're doing better or worse than in bygone days?

In truth, we have no solid, longitudinal data on cognitive learning for the nation as a whole prior to 1971. Statistics for earlier years involve tests—such as college entrance exams—given to unrepresentative and shifting populations. We do, however, encounter lots of anecdotal evidence suggesting that American education standards were generally much higher in decades past, at least for those who stayed in school. Avis Carlson's memoir of life in Kansas in the early twentieth century, for example, contains this recollection of the exam by which one qualified for an eighth-grade diploma in 1907:

> The "orthography" quiz asked us to spell 20 words, including "abbreviated," "obscene," "elucidation," "assassination" and "animosity.". . . Two of Arithmetic's 10 questions asked us to find the interest on an 8 percent note for $900 running two years, two months, six days. . . . Among Geography's 10 were . . . "Name three important rivers of the U.S., three of Europe, three of Asia, three of South America and three of Africa. . . . In History we were to "give a brief account of the colleges, printing and religion in the colonies prior to the American Revolution . . . and to name the principal political questions which have been advocated since the Civil War and the party which advocated each."[23]

That was in eighth grade, mind you. To be sure, some youngsters at the turn of the century could not pass such a test—thus the principal's 1905 complaint about bad grammar. In those days, many did not make it even through eight grades, and high school was largely an elite precinct. As we have gradually widened and universalized access to a greater quantity of education, it has grown more difficult to know what to compare with what in terms of quality. But this is far too easy an evasion of our contemporary shortcomings. To me, it is sufficient to know that today's children are not learning nearly enough. Yesterday's probably learned more, at least most of those in school did. That we cannot conclusively prove this, however, is interesting mainly as research challenge and debating point, not as guide to policy or action.

• *Why fault the kids when the adults know so little and hold education in such low esteem?* When Diane Ravitch and I published *What Do Our 17-Year-Olds Know?* in 1987, several reviewers criticized it (and us) for not dealing with what Professor Stephen Graubard of Brown University called "fundamental questions," such as whether it is "possible that American 'children' are not all that different from American adults, that we are finding fault with one when we ought to be looking at all?"[24]

Benjamin Barber of Rutgers was even more inclined to let the kids off the hook. "They are society-smart," he asserted,

> rather than school-smart. What our 17-year-olds know is exactly what our 47-year-olds know and, by their example, teach them.
> . . We honor ambition, we reward greed, we celebrate materialism, we commercialize art, we cherish success and then we bark at the young about the gentle arts of the spirit.[25]

The nub of this complaint is the familiar radical critique of American society as a corrupt and corrupting place, dominated by materialism and philistinism and hostile to the life of the mind. As we will see in chapter 7, many of today's young people may have made a "rational" decision not to learn much in school. In that sense they are responding to signals sent by the society, and we will have to pay close attention to those signals—and, more important, to the tangible rewards and incentives we accord to education—if we want learning levels to rise. Beating on the schools alone won't get us far enough.

To that extent the radical critique merits attention. But the suggestion that the society itself is fundamentally misguided, hence that revolutionary changes must be made in it before we can reasonably expect children to acquire more knowledge or cognitive skills, is as unhelpful and defeatist a guide to action as the assertion that more money must be put on the table up front. It is to set such onerous and unrealistic preconditions for education reform that they will never be met. Once we accept this reasoning, therefore, we do not have to fret about our failure to improve. In truth, we don't really expect to try!

• *Can't we just emulate the Japanese?* This is as much an illusion as the frequent rejoinder by American educators that our culture and population are so different from Japan's that we have nothing to learn from their schools.

Postwar Japan has been an extraordinary success along many dimensions. In elementary-secondary education, their great dual accomplishment has been the simultaneous achieving of a lofty level of cognitive learning by the average student together with a very high rate (about 91 percent) of "on-time" secondary school completions. In other words, their academic standards are exacting; practically everyone meets them; and few drop out of school.

Simply acknowledging that this combination *can be* achieved is the main lesson to be gleaned from Japanese education in the late twentieth century, a lesson that American educators are wrong to ignore or scorn. Exactly how it has been accomplished in Japan, however, involves familial, social, and institutional arrangements that are alien to contemporary American assumptions. That is not to say all our own assumptions need to go unchallenged, but mimicking the practices of that small, homogeneous nation is not a very promising course of action for our huge and varied one. Nor is every facet of Japanese education wholly appealing. Most of their colleges and universities leave plenty to be desired, for example. Even at the elementary-secondary level, the Japanese themselves are restive about the scanty attention their schools pay to individual differences, and about their lackluster results in nurturing independent thinking and creativity.[26]

• *What about technology?* Many modern devices have great potential as educational tools. Computers, word processors, interactive videodiscs, calculators, sundry audio and video recording and playback machines, electronic mail, sophisticated duplicating equipment, telecommunications—these and others can strengthen pedagogy, testing, homework, research, classroom organization, school administration, even parent-teacher communications. Some of their uses are as simple as the answering machine that some teachers employ to record a brief message for parents each evening about what the class did that day, what's planned for the morrow, and what the overnight homework assignment is. (Parents can leave messages for the teacher on the same device.) Some are as basic as ready access to a functioning Xerox machine for teachers who want to lighten their dependence on textbooks by creating their own instructional materials, a possibility that contemporary "desktop publishing" procedures keep making easier and cheaper.[27]

Other technological offerings are more intricate, such as the exemplary integrated classroom computer systems developed by Dustin Heuston, and the "distance learning" schemes by which students in remote locations can study German or chemistry with teachers (and classmates) far across the prairie or tundra. Some are tailored to individual needs, such as the devices that handicapped students use for mobility or to communicate. Others help the superintendent track the performance of hundreds of schools and thousands of children.

The potential is there; present utilization lags well behind. Yet technology gives us only the tools, not the blueprints. It is a store-house of means, not a guide to ends. It can multiply, magnify, intensify, and accelerate the efforts of people, provided those efforts are well-conceived, earnestly pursued, and accurately appraised. The automobile is a wonderful device, too, and having one gives you the prospect of far greater mobility than legs, roller skates, or bicycles. But a car does little good if you lack a destination, don't know the way, are not motivated to travel, cannot drive, or have run out of gas. Much the same is true of educational technology. We've tended to reach for the hardware without having a clear sense of how we are going to use it or what we want to accomplish with it. That is why many schools have a lot of fancy equipment sitting around idle. One sees a great many television sets on the premises, for example, yet this modern medium, so very influential in the rest of our lives, has played almost no role in formal education.

I am no Luddite. The failures and missed opportunities to date have more to do with the education system than with the technology itself. Fine tools do not make wonderful creations if those wielding them lack relevant ideas and skills.

• *How about more and better research?* This "solution" (which I admit is rarely voiced on most talk shows) is by no means confined to education. The assertion that "more research is needed" has become a cliché in domains frequented by academics. Not surprisingly, it is encountered in the writings and utterances of those engaged in the enterprise of scholarship more than those who inhabit the world of practice. It is also a convenient, more-or-less unassailable statement when one is not quite sure what else to say or do. We can hardly fault the assertion of the late Lawrence A. Cremin that "we need systematic, dependable knowledge about teaching and learning in school and nonschool contexts. . . ." Nor is there any denying his factual observation that the Pentagon spends a much larger share of its budget on research than does the Department of Education. But what is one to make of Cremin's pronouncement that "until this situation is changed markedly, it is sheer nonsense to talk about excellence in American education"?[28]

That is the sort of statement that only a researcher would make and that only an academic could believe. It's well and good to favor greater outlays for high quality research—and Cremin himself headed a foundation that supports such research. It's even become commonplace to hear pragmatic businessmen urging Washington to invest more in educational R & D. Fine. I agree. The awkward point, however, is that we already possess vastly more research-based knowledge in this field than most educators and school systems are using. Stingy budgets for additional research aren't the real problem. If we systematically applied what is now known about the characteristics of effective teaching and learning, the typical American classroom (and the typical family room, too) would be a far different place.

• *Aren't teachers' unions the heart of the problem?* To be sure, they often reveal priorities and engage in practices that get in the way of good schools. That's not because they are unions, however. It's because they are part of the public school establishment and tend to be as smug, self-interested, and allergic to change as the rest of it.

Unionism per se does not alarm me. Nor do many of the stances and positions that unions take. There aren't a dozen issues, foreign or domestic, on which I have any large quarrel with Albert Shanker, for example. That's why, a couple of years back, I felt comfortable joining his AFT (as an associate member). Sure, he's notably more optimistic about school restructuring than I, and I'm a good deal fonder of private schools than he, but on the really fundamental question of what constitutes an adequately educated young American, there's not a penny's worth of difference between us. I don't mind debating means with people who share my vision of the ends to be achieved.

I can't say that about the NEA, however. That organization continues to oppose "mandated standards" linked to student achievement levels, competency testing for teachers, and statewide school choice plans, even when confined to the public sector. Most disturbing of all, the NEA's vision of what a well-educated person should know, while long on "critical thinking," "global awareness," and "problem-solving skills," is silent about history, geography, civics, literature, even science. The kind of education they dream about is not the kind I want for my children.[29]

Bad ideas, ardently pursued, are very damaging, and we've seen state and local affiliates of both teachers' unions do their (considerable) utmost to foil education reform. We've also seen happy exceptions, in places such as Dade County, Florida; Rochester, New York; Toledo, Ohio; Easton, Pennsylvania; Fairfax County, Virginia; and Hammond, Indiana, where the local union has cooperated in thoroughgoing changes, some of which have meant submerging traditional doctrines and substituting the trappings of professionalism.

We can also observe that union membership isn't inherently incompatible with professional behavior and good education in other countries whose schools we admire and whose teachers are at least as fully unionized as ours—and sometimes as politically active.[30]

The NEA and AFT say they want it both ways, of course. But most of their state and local units are still stuck in the model of industrial actions and have not accepted all the implications of professionalism. If eventually they do, the teacher union of tomorrow may look and act very different than what we're accustomed to.

Today, teachers who behave like bona fide professionals sometimes run afoul of their unions. A revealing episode occurred on Long Island when school opened in September 1990. As reported in the *New York Times*, Laurette Holdridge, a brand-new second-grade instructor, spent the first day getting acquainted with her students. She had devoted many hours of her own time during the summer to selecting library books for the children, had rehearsed the story she would read aloud to them during their first morning, had even memorized the questions she would ask them. The youngsters were charmed and, by day's end, had no desire to leave their wonderful new teacher. "We don't want to go," several cried. But rather than linger over another story, Miss Holdridge escorted them to the door promptly at 2:35 and exited the building herself five minutes later. The Mineola teachers, it turned out, had been without a new contract for some months, and as a result their union had declared a "work-to-contract" job action. So much for eager second-graders. So much for professionalism.[31]

• *If only we distributed school funds evenly, all our schools would be equally good and our children equally well educated.* Something feels inherently unfair and faintly un-American about spending more money on some children's education than on others. In Kentucky, New Jersey, Texas, and several other states, it also violates provisions of the state constitution. Lawsuits pending elsewhere will probably increase the number of states obliged by their courts to revise their school funding formulas. Sometimes, as in Governor Jim Florio's New Jersey, policy preferences or political impulses press redistributionism well beyond anything compelled by judges.

As the state share of school spending continues to grow and the local share keeps shrinking, we can expect per-pupil expenditures to grow more uniform, at least within individual states. This is probably a good thing. In any case, like the tide, it appears inexorable. We should, however, pause over three caveats before succumbing to the belief that redistributing dollars will improve American education.

First, some children cost more to teach than others. Equality of resources cannot be the highest value when determining how best to meet the educational needs of a handicapped youngster, say, or one for whom a tutor or a summer program might make the difference between success and failure.

Second, as we saw earlier, a great deal of sound research over the past quarter century has found no sure link between the resources going into a school and the learning that comes out. I'm not saying "money doesn't matter." Nothing is free. I'm saying we have no reason to expect more money per se to boost cognitive achievement levels in schools where they are low. (On the other hand, people eager to redistribute funds for other reasons can be reasonably sanguine that their actions won't drag down achievement levels in schools that lose resources.)

Third, in some states, the big urban school systems have per-pupil expenditures that are way above the statewide average. Straightforward equalization in those states could result in *less* money for districts with the most severely disadvantaged students.

• *I hear that the ABC project is succeeding in the XYZ schools. Why not install it everyplace?* Replicating successful strategies, programs, and projects is irresistibly attractive. And more than a few people earn their livings—sometimes quite handsome livings—proselytizing for their particular approach to classroom effectiveness, assertive discipline, cooperative learning, you name it. An entire federal program—the National Diffusion Network—provides modest subsidies to the developers of projects that have been vetted by a government panel.

The field of education reform today has more nostrums and cure-alls than a herbalist's shelves, and there seems to be a new one every month or so. Issues and enthusiasms sweep like hurricanes through the journals, professional meetings, and teachers' in-service education sessions. All of them appear well intended. Some of them have had good results in one or two places and may or may not function well in other settings. Replication is never guaranteed. And the evaluation criteria by which those projects are deemed to work are grotesquely softer than we permit in other domains. American medical science is occasionally faulted for being too slow and fussy in approving new drugs, procedures and devices. Just the opposite situation obtains in education. Anything that can be described as "innovative," or accompanied by a single success story or a couple of testimonials, is fair game to promote and market. Is it any wonder that the best teachers tend to be wary of change?

• *Isn't the problem really all the fault of the (complete the question by filling in your choice of dumbed-down textbooks, vapid teacher-training programs, the inherent rigidities of the public sector, entrenched racial segregation, Eurocentric curricula, a shortage of minority instructors, the decline of religion, overemphasis on testing, violence, drugs, homelessness, and so on)?* The quest for scapegoats and villains in education goes on seemingly forever. The targets occasionally change, but never the large goal of fingering some readily identifiable culprit other than ourselves. Recall Lester Maddox again, and his "better class of prisoners." There is plenty wrong in education, it seems to me, and plenty of blame to mete out. But as we shall see in the next chapter, a goodly share of it belongs on our own doorsteps.

6

℘

The Lake Wobegon Effect
Ignorance Is Someone Else's Problem

Where ignorance is bliss, 'tis folly to be wise.
—Thomas Gray, 1742

We display the symptoms of a curious national schizophrenia. Nearly everyone now acknowledges that the United States has lapsed into a grave state of educational and social decay from which it urgently needs to extricate itself. Yet most Americans are also satisfied with their own immediate situations, the education of their children, and the performance of the schools they know best. As a result, few of us feel a strong impulse to alter our own behavior or educational circumstances. Other people should definitely change *theirs.* The schools on the other side of the state must be dreadful. That's why the nation is at risk. As for me, however, I'm all right, Jack.

The most dramatic manifestation of this gap between reality and self-perception among students themselves was the 1988 international achievement test, on which American thirteen-year-olds earned the lowest scores among participating countries in actual mathematics proficiency, but, when asked on a background question whether they judged themselves to be good at math, awarded themselves the highest marks in the world.[1] Children in other lands performed better on the test itself, yet held lower opinions of their own mathematical prowess.

Harold W. Stevenson, professor of psychology at the University of Michigan, has spent years comparing the performance of elementary school students in the United States with that of youngsters in Taiwan,

Japan, and China, and his research includes surveys of the children's opinions and attitudes. American girls and boys, he has found in one brilliantly conceived study after another, give themselves top ratings when questioned about such characteristics as their own abilities, their educational attainment to date, and the performance they expect from themselves in the future. "When we asked American first-graders how well they believed they would do in mathematics next year," Stevenson reports:

> 75 percent said they would be among the best students. Only 37 percent of the Sendai [Japan] and 50 percent of the Taipei first-graders were this confident. . . . Similarly, 58 percent of the American fifth-graders expected to be above average or among the best students in mathematics in high school, percentages that again were much higher than those of their Japanese and Chinese peers, among whom 26 percent and 29 percent, respectively, anticipated this degree of success.[2]

Older students appear contented, too. When 2,600 Minnesota youths were queried in early 1990 about the education they were receiving, 63 percent pronounced themselves satisfied or very satisfied with it, and 25 percent said their education was OK. Only 12 percent voiced discontent. Though twelfth-graders were more apt to complain than were younger students, even in the last year of high school the dissatisfaction rate was less than one in five.[3]

We can't be sure they're even aware that the *country* has a problem. Perhaps because they pay scant attention to public affairs, many of these young people are oblivious to the evidence of national decrepitude. A friend who teaches college at a highly regarded private institution presented her sociology students with some recent international comparisons of education achievement. "They were aghast," she reports. "They had no idea that we ranked last."

Their parents are of two minds on the matter. For years, we've seen a recurrent pattern in the annual Gallup education survey questions that ask people to grade U.S. public schools in general and then, separately, to assess the schools of their community and those attended by their own children. Year in and year out, the parents of public school students give higher ratings in all these categories than does the general public. And year in and year out, parents award better grades to local schools than to public schools in general and higher marks still to the schools their own youngsters attend. The closer the school is to them, it appears, the more favorably they regard it.

On the most recent of these surveys (1990), just 21 percent of the public gave "honors" grades (A or B on the traditional scale) to American schools in general. Parents of public school students upped that slightly to 23 percent. But when asked about schools in their own communities, the parents conferred honors grades 48 percent of the time. And when asked to appraise "the school your oldest child attends," a whopping 72 percent awarded As or Bs. Most of the rest (19 percent) gave their child's school a C. Only 9 percent conferred lower marks or professed not to know.[4]

Stevenson has found American mothers to be more sanguine about their children's academic performance than are their Asian counterparts.

> Not only did American mothers generally have the most favorable evaluations of their children, they also were the most satisfied with their child's current academic performance. . . . Mothers also were asked to evaluate the effectiveness of the schools in educating their children. American mothers were very positive: 91 percent judge the schools as doing an "excellent" or "good" job. This was more than double the percentage of Chinese mothers (42%) and Japanese mothers (39%) who chose these categories. . . .
>
> In summary, American children had to do less well than Chinese and Japanese children for their mothers to be satisfied and much worse before their mothers expressed dissatisfaction with their academic performance.[5]

What is more, Asian parents tend to believe that all children can do well if they work hard. "The slow bird needs to start out early," says the Chinese proverb, "but it can reach the same destination." Hence when Asian children perform poorly in school, their parents ascribe the problem to lack of diligence and effort—curable conditions. American parents are more fatalistic. They are apt to cite differences in innate ability as the reason some children learn more than others. Children faithfully absorb these beliefs from their parents and the culture—and conduct themselves accordingly. (If you and your mother and father think your reading or math achievement is unrelated to effort and thus largely beyond your control, well, why lose sleep over it?)

If you want to worry anyway, fine, but don't expect your teacher to. Most American teachers also feel good about the quality of education in their schools. On a Harris poll released in late 1989, a stunning 92 percent of them said that their present school was providing its students a good or excellent education. Just 7 percent rated that education "fair," and virtually none said it was "poor." Though teachers in inner-city and heavily minority schools weren't as likely to say "excellent," fewer than one in five evaluated the quality of education as less than "good."[6]

That is not to say teachers are content with their lot, satisfied with their schools, or oblivious to student problems. Drugs, dropouts, absenteeism, meager basic skills—these and other concerns rank high on teachers' lists of difficulties confronting the public schools and the children enrolled in them. Though most secondary teachers also believe such woes are worsening, they *still* think well of the education provided by their own schools.

As for administrators, an Allstate survey reported in early 1990 that 91 percent of them believe that American public education today is doing an excellent, very good, or good job at turning out an educated population. (Business executives asked the same questions came in at just 23 percent, a massive difference in perception.)[7] Feistritzer's 1987 study found 71 percent of superintendents and 60 percent of principals awarding "honors" marks to public schools in general. Asked about their local public schools, the administrators' replies grew still rosier: 90 percent of the superintendents and 88 percent of the principals conferred A or B grades on their own schools, while fewer than 2 percent gave marks below C.[8]

Local school board presidents are interesting hybrids. When asked in 1989 to appraise public education in the nation as a whole, the scores they gave resembled those of the general public: just 33 percent handed out "honors" grades. But when asked to evaluate the schools in their *own* community—institutions over which they preside as school board leaders—they echoed the teachers and administrators: 79 percent conferred A or B grades and none gave failing marks.[9]

Consider the implications for educational improvement. If the children think they're doing pretty well; if parents think their children are doing well enough (and that any shortcomings are God-given rather than self-induced); if people believe their local schools are doing well; and if the teachers, administrators, and policymakers in those schools agree with that appraisal, why should any people feel moved to alter their actual behavior, demand different results from themselves or their children, or press for significant change in the schools their daughters and sons attend?

Yet if individual behavior does not change in millions of individual cases, if hundreds of thousands of families do not raise their educational standards and the cognitive obligations they lay on their children, if the staffs in tens of thousands of schools do not radically boost the educational productivity of those institutions, and if policymakers in school systems all around the country do not sharply alter course, there is no reason whatsoever to expect our lackluster averages and totals to brighten.

WHY THE SCHIZOPHRENIA?

Decades of survey research have shown that Americans tend to feel good about themselves and to be more pleased with the concrete example that they know—be it a congressman, a school, a church, or a newspaper—than with the distant and more abstract institutions of society: Congress, the education system, organized religion, the media, and so on.[10] We seem to favor incumbents, too. Whether out of mere laziness, genuine satisfaction, or fear of the unknown, we are seldom inclined to trade in the familiar—however many warts it may have—for the alien.[11]

We tend to be fairly content with our own personal situations, too, even when fretful about the state of the nation, the quality of our leaders, and the performance of major institutions. "Severe criticism of institutions," Seymour Martin Lipset and William Schneider observed in 1987, "has coincided with a high degree of satisfaction with personal and family situations and with optimism about the future."[12] This has been true in economics (my family is comfortable, though the national economic picture is bleak), health, housing, and evaluating the overall quality of one's life. Though we have seen some decline in recent decades in Americans' appraisals of their own well-being, Lipset and Schneider report that this "has been modest in comparison with the fall-off in evaluations of the country's well-being."[13]

It appears, then, that the widely acknowledged dismay most of us feel with respect to American education does not spring primarily from our own immediate experiences with that system or from acute displeasure with the schools we know best. This is so, I believe, because of the dissonant feedback we have been getting. On the one hand, our national leaders, the news media, and sundry other sources that report evidence and conclusions beyond our direct experience have been telling us that education is in a mess. We tend to believe them. Yet we feel good about our own schools because the feedback we've been getting about them—and our children's progress within them—is of a very different sort. Simply stated, we've been hearing for some time that the system is failing at the "macro" level, but we've been told for even longer than Steven and Janet and Carlos and Tawana are doing satisfactorily. And we've accepted both reports.

"The public," Schneider and Lipset say, "is inclined to believe that the system works unless it receives compelling evidence to the contrary."[14] For a decade or so now, we have been drenched in evidence that the nation's schools are working poorly, and this shows in public opinions. In 1974, when Gallup first asked the American public to grade the schools, the average grade was B−. By 1983 it had fallen to C−.[15] Those nine years, of course, spanned the revelation of falling SAT scores, the beginnings of the "back-to-basics" movement, the declaration of the Excellence Commission that the nation is "at risk," a great many other studies and reports saying essentially the same thing, and a vast amount of media attention to our education failings. It would be remarkable if the public's wholesale appraisal of schools in general had not declined.

Yet, during the same period, we have continued to receive upbeat reports about the education of our own children and many claims that our local and state school systems are doing a good (and ever-improving) job. Unfortunately, much of this retail information is untrustworthy, the product of the system's preference for favorable public relations and the profession's fervent belief in positive reinforcement and encouraging feedback, reality to the contrary notwithstanding.

TEST SCORES

Several times a year, in practically every community in the land, the press pays close attention to test results. Most Americans are accustomed to gauging the performance of their school systems by whether those scores are rising or falling and by how well the children in their town or state compare with national norms and averages.

We derive our sense of how the country is doing by inspecting nationwide results on the SAT, NAEP, American College Testing Program, and intermittent international comparisons. These wholesale outlets have conveyed plenty of bad news in recent years, but such data are never available for our own city or town. Most of the time they are not even accessible for the state and, when they are—as with college entrance scores—test makers and educators sternly warn us not to use them as indicators of school performance. Hence we are likely to form our retail opinions about state and local educational progress from the results of testing programs organized and administered by those selfsame states and localities, most often from standardized, norm-referenced tests that are commercially produced and vigorously marketed. These include such familiar names as the Stanford Achievement Test, the Iowa Test of Basic Skills, and the Comprehensive Test of Basic Skills. Especially if we have no children of our own in school, aggregate scores on these instruments are apt to constitute practically all we know about the condition of public education in our community. In practice, since few of us have the time or psychometric sophistication to analyze the actual data, our opinions are most likely to be shaped not so much by the scores themselves as by what those issuing them *say* they show.

In chapter 9 we will examine why these testing programs do not work well as dynamic accountability mechanisms for the education system. For now, the essential fact about them is that they customarily relay cheery news, both about how the children in our state or town are doing compared to the rest of the country and about how they are doing today compared with yesterday.

In 1987, Dr. John James Cannell, a previously obscure West Virginia physician, staggered the education and testing communities when he issued a little report asserting that he "had surveyed all fifty states and discovered that no state is below average at the elementary level on any of the six major nationally normed, commercially available tests." He also announced that 90 percent of local school districts claim that their averages exceed the national average and that "more than 70 percent of the students tested nationwide are told they are performing above the national average."[16]

How could that be? Surely this Dr. Cannell must be wrong. He had no track record as a psychometrician, after all, or as a survey researcher. Perhaps he made methodological errors. Maybe he is some sort of demagogue. States and localities certainly would not dupe their own citizens about their educational performance! And even were they tempted to do so, those highly regarded test publishers would demand honesty and integrity. Well, wouldn't they?

I was working at the U.S. Department of Education at the time, and we engaged several of the nation's foremost testing experts to see whether they could replicate Cannell's results. If he was onto something real, the country needed to know it. If he was not, his sweeping allegations should be laid to rest.

It turned out that Cannell was essentially correct. "There can be no doubt," says the RAND Corporation's Daniel Koretz, "that current norm-referenced tests overstate achievement levels in many schools, districts, and states, often by a large margin."[17] In measured language, scholars at UCLA's Center for Research on Evaluation, Standards, and Student Testing concur:

> Clearly it is the exception rather than the rule for a state to report that its students, particularly its elementary school students are performing below the national average. Although it is somewhat more common for a district than a state to report that less than half of its students are scoring above the national median, a substantial majority of districts reports that their students are performing above average (i.e. more than 50% of the students are reported to be above the national median).[18]

Cannell's study quickly became known as the "Lake Wobegon" report, after the mythical Minnesota town popularized by Garrison Keillor, in which "all the children are above average." But it was not really funny, at least not for anyone concerned about the condition of American education. How could it be, we wondered, that the nation was receiving such glum reports about its overall educational performance while those living in particular states and localities throughout the same nation were awash in good news about the achievement of their own children? The whole seemingly bore no resemblance to the sum of its parts.

There are multiple reasons for the discrepancy, most of them technical, bound up with the selection, design, administration, and scoring of the commercial achievement tests utilized by most school systems and with the state assessment programs used in some jurisdictions. It matters, for example, how many times a particular version of a test has been administered, how old its "norms" are, how faithfully the norming population mirrors the youngsters taking the test, how many children are excluded on account of handicap, and so forth. The inflated results—and the unwarranted sense of well-being they induce—can also be traced to the behavior of teachers and pupils, many of whom try to outfox the tests and some of whom, regrettably, do cheat. But the simple underlying reason for it all, the wellspring of the Panglossian message that our schools, if not yet perfect, are surely good and getting better, is that those issuing and interpreting the results have a large stake in presenting their constituents with good news. Were that not so, the "Lake Wobegon" effect would be as insubstantial as the place after which it is named.

With rare exceptions, the testing program is designed, managed and financed by the same people who are responsible for running the education system on which it purportedly provides feedback. They select whichever test they like—and Cannell alleged a quiet conspiracy among test makers and test users to shade that choice in the direction of the desired results. When the time comes to disclose the scores, the same people stage the event, write the press release, and organize the first round of interpretation and commentary. Few state and local education systems have counterparts of Washington's General Accounting Office (GAO), with its responsibility for independent appraisal and frank evaluation of the work of other government units and programs. Nor do we have the tradition of an independent education "inspectorate," as in England. Though a specialized division of the education department may be responsible for testing and assessment, when the time comes to present the latest results to the board, the governor, the legislature, and the press, we can be sure that the state commissioner of education (or local superintendent) will put his or her own "spin" on them. Even where there is an outside watchdog group of some kind, as in South Carolina, its members and staff are apt to have a sizable investment in the success of the reforms whose progress they are monitoring. That is no reason to question their integrity or to fear that they will cover up contrary evidence, only to understand why they must contend with a powerful temptation to put the best possible face on their reports. If, in the process, they hype the good news more than the other kind—well, don't we all tend to do that?

Those running an education system—any system, really—are obviously best off when their bosses, clients and constituents believe that system is working well and getting better. Warm feelings of pride and contentment on the part of the public make it a great deal easier to retain one's job, pass the next bond issue or tax levy, burnish one's reputation, advance one's career, and avoid ulcers. If one has been centrally involved in changing the system, one has also gained a personal stake in the fruits of those reforms.

The slippery aspect of psychometrics is that it is seldom necessary to lie or even distort the data in order to impart favorable impressions to unsophisticated audiences. So long as one selects the right measures, analyzes the results imaginatively, and interprets them in the most favorable light, one can readily convey the impression that the schools in Kansas or Portland or wherever are doing a respectable job. And as the stakes rise, as the idea of accountability for results sprouts incentives, rewards, and perhaps also punishments, as pleasant or painful consequences begin to be associated with one's test scores, the temptation to echo Dr. Pangloss mounts in proportion.

Most of us are untutored in test lore and psychometric convention. Take, for example, the matter of "grade level." Perhaps the single most common boast of test score press releases concerns the (always-sizable) fraction of the pupil population in one's school, district, or state whose results are said to show them "at or above grade level." Told that 64 percent, say, of fourth-graders in the Springfield public schools are in this enviable condition as shown by the latest nationally normed test results, the man in the street is likely to suppose that the Springfield school system is doing fine. That, of course, is exactly what he is meant to think.

What few realize is that "grade level" has no fixed or prescriptive meaning. It has nothing whatsoever to do with what a well-educated fourth-grader *ought* to know and be able to do. To the contrary, it simply indicates the performance of the *average* fourth-grade student on this particular test, based on the results of a national norming population which may or may not even be statistically representative of all fourth graders and whose members may or may not have studied the same things in fourth grade as the Springfield students. There is also the matter of when the norms were constructed; though this particular administration of the test doubtless yielded the "latest" results, if the national norm to which today's students are compared was itself established six or eight or ten years earlier, then we are seeing the performance of today's Springfield child described in relation to the attainment of yesterday's students, which may not be a trustworthy guide to the present.

To be "at or above grade level," when grade level is denoted in these questionable ways, is not necessarily something to take much pride in. Forget the statistical reality that, so long as grade level is defined as an average, half the students are supposed to be beneath it. We want to think of grade level as something fixed and reliable, a real standard like a yardstick or measuring cup. Most of us also want to be told that our child and the other children in our town and state are doing well, preferably that their scores are high and rising. Will we really be grateful to educators or elected officials who advise us otherwise? Or who patiently explain to us that "grade level" is only a statistical happening, not proof of educational success?

I cannot get too angry at school administrators who emphasize good news. Nor is there much point in beating on the American public for its spotty understanding of the nuances of testing and assessment. Let us instead recognize that no properly functioning accountability system would be organized this way. "It is not permitted to the most equitable of men to be a judge in his own cause," Pascal wrote in the seventeenth century.[19] Yet in American education in the late twentieth century, we look to those who run the system also to judge it, to determine what evidence is germane to the case, and then to background the press on the significance of the verdict. Is it any wonder that we've grown accustomed to annual accounts of how well the schools in our community and our state are doing, how much better than before, how much better than the rest of the country? And, since we tend to believe educators and to possess few independent sources of information on the matter, is it any wonder that we are apt to think well of our local schools even while paying lip service to the proposition that the rest of the nation is "at risk"?

OUR OWN CHILDREN

Those same standardized test scores constitute a major source of information on the educational achievement of our sons and daughters, nieces, neighbors, and grandchildren. If the school district issues a press release boasting that 73 percent of its elementary school students are above the national median in math and 67 percent surpass it in reading, that customarily means the same proportion of local parents are also getting laudatory reports of their children's performance on that test, reports that show them—Ricardo and Sharon and Bruno—to be above the national average (and therefore above "grade level"). These individual scores, expressed in "percentiles," "stanines," "deciles," and the like, are often confusing to parents but the impression we are apt to glean is that our kids are doing well.

Not everyone's scores are above average, to be sure, and some people are less pleased with the schools their children attend. If 72 percent give high marks to those schools, 28 percent grade them C or lower. Minority and inner-city parents indicate more dissatisfaction. Though interdistrict choice plans have not had many takers, "magnet" programs that allow families to change schools within their own communities are often oversubscribed. The registration lines sometimes start to form several days ahead of time. Parents who were entirely content with their children's present arrangements presumably would not camp out on the administration building lawn in order to effect a change. Nor would the kinds of radical reforms we have seen beginning in places like Chelsea, Milwaukee, and Chicago have happened without considerable popular dissatisfaction in those communities.

Some children receive direct signals from school authorities that their achievement is unsatisfactory. Though the practice of grade retention is unpopular within the education profession, most Americans believe that children ought not be promoted until they are academically ready for the work of the next grade.[20] Accordingly, 18 percent of all 1988 eighth graders had repeated at least one year of elementary school.[21] This plainly indicates that some youngsters are not cutting the mustard. Those students and their parents undoubtedly come to realize this.

They may be learning it the hard way, however, and may even be surprised when the end of the year rolls around and they are not promoted. For so far as one can tell from talking with educators, reading their professional journals, and attending their conferences, most American teachers and principals strive to give students and parents only positive feedback, encouragement, and reinforcement.

I could not eavesdrop on parent-teacher conversations, but in preparing this book I was able to inspect a selection of the comments that teachers put on children's report cards during the past two years in a well-regarded middle-class school system. It is not a scientific sample, but I believe that the 150 or so student reports I examined from that system's elementary schools are indicative of the messages teachers transmit to parents and, of course, to the youngsters themselves.[22]

The report cards contained a mishmash of letter grades, numbers, and symbols, the code varying from school to school, sometimes even within a single building. The system evidently has no uniform grading scale or standard. Hence the written comments from teachers are doubly important for divining how one's child is actually doing.

Those I inspected were quite varied, some brief to the point of terseness, others filling a full page each marking period with single-spaced typing. Some teachers strove to tailor their remarks to each child; others adopted formulas or standard phrases. (One solemnly reported to the parents of about half her students that their progeny are doing "some of the best work in the class." Lake Wobegon occasionally floods the classroom, too!) Though some are dryly impersonal, others gush with affection and are peppered with exclamation points and decorated with little "smiley faces."

When it comes to academic performance, however, while it was not uncommon for the teacher to indicate some direction in which the child might improve, almost never did I encounter any comment designed to alarm parent or child about the youngster's performance to date. There were no statements calculated to stop them in their tracks, to rattle their complacency, or to demand—with all the authority of teacher and school looming in the background—that a whole new leaf must be turned immediately or dire consequences will follow. To the contrary. It was as if teachers had practiced how to avoid giving offense, raising blood pressure, or causing Mom and Dad to confront Junior about the sorry state of his schoolwork.

I've drawn the following nine extracts from report cards that indicated shortcomings in pupils' performance during the year. Bear in mind as you read them that many others contained only praise, or factual recitations of what youngsters had (and sometimes had not) learned, the books they were reading, and the topics their papers and school projects had addressed. The latter reports were often written in neutral language that let slip few adjectives or judgmental remarks by the teacher.

Ethan is an excellent reader who really enjoyed his novel selections this quarter. His log was accurate and showed incite [*sic*]. His attention span in the afternoon when we have science, health and social studies showed a marked improvement and his grades reflect this. (Grade 3)

Michael does very good work when he chooses to participate in class activities and complete assignments. It is hoped that next quarter Michael will participate more actively. (Grade 6)

Alix should be very proud of her fine progress in Social Studies. She has also shown some good growth in Social and Work Characteristics. Alix shows a great deal of responsibility for her school work but needs to accept more responsibility for her social behaviors and the resulting effect on interaction with peers. (Grade 6)

Sam continues to work hard. Progress in all areas is good; however, we need to encourage him to review and proofread his work. Many careless mistakes can be avoided if he take [*sic*] the time to do this. He has had some socialization problems. The support from home is appreciated. (Grade 5)

Wendy is a very capable student. She is an excellent writer and she contributed much to our "National Deficit" project. Wendy had a difficult time with long division. She needs to spend more time reviewing math and scientific principles next quarter. She did not submit a social studies notebook. Wendy did a fine job on her George Washington report. Wendy served as our class treasurer this quarter and did a terrific job. (Grade not known)

Although Gustav is making satisfactory progress, greater effort would improve his achievement in all subject areas. He should focus on completing quality assignments on time and on the efficient use of school time. He repeatedly does not see assignments through to a successful completion. If he applies himself to his work this last nine weeks and adequately reviews and prepares for tests, he can bring all of his work up to his full capacity. I will work closely with him the last nine weeks to help him succeed. (Grade 6)

Toby's reading grade has fallen since the beginning of the year because he will not devote a daily, consistent effort to his work. I am proud of his achievement in spelling and language this grading period! A review of math skills over the summer would be helpful as a reinforcement before seventh grade. Toby, enjoy seventh grade, work hard, and never lose your sweet personality and cute smile! (Grade 6)

Sonya has many fine qualities, among which are her cheerfulness and good humor. She is capable of doing better work than she has demonstrated during this grading period. She often lets talking to her neighbors interfere with her work. She will make better use of her abilities when she realizes how important it is to listen when directions and explanations are given. I hope to see Sonya put more pride and effort into her written work and to ask questions when she needs further explanations. (Grade 4)

Jason continues to make very good progress in the integrated language arts curriculum. . . . Jason is encouraged to employ correct punctuation in all curriculum areas as his thoughts are impressive but often difficult to follow without capitalization or punctuation. . . . Jason enjoyed the "hands on" approach to learning the metric system in science. . . . His progress in Science is satisfactory. Achievement could be improved by a more responsible attitude, more careful organization of materials, and wiser use of time during daily experiments. (Grade 4)

As a parent receiving reports such as these, most of the time I could make out that my child is not perfect (something I probably already knew), but in few cases would I deduce that he or she is in any serious academic trouble. What I need to hear from the teacher is what's wrong, how bad it is, and what is the price (if any) if nothing changes. As one with some practice in education jargon and reading between the lines of school communications, I am probably better equipped than many parents to draw inferences from report cards like these. But what is a recent immigrant, "underclass" parent, or person without much education to make of such comments?

There are several reasons for this situation, I believe. Bad news about a student's performance is apt to reflect unfavorably on teacher and school, too, even to invite parents to say "Well, if that's the situation, why didn't you folks *do* something about it instead of just complaining to me about Chrissy?" What teacher wants a mob of angry moms and dads demanding to see her, phoning her at home in the evening, or griping about her to the principal or school board? How many times must one be burned before concluding that a cold stove is safer?

Teachers have also been admonished from their earliest days in the college of education that it is vital to provide youngsters with positive reinforcement rather than criticism. "Elementary school teachers are being taught," reports Rita Kramer after an extended examination of teacher education programs around the nation, "to concern themselves with children's feelings of self-worth and not with the worth of hard work or of realistically measured achievement."[23] This belief is strengthened by what they subsequently read in their professional journals, what they learn from mid-career education programs, their own peer culture, and their unions. The NEA, for example, admonishes its two million members that they "must modify the school culture to eliminate any negative effect it may be having on students."[24]

What is more, teachers, especially at the primary level, tend to be kindly, warm, empathic people. Judgmentalism is not their bag. They have bought into the therapeutic ethic. The last thing on earth they want—probably even more fervently than they don't want ignorance or illiteracy—is to be cruel or destructive. Negative comments are believed to damage children's frail egos, to lower their self-esteem, to alienate them from learning, and to cause stress and anxiety. Moreover, angry parents may do them emotional, perhaps even bodily harm. Far safer to say what is good about students' schoolwork and either leave the bad to be inferred from close readings or not to be noticed at all. That such well-intended kindness surely contributes over time to the production of individual and national "dumbth" is someone else's concern. I do retail, not wholesale. It's that mischievous ten-year-old Sam and his up-tight parents I have to contend with.

Then there is the matter of educators' expectations. One of the major findings of "effective schools" research is that schools in which children learn a great deal are schools in which they are *expected* to learn a great deal. The evidence, writes former Education Secretary Lauro Cavazos, "confirms common sense: Youngsters seldom achieve more than what parents, their teachers, and other adults expect of them."[25] In most realms of our lives, most of us work about as hard—and accomplish about as much—as we are obliged or expected to by whomever sets the rules of the activity and establishes its rewards and incentives. This is a truth about human behavior that goes far beyond formal education. Much as one might yearn to live in a society of self-starting, inner-directed, highly motivated strivers, we are destined to inhabit a world in which external standards, minimums, and requirements have more to do with actual attainment levels, especially in domains such as academic learning, where the intrinsic reward is, shall we say, so subtle as not to be a strong incentive for most people.

The expectations that teacher and school communicate to child and parent thus matter hugely. And it is those expectations alongside which the youngster's actual performance is placed for purposes of appraisal and feedback. If Mrs. Turner does not really think Tabitha can handle much science, Tabitha may well earn a good grade (and gushy comment) from Mrs. Turner while wrapping her mind around only a smidgen of scientific knowledge. She has met the system's expectation and thus deserves praise. That she knows little science is something she and her parents will discover only much later, if at all.

This unholy marriage of low expectations and high marks is especially devastating for disadvantaged and minority youngsters. When a communitywide task force in Prince George's County, Maryland, analyzed the large performance gap between white and black students in that school system, it found, reports Superintendent John A. Murphy, "that the root cause of the gap was negative attitudes about the potential of black students."[26] Famed Los Angeles math teacher Jaime Escalante, whose experience is mostly with Hispanic youngsters, puts the matter even more starkly:

> Our schools today . . . tend to look upon disadvantaged minority students as though they were on the verge of a mental breakdown, to be protected from any undue stress. . . . Ideas like this are not just false. They are the kiss of death for minority youth and, if allowed to proliferate, will significantly stall the advancement of minorities.[27]

There is some evidence that this has already occurred, that minority youngsters and their parents have absorbed more than their share of illusions concerning the actual quality of their school performance. Harold Stevenson and his colleagues tested samples of white and minority elementary school pupils in the Chicago area and also interviewed the children and their mothers. Here is part of what they found:

> Black mothers were positive about their child's skills and abilities and had high evaluations of the child's achievements in reading and mathematics. This was also the case with the black children. In comparisons of themselves to other children in their class, they believed that they worked hard in reading and mathematics and that they were doing well in these subjects. Surprisingly, however, their self-evaluations of their skills in reading and mathematics were unrelated to their actual level of achievement. Such a lack of validity in the black children's self-ratings of their academic status seems to indicate that the children had not received, or had not effectively incorporated, reliable and appropriate feedback about their performance in school. . . . [I]f the norms are low, parents and children may tend to overestimate children's degree of success in school. This would result, therefore, in a tendency for many minority children to evaluate themselves on the basis of standards that are not appropriate for students in their grade in school.[28]

Why educators tend to set lower expectations for disadvantaged and minority children entails a poisonous brew of humanitarianism and condescension. We want them to feel good about themselves and to succeed. We certainly don't want thousands of them to flunk, creating untold logistical and political troubles for the school system and for us. But we may not really think they can learn very much. So let's slow the pace, temper our demands, and provide full rewards and ample praise when these lower standards are met. "The existing model of intervention," Stanford's Henry Levin perceptively observes, "appears to be both rational and compassionate, but it has exactly the opposite consequences."[29]

The upshot is that even children doing none too well academically are given positive reinforcement and favorable feedback in the form of encouraging teacher comments, upbeat report cards, perhaps also standardized test scores "at or above 'grade level.'" Is it any wonder that such youngsters overrate their accomplishments? How ironic and sad that those for whom a high-quality education matters most are those of whom we are inclined to ask the least—and to deceive the most about their true accomplishments.

This phenomenon is not confined to the disadvantaged, however. Many a teacher in middle-class schools joins with his or her students in what Theodore Sizer calls the "conspiracy of the least," a tacit pact under whose terms the instructor does not demand too much of the pupils if they, in turn, do not hassle the teacher. We thus wind up asking less of boys and girls than they can deliver. Behind "a facade of orderly purposefulness," Sizer writes, lies "an agreement that reduce[s] the efforts of both students and teacher to an irreducible and pathetic minimum."[30]

Nor is undervaluing by the teacher a uniquely American occurrence. In pilot-testing the assessment systems to accompany England's new national curriculum, test makers have found youngsters succeeding with more difficult exercises than their teachers believed them capable of. As one of the assessment architects described the experience: "We had a lot of comments from teachers last year during the early trials, like, 'I wouldn't have given him that to do but he has succeeded.' "[31]

If educators are quick to praise, slow to find fault, generally as undemanding in the standards they set for students as they are generous in the feedback supplied to children and parents—and if this is combined with glowing reports from the superintendent concerning the performance of the city or state as a whole—is it really any wonder that many of us see no urgent need to change anything in our own educational lives? Why be miserable when there is so much good news? Why bestir ourselves to alter our children's behavior or the practices of the school down the street when it is far less taxing to believe that they're okay the way they are? It's fine for pundits to declare, as David Gergen did not long ago in *U.S. News & World Report*, that "We must stop lying to ourselves about our schools."[32] He's right, of course. Self-deception *cum* complacency is a major contributor to the U.S. education disaster. Gergen is also correct, a few paragraphs later, when he says that "Lake Wobegon is a nice place to visit, but we can't afford to live there." No indeed. But what a comfortable and happy community it is, and how little reason we've been given to go to the great bother of moving elsewhere. Other people, of course, should relocate.

7

❦

Rational Fools
What's in It for Me?

*Coast and get into college and have the same opportunities
as someone who worked hard. That is the system.*
—Virginia high school student, 1990

In the last chapter we confronted the paradox of a wholesale education crisis coexisting with a high degree of retail complacency.
Now we take up a more tragic possibility: that young Americans
are making rational choices when they slip into a pattern of academic
apathy and ease rather than opting for intellectual challenge and
hard work.

In a thoughtful 1990 *Daedalus* article, University of Chicago education professor Mihaly Csikszentmihalyi recalls an ecological paradigm
known as the "tragedy of the commons":

> If say fifty families each have a cow grazing on a common pasture,
> it makes sense for a family to invest everything they have in buying
> another cow, thereby doubling their capital while increasing the
> pressure on the common supply of fodder by only a tiny fraction.
> The problem is that if every family acts rationally, soon there will
> be 100 cows grazing, the pasture will be exhausted, the cattle
> will die, and the farmers will be ruined.[1]

Societal disaster can thus result from the accumulation of individually rational choices. The education equivalent is, of course, millions
of separate decisions not to press oneself hard at academic pursuits
and thus not to learn much in school (or college), confident that
one's access to the good life will be unimpaired. As these choices
pile up, we gradually find ourselves with a population full of semiliter-

ates and ignoramuses, collectively lacking the skills, knowledge, and wisdom to sustain the good life for all. Generalized impoverishment, social decay, and cultural collapse must in time follow. Some has already occurred. There is good evidence, for example, that faltering academic achievement between 1967 and 1980 sliced billions of dollars from the U.S. gross national product.[2]

As these decisions are made (or, more likely, drifted into), student by student, one after another, there never comes a point at which those making them apprehend that they are committing a grave blunder. To the contrary. "Many young people nowadays think it isn't sensible for them to learn too much," Csikszentmihalyi writes, "because the social system will not reward their knowledge anyway and they can live very well without it."[3]

Much as we may wish otherwise, there is reason to think that these young people are coolly weighing the evidence before their eyes. The decisions they are reaching, while profoundly harmful in the aggregate for the nation as a whole, are defensible, even astute, from the standpoint of the individuals making them.

THE COLLEGE-BOUND STUDENT

Forget for a few paragraphs the children of ambitious immigrant parents and the offspring of Yuppie families. Those relentlessly vying for admission to Stanford, Swarthmore, and Brown still have reason to strive in school (which is not, of course, always the same as growing in knowledge, wisdom, and character).

Forget them not because they are unworthy or unimportant, but because there are not many of them. The number of highly selective colleges and universities in the United States—institutions that accept fewer than half their applicants—is under 50 out of some 3,400 degree-offering campuses and an additional 8,500 "noncollegiate" providers of postsecondary education.[4]

Perhaps 200 more institutions are somewhat selective, accepting 50 to 90 percent of those who apply, and still others impose preconditions for entrance, usually in the form of courses one must take in high school even to become eligible to be considered. I do not suggest that all who feel like it can stroll from their high-school graduation ceremonies into the gates of any college in the land. Yet the great majority of our institutions of higher education (and virtually the entire noncollegiate sector) are essentially open to all comers. As a society we pride ourselves on being the only country in the history of the world with near-universal access to postsecondary education; we applaud the boost this gives to equal opportunity and social mobility; and we cheer the forgiving nature of a system in which it is never too late to make a fresh start or go back for more.

The upshot is that if you have the price of admission—very low in the state-subsidized schools attended by almost 80 percent of American college students—and can display a high-school diploma or equivalency certificate, you need not do much more in order to matriculate. Nor are you beyond hope if you *lack* those two basic qualifications. If you cannot afford the price of admission, sundry student aid programs exist to help with grants and loans. And in at least 250 institutions—many of them community colleges but also including the likes of Stanford, Wellesley, and Yale—high-school completion is not an immutable precondition for entry.[5]

Most young Americans apply to just one college, and for the majority of them it is a nearby institution that they can attend while living at home and, frequently, working at a job. Four out of five freshmen enroll within their home states. Only one undergraduate in five occupies college-provided housing. The person who "goes away" to college and lives on campus is the exception.[6]

In recent years the combination of a vastly expanded higher-education system and a diminishing stock of young adults has made it easier than ever to matriculate. The number of eighteen-year-old Americans in 1986 was just 83 percent of what it had been a decade earlier. It will continue declining until about 1994, when it will be three-quarters of its 1976 level.[7] With the ratio of high-school graduates to eighteen-year-olds fairly stable, the impact of this population shrinkage on the supply of traditional college students is evident.

Meanwhile, the higher-education industry has continued to grow—adding about two million students between 1975 and 1990. Putting the matter simply, that enterprise is now so capacious that if every single U.S. high-school graduate went straight to college and stayed there for four years, we still would not have quite enough students to keep the dorms and classrooms full—and there would be nobody left for the "noncollegiate" sector.[8] Because the supply exceeds the natural demand, additional demand must be stimulated.

Under such circumstances we should not be surprised that admission to higher education, far from being a bottleneck through which few young people pass (as in all other countries), is more akin to a free flow, perhaps even a vacuum, drawing prospective students in. Many colleges now go to great pains (and expense) to "recruit" enough students of every size, shape, age, and talent, tailoring programs to their changing interests and enthusiasms and offering such lures and incentives as a year or two of degree credit for "life experience" prior to matriculation.

This is not the place to judge such strategies as they bear on the quality and integrity of higher education. The essential point here is that college entrance now requires very little of the applicant. Save for the small fraction of the secondary school population hoping to thread themselves through the eye of the selective college admissions needle, people know that they can go to college—some college—no matter how little they learn in high school.

Even those aspiring to Ivy League universities and other highly competitive campuses may not feel powerfully impelled to maximize their learning levels in secondary school. Insofar as admissions decisions in the most selective institutions hinge on aptitude-test scores such as SAT and ACT results, they have more to do with innate ability and general cognitive functioning than with particular courses taken or subject-specific knowledge and skills acquired in school. That, of course, is precisely why the College Board tells people not to waste time and money on "test prep" programs and cram courses; the tests are intended to be immune to just the sorts of intense study and rigorous preparation that, in other countries, are key aspects of readying oneself for university entrance exams.[9]

To be sure, selective colleges do not confine themselves to aptitude test scores. Most also inspect one's academic standing, for example. Is Jessica in the top quarter of her class? Yet while such rankings plainly depend on the grades one has earned in school, these, too, bear little relationship to what one *learned* in those classes. That is why some able students eschew "honors" and "advanced placement" courses; their grades and class standings will be higher if they enroll in easier courses. Class rank also has an insidious effect on students' peer culture, notes Professor John Bishop of Cornell University, the foremost analyst of these dynamics. Because it creates a "zero sum competition among classmates," students may opt not to vie with their friends. "All work groups," Bishop explains, "have ways of sanctioning 'rate busters.' High school students call them 'brain geeks,' 'grade grubbers,' and 'brown nosers.' "[10]

Conscientious admissions committees in elite colleges scrutinize the courses displayed on the applicant's transcript, as well as essays, teacher recommendations, and scores on achievement tests and AP exams, both of which *are* linked to what is learned in school. Yet nearly all of them also heed aptitude test scores and class rank. Hence it is not unfair to say that even these institutions at the prestige pinnacle of higher education, the very campuses that Yuppie parents would die for their children to attend, are sending mixed signals to prospective students about what constitutes success in the first twelve grades.

All college-bound students are wise to endure school long enough to obtain a diploma (although an "equivalency certificate" has as much practical value), but for most it is not necessary to take any more courses than the state mandates, to choose classes harder than the high school requires, or to fuss about grades—so long as they pass the course and get credit for it. From the standpoint of an individual high-school student contemplating her own future, going to college presents few hurdles, academically speaking, provided she has sufficient stamina. (It may pose economic or psychological barriers, but that's another story.) The "excellence movement" is far away and abstract. It rarely intrudes on the transaction between the student and her chosen college, hence has no large bearing on the calculus by which that student gauges what she must do while in school in order to matriculate.

In recent years we've seen some evidence that this form of pressure, hit or miss as it has been, is actually diminishing. "Colleges Scramble to Fill Openings in Freshman Classes" read a headline in the *Chronicle of Higher Education* in mid-June 1990. Eighty-four percent of the institutions surveyed by the National Association of College Admissions Counselors reported that as of May 1 they had empty spaces in their entering classes.

One result, of course, is that in today's buyer's market, even colleges accustomed to being fussy about the qualifications of their incoming students cannot always maintain their previous standards and still expect to wind up with enough matriculants. High-school guidance counselors accordingly reported in mid-1990 that "many colleges and universities are admitting students who probably wouldn't have even been placed on their waiting lists a few years ago."[11] Said one counselor:

> Kids would come into my office and announce that they had been admitted, and the first few times I almost fell off of my chair. In the six years I've been director of college counseling here, it was the weakest class we've had academically. But we've had the best college-admissions results we've ever had.[12]

Young people are pragmatic about things like this. If there is no payoff, no reward, no real-world incentive, why take that extra-hard math course? Why spend Saturday at the library beefing up the bibliography of the history paper? Why read the whole novel instead of a plot summary? Why enroll in a third year of science or lose sleep in pursuit of an honors grade? Just by putting in one's obligatory time in ordinary courses—the minimum number of them—and getting passing grades, one can virtually ensure admission to a serviceable college that will be glad to open its doors.

THE NON-COLLEGE-BOUND STUDENT

For the minority of students who are not pointed toward post-secondary education, the incentives for academic excellence in school are even fewer. In study after study, Bishop has expertly probed the hiring practices and reward structure of the employment market for high-school graduates. His overall conclusion is that grades do not matter very much, nor do the specific courses taken, since there is practically no payoff for learning a lot in school rather than learning a little.

> During the first 8 years after leaving high school, young men who do not go to college receive no rewards from the labor market for developing competence in science, language arts and mathematical reasoning. . . . For the non-college bound female, computational speed and competence in mathematical reasoning increase wage rates but competence in science, language arts and the technical arena does not. The tendency of so many American high school students to avoid tough math and science courses and their poor performance on international science and mathematics exams, therefore, appears to be a rational response to market incentives.[13]

Judged by their demonstrated cognitive skills and knowledge, young Americans are plenty ignorant, but when it comes to figuring out how hard to work in school they are wonderfully savvy. Few employers ever ask to see their high-school transcripts. Though the diploma itself remains a necessary credential for most jobs, as it does for admission to most colleges, one can safely gamble that nobody in the personnel office will investigate what courses one took or what grades one received along the way.

Today's high-school diploma, according to the Commission on the Skills of the American Workforce, is regarded by employers not as evidence of educational achievement but rather "as a sign of the applicant's reliability and staying power," more a clue to character than proof of cognitive learning. Employers simply do not see it as a trustworthy indicator of academic accomplishment. "They realized long ago," the commission tartly notes, "that it is possible to graduate from high school in this country and still be functionally illiterate."[14]

But literacy levels may not matter very much to those doing the hiring. "While businesses all over complained about the quality of their applicants," reports the commission, "few talked about educational skills." Instead, eight out of ten sought mainly to employ "workers with a good work ethic and appropriate social behavior—'reliable,' 'a good attitude,' 'a pleasant appearance,' 'a good personality.' " The commission believes this is because few U.S. firms have reorganized their production systems from the assembly-line model of yore into modern high-performance arrangements that confer greater autonomy on workers but also demand more from them by way of skills and judgment. Employers, in other words, are getting by with relatively poorly educated workers because many of them are running antiquated workplaces. This obviously weakens their productivity and competitiveness, but it inevitably eases the pressure on schools and students—and reduces the payoff for academic success.

Those with no education beyond high school may be caught up in a particularly vicious circle with those who hire them. For the most part, these are not, as we have seen, highly skilled or knowledgeable individuals, and the jobs available to them naturally tend to be those with meager knowledge and skill requirements. Needless to say, they are also poorly paid jobs. Though one is still better off with a high-school diploma than without, the economic picture has been dimming for those who acquire no further qualifications.[15] Hence to observe that youngsters who study hard and do well in school gain little tangible reward for their efforts is to describe only part of the picture. The other part is that young people who see their education ending when they graduate from high school are usually contemplating such unappetizing employment prospects that we cannot term them irrational for deciding to treat school as a minimalist activity.

Thus the diploma is still a desirable credential, perhaps even an essential one, for the new job seeker, but not in the way we commonly think. If it is a ticket only into low-pay, low-skill jobs, if it does not matter to employers which courses a person took while in school, or the marks he earned in them, or how much he learned, why should it matter to students? To repeat, young people are pragmatic about these things. "Adolescents are like adults," Albert Shanker observes. "They do as much as they have to in order to get what they want."[16]

A determined employer may, of course, ask to examine a job applicant's school transcript. Yet few do. Employers, it seems, mistrust the quality of high-school courses, are skeptical of the link between a course title and its content, and have encountered difficulty laying their hands on school transcripts when they try to.[17] Fewer than 20 percent of high schools even respond to requests for transcripts. Bishop reports that an insurance company for which he consults received only 93 actual transcripts in response to twelve hundred written requests that it dispatched.[18] Given this sorry rate of return and the uncertain reliability of the transcript, employers with stringent skill requirements are apt instead to demand some college experience as well as a high-school diploma, to administer a test of their own devising, to put applicants through an elaborate screening procedure, or to hire them first in probationary status.

If one's academic record in school plays no substantial role in one's employability, and if graduation is treated more as a testimonial to character than as a gauge of cognitive learning, we should not be surprised that, in the words of the Skills Commission, "the non-college bound know that as long as they get their diploma, their performance in high school is likely to have little or no bearing on the type of employment they manage to find."[19] Course selection does not have much impact either, at least as viewed by the students. When Bishop asked pupils in fifty high schools which math courses they thought they needed to take in order to qualify for their preferred job, more than 70 percent of them did not believe they needed to take any.[20] Is it any wonder that so many study so little math in school?[21]

"If . . . a substantial proportion of the youth in our country does not expect to benefit," Csikszentmihalyi writes, "from acquiring high levels of literacy beyond what is needed to get a driver's license or to read the sports pages, then a very strong incentive for learning is not operating."[22]

We who believe in the value of education as an article of faith are wont to assume that young people are simply shortsighted, hedonistic, and ill-informed about the baleful consequences of coasting through school. If only they knew better, we assure one another, surely they would behave differently. In reporting the results of a survey of eighth-graders, for example, the U.S. Department of Education dwelt on the gap between the children's educational hopes and their concrete plans. "Two-thirds of the 8th graders planned to finish college or attain higher degrees," the study solemnly concluded, "but only about one-third planned to enroll in a college preparatory program in high school."[23]

In the same vein, a California study of student course-taking patterns found many displaying a "lack of congruence between their career goal and their high school program." Nearly half the students who enrolled in the general rather than the academic track of their high school, for example, "had career goals which required at least a four-year college degree."[24]

Shocking, no? Indeed yes, when read as a portent of widespread mediocrity and slipshod educational achievement. The surest way to end up not knowing something is never to study it. If one has an unrealistic notion of one's accomplishments in relation to the prerequisites for the next stages in life, one also runs a considerable risk of dashed hopes, frustration, and alienation.

But how many of these youngsters are out of touch with reality as it actually impinges on them? Perhaps they sense a reality that we wish did not exist but cannot honestly deny—namely that the "lack of congruence" is mostly in the minds of adults committed to education, not in the nitty-gritty arenas of college-entrance norms and job prerequisites. "Eighth graders know very well," writes Paul Regnier of the Fairfax County, Virginia, Public Schools, "that following a 'general' or other non-college-preparatory course may keep them from entering the few selective colleges but will be no barrier to admission at thousands of others, public and private. The 'disparity' is in the thinking of educators."[25]

OTHER STUDENTS

If students' friends and classmates also make light of academic achievement, the likelihood of many young people swimming against that powerful tide is further diminished. According to a synthesis by Judith K. Ide and associates of much research, "Peer influence is a strong, consistent determinant of a wide range of educational outcomes for elementary and high school students."[26] In fact, it often serves to depress those outcomes. The peer pressure, says Kristin Steurle, an Alexandria (Virginia) high-school student, "is to slide by and do the least work possible. People see others doing that and still getting into good colleges and getting good jobs. There's pressure to beat the system."[27] One of her classmates' comments on the matter is the epigraph that opens this chapter.

For disadvantaged and minority youngsters in particular, the norms of the peer group may be strongly antiacademic. The research of Signithia Fordham and John Ogbu buttresses the impressions conveyed by innumerable anecdotes: A black youngster who does well in school invites worse than being labeled a "nerd" or "geek." He or she risks being accused of "acting white," and he, perhaps, of having his masculinity doubted. The relatively few black students who nevertheless display high achievement generally devise elaborate stratagems to conceal or compensate for their intellectual accomplishments. These ploys may include clowning, "acting crazy," hiding evidence of hard work, associating with "bullies" and "hoodlums," emphasizing sexual or athletic prowess, avoiding academic competitions whose winners would find themselves in the school spotlight, and downplaying their talents, even by consciously doing less well in courses—or taking less-advanced courses—than they are capable of.[28]

It's not that our young people are lazy or incapable of hard work and great accomplishment. One need only look at the remarkable efforts of student athletes and the acclaim that the whole community accords to winning teams. A great many youths also work, as we have seen, earnestly and conscientiously at after-school jobs. The problem is that *academic* success yields few such rewards—and indolence brings few sanctions. Once in high school, moreover, it is usually clear to students which of their classmates are likely to harvest the available prizes. "By 9th grade," John Bishop observes, "most students are already so far behind the leaders, that they know they have no chance of being perceived as academically successful. Their reaction is often to denigrate the students who take learning seriously and to honor other forms of achievement—athletics, dating, holding their liquor, and being 'cool'—which offer them better chances of success."[29]

OTHER LANDS

Americans, even in the throes of adolescence, are not by nature apathetic. Observe the passion for success, the energy, and the persistence that students, parents, and neighbors bring to Christmas pageants, school carnivals, and sports. We are among the least phlegmatic of people. We like excitement, revel in heroism, are tantalized by celebrity. We admire great achievement, whether in business, the arts, the research lab, the launch pad, or the playing field.

Yet even a culture of achievement can be reduced to lassitude and apathy if it imposes on itself institutional arrangements that yield scant reward for accomplishment, little incentive for effort, and few adverse consequences for mediocrity.

We saw a nearly pure example of this in 1989 and 1990 as the

Berlin Wall came down and East and West Germany moved toward unification. Early in that sequence, tens of thousands of people left East Germany. No modern nation has a stronger tradition of high achievement or a more deeply rooted norm of hard work than West Germany, with its remarkable reconstruction of war-ravaged economic and social institutions into the most vibrant and efficient in Europe. Yet despite inheriting the same gene pool, the same traditions, and the same culture, after nearly forty-five years under a repressive Communist regime, the people of East Germany appeared to have lost their edge. Those moving to the West underwent profound cultural shocks. So did those receiving them. Consider this perceptive account in April 1990 by a *New York Times* correspondent in East Berlin:

> While many have found jobs, the Federal Labor Office in Nuremberg said that more than 150,000 East German immigrants were unemployed and that the number was rising. The figure is being swollen, officials said, not only by new arrivals, but also because West German businessmen are dismissing the immigrants in increasing numbers out of frustration with their lax attitude toward work.
>
> For their part, East Germans often call West Germany "the elbow society," because of the aggressiveness of daily life on and off the job. If nothing else, East German workers had a far easier life than their West German counterparts.
>
> But a second German economic miracle, the hope of East Germany's 16 million inhabitants, cannot be built on four-hour days, many point out.
>
> "It's unfortunately true our work ethic has eroded," said Eberhard Engel, an economist who heads the East German Christian Democratic Union's economics section. "People work shorter hours and more slowly, while discipline is often lacking in the workplace."[30]

The explanation, of course, is that East Germany's socialist economy did not reward individual effort. It was a no-fault/no-reward/no-consequence arrangement. Everyone got food and shelter (though not much of either) whether they worked or not. And when this economic arrangement was appended to a totalitarian political regime, all manner of entrepreneurial impulses and personal initiatives were suppressed.

I do not suggest an exact parallel between American elementary-secondary education and East Germany under communism. But the comparison encourages us to reflect on how institutionalized incentive-and-reward systems can squeeze out the very attitudes and behaviors we presently fault our schools and students for not having acquired. The East German system produced a "deep passivity" in Peter Schmidt, a young émigré to the west who was profiled at considerable and poignant length in *The New Yorker* in June 1990:

> He told his Hamburg friends that West Germany was too ambitious, too aggressive. . . . At first, they thought he was exotic. They did not know what else to make of him. They thought he was laid back and supercool—that suffering had "detached" him, that it had given him a special claim on truth. . . . But in the end they got impatient with Peter. They decided he was lazy, indolent, maybe a little strange. They did not know what he was waiting for, or why he expected to be taken care of—why he did not get up and go out and participate, like his roommate . . . who was getting a doctorate in history and played guitar with a heavy-metal band and, whenever he was broke, went out and found himself a job. . . . He could handle the system, whereas Peter Schmidt refused to take a job in the system. Peter refused to study in the system, or find a girl in the system, or even do the dishes in the system if he was not instructed to do the dishes. He could follow instructions, but it turned out that he could not easily be free.[31]

We have a lot of Peter Schmidts in American schools nowadays, and I think their apathy and passivity have some common roots.

Other industrial democracies handle their educational arrangements differently than we do. "Overseas," John Bishop writes, "the rewards for studying hard in high school are quite substantial." Students in many industrial nations take demanding external examinations based on the content of the subjects they have studied, and their performance on those exams is the greatest determinant of whether—and where—they will attend university. For those not headed into higher education, Bishop notes, "Large firms in Japan and Europe hire many entry level workers directly out of high school and base their selections on grades and exam scores." The standard résumé that job applicants in Ireland present to prospective employers, for example, even for blue-collar and clerical jobs, includes their exam results, subject by subject.[32] Some wary personnel offices in the Emerald Isle insist that official copies of applicants' exam scores be sent directly from the National Certification Board. This does not, of course, prove that all Irish employees are well-educated, only that those doing the hiring evince a clear interest in how well they did in school.

In Japan, this transition is handled differently. There, high-status private firms in effect delegate to secondary schools the responsibility for selecting which graduates will be hired. If the school is less than forthright about a student's capacity or attainments, the firm will find this out soon enough, and may not return to that school for future workers.

In a number of countries, Bishop explains, parents "know that a child's future depends critically on how much is learned in secondary school." Since not all schools are equal, and access to the better ones is competitive and exam based, the pressure to succeed academically is apt to reach down into the early grades. Because the important exams are national, a particular child's performance is appraised alongside the achievement of youngsters throughout the land, not just classmates in his or her own school.

After scrutinizing the school-to-work transition in some of the countries that boast very strong economies, the Commission on the Skills of the American Workforce made similar observations. "Academic expectations" in those lands, the commission reported, "are high for *all* young people. Both college bound and non-college bound students attain high standards of educational achievement." This is not done by discarding non-attainers along the path. "Students are not easily permitted to fail," the commission declares. Tutoring schemes; after-school, weekend, and summer remediation; academic instruction at the work site; and alternative schools for past and possible future dropouts—all are part of the education incentive-and-support system.

Nor does it go easily with those who fail. Succeeding in school, getting high marks on exams, and completing job-related technical and vocational programs are the paths—sometimes the only paths—to status and prosperity in these lands. To drop out of school is to drop into some sort of backup education and training system that doesn't loosen its grip. These societies are less forgiving than ours but benefit from real leverage over the behavior and motivations of their young people.

INTERNAL OR EXTERNAL INCENTIVES?

I have focused on extrinsic motivation, the kind that provokes one to behave in a certain way because something good is apt to happen to those who do and something bad may befall those who do not. When it comes to academic learning, I believe that external consequences are the main determinant of how hard most of us work and how much we accomplish. The problem with extrinsic motivation as an education reform strategy, however, is that schools themselves possess only limited ability to shape it. Youngsters know when they are being duped and, under present circumstances, teachers cannot honestly say to most American children that their short-term prospects will be much affected by how well they do in school. Yet schools alone cannot change these incentive structures. They would have to be joined, at a minimum, by colleges and employers.

That may be why so astute a critic as Professor Csikszentmihalyi shrinks from hinging all educational motivation on extrinsic rewards, even though he concedes that historically "reading, writing and computation developed because they provided economic and power advantages to whoever knew how to use such information."[33] He and other educators are sure it is possible to imbue learning with *intrinsic* reward in the form of enjoyment. Waxing a bit rhapsodic, he declares that a "matching of challenges and skills, clear goals, and immediate feedback, resulting in a deep concentration that prevents worry and the intrusion of unwanted thoughts into consciousness, and in a transcendence of the self, are the universal characteristics associated with enjoyable activities."[34]

This is doubtless true of many enjoyable activities, though I can think of one or two whose pleasures may be described more simply. But nobody would deny that expert teachers can often turn academic learning into something that offers intrinsic satisfaction. Anyone who has reveled in a great novel, play, or poem under the tutelage of a gifted instructor has a sense of this. The teachers we are apt to recall as having influenced us most are people who stimulated our interest in what we were learning, rather than just making us learn it.

Well and good. To the extent that we can invest the acquisition of cognitive skills and knowledge with intrinsic rewards, we should certainly do so. To watch a child get truly absorbed in a history project, a science experiment, writing a story, drawing a picture, even solving a math problem, is to see that this is no impossible dream.

If the use of extrinsic motivation as leverage for education reform has the drawback of needing cooperation from powerful institutional forces beyond the schools, any purposeful campaign to beef up the intrinsic rewards of education brings difficulties of its own. Just how many children can be "turned on" to the pleasures of high achievement in how many different subjects and skills? This is something that intellectuals and educators, devoted as they are to the life of the mind, tend to overestimate. There is the further question of how many extraordinarily gifted teachers we can reasonably expect to find in a system employing two and a half million classroom instructors. When I offer Escalante as a role model, educators usually complain that it is naive and unfair of me to pick the rare exception and suggest that it might become the norm.

My biggest concern about intrinsic motivation, however, arises from the admonitions of Csikszentmihalyi (and many other educators) about what we will have to refrain from doing if this reform strategy is to be pursued. The surest ways to destroy the "spontaneous interest" of the child, he writes, are for adults to "attempt to control the child's performance as much as possible"; for evaluation, competition, reward and punishment to be emphasized; and for individuals to be made self-conscious about their own accomplishments, which may cause them to do only things they're sure they're good at rather than to take risks.[35] Therefore we are urged to cease and desist from all such practices.

To refrain from pressing children to learn, in the hope that more of them will come to love their studies and reap the innate benefits of intellectual effort, is quite consistent with a long tradition of progressive education doctrine and practice, but also seems to me to fly in the face of much other wisdom and experience in the United States and abroad. Instant enjoyment is assuredly a motivator, but it is not the only kind, else few people would ever climb mountains, plant gardens, fight wars, give to charity, train for the decathlon, go to church—or roll out of bed early to get to work on time. Most of us do much of what we do—and perhaps even more of what we're proud of doing—not because it yields fast gratification but because it will bring some greater benefit later. If we confined ourselves to activities yielding immediate intrinsic rewards, we would not be very active, we would not be very productive, and we would not live in a very satisfactory society.

Moreover, if we settle for spontaneous interest and intrinsic enjoyment as motivators for children to learn more in school, we'll find ourselves competing with some potent adversaries. For how many youngsters do we really think we can make algebra more seductive than television, chemistry more beguiling than rock music, and literature more alluring than romping with their pals? Recall that school has them inside its walls just 9 percent of their lives. The rest of their time is spent under other influences.

"The children in junior high school know no other life except one of comparative ease," a veteran science teacher recently wrote to the governor of his state:

This attitude has become so pervasive that the work ethic has been severely compromised. . . . [W]e can see the productivity decrease as students find less and less reason to study since there are so many other "fun" things to do. . . . I do not mean to imply that they are fighting us. They are not. They simply are losing the ability to focus, to internalize, to associate, etc. These self indulgent attitudes lead to behaviors which tend to short circuit the learning apparatus. No matter how hard we try, teachers cannot teach if the students do not want to put forth the necessary effort required to learn.

The Calvinist ethic is not fashionable in education circles, dominated as they are by the precepts of progressivism, and to say that children must be induced to put forth greater effort and learn more, whether they wish to or not, can easily be made to sound paternalistic and even a bit menacing. I do not suggest that we should employ whips or the rack. Insofar as we can make learning pleasurable, we should of course do so. Gifted teachers, stimulating curricula, irresistible technology, lively lessons, and ample feedback are much to be desired in American classrooms, and any reform scheme that ignores them is unlikely to succeed. But this approach will get us only so far before we bump into the admonition to avoid competition, to eschew evaluation, and not to put so much emphasis on success. At that point I—and most of the American people—bid adieu to Professor Csikszentmihalyi and his associates. I have no doubt that we will make greater gains by facing up to the considerable challenges of revamping our extrinsic incentive-and-reward systems than by abandoning the principles of goals, standards, and accountability. It is to these that we turn in the next several chapters.

8

※

Journey Without a Destination

*If a society won't clearly say what it wants from its schools,
it won't get any clear performance.*

—Lester C. Thurow, February 11, 1990

By 1989 it was dawning on education critics and policymakers
that the school reform efforts we had undertaken thus far were
crippled by the absence of clear objectives and the dearth of benchmarks by which progress could be gauged. What would a properly
functioning education system look like, anyway? What skills and
knowledge do well-educated children possess? What results should
schools yield? How much is good enough? How do we know when
we've got it?

We had not paused even to answer those questions, much less
to build the answers into our reform strategies. As a consequence,
some portion—a hefty one, I believe—of the responsibility for the
excellence movement's skimpy results in the 1980s is attributable
to the fact that we were busily dashing about, sure that there was
something wrong with the status quo but uncertain quite what we
wanted to accomplish instead. Education, former U.S. Commissioner
Ernest Boyer told the Business Roundtable in June 1989, is "like an
industry that's unclear about its product and thus is hopelessly
confused about quality control."[1] Without product specifications,
every industrialist knows, one can fiddle endlessly with the assembly
line, revise workers' duties and pay, designate new foremen, contract
with different suppliers—but only by happenstance will the results
be any better. First one must be able to describe the results he
seeks. Yet few states or localities had such specifications for their

own schools. For the country as a whole, there were none worth mentioning.

GOALS—AND GOAL STATEMENTS

It's not that schools lacked "goal statements." To the contrary, the American education landscape is littered with them. Practically every state and local system can dust off ponderous and dull documents, jargon-rich tomes that purport to delineate the regnant educational "philosophy," "purposes" or "objectives." Though committees of school professionals and outside consultants labor endlessly to prepare these and, at intervals, to revise them, and though they are routinely circulated to principals and teachers, they resemble what ordinary people mean by goals as an atlas resembles a route map or a dictionary simulates a sonnet: If you superimpose your own judgment and priorities on the material contained therein, you can mold it into specific contours that could be treated as real targets of attainment. In its naturally occurring form, however, such a goal statement has so little shape that it might better be termed an expression of general direction. As such, it has little effect on what happens in the classroom and cannot function as an accountability mechanism. That is why the innumerable management-by-objectives workshops that school administrators attend have had so little impact on educational achievement.

Traditional goal statements for American schools are composed in terms either abstractly unimpeachable or mundanely desirable: Help each child to realize his full potential, infuse more writing "across the curriculum," extend various services (for example, full-day kindergarten, earlier foreign-language study, souped-up guidance counseling) to more youngsters, ameliorate sundry logistical problems (overcrowding, too few library aides, antiquated gyms, ill-equipped labs, shabby audiovisual equipment), pare the dropout rate, slash the incidence of vandalism, reduce absenteeism, increase this, modify that, minimize the other. All doubtless worthy, reasonable, even important, but seldom a word about what youngsters emerging from that system should be expected to know and be able to do.

Such goals were tolerable so long as the nation was generally content with its education system. When your team is winning, you do not give the coach a hard time about his offensive strategy. You may not even care whether he can articulate one. But when the team loses game after game, owners and fans eventually ask whether those plotting the moves even know which end of the field to head toward, much less how to organize successful plays.

The vagueness and banality of the typical school-system goal statement has four roots:

First, it is moored to a concept of education that construes quality in terms of quantity; progress in terms of enhanced inputs, resources, and services; and reform in terms of hopes and intentions. So long as you spend enough, do enough, care enough, and try hard enough, you are delivering superior education.

Second, it rests atop a "child-centered" philosophy of education. At least since the "Cardinal Principles of Secondary Education" were promulgated by the NEA in 1918, this brand of progressivism has ruled the minds of most American educators. Far from setting concrete targets of attainment, the "Cardinal Principles" insisted that educational objectives be relative, variable, and situation- (and child-) specific, tailored to the "needs of the society to be served, the character of the individuals to be educated, and the knowledge of educational theory and practice available."[2]

Third, all school goals are deemed to be equal—but there are far too many of them. When you are swimming in desirable objectives, some of them cosmic, some minuscule, when you have no clear indicators of progress toward most of them, and when nobody says which take precedence, it's difficult to resist adding to the list whenever another issue or problem rolls along that someone thinks the schools should take a hand in solving—and it becomes still more difficult to regard such hodgepodges as serious guides to action.

Fourth, the people devising the goals are not accountable for attaining them, nor do they wish to be. Accountability is not something most of us crave. The more general and flexible the goals, the less apt are institutions and their employees and managers to be hassled about the results. When, on a bright Saturday morning, you sally forth to "go shopping," it is practically impossible at day's end for anyone to claim that you failed in your mission. If, by contrast, you announce your determination to procure a new, blue woolen blazer, with charcoal skirt and white silk blouse to accompany it, the extent of your success will be obvious upon your return. American education has been "shopping" for most of the twentieth century. Who was to say it had not made sound purchases?

It's pleasant when one's self-interest coincides with one's philosophy. For educators, this congenial arrangement was also gift wrapped in the certainty that liberal ends were being served, and that anybody suggesting otherwise must be misguided. As Diane Ravitch explains:

Anyone who protested that the schools were supposed to give children intellectual power, to transmit the accumulated wisdom of the past, and to empower young people to make their own decisions about how to be socially useful was apt to be dismissed as a conservative, imbued with reactionary and individualistic ideas. In order for schools to take their place as agencies of social change, educators had to shed antiquated views about the transmission of knowledge.[3]

Much water has passed over the education dam between 1918 and modern times, of course, including some lively challenges to the prevailing philosophy. But progressivism proved as resilient as it was undemanding. Most school goals accordingly remained abstract, earnest, and soft.

LOCAL CONTROL

The much-worshipped creed of "local control" lent further legitimacy to the hazy, general, and process-heavy character of these objectives. Though states bore formal constitutional responsibility, essential decisions about what—and how much—should be taught and learned were presumed to belong to city, township, and county. With its tradition of domination over curricular matters by the Board of Regents and its statewide exams for high-school students, New York was the only important exception to the prevailing pattern until the "minimum competency" movement caught on in the 1970s. "Although the individual state reigns sovereign over its schools," education historian Adolphe E. Meyer wrote in 1957, "it has generally wielded its scepter magnanimously, so that the republic's myriad Main Streets, through their communal school boards, enjoy comparative educational freedom."[4] This pattern grew straight from the nineteenth-century roots of American public education. Until the late 1970s it was also faithful to the prevailing fiscal arrangements. So long as the local taxpayer was responsible for paying most of the piper's wages, local authorities picked most of the tunes he would play.

There had always been tension between state and locality. Meyer recounts several staunchly resisted moves toward "stiffer state control" even before the Civil War.[5] But in core matters of curriculum, philosophy, norms, and standards, the locals had not yielded much. As recently as 1969, when political scientist Alan Rosenthal assembled a collection of essays on education governance, it was accurate for

him to cite as examples of enduring local "discretion" such funda-
mentals as "the major purposes and goals of the schools" and "the
nature of the curriculum."[6]

Few disagreed with this description, at least in public, until very
recently. There was risk in suggesting that important education policy
decisions should be made at higher planes of the federal system.
Even no-strings money from above had sometimes been deemed
unAmerican. While at the helm of Columbia University (1948–52),
future president Dwight D. Eisenhower wrote that federal aid to
education was "another vehicle by which the believers in paternalism,
if not outright socialism, will gain still additional power for the central
government."[7] In the 1960s Senator Barry Goldwater declared that,
in the struggle to control the schools, "I fear Washington as much
as Moscow."[8] When this political squeamishness about nonlocals
setting education norms was joined to educators' own preferences
for relativism and situationalism, it's easy to see why school goals
had few teeth. But, of course, our team had been winning—or so
we believed.

HESITANT REFORMERS

Even as the excellence movement gathered steam in the early
1980s, critics were readier to berate the status quo for implicit standards not yet reached than to specify outcomes that *ought* to be
attained. The National Commission on Excellence in Education itself
was curiously ambivalent. Its famous report cited numerous shortcomings of a kind that are truly lamentable only if you have previously
embraced clear standards and expectations against which the status
quo is manifestly wanting. "Many 17-year-olds," the commission
noted as one indicator of looming calamity, "do not possess the
'higher order' intellectual skills we should expect of them. Nearly
40 percent cannot draw inferences from written material; only one-
fifth can write a persuasive essay."[9] In the background of such statements, there obviously lurked a sense of just what skills we should
expect of everyone.

Yet in introducing its prescriptions, the commission penned statements evocative of 1918 and the "Cardinal Principles":

We must emphasize that the variety of student aspirations, abilities,
and preparation requires that appropriate content be available
to satisfy diverse needs. . . . Attention must be directed to both

the nature of the content available and to the needs of particular learners.[10]

The commission's reform guidance included talk of schools adopting "more rigorous and measurable standards," of teachers who will "demonstrate an aptitude for teaching and . . . competence in an academic discipline," and of holding educators and policymakers responsible for results. Yet nearly all of the panel's recommendations may more aptly be described as emphases, directions, and priorities than as specific norms, tangible targets, or measurable goals. The most important exception—the commission's list of six "new basics" that every high-school student should study—was expressed in terms of course credits appearing on one's transcript (educators call these "Carnegie units") rather than as skills and knowledge one would end up possessing.[11]

Other analyses of the period displayed similar uncertainty. What was wrong, everyone acknowledged, plainly had to do with weak outcomes. Only if one has a sense of what results are wanted does this critique make much sense, let alone point toward an alternative path. Yet few reformers of the mid-1980s complained about the nebulous (or absent) goals by which schools were steering.

One notable exception was Ernest L. Boyer, now president of the Carnegie Foundation for the Advancement of Teaching. In an important 1983 study of secondary education, Boyer reported his conclusion that high schools lack a "clear and vital mission." He and his team had visited a number of schools, had examined their goal statements, and had encountered too many like this:

> The Prairie View Public School is vitally aware that the school of today is the school of the people it serves. The school provides educators who are knowledgeable in their subject matter and who are dedicated to serving all students and their needs.[12]

Another school that the Carnegie group called on had seven goals, ranging from providing "substantial and varied learning experiences that will facilitate life in a multi-cultural changing society" to teaching "skills that will enable the student to function both effectively and affectively in a changing society."[13]

Though we don't often encounter this sort of pap when we ask bank managers, baseball coaches, or thoracic surgeons what they're trying to accomplish, education is rife with it. (And not just in its lower echelons. Take another look at the institutional mission statement printed in the catalog of your favorite college or alma mater.)

Nor did those whom Boyer interviewed seem perturbed by the stream
of banalities. When asked about their schools' goals, he wrote, the
"response frequently was one of uncertainty, amusement, or surprise." One teacher suggested that goals and objectives were something "to be learned in teacher education courses and then forgotten."
Another said, even more cynically, "If we had goals, we wouldn't
follow them anyway."[14]

Boyer was duly alarmed. The nation's high schools, he declared,
"are unable to find common purposes or establish educational priorities that are widely shared. . . . The institution is adrift."[15] He urged,
sensibly enough, that every school adopt "clearly stated goals and
purposes that are understood and supported" by teachers, students,
parents, and administrators. He even made so bold as to suggest
what these might be. So far, so good. But Boyer then stumbled into
the same trap as the Excellence Commission. Instead of precise,
measurable, concrete objectives, he offered a quartet of goals that
could have been lifted from the "Cardinal Principles" of 1918, talking
of the need for schools to "help all students develop the capacity
to think critically . . . learn about themselves . . . develop individual
aptitudes and interests . . . [and] fulfill their social and civic
obligations."[16]

As in the case of the Excellence Commission, Boyer's critique
was more trenchant than his alternatives were specific. It was left
to the governors in mid-decade to move the nation toward education
goals of the kind that are suited to leveraging real change.

GOALS AND GOVERNORS

Elected officials are accustomed to this way of proceeding. If they
promise to build a new highway, people expect them to be able to
say where it will start and end, what route it will follow, and how
many exits and rest areas it will have en route. If they offer better
law enforcement, voters will want evidence of lower crime rates.
They set environmental standards in terms of how many parts per
million of this or that pollutant will be tolerated in the air or water
supply, and policy-making in this domain consists in substantial
part of epic arguments about how much is too much. Billions of
agricultural dollars are spent to maintain prices at fixed levels, to
hold soybean production to an agreed-upon quantity, or to ensure
that the lamb chop encased in plastic at the supermarket meets
precise sanitation norms.

Politicians bicker and vie with each other about where such stan-

dards should be set, whether the benefits of more stringent requirements equal the costs, and where to locate the intersection between
conflicting desiderata. Trade-offs and choices, after all, are what politics is about. More concerts in the park may mean fewer policemen
to protect music lovers from derelicts. Killing fewer dolphins in the
Pacific means costlier tuna sandwiches in St. Louis. There are difficult
priority decisions, diverse valuations of costs and benefits, indirect
(and sometimes unexpected) consequences, and more. This is why
we elect people to make public-policy decisions and why, if they
make foolish or extravagant decisions or fail to deliver on their promises, we elect others to replace them. Clear goals, accurate information
feedback on the attainment of those goals, and consequences tied
to success or failure—these are the essence of "accountability" and
of effective management.

As public officials, particularly governors and legislators, probed
deeper into the education problem in the 1980s, it was predictable
that the ways of government and the habits of politicians would
start to loom larger in the schools. Superintendents and principals
might be comfortable with goals of "meeting individual needs" and
facilitating "life in a changing society," but elected officials are apt
to think such notions soft and unworldly, especially alongside such
tangible projects as bringing a high-tech electronics plant to one's
state or attracting an airline hub to one's city. It is results that they
need to be able to display—hard, palpable, measurable results, preferably in accord with their blueprints and promises.

It was "time for results," in the impatient phrase with which the
National Governors' Association titled its 1986 report. "The governors," Tennessee's Lamar Alexander wrote in the chairman's summary, "want to help establish clear goals and better report cards,
ways to measure what students know and can do."[17]

Behind the bland language of "helping" there was some steel forged
in the heat of practical experience. The governors who had been
most deeply engaged in education reform had concluded both that
the system was not going to orient itself spontaneously to results
and that without such reorientation, improved outcomes would not
emerge. "As the education reform movement gathered steam," New
Jersey's Kean wrote, "it became clear that states must demand results." He knew whereof he spoke. Here is part of Kean's account
of his coming-of-age about education:

> As part of my blueprint for reform, I proposed a much tougher
> test, this time to include writing skills that would be mandatory
> for high school graduation. . . . The initial reaction of educators

to the new test was extremely negative. Educators lobbied me strenuously to delay the test, or better, to cancel it. A close look at the argument shows an insidious tendency to put the image of schools above the welfare of the students. . . . We went ahead with the test despite the critics. . . .[18]

Kean wanted results. Alexander wanted results. So did Arkansas' Bill Clinton, Florida's Bob Graham, South Carolina's Dick Riley, Missouri's John Ashcroft, and the others who knew this domain best. They had been struggling with the education problem in their states for some time and thought they now understood what was needed in order actually to solve it. What was less predictable was that the governors were also gearing up to place demands on American education as a whole.

DID YOU SAY "NATIONAL"?

As they talked to one another, compared notes, shared concerns, organized themselves into task forces, and started to list common problems and mutual objectives, the possibility arose that after two centuries of decentralized schooling, the elected policymakers of the several states might devise some worthy education goals that were both concrete and nationwide.

Authentic objectives that individual states could act on would themselves have been a marked improvement. State education laws were voluminous but, when it came to enumerating results, they were either incredibly abstract or absurdly specific. The statutes resembled archaeological sites, with layers of accumulated detritus from eras, fads, and interest groups spanning many years and legislative sessions. Governors had paid little attention to these compilations. Lobbyists and legislators had wantonly added their enthusiasms of the moment. And, since nobody gave these provisions more than lip service anyway, educators had gone along. As a result, Illinois expected all its school graduates to "have had adequate instruction in honesty, justice [and] moral courage," while Mississippi wanted "experiences to promote the optimum growth and development of youth." California demanded "true comprehension of the rights, duties, and dignity of American citizenship, including kindness toward domestic pets." Ambitious Maine wanted its schools to teach "principles of morality and justice and a sacred regard for truth, love of country, humanity, a universal benevolence, sobriety, industry and frugality, chastity, moderation and temperance, and all other virtues that ornament human society."[19]

No wonder few heeded such goals. As guides to action, the typical state requirements were as quirky and overwrought as the profession's "Cardinal Principles" were cosmic and vague. Any governor opening this particular Pandora's box could anticipate all sorts of strange creatures flying about. Yet a governor or legislator worth his salt *had* to pry off the lid, swab out the box, and refill it with sensible, tangible, and measurable objectives.

This implied shooting holes in the doctrine of local control—a target one might have expected to be off limits. It turned out to be politically difficult, of course, inasmuch as there was stiff resistance, issue by issue and case by case, from local superintendents, school boards, and countless other professional factions and interest groups. The governors lost some of those political battles and had to negotiate truces in others, but it's more revealing that we seldom heard anything about the *principle* of local control and, even when we did, it seemed to sway few minds. Journalists did not thunder their abiding support for it. Nobody took to the Senate floor to denounce those who were undermining it. If it became an issue in election campaigns, it certainly failed to draw much attention. Though many were pressing for increased parent involvement, and whole armies sought more school-site authority over key education decisions, the traditional American concept of "local control" appeared, by the late 1980s, to rouse very little passion, save from those whose powers and prerogatives were directly menaced. For most people, as we saw in chapter 4, improving what—and how much—children learn in school had come to count for more than tedious disputations about who's in charge. A governor could still find himself in a power struggle over specifics, but the taboo had vanished.

Somewhat the same fate befell the parallel doctrine that, because education is a state function, the country as a whole has no business addressing itself to what happens in schools. The Tenth Amendment remained in the Constitution, of course, and the states retained their responsibility for providing education. But when it came to goals and standards, was there any sound reason to confine one's horizon within state boundaries? Why should Connecticut's education objectives be much different from Oregon's? It was the whole country that had been declared at risk, after all, not fifty separate jurisdictions. It was the entire nation whose competitiveness and productivity needed strengthening. In an era of ceaseless population mobility, moreover, there was every reason to want a youngster leaving sixth grade in Cincinnati to be able to plunge smoothly into seventh grade in Tucson or Tulsa or Anchorage.

Though states always compete with each other to some extent, and the Education Department's annual wall chart encouraged comparisons, it made ever-less sense in the late twentieth century to erect educational barriers along state borders. In truth, it made no sense for their central educational goals to diverge. Texas would likely keep making its schoolchildren study the history of the Lone Star State, and other jurisdictions would retain their own idiosyncracies. But when it came to the core of the curriculum and the standards that youngsters should attain within it, was there any sound rationale in the late 1980s for big differences from one place to the next?

These had mostly lapsed into pseudo-diversity, anyhow. Instant communications, the mass media, huge textbook and entertainment conglomerates, and countless national conferences had built an informal coast-to-coast education system. Ten-year-olds in Kansas City and Seattle watched the same television shows and scribbled in the same fourth-grade workbooks. High-school seniors in Savannah and Albuquerque took the same SAT and Advanced Placement tests. Teachers in Miami and Toledo belonged to the same unions and read the same professional (and recreational) magazines. Everybody ate the same Big Macs, bought the same national newspapers, and lined up for the same movies and rock concerts. For better or worse, American culture was homogenizing—indeed, was colonizing most of the planet. The de facto curriculum encountered by American children was much the same, in school and out, from sea to shining sea. We still mouthed the mantra that states and localities controlled the schools, but their boundaries could no more contain these developments than the highway patrol could keep out the Medfly. What had been missing was the will to transform our de facto national curriculum from the flabby, standards-free version that had placed the country at risk into a purposeful one that corresponded to sound ideas about what children should know and be able to do on entry into adulthood—a muscular curriculum that could be aligned with specific goals and married to clear indicators of result.

Though superintendents and school boards might still harrumph about territorial prerogatives, by the late 1980s some thoughtful educators were also acquiring a national perspective on school goals and content, even on issues of structure and control. In 1986, the Carnegie-sponsored Task Force on Teaching as a Profession urged the creation of a "National Board for Professional Teaching Standards," intended to establish new nationwide norms for quality teaching and to confer nationally valid certificates on expert instructors, much as medical specialty groups designate obstetricians and dermatologists to be "board-certified."[20] Since every aspect of teacher licensure and certification was firmly in the hands of the fifty states, and reciprocity among them was the exception, not the rule, this was an unprecedented notion.

On the curricular front, several organizations recommended new nationwide goals, guidelines, and norms for their disciplines. This was revolutionary, too. But the National Council of Teachers of Mathematics, the American Association for the Advancement of Science, the Bradley Commission on History in the Schools, and similar groups were not deterred by the traditional boundaries. Each was clear and exacting about what would constitute good education in its field, and forthright in urging this vision on the entire country.[21]

From one side of the political spectrum, Education Secretary William J. Bennett drafted model curricula for American students from kindergarten through twelfth grade. He called them "James Madison Elementary School" and "James Madison High School." This was an extraordinary move for a conservative Republican administration, but Bennett was serene. It was not, he wrote, "a monolithic program to be uniformly imposed or slavishly followed. Neither is it a statement of federal policy." It was only "my views on an important matter."[22] That he took this step at all, however, suggested the extent to which the climate had altered.

Some distance across the spectrum, teachers' union chief Albert Shanker and Stanford Education Dean Marshall Smith urged the American Educational Research Association in 1990 to press for a bona fide national curriculum. Local control, Shanker said, was already a "myth." "We may end up going in the wrong direction," he conceded, "but on balance, I believe we ought to move forward."[23]

Most surprising of all, the American people concurred—or said they did. As we saw in chapter 4, the 1989 Gallup education poll disclosed that the public, by whopping margins, is comfortable with the prospect of nationwide goals and norms, even with a national curriculum and testing program to accompany them.[24]

Nobody expected these opinions, and their implications are momentous for an education system long anchored to the belief that Americans want all important education decisions to be made close to home, ideally in their own communities and certainly no farther away than the state capital. This anchor may, of course, have been dragging for quite a while and we simply didn't know it. Or opinion may recently have shifted. Whatever the case, when one recalls how often the cry of "local control" had been raised in education policy arenas, and with what political potency, one wonders whether we were deliberately kidding ourselves. Perhaps this, like so many other mossy assumptions about American schooling, had functioned more as a convenient shield for the status quo than as a reflection of strongly held popular sentiment.

A few weeks after the Gallup results were released, President Bush and the fifty governors held their high-profile "education summit" in Charlottesville, Virginia, and there resolved to develop national goals to which the education reform movement ought aspire. Nobody said these would be promulgated, much less enforced, by the federal government (by now a lot of people had grasped the distinction between "federal" and "national.") But nobody tried to disguise the idea, either. It was *national* goals they said they wanted, not just goals. And these goals were meant to catalyze changes, not sit on a pedestal to be admired. Accordingly, the president and governors also announced their commitment to a much-improved monitoring and information-feedback system, and vowed to issue annual report cards on the progress being made by state and nation.

In January 1990 President Bush outlined the six national education goals "for the year 2000" that they had agreed on, and a few weeks later the National Governors' Association ratified and elaborated these. With one or two exceptions, they were clear and concrete about the outcomes they sought. By the year 2000, for example, they pledged that "the high school graduation rate will increase to at least 90 percent" and that "students will leave grades four, eight and twelve having demonstrated competency over challenging subject matter including English, mathematics, science, history, and geography."[25] They did not say that only some students should do this or that the standards ought to be tailored to individual needs. These goals were meant to apply to everyone and, it appeared, to be the same in every place.

CONTINUING RESISTANCE

It is too soon to tell whether goal setting will turn out to be an efficacious reform strategy and impossible to know whether the specific objectives set by "education president" George Bush and the governors will rally the nation to action. Goals are not self-implementing. The system must direct itself toward their attainment, and the daily routines of thousands of schools, millions of teachers, and tens of millions of youngsters must be changed in purposeful ways. For that to happen, both the public and the profession must concur that achievement norms are a good idea, that the specific objectives chosen are worthy, and that the actions necessary to realize them are more important than the other matters that habitually fill up one's week.

The early responses of professional leaders to the post-Charlottesville education goals scarcely filled one with optimism. With a few conspicuous exceptions, they indicated that only if—and when— the president placed a large additional dollop of federal funds on the table would they begin to look seriously at his and the governors' goals. The money must come first.

"The President has provided us with a hearty menu," said Keith Geiger of the NEA, "but has left the cupboard virtually bare." The head of the national high-school principals' group said of the goals that "without resources, they are merely wishes."[26]

Especially in the current federal fiscal climate, to say that we need gobs of new money up front is practically equivalent to staking out one's excuse, far in advance, for not achieving the goals, perhaps for not even striving toward them. But that was the message sent by the heads of most of the major professional organizations.[27]

Nor can we be sure that the governors and president have the needed stamina and resolve. Six months after their unveiling, the goals were finally joined—at the 1990 summer meeting of the National Governors' Association—by a report suggesting possible state strategies for achieving them.[28] A commendable set of guidelines, provided one subscribes to the contemporary passion for vaguely defined school "restructuring," it was entirely hortatory. It carried no timetable for action, no model legislation, no specific outcome measures. Nor were the states individually rushing to embrace the new national goals. As of December 1990, only a few had enacted them into state law, and just a handful of localities had adopted their own versions.[29]

As for the expanded data gathering and assessment that everyone knows are vital if progress toward the goals is to be tracked, all that had happened by late 1990 was the naming of a fourteen-member bipartisan panel to work on the matter. Not another datum was actually scheduled for collection. The U.S. Department of Education, wary of making waves, and taking its signals mainly from interest groups, was all but paralyzed. Congress was irked that it had not been included in the goal-setting process and attempted to get even by threatening not to approve any more data gathering and by fussing over the provenance and membership of the monitoring panel.[30]

At the National Governors' Association summer meeting in Mobile, talk of the environment and health care filled the humid air and, with thirty-six governorships at stake in the November elections, few incumbents appeared to give top priority to stumping their states on behalf of the education goals. The pragmatic and soft-spoken Bush administration engaged in long behind-the-scenes negotiations with the governors about structures and procedures but, on its own, was not battling with audible gusto or determination for public acceptance of the goals themselves or for improved monitoring instruments. At one education conference after another in the summer and fall of 1990, it seemed that participants were either unaware of them or disinclined to take them seriously.

Even if Congress were well disposed and the president, his education secretary, and the governors were giving their all to this endeavor, they would still encounter wide and deep resistance within the profession. Concrete goals and uniform standards remained as unpalatable to many educators in 1990 as they had been to the authors of the "Cardinal Principles" in 1918. At the meeting where Shanker and Smith pressed for a national curriculum, for example, the NEA's Geiger voiced his opposition. Schools were different and children had unique needs. A national curriculum would not "do anything for [students] who really need help," he said, and would move away from the kinds of school-site management and decentralization that the NEA favors.[31]

Eighteen months earlier, in the main auditorium of Columbia University's Teachers College, I had one of the more illuminating—and dismaying—experiences of my professional life. The afternoon symposium had been organized to commemorate the college's centennial. The question before us was whether "uniform standards for American education" are a good idea. My seven fellow panelists included such academic luminaries as Jerome Bruner, Sara Lawrence Lightfoot and Maxine Green, former Atlanta school superintendent Alonzo Crim, MacArthur Foundation "genius award" winner (and famed school principal) Deborah W. Meier, SUNY-Buffalo professor Harold Noah, and commentator Bill Moyers.

Tom Kean had been scheduled to participate as well, having journeyed to Morningside Heights that morning to receive an honorary degree. But he had had to get back to Trenton in a hurry, we were told. (I was sorry he had gone and wondered whether he had prudently determined that he did not need the misery to follow.)

To all intents and purposes, I found myself isolated on the panel, the lone proponent of any sort of external norms for children or schools, much less uniform national standards. Professor Green favored "relativism," "contingency," "flexibility," and "responsiveness." Professor Lightfoot found her mind full of "ominous images" at the prospect of national standards. Harold Noah was troubled by the myriad complexities he saw on the horizon. Bruner thought the movement was "terribly irresponsible." Ms. Meier averred that "working out ahead of time what everyone should know by twelfth grade is not a solution" to the problems of American education. Bill Moyers spent most of his time reading aloud a batch of letters that viewers had sent, but he at least recognized some validity in my "concern that it is hard to have a cooperative society unless you have certain things that we know in common."[32] That was a wee bit encouraging. The audience reactions were not, however. My remarks were politely received, but it was evident from both applause levels and questions put to the panel that in this chamber full of hundreds of current and future education professionals, practically everyone believed that education standards are a rotten idea.

So far as I could tell that afternoon, and yesterday afternoon, and today as I write, it's still 1918 in most of the profession. The "Cardinal Principles" are in. Goals—real ones—are out.

Nothing yet stirring among politicians and business leaders is powerful enough to overcome this attitude. In the state capitals we observe well-intended, generally commendable efforts that are occasionally visionary and sometimes noble but for the most part half formed and perhaps impermanent. In Washington we see education interest groups, Congress, and the executive branch engaging in their familiar rituals, though of late the spectacle has been made more interesting by the novelty of national goals, by the unique (if shaky) alliance between the White House and the governors, and by the awkward moves of congressmen unsure what to do with a large idea that doesn't translate neatly into a federal program.

It is none too clear where the public is in all this, beyond its steadfast enunciation of commonsensical but—in the education context—radical views every time its opinion is asked. People are ready for big changes, mindful of the need for direction, unconcerned about local control, comfortable with the idea of national education goals, and supportive of the particular goals that emerged from the "summit" process. Yet neither these nor any other specific objectives appear to have fired John and Jane Doe with a clear sense of direction for the schools of their community or new standards for the education of their children. Unless that can be made to happen, I suspect we aren't likely to see changed behavior in tens of millions of households and hundreds of thousands of classrooms. And until people change their behavior, we cannot expect different results.

9

❦

A System Without
Accountability

*There are greater, more certain, and more immediate
penalties in this country for serving up a single rotten
hamburger in a restaurant than for repeatedly furnishing
a thousand schoolchildren with a rotten education.*
— U.S. Education Secretary William J. Bennett, 1987

If we handled academics as we do athletics, our children would learn more. On the playing field, we find clear goals and high expectations, uniform standards, explicit rules, and referees to enforce them. We savor the keen sense of competitiveness and we applaud the resolute drive toward success and victory (so long as these operate within set limits of acceptable behavior and fair play). We employ coaches who understand that they must balance multiple objectives but that their top priority is to build a winning team. And when it comes to that team's actual performance, we receive prompt, ample, and precise information, data we can easily analyze a hundred ways: in relation to the immediate event, in the context of past performance, and in comparison with the performance of other teams.

In sports we also acknowledge the link between effort and results. Though luck intrudes now and again, players and coaches seldom attribute the final score to forces beyond their control or claim that they are hapless victims of broader social trends. Nor do we expect the score to go unnoticed. We know it matters. We believe it *should* matter. Only in classrooms do adults downplay results. Only in colleges of education are we told to de-emphasize them. In the "real world," as on the athletic field, everyone understands that predictable consequences follow from success and also from failure.

Those features do not deter many youngsters from participating in athletics or discourage most schools from fielding all the teams they can. In fact, I suspect these very qualities help account for the immense popularity of sporting events and the status accorded successful athletes by classmates and community. Nothing elicits more school spirit, parent involvement, and enthusiastic attendance than a varsity game. Few accomplishments bring a warmer glow to the entire school than a championship team or winning season.

Sure, it can be carried to excess. Feelings as well as bodies may be bruised. The norms of sportsmanship may be bent too far. The youngster with little natural talent may be excluded. Still, if you believe that almost every gain entails some pain and every goal some risk, you have to admire the world of organized athletics for its sure and virtually automatic accountability system.

We take similar arrangements for granted in many other human endeavors. The entertainment industry is highly accountable to its audiences, whose reactions (duly influenced by reviews, ads and hype) determine box office sales. Though we prefer to avoid wars, the military services are ultimately held to account for winning— or losing—them. Physicians and hospitals are judged mainly in terms of their success in curing people, as trial lawyers are evaluated according to their courtroom results. Businesses of every sort are answerable to shareholders for profit and loss, recorded at least quarterly in the well-known "bottom line," which cannot slope downward for too long without a change of management—if not a bankrupt company.

THE IDEA OF ACCOUNTABILITY

Accountability in any endeavor today means that specified goals or outcomes are supposed to be achieved, and that people throughout the organization are responsible for achieving them. Not just for following set procedures, putting in time or going through the motions, not even for making a valiant effort, but for *actually producing* the desired results.

To be responsible for outcomes includes knowing that consequences will follow from one's success or failure. These may be pleasant or not, but without predictable and sure consequences there can be no true accountability.

Some consequences are internal, such as the pride or shame that one feels in a task deftly completed or egregiously bungled. As professionals, we like to think that this alone will motivate us. For some, well fitted-out in ambition and superego, it probably will. Many more of us want to believe that it will. That is why we thrill to the famous exchange between Sir Thomas More and young Richard Rich in *A Man for All Seasons:*

> More: Why not be a teacher? You'd be a fine teacher. Perhaps even a great one.
>
> Rich: If I was, who would know it?
>
> More: You, your pupils, your friends, and God. Not a bad public, that.[2]

An accountability system, however, cannot rely exclusively on the incentives cited in Robert Bolt's memorable play to shape the behavior of adults, any more than we can count on love of learning alone to motivate youngsters to do their utmost in school. What transpires between one's conscience and one's Creator is irreplaceable, but it is never systematic and it isn't always sufficient. Most grown-ups pay the taxes they owe, but how scrupulous would we be if only God were watching and there were no earthly consequences one way or the other? Many people edge over the speed limit now and again, but think how much worse the highway carnage would be if every driver answered exclusively to his or her passengers and con-science and there was no possibility of a patrol car waiting around the next curve. Most mail carriers conscientiously deliver the mail, but how many homes atop steep hills would receive it on an icy winter day if there were no consequences for skipping them? The more important the outcomes for society, the more imperative it is to intertwine their accomplishment with sure rewards and punish-ments. Good things should happen to those who meet stated goals. But when targets are not reached or necessary results produced, interventions must occur. Something has to change, else the failure will repeat itself.

The purpose is not punishment or retribution. Accountability sys-tems aren't criminal justice systems, and we do not build them because we are vengeful. We construct them because we want good results, and in this world we have greater likelihood of producing good results if consequences follow from bad results as well.

Back on the playing field, this is well understood. The champion athlete is applauded, hugged, slapped on the shoulder, lionized. She may receive a medal, see her name inscribed in the record books, be offered a college scholarship or a lucrative professional contract. The successful team has a victory party and goes on to the semifinals. The losing side receives clumsy condolences, forfeits its chance for the pennant or the opportunity to try for the Olympics. Its practice schedule may be doubled, its coach replaced. Attendance at subsequent matches declines. The quarterback is not recruited by the talent scout for the Big Ten team or the pitcher by the professional ball club. Perhaps the lineup is rearranged before the next game. Weak players may be banished to the junior varsity. Young Tabitha, last seen in chapter 6 where she garnered high marks and praise from her classroom teacher even though she hadn't learned much science, is far less apt to be applauded by her basketball coach or teammates if she consistently fails to sink the ball. Instead she will probably be advised to work on her game, practice a lot, and try out again next year. Nobody calls this an accountability system. But that's exactly what it is.

Lodged between goals and consequences in any functional accountability scheme must be solid information about how well the goals of the enterprise are being achieved. In sports, this is as simple as the scoreboard and as complex as the lifetime batting averages and other intricate statistics kept by fans, journalists and league officials. Without such information, goals are wishful thinking, not prods to action. Absent reliable feedback about the adequacy of one's performance, any consequences are apt to be capricious, inappropriate—and probably ineffective. I see accountability systems as tripods. To stand upright, all three legs must be in place: clearly stated goals, prompt and accurate information about progress toward them, and positive and negative consequences that follow from the information.

This sounds more complicated than it is. In many realms of our lives we have come to take it for granted. We engage in certain actions in order to achieve a desired result. (Wanting to please my friends with a delicious meal, I take considerable pains to prepare a gruyere soufflé with fresh tomato sauce.) We get information about the extent of our achievement. (What do they say when they eat it? How does it taste to me?) And we incur consequences. (Was the evening enjoyable? Did the friendship survive? How eager are they to return for more of my cuisine? Does my wife threaten to replace me with a caterer?)

IN THE PUBLIC SECTOR

Government agencies and public services are generally less accountable than private organizations for the effectiveness of their performance and the quality of their results. We often explain this by noting that they enjoy near monopolies and have no need to break even, much less turn a profit. That combination can devastate efficiency and quality control, especially if the agency is staffed by people keener on job security than entrepreneurship or advancement.

These familiar explanations for public sector mediocrity are true to my own experience. During my years at the Education Department, for example, it appeared to me that little was done quickly, much was done sloppily, and when rapid, careful work was done, perhaps 10 percent of the employees did 90 percent of it. There were virtually no consequences, there was no competition, and the taxpayer paid the bills regardless. When the money ran out, people took fewer trips and made do with older computers. When the duplicating machine went on the blink, no copies got made. When it snowed, people stayed home. (It was remarkable how often snow and illness struck on Friday or Monday.) When, occasionally, the agency ran out of envelopes, it simply stopped mailing things.

Par for the course, I surmised. There is only one federal Department of Education, after all, and its clients had neither recourse nor redress save to complain to Congress. Harvard Professor Steven Kelman offers a different analysis, however—namely that government agencies are plenty accountable to the public, but for the wrong things. They "get attention," Kelman writes, "when they do something scandalous rather than when they perform well." Therefore they develop organizational rules and norms that reward caution, regularity, and impartiality rather than courage, creativity, or zeal. Kelman calls this the "bureaucratic paradigm," and suggests that if we want *efficient* government instead, we must "insist on good service with the same persistence [with which] we currently pursue corruption."[3]

This is a shrewd insight that also corresponds to my experience. One reason so little gets done with flare or zeal in public agencies is that so many people are checking to make certain that all rules and precedents are slavishly adhered to. At the Education Department, we never got into serious hot water with clients, constituents, or Congressional committees (or with the department's umpteen internal watchdogs) for being sluggish, unimaginative, and repetitive. Trouble could be counted upon to descend in minutes, however, whenever we attempted to change an ancient routine, alter a priority, or decide something in a fresh way.[4]

Holding government agencies accountable for results grows even trickier when the services they provide are the kinds we need in reserve but would rather not have to use. Indeed, the longer some service providers are idle, the better off we are. Think of lifeguards, nuclear submarines, fire departments, or airplane crash investigators.

When services such as these are necessary, however, much as we prefer to minimize their use, we also want efficiency and good results on demand. A submarine that sends its missiles in the wrong direction is as useless as a police department that never solves a crime or a municipal hospital whose staff cannot suture a wound without infecting it. Indeed, one cannot think of many public-sector enterprises today that are immune to judgments about their efficacy and productivity. Save for a handful of essentially custodial institutions—prisons for the criminally insane, for example, where we are probably content with the responsible delivery of services—we otherwise insist that public as well as private endeavors be able to display outcomes as well as activity, that they yield value for money, and that they generate results that bear a palpable relationship to their goals. We are also inclined to reward and punish elected officials at the ballot box for the efficiency and quality of the public services over which they preside.

Yet we're still so far from successfully implanting the ethic of accountability in most government services. That is why many people remain disgusted with public-sector waste and ineptitude, why it is possible to gain public office by running as an outsider or "against the government." Few agencies have internalized an obsession with results. The "bureaucratic paradigm" is so well entrenched that where it endures, the public employee feels responsible mainly for staying out of trouble, impartially delivering services, obtaining and deploying the necessary resources with regularity and evenhandedness, and not rocking boats. Anyone who cut his or her professional teeth on those norms is sure to be confused and troubled by the changeover to accountability for results.

SCHOOL ACCOUNTABILITY

American education is slowly evolving into an outcomes-oriented enterprise whose institutions, employees, and policymakers will be held responsible for their results by the public they serve. That is the only kind of accountability worth having in 1991, certainly the only kind that bears any relationship to the premier education problem we seek to solve—namely the weak academic achievement of our children. And in twenty years or so, I expect that the education system will have taken this to heart.[5]

But what a misery we are enduring in the meantime! It is no

easier in public education than in any other government activity to replace the bureaucratic paradigm with a passion for excellence. We've been unwilling to trust the marketplace to do this for us. And we haven't often summoned the courage either to "throw the rascals out" or to provide large incentives for superior performance.

For a very long time, schools and their employees were judged in terms of efforts, intentions, resources, and service delivery. They were accountable, to be sure, but for compliance with rules, orderly procedures, and resource allocations. Their customers thought of them that way. Their own staffs and governing boards believed these were proper criteria by which to gauge their work. Besides, education is one of those public services with multiple missions. Who is to proclaim any of them supreme?

The result is a system unaccustomed to organizing itself around the efficacy of its efforts or the quality of its results.[6] Worse, our efforts to reconstruct it along different lines are occurring at the least propitious time imaginable: While our "no-fault" culture is insulating people from a sense of responsibility for the consequences of their own actions by encouraging everyone to believe they are the innocent prey of broad social trends and ineluctable forces. In the name of accountability, we are asking education to swim against its traditional paradigms and internal organizational norms while also battling the shifting currents of the zeitgeist.

My twenty-year forecast may therefore be too rosy. If an accountability system resembles a tripod, it must be said that in American public education today, none of the three legs is sturdy. As we saw in the previous chapter, achievement goals are vague, inconstant, and suspect. Reliable information feedback, as we shall discover in the next few pages, is extremely hard to obtain, and the profession resists most ideas for augmenting its flow. As for consequences, we observed in chapter 7 that, from the student's perspective, academic achievement is not a prerequisite for much, few tangible rewards come to those who study hard and learn a lot, and little suffering or ignominy befalls those who slide by with minimum effort.

Even deadlier for the quality of American education, the schools are not accountable for their institutional results, nor do those who lead and teach in them face large consequences for success or failure. "Teaching," noted Lamar Alexander, "is the only profession in which you are not paid one extra cent for being good at your job." "If you do a good job educating a group of students," Education Secretary William J. Bennett wrote in 1987, "nothing happens to you or for you. Similarly, if you do a bad job educating a group of students, nothing happens to you or for you."[7]

At the extremes something may happen these days, especially at the top end. An outstanding public school may get "recognized" by the Department of Education, win a grant from Coca-Cola or RJR Nabisco or the Joyce Foundation. A great classroom instructor may be designated "teacher of the year," honored by the National Science Foundation or feted by Burger King. A dizzying array of recognition and accolade programs has sprung up in the past decade. Though these are welcome additions to an enterprise that paid scant attention to success over the years and that showed little respect for quality, they hover on the outside of that enterprise and are not part of its basic structure, its routine management, or its internal reward system. Most of them employ as criteria a generalized notion of "excellence," retrospectively applied, rather than concrete targets toward which one can aim. There are not enough of these programs for one hundred thousand schools, in any case, nor are they big and intrusive enough to influence the actions of most U.S. educators.

If such honors and rewards are not felt in advance, they cannot serve as strong inducements to alter one's behavior toward particular goals. They are more like lucking out in a game of chance than winning the blue ribbon for the best fig chutney at the state fair. Receiving one is akin to winning the lottery or a MacArthur "genius award." It's a marvelous windfall when it happens, but there's practically nothing you can do ahead of time to improve materially the odds that this will happen to you. When tangible rewards are not winnable through the successful attainment of predetermined goals, they do not exert much incentive effect. Hence they will not make a great difference in people's actual behavior and performance and are not apt to boost the effectiveness of the enterprise as a whole. By my lights, therefore, they do not qualify as an accountability system for American education.

If we have not made satisfactory provision for fostering success through incentives and rewards, we're light years further behind when it comes to predictable interventions in cases of failure. Negative consequences are few and far between in public education. If a teacher commits a felony or is chronically drunk, he may be disciplined or dismissed. But when did you last hear of a teacher being fired, fined, or even reprimanded because her students did not learn enough geology or German?

In a few jurisdictions, a chronically bad school or local system may be "intervened in" by higher authority. New Jersey's management takeover of the Jersey City system is the most famous instance of this rare occurrence. South Carolina has engaged in less drastic (but more frequent) interventions, Indiana runs a performance-based accreditation system that functions similarly at the building level, and Kentucky has built a version of this idea into its statewide reform scheme. As the 1990–91 year opened, the Massachusetts commissioner of education threatened to take over the Boston schools. "I would argue that the time is upon us," he said, "to question whether Boston has the capability of running its public schools."[8] Yet despite these and similar moves (or threats) in other places, we have no generally accepted doctrine of educational malpractice in the United States. We have constructed innumerable job security protections for school employees, but we have not made systematic arrangements for safeguarding students and taxpayers from pedagogical nonfeasance. For several years, the federal government has reported hospital-by-hospital death rates, and in 1990 the Department of Health and Human Services launched a national directory of incompetent physicians.[9] Yet "a poor surgeon," as Ernest Boyer has remarked, "hurts 1 person at a time. A poor teacher hurts 130."[10]

When a pilot takes off with a load of passengers after a late-night binge at the local saloon, we don't settle for being outraged; we bring him to trial, fine or jail him, strip him of his license, and dismiss him from his job—all this even though no mishap occurred. When Joseph Hazelwood ran the Exxon *Valdez* onto the reef in Prince William Sound, loosing an immense oil spill, he lost his job and, after a trial, was sentenced to one thousand hours of community service and fined fifty thousand dollars. When schools are operated in an unsafe manner, however, we do far less. Grinding onto an educational reef and spilling children's futures into the sea doesn't lead to much trouble for those in charge of the errant craft. In some systems the principal may be transferred to another building or demoted back to classroom teaching (in which role he or she almost surely possesses tenure protected by state law.) But this cannot be taken for granted. Until new Education Chancellor Joseph Fernandez prevailed in the state legislature in 1990, for example, New York City's school principals had long enjoyed "building tenure." Try to imagine a law giving pilots "airplane tenure" or doctors "operating-room tenure."

As Bennett noted in the epigraph that opens this chapter, restaurant inspectors can close down a sandwich shop that serves spoiled food or does not maintain sanitary conditions. And this happens regularly. Every week or so, in many communities, the newspaper lists eateries whose doors have been locked for such offenses. When did you last hear of a public school ordered to close because the instruction it served its pupils contained the educational equivalent of mouse droppings?

A somewhat different situation obtains in private education. Though school goals may still be vague and information feedback sketchy, education's nongovernment sector functions amid palpable consequences. By whatever criteria parents and students appraise the performance of a private school, if they judge it to be educationally unwholesome they can take their business elsewhere. The marketplace thus creates demand-side consequences for private schools (and their employees) as tangible as those for restaurants, florists, automobile manufacturers, and magazine publishers. Those institutions that satisfy their customers flourish and—if they wish—grow. Those that deliver unsatisfactory products, poor service, or weak value for money must either change their ways or shrivel and die. Marketplace forces, coupled with the flexibility of private schools to respond to them, create a partial accountability system for private education. This is the core of the closely reasoned and generally persuasive arguments of John Chubb and Terry Moe for revitalizing public education by building kindred features into *its* structure.[11]

But student achievement can remain mediocre in "successful" private schools if their objectives are modest, standards low, information feedback incomplete or misleading, or the customers too readily satisfied. This is my main quarrel with those who view school choice as a silver bullet, a sufficient precondition for excellence. Fast-food outlets come and go as consumers choose among them, and nobody doubts that their marketplace is lively and responsive. But we can still wind up with an obese and malnourished populace if most of their customers are happy with a diet of burgers and fries.

Accountability in education does not consist entirely of pleasing the consumers, any more than it consists of cosseting the providers. The real stakes are higher. Sating millions of individual appetites may not add up to a society that is well prepared for the twenty-first century. I do not mean this as an elitist or undemocratic argument. Rather, it recognizes that education serves both private and public purposes and that it is possible to satisfy the former, at least in the short run, without doing justice to the latter, especially when so many people are content with the present performance of their children and schools. An accountable education system that also meets the larger society's quality needs has to have goals that are worth achieving, consequences that affect individuals and institutions at every stage and level of the system, and accurate information feedback that connects consequences to goals.

THE INFORMATION VACUUM

American education is drowning in certain kinds of data about itself. The 1990 edition of the principal federal compilation of education statistics has 462 large pages displaying 31 figures and 360 tables. That's more information than we know what to do with. Yet nearly all of it harks back to the "bureaucratic paradigm" of government in general and the traditional input-orientation of our education system in particular. Practically all of this flood of information has to do with resources and services. Where outcomes are tabulated, the measures mainly involve time spent, courses taken, diplomas and degrees received. These are worth knowing, to be sure, as they relate to some of the schools' multiple purposes. But they do not fill the bill in an era when our top priority is boosting cognitive achievement. It is learning outcomes, however, about which information is hardest to come by. And where we have relevant data, they nearly always suffer from two basic weaknesses. Either they report results only for the country as a whole—data that are good to have but do not lend themselves to accountability in a government structure where most management decisions are made below the national level. Or they report the achievement of youngsters in individual states and localities in ways that make it impossible to compare them with those in other jurisdictions, with national standards, or with international competitors.

Most exasperating of all, in few jurisdictions can Mr. and Mrs. Hopkins obtain trustworthy information about Megan's and Thad's educational achievement in terms they can understand. Nor can they determine how well the Ralph Waldo Emerson Elementary School is doing in relation to other schools in town, to state and national goals, or even to its own past performance. When it comes to consumer information about outcomes, the American education system has been engaged in a massive cover-up. If the Securities and Exchange Commission allowed publicly traded corporations to conceal this much data about their profits and losses, we'd have a crisis of investor confidence—and a lot of ruinous investments.

There are honorable exceptions, sometimes at the instance of education officials, sometimes because state legislatures have demanded greater disclosure. Half a dozen states now issue or are developing "building report cards," by which parents (and the press and general public) can obtain important data concerning the performance of individual schools. California and Illinois pioneered this, and they've been joined by Connecticut, Louisiana, South Carolina, Alabama, and, for a time, New Jersey. Kentucky's ambitious reform agenda also includes this feature. Properly done, such report cards are rich sources of school-specific information, including attendance and graduation patterns, honors and AP course-taking rates, the incidence of discipline problems, the placement of graduates, and, of course, the school's results on various tests and assessments.

Building-level reports remain the exception, however, and even when available they can only present such data as are gathered. Nowhere do they show employers how the performance of a job applicant relates to standards such as those set by the governors and president in 1990. Despite California's generally exemplary work in student assessment, the head of the education task force of the state business roundtable advised a key legislator later that year that "we have no state test results that are meaningful to us in assessing prospective employees."[12] Nor do school-level report cards make comparisons to neighboring states or foreign countries. Nowhere can American parents get their hands on such information regarding the particular schools their children attend. Often, they can't get clear guidance on how their school *system* is really doing, perhaps because some of the people providing the explanations don't know which end is up. "I'm not sure what is reasonable to expect," said the assistant superintendent for research and evaluation in Dallas, after test scores in that city declined in 1990. "It's a complicated issue that I don't pretend to understand, and I know more about it than most people in the country because I work with it every day."[13]

As for the Hopkins family's desire to know how Megan and Thad are faring vis-à-vis such gauges of success and adequacy, don't even bother asking. Unless, of course, you want the commercial standardized test results on which we can practically guarantee that your children will be above the national average. Or possibly you would care to move to England, where the Thatcher-era reforms include individualized annual written reports to parents that evaluate their children's performance in each subject of the new national curriculum—measured in relation to the new nationwide "attainment targets" for various age levels.

That we do nothing of the sort for Mr. and Mrs. Hopkins, or for the families of forty-five million other U.S. students, means that our school reform efforts are unlikely to improve student achievement, because they will not alter the behavior of all those complacent children and parents who today do not believe they have a problem that warrants change. They don't believe it because nobody has given them—and they generally cannot obtain even when they ask— the kinds of performance information that are most likely to get their adrenaline flowing. It's grand for the country to have goals expressed in terms of outcomes. But until those have some clear link to Thad's and Megan's individual performances, the education reform rubber is not really going to be in contact with the road.

I have observed and struggled against this unconscionable situation long enough to have grown a bit paranoid. I no longer believe that the data gaps and information flaws in American education are inadvertent or coincidental. Yet the reader new to this topic may think I exaggerate. After all, do we not see in the news every few weeks yet another account of yet another alarming study of educational outcomes? How could there possibly be a dearth of data?

Let me enlist as witnesses some of the policymakers who are living with the situation—a goodly distance from the Hopkins family, to be sure, but illustrative of how this problem looks on the big screen:

"Indicators of the quality and effectiveness of American education have consistently been lacking, especially at the state and local levels," reported the National Governors' Association in 1989. "Only at the national level have data been regularly collected on American students' knowledge and skills in various subject areas."[14]

In the words of the Council of Chief State School Officers in its 1989 compilation of education indicators:

> Missing entirely from this report are state-level measures of student outcomes, the ultimate accomplishments of the educational system. Even the most rudimentary accomplishment—succeeding in getting students to school—is plagued by inconsistencies. . . . Most states have comprehensive programs in place for testing student achievement, but each state uses a virtually unique combination of tests and testing procedures.[15]

The SREB has identified sixty different gauges of educational progress that its member states are urged to use to track their own performance. "Pursuing educational goals without indicators of progress," the SREB astutely notes, "is like traveling a highway without mileposts. We do not know where we are or how far we have to go." Yet in appraising the extant data base in its region in 1990, the board ascertained that "for many of the indicators, information is not collected or analyzed by states. The lack of common definitions . . . is a major obstacle for obtaining reliable comparative information. . . . [T]he wide variety of tests used by states to measure student achievement makes state-by-state comparisons impossible."[16]

"No state," concludes Dr. Susan Fuhrman of the Center for Policy Research in Education,

> has a fully developed system of indicators that relate educational inputs, process and outcomes. Hence, we are hindered in our efforts to describe the educational system (to assess the quality of teachers, for example), to measure progress toward policy objectives (to tell how much and what kind of math students are taking in response to graduation requirements, for example), and to examine interrelationships between policy and outcomes (to tell if increased coursetaking is associated with student achievement, for example).[17]

This acute shortage of outcomes information has devastating implications for any serious attempt to move American education toward specific goals, including the brash effort by President Bush and the governors. Goals fast turn to mush if we have no practical way of tracking progress toward them. Yet that is our present situation. When federal officials set out in early 1990 to identify indicators by which movement might be monitored toward the goals and objectives specified after Charlottesville, they came up with ninety candidates. For the great majority of these, some data are flowing for the nation as a whole. But even by the most generous interpretation of current activities and plans, there were only sixteen for which *any* state-by-state information was visible in 1990; for most of these it is incomplete; and for some it is only a gleam on the horizon. Yet the states bear primary policy responsibility for *achieving* the national goals. Without relevant data, their prospects for success are greatly reduced. As for wanting trustworthy information about where one's own child or the school down the road stands vis-à-vis these national goals, one must be ingesting something illicit even to conjure such a fantasy.

At the other end of the data continuum, we're in no better shape. Though international comparisons of student performance are probably the most revealing and motivating of all to policymakers and education officials, the world has no mechanism by which to assure that any more of these will produced in the future. A quasi-private organization called the International Association for the Evaluation of Educational Achievement and the wholly private Princeton-based

ETS have been the sources of most such data in the past, but each depends for successive assessments on uncertain grants from government agencies and private foundations. No established international organization generates information on student learning. And nobody in Washington is responsible for changing this situation, even though one of the education goals set by the governors and president cannot be monitored at all without comparative international data and another loses most of its oomph in the absence of such data.

These information vacuums, I suggest, are no accident. They result from omissions, hesitation, and avoidance over many years at every level of the education system. Especially with regard to cognitive achievement by students, I see little reason to expect the situation to improve soon, for reasons to which we now turn.

10

🔥

The War on Testing
A Dead Messenger Brings No Bad News

*Testing, of course, always embarrasses somebody. . . . But
the inconvenient fact remains that we will never be able
to do anything for the schools until we figure out exactly
what is going on there, and if anyone is serious about meeting
goals 'by the year 2000,' the time to start was yesterday.*
—*Washington Post* editorial, June 1990

In chapter 6 we saw that "standardized" student achievement tests, as deployed in most American school systems, deliver inflated and misleading feedback to parents, policymakers, and the public. The result is dangerously deceptive, as if the greaseburgers and shakes at the fast-food emporium came with certificates citing their superior nutritional properties.

Yet testing and assessment results are our greatest single source of information on academic performance. We use them at all six levels of American education for which we crave performance information: the child, the classroom, the school, the local system, the state, and the nation as a whole.

If accountability for performance at all those levels is a vital component of serious education improvement, if sound information about cognitive outcomes is the keystone of the accountability arch, and if tests are our primary information resource, one might suppose we would take pains to assure that our testing programs yield timely and trustworthy data at every level.

This we have not done.

Imagine embarking on a weight reduction program without trust-worthy scales, planning a space shuttle launch (or even an office picnic) without decent weather data, managing one's checking account without monthly bank statements, making national economic policy without timely manpower statistics, or trying to sell ad space for a magazine without any circulation figures to show prospective buyers. You would be crazy to try—and your odds of success would be slender.

There are a few domains—art and music come to mind, as does cooking a souffle—in which creativity, subjectivity, and individual taste reign supreme. But I can think of no large enterprise, and certainly no major public function, that can even be successfully managed let alone made more efficient and productive, without hard information about its performance in relation to its goals.

Yet the $230-billion enterprise of American elementary-secondary education has little such information.

SHOOTING THE MESSENGER

Instead of rectifying that grave situation as a matter of supreme urgency, much of the education profession has been—and is today—waging war on testing and on the outcomes emphasis associated with it.

This is not an all-out assault so much as a series of persistent and damaging guerrilla attacks. Rarely does anyone declare himself opposed to all imaginable forms of measurement and assessment. What we often encounter, however, are complex criticisms, whose gist is that "testing may be fine in its proper place, but I've never met a test I liked, or one that satisfies all the criteria that I believe are necessary."[1] This is akin to condoning just wars while never having seen one that deserved to be fought or claiming that you are without prejudice but not so fortunate as ever to have met a Jew or black with whom you care to associate. "When it comes to testing and evaluation," Ernest Boyer bluntly comments, "educators have, for years, been playing blindman's bluff [sic]. They have criticized almost every test that has been proposed while failing to develop useful yardsticks of their own."[2]

One cannot be sure how many of these attacks are prompted by the impulse to sidestep accountability for results, but it certainly lies behind some. "Killing the messengers of bad news is nowhere more popular than in education," writes Robert J. Braun, veteran education reporter for the Newark *Star-Ledger*, "but the perpetrators are especially adroit at justifying their deeds."[3] More than any other single factor, test scores have brought American education into bad odor, and test scores are most likely to keep the public discontented with its schools and crotchety about those who run and work in them. To be unable to identify any test worth giving is to suggest that no more tests *be* given, at least not now; not to test is not to know how much the children have learned or how good a job the system is doing with respect to cognitive outcomes; and for people not to know this is greatly to reduce the chances that one will be criticized, blamed, or suffer unpleasant consequences in light of those outcomes. Though those waging it protest otherwise, the war on testing is in considerable part a sustained battle against enforceable standards and an informed public. "The anti-test, anti-public disclosure folks," Braun explains, "have converted anxiety about consistently poor test results into an ideological crusade: Poor schooling is not the problem; the bad tests are the problem." (Expanding girth is not my problem; it's the wretched scales and the misinformation they give. Best not weigh myself again until the scale people come out with a better product.)

TEACHING TO THE TEST

Testing is an immense topic, and some of what needs to be said about it is properly critical. Some tests do have undesirable side effects; we misuse them sometimes, too, at least we use them for purposes other than they were meant for. The crucial point, says UCLA evaluation expert Eva Baker, is to obtain "assessment devices that measure what we think is most important for students to learn." What is measured and monitored in any system is what gets attention. What is tested is almost surely what the schools will emphasize in their teaching and, one hopes, what the children will learn. It is, therefore, right to demand that the tests used in one's schools be carefully calibrated to the educational goals one seeks. This sounds self-evident, but in the real world of American education it's remarkable how seldom our curriculum objectives, our instructional materials, our pedagogy, and our testing programs are aligned with one another.

One reason is that most "standardized" tests are purchased ready-made from a half dozen commercial vendors that make them up without direct reference to what is being taught in particular places.

A few states and localities have developed their own tests, and some of these are quite good, but it's a costly and complex endeavor. Moreover, the commercial products afford easy comparisons between one's students and the country as a whole—via those treacherous "norms" and "grade levels"—while the homegrown product, since it is tailored to one's own objectives and not of much interest elsewhere, seldom permits comparisons beyond one's borders. Not surprisingly, therefore, most states have turned to publishers of the Iowa Test of Basic Skills, the Stanford Achievement Test, and their ilk. So have local test directors in jurisdictions where these decisions are decentralized. But only by happenstance is such a test closely matched to the school's instructional objectives.[4]

That mismatch, combined with a heavy emphasis placed on the scores, is what prompts teachers and principals to depart from their curriculum and "teach to" the test. This is regarded throughout the education profession as a heinous act, ranking on the infamy scale somewhere between denouncing Dewey and abusing children.[5] The irony, of course, is that teaching to the test is a grand thing to do so long as the test does a good job of probing the knowledge and skills one wants children to acquire. If our objectives are sound and our exams carefully aligned with them, we should praise teachers who successfully prepare children for those exams. Obviously, that doesn't mean drilling them on actual test questions; that's cheating in anyone's eyes. I mean ensuring that one's students learn the content and skills of the subjects (and domains within subjects) that the exam will plumb.[6] That is the proper function of testing within an accountability system—and the proper classroom response to such an accountability system.

That is also the way most other countries handle testing, at least at the end of secondary school. In France, Germany, England (and many Commonwealth countries that cling to this system), and in much of the rest of Europe and Japan, exams are regularly given and one's results on these have immense bearing on one's future, beginning with university admission. Such exams do not look much like American-style "standardized" tests. They are typically essay format rather than multiple choice. More remarkably, teachers are *supposed* to prepare their students conscientiously and meticulously for them. Each subject has a preset curriculum or syllabus, and it is understood by all that the way to do well on the exam is to learn what's in the syllabus. In this sense, "teaching to the test" dominates the last couple of years of schooling. It is taken for granted that preparing young people for this important rite of passage into the world of educated adults is the chief mission of those years. And, where high-stakes exams come earlier (as in the transition from junior to senior high school in Japan), an analogous pattern is visible at younger ages.

The New York "Regents" tests follow a similar approach, but for the closest U.S. facsimile of European-style examinations we must turn to the privately administered AP tests. Some 450,000 of these are taken by high-school students each year, divided among twenty-two subjects. As in Europe, each is keyed to a course syllabus that is well understood by veteran teachers. They know approximately what the exam will cover and what its form will be, though not what questions will be asked. Their job is to prepare their students to do well on it. If the syllabus was well planned, it's impossible to do a good job of preparing students for the test without simultaneously teaching them a great deal about the subject at hand.

The International Baccalaureate (IB) works similarly. Secondary schools in many countries that participate in this demanding program make sure that their students master a predetermined body of subject matter knowledge and intellectual skills in anticipation of rigorous exams that arrive at year's end from IB headquarters. As with the AP tests, and their European and Japanese counterparts, these are "external" exams; the questions are devised and test papers scored by educators outside one's own school.[7]

In the United States, we've generally shunned that approach. We prefer to think that the best and most important tests are created and marked by individual classroom teachers. Where we use external exams, they are almost always voluntary.[8] Because most are also privately organized, outside the public school apparatus itself, students taking them pay a fee. Ironically, the best and most challenging of these exams are confined to our quickest and most accomplished students. Youngsters who need to make the greatest advances are usually given the drabbest tests, which also turn out to be the kind most apt to yield misleading results.

When the stakes are high, however, even a conventional test can influence what happens in school, can concentrate one's mind and shape one's priorities. (If it did not, we would not see so many educators deploring the potent influence of testing on what happens in the schools.) Individual classrooms, entire districts, even whole states that place heavy emphasis on test results have reoriented themselves to ensure that their children acquire whatever knowledge and skills the test taps. Fashionable education doctrine holds this to be lamentable. In fact, it is one of the few approaches to school reform that is virtually guaranteed to alter the behavior of grown-ups and children.

Assessment expert Barbara Lerner contends that the "minimum competency testing" movement of the 1970s was the only truly successful education reform effort in recent decades, that American youngsters now acquire basic cognitive skills precisely because they had to pass these state tests in order to graduate from high school, that individual and institutional behavior changed accordingly, and that the only big blunder was setting the standards too low. A round of tests with loftier expectations—and continued high stakes—would, Lerner argues persuasively, alter behavior once again and boost student achievement higher.[9]

It works at the building level, too. The *Washington Post* recently profiled a low-income and predominantly minority elementary school in Prince George's County, Maryland, where "the message that tests are important reaches children in many ways." From pep rallies before the major national achievement test (administered in grades three and five) to Friday-afternoon conferences at which all teachers demonstrate to the principal the progress their students made that week, this is a school that has systematically organized itself to do well on these exams. Scores have risen, too, both in District Heights Elementary School and in the county as a whole.[10] Some critics fault Superintendent John Murphy for the heavy emphasis he has placed on such test results. But he makes no apologies. To the contrary, he uses these scores (and other outcome indicators) as one of his primary modes of motivating his staff, monitoring school performance, and communicating with parents and taxpayers. "I don't see education as any different from any other major business," Murphy says. "If it can be taught, it can be measured."[11]

The state of Connecticut structures its first eight grades around a set of achievement goals against which performance is measured (at the student, classroom, school, and district levels) by a statewide Mastery Test given in grades four, six, and eight. (Tenth grade will be added in 1993.) "Like a Japanese factory," reported the *Wall Street Journal* in an account of changes under way in one Connecticut town, "Bloomfield has lifted school performance by responding to test results with relentless detail." "We found some areas we could improve upon," explained Bloomfield Superintendent Paul Copes, after analyzing slippage on the sixth-grade writing test. "The frequency of writing, the monitoring of writing folders and the variety of writing wasn't what we thought it should be." So changes were made.[12]

That tests wield so much influence is partly due to the absence of other trustworthy indicators of student achievement. Even so outspoken a test critic as Grant Wiggins understands that "mass assessment resulted from legitimate concern about the failure of the schools to set clear, justifiable, and consistent standards to which it would hold its graduates and teachers accountable." Nor, as Wiggins acknowledges, has the situation resolved itself:

> The problem is still with us: high school transcripts tell us nothing about what a student can actually do. Grades and Carnegie units hide vast differences between courses and schools. An A in 11th-grade English may mean merely that a student was dutiful and able to fill in blanks on worksheets about juvenile novels. And it remains possible for a student to pass all of his or her courses and still remain functionally and culturally illiterate.[13]

If "grade level," for example, really meant something concrete throughout American education, if there were a nationwide standard of intellectual prowess that had to be met in order to receive a high-school diploma, or if courses had predictable content and course grades had uniform meanings, we would pay less heed to tests. But none of those conditions obtains.

So long as we look to test results for information on learning outcomes and consider them the basis for accountability at the several levels of the education system, it stands to reason that the nature and content of the particular test we use are quite important. It should be a test *worth* teaching to. That's what gives it a catalytic quality and transforms it into a participant in education reform, instead of an exercise in monitoring and bean counting.

An immense amount of research and development is being done these days on improved modes of testing and assessment. Some use computers, which are fun for students, allow the simulation of some "real world" situations, and quickly move past the questions that are far too easy or difficult for a given test taker in order to focus instead on items that reveal more about what she has and hasn't learned.

Other pioneering developments include various forms of what educators now call "authentic assessments," in which students are asked to engage in tasks or exercises that closely resemble their "real world" counterparts. In science, this might mean an actual experiment; in history, perhaps the preparation of a research paper; in art, maybe the creation of a sculpture or painting.

A variation on this approach, under active development in Vermont and several other places, is "portfolio assessment," in which students, rather than showing what they can do under pressure of time in the controlled setting of an examination, are asked to assemble a collection of their work in a particular field or subject, possibly spanning many months and presumably including what the students regards as their finest products.

Even the familiar college admissions tests are undergoing major revision. The American College Testing Program introduced a new version of the ACT in 1989–90. Late in 1990 the College Board disclosed plans for changes in the venerable AT.[14] So much is bubbling in the assessment world that five or ten years from now we'll probably have options and variants that today are hard even to visualize. This is all to the good. But testing and measurement are neither unexplored territory nor technically so very difficult. "We cannot measure everything that matters to us in the world of education—" Lerner wrote in 1986, "we do not yet live in a world in which every hope has a number—but we can easily measure one important thing, their cognitive development."[15]

Why, then, all the uproar about testing? Why are so many people so agitated on the subject? As journalist Robert Braun insinuated, more than a little of this static arises from discomfort with outcomes accountability itself. Some also reflects disquiet over specific results that tests have been revealing. Before I take up several of the criticisms heard most often these days, however, one distinction is necessary.

INDIVIDUAL TESTING VERSUS INSTITUTIONAL ACCOUNTABILITY

College admissions tests produce individual scores, as do the commercial tests used by most school systems. So do Advanced Placement and International Baccalaureate exams. Martin and Muffy find out in midsummer how they did on the AP calculus or Spanish or European history tests. Weighty consequences follow, since colleges usually award credit for high scores, and many permit students to skip required or introductory courses.

Individual scores are essential when checking on Martin's or Muffy's achievement, when seeking to apprise parents of their progress, or endeavoring to help a teacher pinpoint their instructional needs. Individual scores are *not* necessary, however, when checking on the performance of a school, school system, state, or nation. For those purposes, we do not need information on Martin or Muffy in particular. We need instead to know how the Emerson Elementary School, the Cleveland public schools or the state of Arkansas is doing.

Such data can easily (and economically) be generated by a test administered to a statistical sample of the larger population involved. That is how NAEP works, for example, as well as the California Assessment Program.

The difference between testing individuals and assessing the performance of institutions and systems gives rise to much of the confusion that surrounds testing in the United States today, and to lots of the redundancy and burden. How much more efficient it would be if we could learn many different things from the same instruments; then we'd only need a few tests. But today we usually employ separate measures for each purpose we're trying to serve and a different test for each level about which we want information. That can mean imposing half a dozen assessment programs on the same classrooms.

This lack of coordination is the main reason so much testing is now being done in American schools. I know of no instance—not one—where a single instrument produces data for all levels. We can determine something about the individual youngster, the state, and the nation, for example, from college entrance test results, but cannot in this way learn about the classroom, school, or school system. States such as Connecticut successfully interconnect several levels, but they cannot compare their students' performance with those of youngsters in other states, in the country as a whole, or in nations overseas. California has a state-of-the-art assessment that integrates the middle four levels but furnishes no information to the Hopkins family about Thad and Megan, nor can California easily relate its statewide results to national performance levels. Several states, including Virginia, have devised means of administering international tests to samples of their students for comparison purposes, but rarely in more than one or two subjects and only on a highly irregular schedule.[16] For the United States as a whole, as I noted earlier, there is no systematic mechanism by which to obtain comparative international data on cognitive achievement. Our information base, in sum, is full of holes. That means we have a mighty shaky foundation on which to construct a real accountability system.

Yet efforts to strengthen that foundation run into guerrilla attacks on testing. Let me briefly state eight of the criticisms most frequently encountered in these sorties and offer a brief comment on each.

• *Overreliance on multiple-choice formats.* If what is tested determines what is learned, we should not limit ourselves to the knowledge and intellectual skills that can be appraised by filling in little "bubbles" with a number two pencil. Such important intellectual acquisitions as the capacity to analyze, reason, reflect, and persuade cannot be fully judged this way. Neither, of course, can one's prowess in the biology lab, agility on a computer, or organized imagination in the preparation of a research paper, nor such relevant traits as persistence, creativity, and conscientiousness.

But there's no need to throw out the baby, too. Much that is worth finding out about student achievement *can* be ascertained from multiple-choice questions, and it disserves the public to suggest that all such tests are evil, as Monty Neill of an advocacy group called FairTest told a group of education journalists in 1990. "They are destructive," he said, "and lead to cheating, coaching and early sorting of kids."[17] In fact, basic skills and factual knowledge can be efficiently and cheaply evaluated via multiple-choice testing. The better of these instruments, says Blaine Worthen of the Research and Evaluation Methodology Program at Utah State University, also "measure more complex mental processes" such as logic puzzles, reading comprehension questions, and math problems that require several steps to solve.[18]

For some purposes that is sufficient. For many others we want to probe deeper into intellectual domains and processes that multiple-choice items cannot satisfactorily reach. The difficulty is that the other kinds of tests and evaluations one would like to see given are more cumbersome, time consuming, costly, and at least as vulnerable to manipulation. They are subject to uneven standards among those conducting and evaluating them—people rather than machines—and, to the extent that they are not administered in a controlled setting, may invite more cheating. I believe that all those problems will in time prove soluble, however, indeed that this is where we'll likely see the greatest payoff from the R & D now under way. As we acquire more sophisticated student assessment alternatives that skirt such obstacles, we will be better able to confine multiple-choice testing within its proper bounds.

• *Excessive reliance on standardized tests.* Since these are nearly always multiple-choice tests, this criticism bears similarities to the last one. But it is more confusing, inasmuch as two different meanings of the word *standardized* are involved—and neither is what the man in the street may suppose.

One meaning has to do with uniformity or homogeneity in the skills and knowledge that the test probes; framed in this way, the objection really springs from opposition to the view that all children should learn the same things. Here is a typical version of this argument, found in a 1990 paper presented to the AERA by a pair of analysts at a federally funded center in Philadelphia called Research for Better Schools:

> Existing statewide tests reinforce a number of traditional values and beliefs about education—namely, that there is a body of content students must master and a set of skills students must demonstrate by a particular age, that this content and these skills can be reflected in student responses to paper and pencil tests, and that student failure to respond successfully on tests is the school's responsibility to correct. . . . There will be no room for reforming schooling until the purposes of education are rethought.[19]

This is a debate worth having, not least because I believe most Americans strongly affirm those "traditional values and beliefs about education" that the researchers deplore. It's really an argument about mission, goals, and content, though, not about testing.

The second meaning involves the "standards" or "norms" that are supposedly built into the tests, the markers by which we determine how many of Middletown's children are "at or above grade level" (or the "national average") or that tell us David is in the fourth decile while Amanda is scoring at the seventy-second percentile. On this matter, there is ample reason for disquiet. Averages, as we have seen, can be profoundly misleading, and "grade level" is not what people think. What John Q. Public means by "standards" and "norms"—what students need to learn and how good is good enough—is not what "standardized" tests incorporate. This is a problem in urgent need of solution. But it should be solved by building real standards into the tests that are given, not by carpet-bombing the idea of standards.

• *The temptation to cheat on a "high stakes" test is nearly irresistible*, and the heavier the consequences attached to the results, the greater the risk. This is one of those curious arguments that is perfectly true, yet most people making it come to just the wrong conclusion. Nobody wants a situation in which lots of teachers and students cheat. It's contrary to our principles, it's bad for their character, and it yields inaccurate data to boot. But one deals with the temptation to cheat on a test by making cheating more difficult and costly, not by scrapping the test or refraining from using it for accountability purposes. Good test security will boost the price of testing—as good security does in any human endeavor. Even when great pains are taken, there will still be slippage, hence some cheating. The way to deal with this, once again, is through consequences. Anyone caught in the act will suffer in various ways. We do not deal with the threat of aircraft hijackings by grounding all flights or with the risk of botulism by banning all canned goods. When we care about security, we create systems to strengthen it. Some schools have installed metal detectors at the door to keep students from bringing guns and knives to class. Guards in the corridors, while costly and lamentable, are not unusual. Test security needs to—and can—be handled with equal gravity.[20]

• *Tests are biased and discriminatory.* It's true that most cognitive tests yield different average scores for the members of our many racial, ethnic, linguistic, and socioeconomic groups. Most also yield different results for boys and girls (though which gender gets the higher score depends on the subject being tested).

Is this proof that the test is biased, or that the skills and knowledge it probes have not been acquired in a uniform way? I believe the latter is generally the case and that it ought to be cause for concern and corrective action, not for suppressing the evidence. Yes, there have been test questions over the years that, because of the nature of their content, would more likely be answered correctly by some groups than by others. But we have learned how to minimize this problem. Test items that are systematically biased by race or gender can be spotted and eliminated. All reputable test makers now do such screening as a matter of course. If certain knowledge or skills are important for everyone, however, the revelation that they have been unevenly acquired is evidence of trouble in the education system, not in the testing system. The divulging of data is part and parcel of accountability, which is why some minority leaders now ask that test results be displayed by racial and ethnic group; far from masking differential scores, they want to use them to leverage changes in the schools.

• *Some children do not "test well," and it's unfair to make important decisions about their fate on the basis of these scores.* This is a proper concern with respect to *individual* testing used for purposes of admission, placement, employment, and similar purposes. I am the parent of a child who earns honor grades in hard courses at tough schools yet gets mediocre scores on multiple-choice tests administered in pressured settings. (I am also the parent of one whose handsome test results are not always matched by subsequent performance on real assignments.) The remedy is clear:

When evaluating individuals, especially when making important decisions that affect them, we should not rely on test scores as our only criterion.[21]

Parents who know that a son or daughter presents middling or poor results on certain kinds of tests can encourage that young person to supplement the admissions or employment file with additional evidence of other kinds. But they can only do so if parents have access to information about their children's performance.

Our unease about the role of tests in deciding individual fates should not, however, govern our attitude toward testing as a way to monitor the achievement of groups, the performance of schools, and the progress of political units. Even the test-wary National Commission on Testing and Public Policy notes: "More efficient and effective assessment strategies are needed to hold social institutions accountable."[22]

• *Tests show children's cumulative achievement, not how much they learned in particular classrooms or schools.* The more disadvantaged and mobile the student population, the more often we hear how unjust it is to use for accountability purposes test results that are influenced by so many other factors. Yet all kinds of achievement gauges suffer from this infirmity. Asking youngsters to display portfolios of their work—an alternative approach beloved of those most hostile to standardized tests—is inevitably an appraisal of skills and knowledge accumulated over time and from various directions. Let's accept that fact without grumbling. It is, after all, the cumulative condition of the students that we care about, not who did what to whom. As far as rewards or interventions in the lives of individual teachers and principals are concerned, however, it is reasonable not to go overboard in suggesting that they are solely responsible for their students' scores at any given point in time. This dilemma can be eased by administering before-and-after tests to children each year so as to gauge the cognitive "value added" by a particular teacher. But this prospect horrifies those who think there is already too much testing.[23]

• *Comparisons are odious.* Every child is unique. No two of them learn the same things in quite the same way. Each community is different. Tests obscure or ignore such nuances and foster invidious competition among youngsters, schools, states, even nations. "In the United States today," complains Colorado education professor Lorrie A. Shepard, "standardized testing is running amok. Newspapers rank schools and districts by their test scores. Real estate agents use test scores to identify the 'best' schools as selling points for expensive housing. Superintendents can be fired for low scores, and teachers can receive merit pay for high scores."[24]

Exactly right, many Americans would say, and let's have more of it. We're accustomed to league standings in the world of baseball, price–earnings ratios in the stock market, and circulation figures in the newspaper business. Comparisons of precisely this kind in the field of education have been propelling the contemporary excellence movement; they are most apt to rouse the public; and policymakers are keen to make them. Test critics (and many other educators) deplore comparisons and competition, however, and they—correctly—see test results as the basis for these unwelcome practices. This mind-set is characteristic of the child-centered philosophy that has dominated the education profession since the early twentieth century. But it is a philosophy that has brought the nation to the brink of ruin.

• *Tests take up too much time that should be devoted to teaching and learning.* They do, indeed. I have a recurrent nightmare that, if we keep laying test atop test and never shake out or rationalize the system, one year we will find children devoting 179 days to being examined on what they learned on the first day of school. The solution to this problem is no mystery, however. We need to link, equate, and amalgamate our testing programs so that each one serves multiple purposes. Though this is technically possible, it is nonetheless staunchly resisted. It portends less total testing (bad for the test industry), reduced state and local sovereignty (bad for state and local education officials), and easier and more frequent comparisons across jurisdictional lines. That, of course, is precisely what some of testing's doughtiest opponents most fear.

The political clout of those opponents is not to be underestimated, nor should the reader assume that all changes being made in these realms today move in the direction of improved accountability. One of the last gubernatorial acts of New Jersey's Tom Kean and his outstanding education commissioner, Saul Cooperman, was to institute the "New Jersey School Report Card," by which citizens of the Garden State would receive outcomes data on each public school, much as Illinois and California were already providing. One of the first steps of Governor Jim Florio was to discontinue that system. He cited budget pressures (even as he was hiking taxes in New Jersey), but it is also true that he was elected with the strong support of the major statewide education interest groups and that he arrived in Trenton committed to cancelling the Kean-era accountability measures those groups deemed most onerous. "Educators," the *Star-Ledger's* Robert Braun concludes, "do not like . . . bad publicity. Obviously, they can either find ways to transform the schools to avoid such results—or they can cut off the flow of embarrassing information. The killing of the school report card showed which way the New Jersey school establish-ment wants to go."[25]

THE SAGA OF NATIONAL ASSESSMENT

One major source of "bad publicity" about the condition of Ameri-can education is the federally funded NAEP. Since its inception in 1969, this project has monitored achievement trends in most key skills and subjects. The resulting data have been illuminating and useful, if frequently depressing. NAEP is far and away our best barome-ter of student performance in the United States as a whole. But its architects in the 1960s had brilliantly—and intentionally—designed an assessment that refrained from comparing states, districts, or schools, let alone yielding any information on individuals. This was a political decision, forced on them at the time by state and local education officials who were dubious of the whole undertaking and profoundly squeamish about comparisons. Hence NAEP has pub-lished data only for regions of the country, as well as for the nation as a whole, even though education systems are organized by state and locality.

By design, in other words, NAEP has yielded few results relevant to actual education practitioners and policymakers or helpful to parents and voters wanting to know how *their* schools are doing. In the mid-1980s, this began to be seen as a problem rather than a virtue. Late in 1984 a (slender) majority of the Council of Chief State School Officers (CCSSO) agreed to develop a system of comparative state-by-state education indicators that would include student learn-ing outcomes. The following year, spurred by the federal govern-ment's wall chart, CCSSO endorsed the expansion of NAEP as one mechanism for collecting better data on cognitive achievement. In 1986, the National Governors' Association signaled its assent.

In the meantime, though not underwritten by the federal NAEP grant, ETS was responding to several requests to piggyback state-specific testing atop the national assessment program.[26] In 1986,

Wyoming and Georgia contracted for such assessments. From 1985 through 1987, a number of southern states also conducted concurrent assessments in a project organized by the SREB. These and other efforts to generate state-specific data via NAEP attested both to the appetite for such information and to the feasibility of gathering it.

In 1986, sensing that the extant NAEP structure and mandate were becoming antiquated, Secretary Bennett formed a prestigious twenty-two-member panel to make recommendations on how national assessment could be improved. He appointed Tennessee's Lamar Alexander to chair the committee and the distinguished educator H. Thomas James, recently retired as president of the Spencer Foundation, to serve as its vice-chairman and study director.

After a year of deliberations, involving advice from nine subgroups and fifty-two commissioned papers, the Alexander-James panel delivered its report in March 1987. Entitled "The Nation's Report Card," its foremost recommendation (among many) was that NAEP begin systematically to provide state-by-state comparisons.[27]

By midsummer, the Reagan administration had concurred and dispatched to Congress a bill that included this feature as part of a thoroughgoing reauthorization of NAEP.

The Senate quickly consented but the House of Representatives balked. Local school administrators and board members, joined by the national PTA and commercial test publishers, had alarmed key House members and staffers about the menace of an expanded national assessment program. Some were skittish about comparisons; others were dismayed by the prospect of additional demeaning data about racial and ethnic minorities; still others were worried about federally subsidized competition for the testing industry. The House Education and Labor Committee has also shown a pronounced tendency to resist in knee-jerk fashion just about everything proposed by the executive branch while the latter has been in Republican hands. It is easy to hide this twitch behind the bland assertion that any additional education money shouldn't be spent on something as unhelpful and politically problematic as assessment at a time when popular direct service programs are not fully funded.[28] And, while I cannot prove it, I have little doubt that some people just didn't want any more messengers bringing any more depressing news about the condition of American education, doubly so if they would be carrying a federal imprimatur, and triply so when bearing data that would give the hated Reagan administration more material with which to criticize educators.

As a result, when the legislation emerged from a Senate-House conference in 1988, the only expansion permitted was a two-phase trial program. In 1990 eighth-grade math would be assessed in states that wished to participate. In 1992 the experiment would cover math in grades four and eight as well as reading in grade four. It would again be voluntary. Participating states would have to share in the costs. And there was inserted into the measure a flat ban on "the use of National Assessment test items and test data . . . to rank, compare, or otherwise evaluate individual students, schools, or school districts." That meant no state could build its intrastate assessment program around NAEP, as several sought to do, and that any city-by-city or school-by-school comparisons would have to be based on other tests.

Under present law, therefore, four of American education's six levels—child, classroom, school, and district—are completely off limits to NAEP. The national data, while extremely useful for domestic monitoring and diagnostic purposes, do not provide any systematic basis for international comparisons, as no students in other countries are tested by this instrument, which has only once been joined to an international assessment. The state-by-state data, moreover, are confined to the two-cycle pilot program authorized in 1990 and 1992. Without statutory amendment, in other words, NAEP will never furnish state-specific information about student achievement in science, history, geography, or writing, nor any about twelfth-graders in any subject whatsoever. Since NAEP is a complex and cumbersome undertaking, slow to organize its tests and slower still to report results, even if Congress were to act in 1991 or 1992 to authorize an expansion, it would be 1994 at the earliest before additional state-level assessments could be administered and probably 1995—halfway through the decade—before we possessed even baseline data from them.

Because NAEP's subjects and grade levels correspond to those the president and governors designated in 1990 (in the goal that says all students will "leave grades four, eight and twelve having demonstrated competency over challenging subject matter including English, mathematics, science, history, and geography"), the present shackles on NAEP will severely cramp policymakers' ability to track the progress of students in their own states and to report to the nation on whether we are any closer to reaching those ambitious targets for the year 2000.

One might think this a soluble problem, and in principle of course it is. But when the NAEP governing board (which I chaired at the time) responded to congressional and executive-branch queries in late 1989 by identifying the statutory and budgetary changes that need to be made if NAEP is to discharge its role in monitoring progress toward the national education goals, it ran into a mob of protesters.

The board's recommendations included regular state-by-state assessment and removal of the ban on intrastate use of NAEP items, so that states wanting to use them for internal purposes could do so. The angry naysayers included a number of familiar anti-testing guerrilla fighters, as well as some who aren't necessarily opposed to outcomes assessment but want future initiatives of this sort to be taken by state, local, or commercial interests. In a snit, Pittsburgh's testing director withdrew his city from the Pennsylvania sample of the 1990 "trial state assessment." The head of the Michigan state testing program was splenetic. The American Association of School Administrators, the national PTA, and the anti-testing advocacy group that calls itself FairTest circulated a letter to education and civil rights groups that said the board's recommendations were "dangerous." Though most major education associations declined to sign it, some seventy-five individuals and organizations did, and the letter was widely circulated on Capitol Hill. Two senior officials of the Department of Education even joined the mob and signaled their displeasure with the board's "pre-emptive strike," notwithstanding that the executive branch had little else to offer the president and governors in its arsenal of outcomes information for tracking progress toward the national goals, nor had it made any move to replenish that arsenal by expanding NAEP. A few months later the House Appropriations Committee cut the governing board's funding almost in half. Though this money was restored by the Senate, a separate piece of legislation that came close to passing in November 1990 would have slashed the board's funding for three straight years. Reliable sources reported that high-ranking Education Department officials raised no objection when this deal was struck by Congressional aides who have long opposed NAEP and its governing board.

That all this happened in reaction to mere policy *recommendations* from a board that has no independent power to implement any of them suggests how sensitive assessment issues remain at the dawn of the new decade. Yet even as these events unfolded, several influential groups and individuals were weighing initiatives on the testing front that go far beyond anything contemplated for NAEP or proposed by the governing board.

The Commission on the Skills of the American Workforce suggested a nationwide certificate that all sixteen-year-olds would have to obtain before going on to further education or employment. They would do this by passing "a series of performance based assessments" keyed to a new "educational performance standard" that "will equal or exceed the highest similar standard in the world" and that is to be developed by a new "independent examining organization."[29] Before the year was out, several key members of that panel, generously underwritten by private foundations, had embarked on an extraordinary effort to develop a national (but not federal) examination system for the U.S.

Albert Shanker also urged the development of new national tests to be taken by *all* fourth-, eighth-, and twelfth-graders. And the President's Education Policy Advisory Committee was busy working on its own plan at the instance of members like Xerox CEO David Kearns, former Labor Secretary Bill Brock, and committee chairman Paul O'Neill (who is also the chief executive of Alcoa), none of whom could see how the new national education goals will make a dime's worth of difference until Thad and Megan Hopkins (and their parents) can ascertain where *they* stand in relation to those targets.

Nationwide tests for all young Americans, at whatever ages or grade levels, would be a truly epochal change in the nature and functioning of our education system, vastly more ambitious than the sample-based NAEP program has ever been and far bigger, costlier, and more intrusive than anything the governing board endorsed. Nevertheless, the idea is consistent with the public's preferences. It parallels changes under way in England, and it is of a piece with the more radical changes in education's basic assumptions and ground rules that we've already seen in several parts of the United States.

With the House of Representatives seemingly opposed to any more assessment, however, with just two or three champions in the Senate, and with myriad education interest groups resolutely hostile, the burden of policy change—if it's to involve the federal government— must be borne by the executive branch, which is, after all, collaborating with the governors in this massive goal-setting project.

Perhaps those seeking more reliable and useful data on education outcomes will yet prevail over the forces marshaled against testing. As of late 1990, however, I am not optimistic, at least at the national level. "Key members of the House and Senate have historically resisted the use of school test scores for accountability purposes," *Newsweek*'s Tom Morganthau reported in mid-1990 after interviewing most of the key Washington players. "The reason is simple, and deeply political. . . . [N]ational scores could be used to show that one state's public-school system is lagging behind another's. That's bad politics."[30] Since we cannot install effective accountability systems unless we possess the outcomes data that also permit such unwanted comparisons, it is entirely possible that those who have been setting goals for American education are indulging in a pleasant fantasy. But until we can assure ourselves that we know how much and how well our children are learning—and can trust the information we are given—we will have no real control over our education system.

11

@

Paralyzed by Design?

*It has been the meanest, bloodiest, and most difficult thing
I've ever been into.*
         —H. Ross Perot on school reform in Texas; September 28, 1984

Yes, Virginia, there is an "education establishment." Full of decent
and able individuals, its principal accomplishment of the 1980s
was nonetheless to deflect the Roto-Rooters of reform from clearing
the blockages and backups in what was already an ill-designed
plumbing system.

Both inside the schools and in the government policy arenas that
deal with education, we find ingrained roles and entrenched relationships, strongly rooted habits, and such organizational complexity
that nobody has the authority to ensure that a change gets made
yet almost everyone has the capacity to prevent it.

DIFFUSED AUTHORITY

American education is a sprawling labyrinth in which reforms
disappear. A thousand interest groups jostle and vie to maintain
their status, power, and revenue flow. The system has been characterized by organizational scholars as "loosely coupled," meaning that
motion in one part of it does not necessarily cause movement in
other parts. The teacher is sovereign when the classroom door closes;
principals can evade central-office directives; localities have remarkable capacity to ignore states, and so on.

Traditional analyses of power and politics in public education
ascribe this situation to a layer-cake governance structure with many
tiers of influence and control, to the multiple and conflicting missions
that society places on its schools, to the school system's inability

to balance so many incompatible assignments, and to the emergence inside the system of factions that mirror those in the world beyond.

All those interests jockey for limited resources. Grow as our education budgets have, this cat never has quite enough milk to satisfy all her kittens. Yet the rivals eventually develop a crude equilibrium in their relationships. Each knows who does what and why, who must be placated and how, and what rough but functional formula governs the division of the spoils. All is well until a crisis flares, a new constituency finds its voice, or someone upsets the equilibrium by maneuvering for more than his share of the booty. These destabilizing conditions must be dealt with, usually by enlarging the total resource pool so that the intruder can be pacified without robbing or vexing the traditional interests.[1]

This explanation works well as history and political science, and if we were content to understand how the present situation developed, we could stop here. But such an account fails as a guide to *changing* the status quo, in part because it doesn't recognize the extent to which the internal dynamics and rivalries of the education system have pushed the public interest aside.

Democratic government is supposed to be the means by which public education is subordinated to the public interest and the suppliers of education are bent to the priorities of their customers. That is what school boards, legislatures, and other policy-making structures are meant to do. Instead, they have been drawn into, and sometimes co-opted by, the intergroup politics of the supply system itself. As John E. Chubb and Eric A. Hanushek comment:

> These bodies are the arenas for battles among teachers' unions, administrators, advocacy groups for students with special needs, business interests, textbook publishers, and others, each of whom has a different idea about how to run schools. However the battles go, some groups are pleased while others are not. Bureaucracy is the winners' instrument for getting the losers in educational politics to comply.[2]

Sometimes the boundaries between internal and external blur, as when schoolteachers run for the state legislature—an increasingly frequent occurrence—and in short order find themselves chairing the education committee.

Cui bono? Whose interests, we must never stop asking, is public education meant to serve? Is it the instrument of the larger society, a form of common provision that requires the continuing and active consent of the governed, or does it exist mainly to serve its own employees, its managers, and the other longtime denizens of its self-absorbed policy arena?

Today major interest groups within public education (as in other fields) wield their immense political power first and foremost on behalf of their own members. To the extent that they see those interests served by embracing certain changes, they do so. But they never stop looking out for number one.[3]

This preoccupation with stability and constituents sometimes produces unexpected twists, as organizations grow so attached to the equilibrium of the system that they abandon their own members' putative interests. The national PTA, for example, pays scant attention to parents' real concerns in such key domains as choice among schools and accurate feedback on student achievement. We might suppose the PTA would fight to free families from the tyranny of being forced against their will to attend bad schools when there are better ones not far away. We might also expect to find the PTA leading the effort to construct reliable, user-friendly assessment systems through which Mr. and Mrs. Brown can readily see how Toby and Rachel are doing in school, how their school is doing vis-à-vis the national education goals, and so on. In reality, however, the PTA has placed so many constraints and conditions on its position with respect to educational choice as to be functionally opposed to most actual choice schemes, and it fields one of the fiercest armies in the war on testing. It has become a full-fledged member of the school establishment, indistinguishable from the professional organizations. In these matters it serves the interests of parents about as well as ivory merchants serve the interests of elephants.[4]

Other education groups devote themselves to the preservation of archaic, supplier-friendly structures and practices. Sound education reform in the 1990s would move a number of key decisions up to the states and devolve practically all the rest to individual schools and parents. What then is the point—or function—of the bulky layers of middle management associated with "local" education agencies: those 13,000 superintendents, 96,000 school board members, and the bureaucracies that serve them? There is no doubt that they were essential elements of the nineteenth-century arrangement, but if we did not already have them in 1991, would we set out to create them? How much money might we save—and how many bureaucratic logjams could we loosen—if they were to shrink radically in size and scope, perhaps even to disappear? Yet we know they are not going to fade away willingly, any more than home economics instructors are going to exit the curriculum voluntarily to make room for more geography and chemistry. The National School Boards Association (NSBA) and the American Association of School Administrators (AASA) and their state affiliates remain among the toughest and most conservative forces in American education.

Though such organizations never come out and say the education system belongs to them, they behave as if it does. They are occupied with defending their turf, fending off trespassers, and engaging in a kind of ritualistic battle with one another. I say "ritualistic" because those in the education establishment never shoot to kill, at least not when aiming at each other. We might think that administrators and teachers' unions would be natural enemies, for example, or that state and local boards would be at one another's throats. Certainly they bicker, snipe, and jockey for position. Their differences, however, turn out to be less consequential than their need to maintain the equilibrium from which they all profit. Hence their battles are more like a ballet or musical—*Billy the Kid*, perhaps, or *West Side Story*—that is choreographed to include gunfire and conflict of the sort that only a naïf would take seriously. Mix it up on stage, but don't draw any blood. Preserving the balance of power is more beneficial in the long run than winning victories in the short. A modicum of peace in the family permits organizational priorities to flourish. It's just that these seldom have much to do with the effectiveness and efficiency of the system or the education of children. Of the five overriding goals adopted by the NSBA, for example, *all* pertain to the group's power, influence, member services, and relations with sister organizations.[5]

When outsiders bring main force to bear through the political process on behalf of the public interest, the situation sometimes changes. That is what Ross Perot and Mark White did in Texas in 1983, what Lamar Alexander did in Tennessee in 1984, what Rudy Perpich did in Minnesota between 1985 and 1988, what the Kentucky Supreme Court did in 1989, what Tom Kean and Saul Cooperman did in New Jersey on many occasions, and what the citizens of Chicago and Chelsea did in 1988. That is what Polly Williams did in pushing the Milwaukee voucher program through the state legislature early in 1990 and what the voters of Oregon almost did on their tuition tax credit and school choice referendum later that year. It is what Margaret Thatcher did in England. Under such circumstances, the closed system of public education can be unlocked. And when political muscle and additional money are combined, as Bill Honig managed in California and Dick Riley in South Carolina, entry can be achieved more easily.

Sometimes real political bullets have to be fired during these alter-cations and occasional casualties are visible. But this does not happen often and, when it does, the changes do not always last. The system can be stretched but, like a giant rubber band, it never stops yearning to resume its previous shape. Alexander's successor, elected with the help of the Tennessee education establishment, has undone a number of reform features that the interest groups liked least and has brought to the legislature a new package of very costly changes that the supplier organizations crave. As we have seen, New Jersey's Jim Florio—with similar allies—speedily jettisoned some of Kean's most impressive changes.

WHO'S IN CHARGE HERE, ANYWAY?

If you were setting out to devise an organization in which nobody was in command and in which, therefore, no one could easily be held accountable for results, you would come up with a structure much like American public education. To find its like, you might try domestic air travel in India, characterized by one recent victim as a system "which is mostly about waiting, about promises no one intends to keep, about solemn information that is wildly inaccurate, and about the dawning realization that since no one is responsible for anything, nothing whatsoever can be done about any given situation."[6]

In most realms of American life, we know who is responsible. If the surgeon bungles the operation, if the Federal Express delivery arrives late, if the gas company calculates the heating bill incorrectly, if the preacher is a sanctimonious bore, if the new car rattles, if the coleslaw is tainted, if an oil tanker goes onto the reef—we have a fairly clear sense of who caused the problem, where to turn for solution or compensation, and how to go about it. I do not say that getting satisfaction is easy, or that those responsible will always admit it. The surgeon may blame the anesthesiologist, just as the supermarket manager may claim the slaw was bad when it arrived from the shipper. The gas company will let the phone ring or put the customer on hold. We're accustomed to such delays and excuses and have varying degrees of patience with them. Yet there is a trail of responsibility we can follow. It may be bumpy and have puzzling detours, but it's not—like Indian Airlines—something over which we throw up our hands in despair because we cannot locate either its beginning or its end.

Education, alas, is not so consumer sensitive. Nobody takes responsibility and everyone can get off the hook. The teacher says she is required to use this textbook, isn't allowed to discipline that disruptive youngster, and doesn't have time during the day to provide individual tutoring for the exceptional child. The principal says the teacher was foisted on him, the textbook decisions are made downtown or by the state, the school board will not allot funds for tutors, and the courts have tied his hands with respect to discipline. The superintendent explains that the principal has tenure (and, besides, his wife's cousin is an alderman); the school board is adamant that handicapped and disadvantaged children receive all the tutorial help, even if that leaves none for gifted youngsters. The board chairman says he is following the superintendent's professional advice, and in any case, is constrained by state and federal law. The governor observes that the schools in this state are locally controlled and the teachers' union and school board association helped elect him. The congressman sends back a polite form letter indicating that your views will be carefully considered the next time pertinent legislation comes before the House. From the federal Department of Education, there is no reply at all for six months; then you receive a pamphlet entitled "How to Help Your Child Improve in Math."

It's an army without a command structure, a pinball machine that always says "tilt," an automaton that seems to move of its own volition. Lynne V. Cheney, quoting philosopher William James, terms the ingrained habits and settled practices of American education "tyrannical machines."[7] This is not an auspicious situation at a time when we urgently seek nonincremental improvement in school productivity.

Our peculiar way of organizing public education in the United States has made change even more difficult—and less apt to yield results. The layer cake is part of the problem, as Chubb and Hanushek observe:

> Three separate levels of government have a hand in setting educational policy. Because federal officials, for example, cannot choose state and local education officials to carry out policy set in Washington, they rely on prescriptive programs to see that their wishes are fulfilled. State officials face similar problems with local administrators. When local regulation is added to state and federal regulation, the confusion and constraints faced by schools can cripple virtually all initiative.[8]

In such circumstances everybody wants to be involved in all decisions but nobody is in charge. Not the president or the legislature or the parents. Not the teachers or the principals or the school board. When leaderlessness is joined to complacency, and there are no satisfactory gauges of outcomes by which that equilibrium might be jarred, the result is systemic passivity and inertia, even in the face of crisis. We managed to remove Perrier from the shelves of tens of thousands of stores within hours of discovering that some bottles contained a mild toxin. Yet eight years after being proclaimed a "nation at risk," we've eliminated virtually none of the hazardous practices, dangerous ideas, or pointless customs of the education system.

THE "VISION THING"

This system, as we have seen, is porous enough that it affords motivated individuals some leeway to try their ideas. That is why we have hundreds of experiments and demonstration projects under way here and there, and dozens of effective schools led mostly by mavericks. Outside a handful of communities, however, the system itself does little to encourage those traits. The mavericks succeed not because they do what the rules say but because they have learned how to bend them. The experimenters obtain grants from large corporations, private foundations, and federal agencies, thus buying a degree of freedom within an enterprise that never has much spare change and is easily wowed by those who bring their own resources. How curious—and how sad—that we have forged a set of arrangements in public education that works worst when it behaves systematically and best when bold souls within it thumb their noses at standard procedures and instead do what they judge to be right for children or expedient for themselves.

But there are not enough such souls. Within the vastness of American public education, most people just follow the rules, even when invited to think for themselves and take risks.

In the aftermath of the National Governors' Association's 1986 proposal for a little "old-fashioned horse-trading"—to curb procedural micromanagement in return for better results—a number of states adopted waiver provisions by which individual schools wanting to improve could obtain exemptions from regulations impeding the changes they sought to make. But such offers found few takers. As journalist Lynn Olson summed up the situation in April 1990:

> Policymakers expected that after years of complaining about
> excessive mandates from above, educators would jump at the

chance to do things differently. But at both the state and district levels, officials are reporting far fewer requests for waivers than they had anticipated. And the requests they have received cover relatively minor rules and regulations.[9]

Maine, for example, provided for as many as ten schools to get extra money and waivers in order to innovate. But no school applied for so much as a single waiver. In Massachusetts, which furnished funds for seven schools to "restructure" their programs, only one waiver request was received. Even in places with more ambitious school restructuring programs, the kinds of regulatory relief sought are minor, even trivial. "The primary reason for the lack of waiver requests," Olson suggests, "may be the inability of educators to imagine doing things differently."[10]

In New York City, schools chancellor Joseph A. Fernandez was hired in late 1989 partly because he pledged to install in our largest urban system a version of the site-based management scheme he had pioneered in Florida. In early 1990 he invited each of the city's 984 schools to submit proposals indicating what they would do differently if they had the freedom to innovate, including the opportunity to waive union contract provisions and school board regulations. Not even one school in six responded, however, and Fernandez found about half their proposals to be acceptable. The result is that in 1990–91, this major change in power and governance is operational in just 8 percent of New York's vast and troubled education system. Many school principals, a *New York Times* reporter explained, "resisted surrendering authority"; teachers were "reluctant to take on the extra hours of work on governing committees without increases in pay"; and local boards and superintendents (in New York's already partly decentralized structure) "were hostile to the process."[11] It's likely that more schools will eventually join the venture, however. In Dade County, Fernandez's last post, only thirty-two schools volunteered at first, but half were eventually included in the site management scheme. (Unfortunately, there's no persuasive evidence yet that the children in those schools are learning more.)[12]

It's not unusual to find such wariness about change among lay policymakers and parents, too. When the staff of Parkway South, a well-regarded suburban high school near St. Louis, set out to turn that institution into a "mastery-based" alternative school, following the educational tenets of Theodore Sizer, parents balked. "We're just not about to let our children be experimented upon," said one. Hundreds turned out to present their concerns to the school board, which has had to slow down the pace of change in the school.[13]

Sizer's Coalition of Essential Schools has encountered similar problems elsewhere. Wary teachers, hostile unions, timid administrators, smug and cautious parents, and sometimes a dearth of imagination or energy among those he is trying to energize have dogged Sizer's spirited efforts to get schools to reform from within.

Veteran Excellence Network staffer Stephen Clements and I observed the beginnings of Chicago's revolutionary education governance scheme in 1989 and 1990 and came away troubled by the limited vision we detected at many newly liberated schools, notwithstanding the parent-majority councils that now run them. Some think their school is doing satisfactorily as is. For them, "reform" may be no more than a new textbook series or summer workshop for teachers. Other schools are manifestly not faring very well, but instead of conceiving wholly different approaches to curriculum, instruction, and resource use, the principal and school council are seeking a part-time guidance counselor, fresh paint in the auditorium, another attendance aide, perhaps some new equipment in the chemistry lab. All are desirable, no doubt, but in a city that is begging its schools for nonincremental increases in pupil learning levels and that has imposed radical alterations on its education structure so as to make this possible, too many of the "reforms" we saw under consideration at the building level were marginal and wan.[14]

Even as we admire the occasional "turnaround" school and its heroic leader, therefore, we need to realize that the American public education system as a whole rewards conventionality and harbors a great many very nice people of modest vision who are more comfortable when routines do not change abruptly and when big decisions are made elsewhere. Such a system regards enterprise and nonconformity (and celebrity) with puzzlement, scorn, or envy, thus we shouldn't wonder that the number of education change-agents is so small: Sizer and his hundred schools; a few inspired local councils in Chicago; a handful of innovative building teams in Rochester, Los Angeles, Dade County, San Diego, and Hammond; the isolated maverick, two here, three there—these among 83,000 public schools in the land.

Interests outside the schools have a conservative influence, too, usually by shackling those administrators and policymakers who are ready to innovate. Every hated regulation is somebody's cherished protection. Each categorical grant benefits at least one organized group with contacts in high places. Any decision made without the involvement of all affected parties (in Washington we call them stakeholders) is one whose legitimacy is open to challenge; yet decisions that appease all affected interests turn out to be the kind that maintain the status quo—and usually cost the taxpayer more money.

"Everyone wants to be a major player" in shaping school policy, says Boston University's Peter Greer, after a year of striving to remake public education in Chelsea, but:

> The kids are never mentioned. When the Hispanic leadership first approached us, just before the contract was signed, they had demands for quotas, for a Hispanic majority on every board, and they wanted a cut of the money we raised. . . . Look at any city. You have the Black Caucus, the Hispanic Caucus. . . . They all fight with each other and try to gain power, and nothing happens in their schools.[15]

Washington plays by similar rules, especially on Capitol Hill. A major goal of the president and governors, emerging from their Charlottesville education summit, was to liberate schools from federal and state impediments to reform and renewal. The Bush administration dutifully asked Congress to authorize schools to combine the federal funds they receive from various programs and to set aside fussy regulations. The initial congressional response was flat rejection. How dare anyone meddle with all those "targeted" categorical aid programs and the carefully crafted procedures and protections associated with them? After much folderol, including heroic efforts by former Vermont Congressman Peter Smith, longtime House Education Committee Chairman Augustus Hawkins finally consented (so long as assistance for the handicapped was excluded from the package) to allow up to fifty local school systems to try this approach if they wanted to. A demonstration program involving a handful of districts was tolerable. Wholesale alterations in basic power relationships in 15,000 districts were not.[16] In the event, this much-weakened measure failed to reach the Senate floor before the end of the 101st Congress.

There is no visible exit from this maze. It's impossible to regulate 83,000 individual schools into excellence. Yet not enough of those schools possess the gumption and imagination to reform themselves from within. While the public as a whole says it's ready for sweeping changes in education, individual factions in each community are reluctant to surrender power or prerogative. Hence they and their elected representatives at every level of policy-making tend to block wholesale revision of the ground rules. Even when they can be tempted, persuaded, or overruled, however, and nonincremental reforms become possible, few building-level educators seize the opportunity. I once remarked to Sizer that he was trying to clean out the Augean stables with an ice-cream scoop. He did not disagree.

A CACOPHONY OF INTERESTS

When he was secretary of education, William Bennett sometimes referred to *the blob,* an unflattering but vivid term with two overlapping meanings. Bennett used it both to characterize the costly human overhead of the school system—two million salaried employees of American public education are neither teachers nor principals— and to depict the bulky array of interest groups and lobbyists whose interlocked relationships, entrenched assumptions, and substantial investment in the status quo make for policy gridlock in public education.

We tend to think of the "establishment" as something located inside the beltway, and it's true that the mass of associations to be found within ten miles of the Washington Monument lends credence to this view. The 1989 *Encyclopedia of Associations* lists 1,221 national and international education associations.[17] These include such specialized ones as the Ceramic Educational Club, the School Projectionist Club of America, and the International Listening Association. Like Orwell's animals, however, some groups are more equal than others. Every few weeks the heads of the most influential of them assemble as the Educational Leadership Consortium and (a slightly different grouping) as the Forum of Education Organization Leaders. The latter consists of top executives in eleven national associations: the American Association of Colleges for Teacher Education, the American Association of School Administrators, the American Federation of Teachers, the Association for Supervision and Curriculum Development, the Council of Chief State School Officers, the Education Commission of the States, the National Association of State Boards of Education, the National Association of Elementary School Principals, the National Association of Secondary School Principals, the National Congress of Parents and Teachers, and the National Education Association. Though their meetings are sometimes interesting and usually amiable, these groups have such a huge stake in the existing equilibrium that, when confronted with ideas for fundamental change in the educational status quo, their collective stance resembles that of the National Rifle Association toward gun-control schemes.[18]

That's the cream of the education establishment at the federal level. Much the same situation is also to be found below. Many of the national associations have state affiliates, and the major ones have local branches as well. Even inside the individual school, the teachers' union is apt to have a chapter with its own elected leader; the principal belongs to an association of administrators; and the lunchroom attendants and building custodians have separate unions of their own. What is more, the levels intersect, so that making any move brings fear of risk, and resistance, from every direction, like playing three-dimensional chess.

The next time you find yourself in a state capital, preferably the low-rise kind like Tallahassee, Pierre, or Annapolis—where there are still small office buildings that identify their tenants with name-plates out front—stroll the streets near the statehouse. If you are relatively new to education politics, I predict that you will be struck by the concentration of education-related associations, unions, boards, and affiliates that maintain offices within blocks of the capitol building.[19] They are there, of course, to keep watch on lawmakers and bureaucrats, to make certain that the priorities of the various supplier groups are operationalized within every state, to lobby for benefits and favors, and to dissuade policymakers from actions that might disadvantage this or that organization. "I was amazed," Ross Perot recalls from his bout with Texas school politics, "at the power of the lobbyists."[20]

What's amazing is not that education is neck deep in lobbyists. It has, after all, become the largest single item in the budget of every state, and we know that substantial public expenditures draw interest groups and their representatives like teenagers to a rock concert. More striking to me is how specialized and fragmented they have become, yet how interdependent. The art educators, the vocational educators, and the custodians' unions have little in common with one another when it comes to the content and quality of what occurs in school. But they share a keen interest in preserving an equilibrium in which no change is revolutionary, in which no faction loses or gains more than its share. The same may be said of school bus drivers, school social workers, and math supervisors. I sometimes visualize education reform as Gulliver and these myriad groups as Lilliputians, hordes of them, each placing its own tiny string over the big visitor to see that he does not make any untoward moves.

ESTABLISHED AUTHORITY

Where does all this power come from? How did "the blob" pin American education to the ground? Inertia, we must remember, always favors established interests. It does not take nearly so much energy to block change in a leaderless system as it does to push an idea all the way to implementation. (That is why Congress gets so little done.) A single stuck gear can keep a complex machine from turning at all. For the machine to rumble off in a different direction, however, requires the synchronous movement of dozens of components.

Like so many major institutions in our society, the education system also rewards incumbency. Job security is part of it, both in the schools and in the executive offices of those innumerable associations. One might think that the excellence movement would have loosened tenure for educators, but—outside of Chicago and New York—just the opposite has happened. Between 1984 and 1990, reports the secondary school principals' association, "numerous states have enacted legislation that has increased the employment protection available to administrators."[21] Teachers, of course, have long enjoyed tenure or something akin to it in nearly all jurisdictions, usually after just three years in the classroom.

Secure jobs, however, are only the beginning. Ideas and practices gain incumbent status, too. Whether out of satisfaction, resignation, or fear of the unknown, we are disinclined to trade in the familiar, whatever its imperfections, for the unknown. It is not hard to persuade us that with just a bit more time or money or whatever, we can set matters right in our school or town without overturning any applecarts. In this way do our own caution and complacency vis-à-vis our children's education play into the hands of those with the deepest devotion to existing arrangements.

Its ability to buttress the status quo, outlast the agents of change, and throw sand into the wheels of reform is perhaps the most valuable possession of any "establishment." But its influence flows from multiple sources. In education, as in health care, the mystique of professionalism is another of these. Though most people have views on schooling, and we're somewhat less awed by the specialized expertise of educators than, say, of oral surgeons, biophysicists, or clergymen, John Q. Public is still unlikely to feel comfortable rejecting "professional" judgment in complex technical matters. These could range from methods of teacher assessment to modes of reading instruction, from the choice of math curricula to the allocation of class time to science.

Educators not only possess expertise, they also control the language in which issues are posed, jargon that other people may not be able to penetrate. They often formulate the options among which decision makers will choose. Because we associate selflessness, moral strength and generosity of spirit with the decision to make one's career in education, ordinary mortals also tend to be deferential. The professionals may not invariably know best, but we are usually willing to give them the benefit of the doubt. Teachers, in particular, occupy a special place in the minds and hearts of most people and in the language and literature of many societies. We want to love and honor them. We're heartened to read of the veteran fifth-grade teacher in Harlem who knows every child's name before the first day of school ends and who—"part earth mother, part drill sergeant and part Catskill social director"—managed to squeeze a poem into the procedures and paperwork that launched the new year at PS 192. "This is my home," Linda A. Friedman says, and we beam. We believe her, partly because we are accustomed to believing teachers, partly because we dream that our children will have teachers like her. The prospect of doing anything that might make these noble souls sad, angry, or uncomfortable—well, best not.[22]

As if such sentiments were not inhibiting enough to our education reform impulses, far more so, at least to veteran politicians, is the unvarnished clout that public school educators have come to wield. Their endorsements, their doorbell ringing, their hefty political-action-committee (PAC) contributions, their influence over what others in the community think—not to mention the actual votes of more than four million of them—are as influential as those of any interest group in contemporary American society. "Teachers," campaign consultant Matt Reese once observed, "are the ideal political organization. They're in every precinct."[23] They're articulate. Their voting rates are high. They're well organized. They have time after school and during the summer. And they're motivated. In New York City's local school board elections prior to 1988, reports the *Village Voice*, "the union always ran its own slate of candidates, mobilized its impressive phone banks, and donated legal help to candidates who needed it. In the 1986 election, the UFT [United Federation of Teachers] endorsed 90 percent of the winning candidates [and] spent $150,000 getting them elected."[24]

When engaged in politics, educators play hardball. It was no Linda Friedman or Mr. Chips or "Our Miss Brooks," the caring teacher of rose-tinted memory, who led Texas tycoon Ross Perot to conclude that it was easier to deal with the North Vietnamese, to elude the Ayatollah's goons, and to build a multibillion-dollar corporation than to change the rules by which the Lone Star State operates its schools. But it may well have been the engravers of "smiley faces" on the report cards of eight-year-olds whose massed votes (and PAC contributions and dues money) kept Mark White from being reelected governor after Perot spent that year working with him on education reform.

The NEA and AFT are much the largest and most politically sophisticated of the establishment organizations, and they're active at local, state, and national levels. Their PACs are among the richest, right up there with the postal workers, the trial lawyers, and the bankers. Their bumper stickers, "public-service" ads, columns, and press conferences are highly visible. The threat of a strike by one of their major locals is enough to bring many a community to its knees. Their political directors and lobbyists are among the smartest and toughest of any organization's. When an issue matters to them, they'll pull out all the stops. (The Oregon affiliate of the NEA devoted a million dollars in 1990 to defeating the state tuition tax credit initiative, a sum vastly greater than proponents had to spend.) They also involve themselves deeply in congressional and legislative races, sometimes running candidates from within their own ranks. When the AFT launched a "Governors Project" in July 1990, designed to "shape the agenda" of thirty-six gubernatorial races later that year, and held out the promise of money and electoral help for candidates the union decided to endorse, we can fairly assume that those running for governor in 36 states took notice. We can also assume that many judged it would be in their interest to win the favor of the teacher unions. Some doubtless had already come to that conclusion.

Educators have long memories, too. Like other shrewd political operatives who expect to be around indefinitely, they recall friendly and hostile acts years later. They don't just have individual job tenure. Their organizations and their policy preferences endure as well. After a great legislative victory, an elected official is apt to feel he has accomplished something. Those he vanquished, however, wait to fight again another day—as the regulations are written, as the funds are (or are not) appropriated, and as the people are hired. They will also be on hand when the next election produces (doubtless with their help) a crop of different policymakers, more amenable to the interests of educators and pleased to make headlines by sweeping out the ashes of their predecessors' decisions.

Elected officials are not the only ones who occasionally try to alter education policy and practice. Business leaders in many states and localities have recently joined the fray as well. As we saw in chapter 3, business "involvement" programs can be found in many communities and, increasingly, at the state level, such as the laudable multiyear effort by the Business Roundtable to persuade its member corporations to "adopt" entire states for purposes of school reform.

Business leaders are less directly vulnerable to conventional political hazards, but they do have their companies' reputations to protect, and few are eager to antagonize thousands of articulate educators. Most, therefore, are cautious about appearing pushy, cranky, or overly demanding vis-à-vis the schools. They prefer to make gifts and grants, to confer honors, rewards, and incentives, rather than to press the education system to alter its basic rules and practices. Instead of wearing their "business" hats when they enter this policy arena, and demanding evidence of an upward slope in the bottom line, corporate chieftains are more apt to don their "philanthropic" or "community relations" headgear.[25] There are a handful of impressive exceptions—David Kearns of Xerox, John Akers of IBM, and William J. Hume of Basic American Foods come quickly to mind, along with Perot. But many otherwise hard-nosed CEOs are likely to entrust this part of their activities to whomever manages the company foundation or is charged with keeping the locals happy. Instead of hiring tough strategists for these jobs, a surprising number of major corporations engage people right out of the education establishment itself. When their choice of staff, proposal reviewers, and the projects they fund is examined, company foundations end up behaving much like conventional ones. Even the leaders of Fortune 500 firms may be vulnerable to intimidation via "expertise." And when they don't succumb directly to this temptation, one can be certain that the various "chambers" and "alliances" and "committees" to which they belong will see to the matter.

Milwaukee, Chicago, Chelsea, and Oregon are not the only places where the establishment has recently mounted a full-court press against fundamental changes in education. Examples of stasis and resistance can be sighted all over. In the remainder of this chapter, I briefly sketch three recent national episodes, one involving the blunting and co-optation of a powerful reform idea, the second illustrating the education system's tendency to exclude innovators armed with heterodox ideas, and the third entailing a much-publicized, educator-initiated change that has been slowed, if not yet stopped, by the professional establishment whence it sprang.

ALTERNATIVE CERTIFICATION

Perhaps the boldest way to attract and keep more able and better-qualified people in schoolteaching is to redefine the pool of prospective instructors. As we saw in chapter 3, many states have responded to the idea, heavily promoted by the Reagan and Bush administrations, that well-educated adults who would like to try teaching should find their paths into the classroom eased.[26]

The idea is instantly attractive. Do not confine entry into teaching to recent graduates of traditional preparation programs. Instead, invite midcareer people (and young college graduates with degrees in academic fields) to try it, providing them with enough on-the-job supervision, mentoring, and pointers on classroom craftsmanship to create a reasonable chance that they will succeed. Retain those who do well; urge those who don't to seek other lines of work.

This is so sensible, endorsed by so many panels and commentators, and so attractive to lay policymakers—many of whom are contemptuous of conventional teacher education—as to be nearly irresistible in the domain of politics. Complementary variants, such as Wendy Kopp's "Teach for America" project, a sort of reborn "teacher corps," have drawn lots of applicants, money, and public acclaim. What is more, the program evaluations now beginning to trickle in indicate that teachers who entered via alternative routes are at least as good as those who followed the conventional path. Yet—as one might expect—the idea is resisted by colleges of education, whose monopoly it menaces; by state license givers, who previously needed only to scrutinize a candidate's transcript and test scores, not to worry about their classroom effectiveness; and by teacher unions, who fear its ominous implication that if anyone can become a teacher, what's the value of specialized professional expertise? If the supply of teachers is sufficiently enlarged, moreover, perhaps the demand can be met without the fat across-the-board salary increases that educators crave.

The upshot in 1990 is that while most states claim to have opened alternative routes to the classroom, in reality, Emily Feistritzer reports, "relatively few of these programs are available to the large numbers of people who would like to go through them."[27]

From a careful survey conducted by Feistritzer's research center, we learn that only about twelve thousand individuals passed through these routes between 1985 and 1990—approximately 1 percent of all new teachers hired in that half decade. It was not for lack of interested candidates, either. New Jersey's relatively large and highly regarded alternative certification program, for example, had seven thousand applicants but certified just fifteen hundred of them. The Garden State is also one of only three states with an alternative route that met Feistritzer's most exacting conditions: a "state-designed" program "available in all fields at all grade levels." In other jurisdictions entry through this route is limited to certain levels of schooling (usually secondary) or restricted to fields with shortages of conventional teachers, or the programs have been turned over to the colleges of education or involve paper credentials more than actual teaching prowess.[28]

In many states the alternative route into teaching is so little used as to be marginal. Arkansas has certified only twenty-one teachers in this way, Oregon three, Hawaii seventy-two. The reason is clear. The people setting them up are not trying to improve education in their state nearly so much as they are seeking to fend off more draconian approaches. As one state education official said to Feistritzer, "If we hadn't designed this program, the state legislature would have, and we didn't want that to happen."[29]

CHANNEL ONE

Communications innovator Christopher Whittle had another brainstorm. He would produce a short daily news show for U.S. highschool students that could be beamed into classrooms by satellite. He would install all the necessary telecommunications technology in the schools at no cost to them. And he would finance the entire enterprise by selling two minutes of commercial time per show to major advertisers eager to reach the teenage market. He promised to run only tasteful ads for such noncontroversial products as jeans and cars.

It struck the young Knoxville entrepreneur as an arrangement by which everyone would win. Millions of American adolescents would get daily doses of news and public affairs. Thousands of schools would each receive about fifty thousand dollars' worth of free equipment (which they could also use for other purposes), as well as a nice addition to their curriculum. Advertisers would expand their markets. Whittle Communications would prosper. As soon as eight thousand or so schools—roughly one in three at the secondary level—signed up, the numbers would work. With six million or so student viewers, the arrangement would become profitable.

That was in 1988. By the time Whittle began running his pilot shows in half a dozen high schools in the spring of 1989, however, the education establishment had nearly had a seizure. Everyone was in favor of the technology; the business partnership aspect was swell; no one minded the generous handouts of hardware; most also welcomed the prospect of students knowing more about what was going on in the world. What Whittle had not reckoned on was the knee-jerk hostility of educators to commercial advertising in the classroom.

"Academic acid rain," the head of the elementary principals' association called it, "trickling down through the years with possible damaging effects."[30] Educational "junk food" resolved the secondary principals' group.[31] A "very dangerous precedent," huffed the director of the ASCD.[32] "Our students aren't for sale," thundered California's Bill Honig.[33] "Will we eventually be selling one-minute spots in fifth-grade geography?" asked an AASA official.

Honig and the New York Regents moved to bar Channel One from public school classrooms in their states. The North Carolina state board of education forbade future contracts between local school systems and the Whittle project (though the state legislature later overturned the ban.) Defying the principle of building-level control in Chicago, General Superintendent Ted Kimbrough announced that no school in that city could run Channel One. Several other states and localities have imposed their own restrictions.

Whittle persevered, however. He sweetened the deal by adding "instructional support" and "professional development" channels, thus offering more (noncommercial) benefits to participating schools, still at no cost to them. He bestowed greater professional legitimacy on the venture by empanelling a blue-ribbon advisory group chaired by former U.S. Education Secretary T. H. Bell.

During the fall of 1989, Whittle's representatives worked energetically to sign up schools, and by the end of the first regular season in 1990 they claimed 4000 participating institutions, approximately half their goal. By December, they had enlisted 5700 schools.

Meanwhile, Turner Communications and the NSBA devised a noncommercial alternative for high schools that wanted a public affairs television show. Their scheme also costs participating schools nothing but does not include the free equipment on which to receive, record, and replay the fifteen-minute "CNN Newsroom" show.

With competition between suppliers, perhaps this sequence will yet result in greater exposure of young Americans to daily news and public affairs information in ways that teachers can help interpret, together with a substantial boost in communications technology in the schools. But it is also possible that Whittle's venture will not be able to overcome the resistance, will fail to sign up enough schools to make good on its claims to advertisers, and will come to naught. Turner's uncontroversial (but unprofitable) alternative could continue as long as the company is willing to subsidize it, yet many schools lack the requisite hardware to avail themselves of it.

There's no denying that Whittle is out to make a buck and that his considerable business success over the years has come from developing unusual communications-cum-advertising niches. His new public affairs program for high schools is by no means perfect; the examples I've seen are lively and well paced but somewhat superficial. Yet the education establishment's rejection of Whittle's idea has had practically nothing to do with the shows' content. Amid the clamor, little was said about their quality. Nor did anyone dare to suggest that the learning gap he proposed to reduce wasn't embarrassingly wide. The 1988 National Assessment civics report revealed that 61 percent of twelfth-graders do not know that Congress can raise income taxes and half aren't aware that the Bill of Rights provides for the free exercise of religion. It's not as if Whittle were offering ice to Greenland.

But that wasn't the issue. Neither was the program's popularity among students and teachers, which turned out to be considerable, or the poll evidence indicating a high degree of public approval for Channel One, or the many editorials and columns in support. No, it all came down to a single strong sentiment: the "leaders" of American public education are viscerally hostile to this kind of capitalism.

What left me gasping, though, was not this primal sentiment. It was the major-league hypocrisy that surrounded it. The fact is that American public schools are awash in commercial advertising of many kinds: from publishers' logos on the spines of textbooks, to the "Dixon" or "Ticonderoga" inscribed on the lead pencils, to the boxes of trademark chalk and erasers up front; from the milk cartons in the school cafeteria to the newspapers and magazines that social studies classes subscribe to; from the ads in such familiar publications as *My Weekly Reader* to the large "Rand McNally" emblazoned on maps hanging around the walls; from the avid quest for ads for the school newspaper and yearbook to the itinerant vendors of graduation photos, athletic gear, class rings, and prom regalia; and, of course, the commercial television shows taped by teachers or students on their VCRs for later use in class.

The profession is steeped in commercialism, too. Almost every conference I've been to has ballrooms full of displays by publishers, software developers, computer salesmen, and the makers and vendors of an awesome range of prizes, premiums, and notions by which schools can raise money. Free samples are readily available. (Oversize candy bars seem especially popular.) These same commercial firms also underwrite the costs of many of the conferences, often including lavish receptions or barbecues, and program organizers repay them by scheduling times when attendees are expected to browse and sample. Most professional journals are full of advertisements, too, for such things as insurance, overseas tours, computer discounts, cut-rate magazine subscriptions, and bargain books. Perusing a representative issue (April 1990) of the largest-circulation journal of them all, *NEA Today*, I also spotted ads for Yugo cars, for an NEA-sponsored gold MasterCard, and—on the back cover—for an NEA-sponsored money market fund promising "above-average yields" and "100% liquidity."

To me there is nothing immoral in such advertising. It's part of the world we inhabit, and nobody is forcing anyone to buy. I see plenty wrong, however, with the sanctimony by which Whittle's offer was rejected *in principle*, denounced as a Faustian bargain, as the beginning of the end of "public" education. I've yet to meet a teenager who can be forced to heed a television commercial. Nor can one reasonably suppose that two minutes of advertising will suck knowledge and skills out of their brains. But it seems that the education profession, for all its breast-beating about inadequate modern technology and weak current affairs knowledge among students, cannot be persuaded to change its ways even when offered a very attractive deal.

THE NATIONAL BOARD FOR PROFESSIONAL TEACHING STANDARDS

The Carnegie Forum on Education and the Economy had a good idea. "A National Board for Professional Teaching Standards should be created," proposed a forum task force in 1986, "to establish standards for high levels of competence in the teaching profession, to assess the qualifications of those seeking board certification, and to grant certificates to those who meet the standards."[34]

The Achilles heel of the teaching profession is that it treats everyone, good or bad, as interchangeable. Professionals, we understand, don't behave this way. With governors and legislators wanting to reward merit, with evidence that big across-the-board salary increases for teachers were going to be few and far between, at least until educators themselves shouldered responsibility for peer quality control, and with more mature professions willing and able to distinguish among their members on the basis of performance, schoolteaching needed to get off the dime. You could have your baby delivered by a "board-certified" obstetrician, your home wiring repaired by a "master" electrician and your college-going daughter lectured by a "full" professor. Why could you not have your eighth grader taught by a "board-certified" teacher?

In time, schools would pay such teachers more, and individuals holding board certification would be more attractive to prospective employers. Teachers would no longer be interchangeable. And these judgments would have been made by the profession itself. The AFT's Shanker embraced this reasoning and has never flinched. Former NEA president Mary Futrell went along with it at the start (amid many footnotes, caveats and qualifications), though her organization has shown less steadfastness.

The crucial issue from the outset, of course, was what sort of standards and measures the new Board would use in making these judgments. If it fell back on paper credentials, graduate school credit hours, time-in-harness, or who liked whom, the new arrangement would lack any credibility. If, on the other hand, the board actually evaluated teacher competence in a rigorous way, maintained lofty standards, and based all its judgments on such criteria, it could be a valuable addition to American education.

But how to judge teacher competence? Four years after the Carnegie Forum recommended creation of such a board, and three years after the 64-member panel was actually formed, that remains an open question. The majority of the Board's members are practicing teachers (and union officials), so it is not surprising that the group has shunned the criterion that most laymen would first reach for: judging teachers' performance by how much their students learn. This approach is not acceptable to the Board, nor are paper-and-pencil examinations for teachers.[35] Once those two obvious possibilities are excluded, what remains is some sort of (live or videotaped) classroom observation system, the inspection of a portfolio of the teacher's work, perhaps some predetermined exercises. But how to appraise these in a fair and equitable way? How to devise standards that recognize competence in both a third grade art instructor and an eleventh grade chemistry teacher?

Much research has accordingly been undertaken by the new Board, many reports written, some prototypes developed. Innumerable meetings have been held and millions of corporate and foundation dollars raised and spent. Lots of energy has also been devoted—and sizable sums paid to lobbying and public-relations firms—to induce the federal government to share in the cost of still more research and development, a quest resisted by both the Reagan and

Bush administrations but likely to be okayed by Congress sooner or later.[36]

According to a recent board report, the first actual teacher certificates are expected in 1993, six years after the board's creation. But these will cover only selected subjects and grade levels, with the others to follow gradually. It appears that the third millennium will dawn before the evaluation battery is complete.

So slowly is this process going, and so thoroughly is it dominated by researchers and practitioners, that one does not have to be terminally cynical to wonder whether the Board really yearns to get about the hard work of distinguishing among teachers, or whether perhaps some of its members are content with the promise that something will happen someday but not yet.

Still, we will be better off with board-certified teachers than without them, even in the twenty-first century, *if* high standards of actual performance and competence are the sole criteria for judging them. This, however, is in considerable doubt today. The politics of board certification for teachers turn out to resemble those of alternative certification. If instructional effectiveness is the exclusive consideration and paper credentials do not count, obviously there is no need for candidates to complete a conventional program of teacher preparation in a college of education, nor is there any obligation to obtain a state teaching license as a precursor to board certification.[37]

Hence the American Association of Colleges for Teacher Education has determined that board certification is a bad idea and—observe the strange bedfellows—has found itself siding with two consecutive Republican administrations in objecting to federal subsidies for the board's work. Also opposing the board's plans are the National Association of State Directors of Teacher Certification, the Association of Teacher Educators, and the Land Grant College and University Deans of Education—the very establishment groups with the greatest stake in this particular corner of the status quo.

A number of local school administrators have been fretting as well, worried that their districts—small and rural, urban and troubled, suburban but poor—won't be able to compete for board-certified teachers and will accordingly be disadvantaged.[38]

Various conservative groups have also opposed the board, especially federal support for it, on grounds that it will give the teachers' unions even greater control of American schools.

Most threatening of all in the political domain was the announcement by the NEA in December 1989 that it objected to the absence of preconditions for board certification. Though the AFT's Shanker remained steadfast, NEA leaders finally succumbed to their initial trepidations and vowed to "take whatever steps are necessary" to link eligibility to possession of a state teaching license and completion of an accredited teacher-preparation program.[39] Twenty of the board's sixty-four members are NEA members. If they allow their union's stand to define their own positions, a serious rift will open within the board over one of the premier issues by which the larger world will judge its integrity.

We cannot yet know what will come of all this. Perhaps some day there really will be board-certified teachers for American schools. Whether they will be good teachers is an open question, but it's already evident that what once seemed like a straightforward reform idea, generated in substantial part by the profession itself, is becoming trapped in the Sargasso Sea of the education establishment. The story has been repeated so often. Each new candidate for significant change in American education, wherever launched and however skillfully navigated, seems fated to sail to that dread region of the ocean, a place where kelp and seaweed flourish and no fresh breezes blow, where momentum is lost, the sun beats down, and even the most seaworthy vessel is eventually reduced to a torpid, drifting hulk.

12

ℱ

Bad Ideas Whose Time Has Come

I speak truth, not so much as I would, but as much as I dare; and I dare a little the more, as I grow older.

—Montaigne, 1595

If we never succeed in sailing the becalmed vessel of American education out of the turbid seas in which it is stuck, the reason may be that we have been navigating by the wrong stars.

Ideas have consequences. When we steer by sensible ones, we end up in desirable places. When we chart our course in relation to eccentric notions and skewed priorities, we find ourselves where we don't want to be.

As we saw in chapter 5, those who dial the talk shows are fond of overly simple diagnoses and one-dose nostrums for education maladies. As we saw in chapter 6, many people are far too sanguine about their own situations. Yet the basic values of the American public are sound, as are its instincts about what constitutes good education. When professionals (or politicians) confront John and Jane Doe with ideas that do not ring true, those notions get ignored or resisted. When too many such notions flow from the same sources, people stop taking those sources seriously.

"What parents seem to want," columnist William Raspberry wrote in March 1990,

> are public schools, traditionally organized, that work as well for the children who attend them as the private and parochial schools work for their enrollees. . . . But mostly the educationists don't ask parents what they want. They merely ask us to support— and press our legislators to finance—whatever vague schemes they

come up with, no matter how little evidence there may be to suggest that it will make any appreciable difference.[1]

Today the field of education is full of "vague schemes" and their earnest proponents. Many of these plans rest atop dubious ideas about how the world works, what is important for children, and the proper mission of formal education.

In this chapter I examine some of those ideas and suggest how they not only undermine the kinds of education most people value but also erode public support for schools and those who work in them. I also cast a critical gaze on some of the beliefs that stir "conservative" reformers.

THREE ANECDOTES

We begin with three recent episodes, true but little publicized, that illustrate the intellectual and ideological infirmities of this field.

The first was recounted in a letter sent to me in 1989 by Edward M. LaMotte, a suburban New York high-school English teacher. I have changed only the names:

> The happening began at 2:30 P.M. a few Mondays ago. Our faculty meeting began with one of the high school assistant principals introducing a Mr. Raymond Short who would run a "Human Interconnectedness Institute."
>
> "Ray," as he wanted to be called, immediately took the mike and said "Everyone stand up and clap." The teachers did. Then, he continued, "Pair off. . . . Pair off and write down the thoughts that come to mind about this day." The goal of this experience would be to find "facilitators." The planned student meeting, however, would be self-directed to enhance the consciousness of self-worth. At this point, Ray asked a faculty member to come forth to describe a personally fulfilling experience of the day.

Mr. LaMotte enclosed a pair of handouts from Short's organization, clearly meant for posting on bulletin boards. One was a well-known collection of aphorisms by Dorothy L. Nolte, a leader of the "self-esteem" movement in education, along the lines of, "If children live with criticism, they learn to condemn. . . . If children live with approval, they learn to like themselves." The other consisted of four "inspirational" quatrains, the flavor of which is adequately conveyed by the last:

The more I learn, the more I grow,
And then the more I see
Just how much more I want to know
The Me I'm Learning To Be!

This, mind you, took place at a high-school faculty meeting.

Anecdote two comes from the Midwest. It is already in the public domain, so these names are real.

The same month that Edward LaMotte sat through that faculty meeting on Long Island, Fred Whitehead, Ph.D., assistant director of preceptorships at the University of Kansas Medical School, wrote to the principal of his child's school:

Dear Ms. Moritz,

My daughter Susannah is an honors student at Sumner. Recently she and I were discussing an aspect of the history of science, and I was quite surprised that she could not give me a correct definition of one of the most important Scientific Laws.

What gave rise to our discussion was my discovery that evening students in Logic and Philosophy at Penn Valley Community College (where I'm teaching part-time) could not give me the definition either.

Therefore, I would like to enlist your help in trying to get a broader "sample" of Kansas City's student population, in one school at least. What I have in mind is a *very* simple one-page form with four questions.

The short quiz he sought to administer asked who had discovered the Law of Gravity and in which land and what century he had lived. It also requested a brief statement of the law in words or as a scientific formula.

Several weeks later Dr. Whitehead received a reply from the school system's director of pupil services and research, denying his request. Here is an excerpt:

In discussing the questions with the Science Supervisor, he . . . stated that the goal is not to teach the immediate recall of facts, since memory does not imply understanding, but rather, to teach for application of science to daily living and to understand its relationship to our environment. He further stated that students are taught the tools to seek out and find laws and formulae when such are needed.

Whitehead appealed to the school superintendent. "I am perturbed," he wrote, "by your Science Supervisor's statement . . . that 'memory does not imply understanding.' Of course, this is partly true, but—if one does not know a scientific law, one cannot be said to understand it."

He got no satisfaction, however. "Stone-walling on this matter" is how Whitehead characterizes the final response of the Kansas City, Kansas school system.

Like Edward LaMotte, Fred Whitehead is an educator. That both were alarmed by these brief encounters is evidence that muddleheadedness is far from universal among professionals in this field. Indeed, survey after survey has shown that schoolteachers and principals have values and life-styles scarcely distinguishable from those of other middle-class Americans. We know, for example, that 72 percent of public school teachers watch television daily and that the magazines they read most often are *Reader's Digest* and *National Geographic*. Eighty-seven percent describe themselves as religious and 71 percent as middle-of-the-road or conservative in their politics. We also know that 62 percent of public school principals voted for Ronald Reagan in 1984, 29 percent for Walter Mondale.[2]

Anyone fearful that our children are in the hands of oddballs can take solace in the benign conventionality of the typical tiller of the education field. But their ideas and the priorities of their schools are eventually influenced by the profession's organizational and intellectual leaders, the people who write the journal articles, address the conferences and teach in the colleges of education. Within *that* population, the sappy "interconnectedness" workshop of Ray Short is thought to be a constructive use of a faculty meeting, much as the animus toward specific knowledge displayed by Kansas City's science supervisor is regarded as a tenet of sound contemporary curriculum policy.

My third anecdote comes from one of those innumerable conferences, in this case the high-status gathering of the Education Commission of the States (ECS) in Seattle in July 1990. The ECS has been around for twenty-five years and is supposed to consist of heavy hitters in state education policy. Its Denver-based staff is led by the capable and droll Frank Newman and its yearly meetings draw six or seven hundred people from across the nation.

Judging from the list of preregistrants for the 1990 gathering, however, most attendees nowadays are staffers of national and state education associations, researchers, itinerant school (and college) reformers, and sundry hangers-on. Only five governors made it to

Seattle, as did a few dozen legislators, a handful of businesspeople, and a lot of legislative aides. But every doubtful idea that enjoys any standing in the profession was well represented.

I was one of four panelists in an afternoon session on "Teaching and Learning for a Democracy." My colleagues were James Banks, professor of curriculum and instruction at the University of Washington's college of education; Mary Diez, professor of education at Alverno College in Milwaukee, Wisconsin; and John Goodlad, director of the center for educational renewal at the University of Washington and a well-known scholar.

The moderator began by asking us about Allan Bloom's allegations in *The Closing of the American Mind*. Professor Banks promptly declared that Bloom was an "exemplar of a person who contributes to the closing of the American mind," a statement that evoked the first applause from the audience of several hundred. Banks then asserted that Bloom's notion of knowledge was "very elitist" and that "the kind of paradigm that Bloom set forth is a factor that contributes to the eradication of democracy." He segued into a standard deconstructionist analysis of education, in which knowledge has no objective existence or neutral meaning. "Kids," he explained, "need to know who formulated the facts, what is the context for the facts." What is important about knowledge is understanding "for what purposes was it constructed, whose interests does it serve." Some knowledge, Banks averred, "erodes democracy rather than supports it." The implication was that we should shun information that "contributes to inequality." If we don't teach knowledge that menaces our political values, perhaps children will never acquire ideas that we deplore.[3]

Concepts got much the same treatment as facts. Professor Banks said he wants youngsters to understand "who formulated the concepts, who participated in the conceptualizing of the concepts [sic]." The ethnicity and motive of the thinker are of greater moment than the originality or value of the thought. He took as an example the unit in U.S. history courses commonly called the "westward expansion."

"It wasn't a westward movement to the Sioux," he said to hearty applause. "They were already in the West. It wasn't a westward movement to the Japanese, from Asia, because it was in the East. If you look at the 'settlers,' they may have been settlers to the European immigrants but they were invaders to the Sioux. So which facts do you teach? . . . We have to understand the whole paradigm from which the facts originate. . . . They can't understand the facts if we only teach them facts from the point of view of the settlers or—should I say?—immigrants." More applause.[4]

My fellow panelists also felt that American schools overemphasize the breadth of students' knowledge. "We fill them so full of facts they can't think," said Professor Banks, who urged the schools to teach fewer things in greater depth. "We can't expect kids to think, and to perceive reality from diverse directions," he explained, "and also cover those five hundred pages." Professor Diez also endorsed the principle of "less is more," noting that in science, for example, "We either keep kids in school forever or we . . . teach science as a process, we teach the relation of science, technology and society, we pull out big principles, and yes, of course, we deal with some examples."[5]

I said this was more like teaching *about* science than conveying the content of science itself, and that there is quite a lot of information we all need to know, both as general background knowledge and as a basis for communicating. Professor Diez demurred, asking: "Who gets to decide what are the important things? How will knowing those things help me solve some of the serious social and political and environmental questions of the day?"[6]

Citizens may think that what ails American schools today—and the reason they are widely criticized—is the wretched job they are doing of imparting knowledge and skills to their pupils. But educators do not like to hear that. It implies that they are responsible, a discomfiting thought that Professor Goodlad was pleased to spare them. He chose to lay most of the blame at the doorstep of the political power structure. The ECS audience clapped warmly when he said that the real problem is "the dissolution of the coalition that built the American common school in large measure because it excluded as part of the decision making structure people in our society" such as the Iroquois and the "involuntary immigrants" and because it had obliged "Latinos" and French Americans to "give up their language." The premier failing of public education, he suggested, is political, not educational.[7]

Goodlad then suggested that we should learn from the recent experience of Canada. The lesson he had in mind, however, is not that a society flies apart when it fails to develop a common language and culture. Rather, Goodlad believes that we should derive from the Canadian example the conclusion that every faction in society needs to be invited to set its own terms for continued participation, notwithstanding the effects on the commonweal.

ALLERGIC TO KNOWLEDGE

ECS conferences are not the only domains of contemporary American education where knowledge is excoriated for being unimportant and inert on the one hand and politically suspect on the other. This attitude among academics and practitioners requires scrutiny. Though it's of fairly recent vintage and appears to be spreading, it's tragically flawed.

Facts are to thinking as bricks are to mortar. Together they can make a mighty edifice; alone neither is of much use. A stack of loose bricks tips over at the gentlest push. Isolated facts, even a lot of them, constitute an incomplete education, Mr. Gradgrind to the contrary notwithstanding. One must know what to do with knowledge and have the intellectual skills to do interesting things.

But pure brainwork, for one whose brain holds no information worth working on, is as feckless as knowing how to read but never picking up a book. A mound of mortar has no strength. Conceptualizing in a state of ignorance is akin to pure opinion, as in those thousand wasted classes where students are asked to express their feelings or make "decisions" about things they do not begin to understand.

Education critic Denis Doyle jests that a think tank is a place where "reality is examined to see if it conforms to theory." The man in the street recognizes that even the agile mind is useless when empty, that opinions without foundations are mere prejudices, and that the most dazzling theory is valueless if one possesses no reality against which to test it. The only place this view is rejected is within the encapsulated world of education. Today, prominent inhabitants of that world rhapsodize about "thinking skills," "higher-order cognitive skills," and "learning how to learn" as if these were sufficient unto themselves.

At first you suppose they are merely forgetting to mention knowledge. In time you realize that it's worse than negligence. Knowledge has become a problem for educators, a minefield to be stepped carefully through when not avoided altogether. If you tread on a bit of information, it can explode in your face, with someone like Professor Banks demanding to know the race and motive of whoever constructed that fact, Professor Diez asking who had the temerity to select it among all possible facts, and Professor Goodlad asking whether the society within which it is used is governed by a fully participatory political system.

Because this is more challenge than most knowledge users can handle, facts are becoming the stuff of smirks, attacks, and burlesques. Today's sophisticated education thinker prefers to shun them.

Ravitch and I encountered some of this in the response to *What Do Our 17-Year-Olds Know?* Though we had taken great pains to dispel the "false dichotomies" of "skills vs. content" and "concepts vs. facts," insisting instead on both bricks and mortar, we were nevertheless assaulted on many occasions for clinging to the retro conviction that factual knowledge is a necessary element of a proper history curriculum.

Ours was a mere drizzle, however, compared to the downpour that has fallen on E. D. Hirsch, Jr. for daring to suggest both that knowledge is important for children to acquire in school (especially for disadvantaged youngsters, who do not get enough of it at home) and that it is possible to come up with a specific list of essential facts needed for "cultural literacy." He did not merely assert the possibility of such a list; he had the hubris to devise and publish one! Worse, this list and its subsequent evolution into dictionaries, tests, and curriculum guides have proved immensely popular. More than a million copies of Hirsch's books have been bought since 1987. Book sales, opinion polls, and cordial reviews in the popular media all suggest that the American public agrees with Hirsch that shared background knowledge is indispensable to the national welfare, not to mention our ability to communicate with one another.

This is self-evident to anyone whose job involves communicating. Political cartoonist Pat Oliphant, for example, grumbled to an interviewer that soon he won't be able to use once-familiar artistic and literary icons as the basis for his mordant drawings. "The problem," he explained, is that "as education becomes more and more of a mess in this country, and people learn less and less about the arts and history, the possibility of using those sorts of metaphors is disappearing. It will get to a stage where eventually you won't be able to use the classics at all, or allusions to historical events."[8]

Thoughtful politicians notice the same erosion. In a speech at Northern Arizona University soon after the 1988 election, former governor (and Democratic presidential aspirant) Bruce Babbitt laid it on the line:

> We've become a nation . . . of short-term, specific education where people are learning more and more about less and less.
>
> I submit to you that that's the problem with education today. How can people even know what questions to ask unless they

are receiving an education in which we have some common ground—and in which we all understand the relevance of the Constitution and the Declaration of Independence—unless we understand the fables and the stories and the shared history of western civilization?

If we don't understand those things, we can't ask our leaders those questions.[9]

Babbitt and Oliphant agree with Hirsch. So does Fred Whitehead. So, I have no doubt, do most Americans—including many classroom teachers. Yet the education establishment thinks otherwise. Hirsch violated four of its favorite tenets. First, he suggested that all Americans have—and *should* have—a common (albeit multi-sourced and richly diverse) culture and language and that schools should reinforce and transmit these. Second, he affirmed a strong commitment to imparting specific knowledge as an explicit goal of education (while also demanding the "thinking skills" by which that knowledge can be deployed). Third, in an era of fashionable relativism, he possessed a "canonical" view of knowledge and culture in which everyone should learn many of the same things because some things are more worth knowing than others, and children can't tell which are which. Fourth, he advocated broad but rather shallow knowledge at a time when the approved view—well stated by Professor Diez, although castigated by Bruce Babbitt—is to select only a smidgen but probe it deeply.

This was too much. "The logical consequences of following Hirsch's lead," wrote a typical education-journal reviewer, "are an increased dependence on rote learning and machine-scored tests, with a consequent decline in teaching the skills of problem solving and critical thinking. Equally ominous is the encouragement the book will give to those opposed to multilingual, multicultural and global education, an encouragement Hirsch clearly means to offer."[10]

Hirsch has since been treated as a pariah by the education establishment and the private foundations that steer by the same stars. Never mind that platoons of parents, voters, and taxpayers are reading his books or that hundreds of individual teachers and principals have joined his Cultural Literacy Foundation and are keen to put his ideas into practice in their schools. The professional elite cannot abide this dedication to something so archaic as specific knowledge. A "serious fraud upon the public," writes Stanford Education Professor Decker Walker, a proposal that "may trivialize debate about improving American education." Bard College President Leon Botstein sniffed: "The maximal power of literacy is replaced by the primitive packaging of minimalist simplification."[11]

Hirsch has not been alone, however. "A high level of literacy," California's Bill Honig pointed out:

> involves more than mastering reading technique; literacy is inextricably linked to content. . . . To build up literacy, then, it follows that one important step is constantly to present significant, new information to students and continually to open up new frontiers of knowledge on which children can exercise their growing linguistic abilities. . . . Unfortunately, we have been doing just the opposite. Children need an orienting core of knowledge about their social, political, and moral worlds, but we have been emptying the curriculum of all content.[12]

Honig set about with energy and fine educational judgment to rectify the situation in California, where he has laid before the state board of education one curriculum "framework" after another as he and his able team worked through the core school subjects. Nowhere in the nation today is there a better-conceived curriculum for elementary and secondary students than in California, one that smoothly blends knowledge with skills, facts with concepts, western civilization with nonwestern, and so forth.

William Bennett also sets considerable store by knowledge. In perhaps his most eloquent address while education secretary, he begged the members of the National Press Club in 1985 to understand that:

> Good teaching does more than teach skills. Skills are important, but knowledge is at least as important, and knowledge can come only from content. . . .
>
> Every student should know how mountains are made, and that for every action there is an equal and opposite reaction. They should know who said "I am the state" and who said "I have a dream." They should know about subjects and predicates, about isosceles triangles and ellipses. They should know where the Amazon flows, and what the First Amendment means. They should know about the Donner party and slavery, and Shylock, Hercules, and Abigail Adams, where Ethiopia is, and why there is a Berlin Wall. They should know a little of how a poem works, how a plant works, and what it means to remark, "If wishes were horses, beggars would ride." They should know the place of the Milky

Way and DNA in the unfolding of the universe. They should know something about the Constitutional Convention of 1787 and about the conventions of good behavior. They should know a little of what the Sistine Chapel looks like and what great music sounds like. . . . These are things we should want *all* our students to know.[13]

Albert Shanker sounds much like Bennett and Honig with respect to curriculum. So do Lynne V. Cheney and James Atlas. This is not a battle being waged by a lone English professor from the University of Virginia. Yet the opposition is mounting. It comes from so-called multiculturalists who want each child to learn about his or her own ancestors but not those of others; from relativists unwilling to declare certain knowledge to be most valuable; from deconstructionists for whom there is no objective reality, only motive, preference, and viewpoint; from educationists convinced that knowing how to think is more important than possessing information worthy of cogitation (a position Hirsch terms "educational formalism"); and from sundry established interests (such as textbook publishers and teacher educators) accustomed to doing things their own way. Perhaps most troubling, opposition is infecting some of the senior figures in the establishment, too. Lawrence A. Cremin, for example, described as "academic fundamentalism" the view that there is some knowledge all children should acquire.[14]

Quite a lot is at stake here. Reflecting on the popularity of Hirsch and Bloom in the 1980s, James Atlas concludes that they "had discovered a potential threat to our society and gave warning. America is foundering because Americans no longer get a proper education. In their attempts to redress injustice, the radicals of the 1960s unwittingly helped to perpetuate it; the assault on the curriculum has undermined the foundation of learning on which our society rests. The problem could be simply put: What we don't know will hurt us. And it has."[15]

ESTEEMING OURSELVES INTO OBLIVION

January 1990 brought the long-awaited report of California's "Task Force to Promote Self-esteem and Personal and Social Responsibility." This twenty-six-member panel was not cowed by multiple *Doonesbury* episodes lampooning it as "the first official study of new age thinking." Instead, it grandiloquently declared self-esteem to be "the likeliest candidate for a social vaccine" and ascribed to it near-magical powers:

> Something that empowers us to live responsibly and that inoculates [*sic*] us against the lures of crime, violence, substance abuse, teen pregnancy, child abuse, chronic welfare dependency, and educational failure. The lack of self-esteem is central to most personal and social ills plaguing our state and nation as we approach the end of the twentieth century.[16]

In its education chapter, the Task Force urged mandatory "course work in self-esteem" for all licensed educators and its integration into the "total curricula" of every school and district. The reformulated program envisioned by the panel, a virtual catalogue of modish education ideas, would include "positive self-esteem, conflict resolution, effective communication, goal setting and goal achievement, time and money management, creative problem solving, leadership, stress management, and decision making."[17]

Self-esteem via curriculum reform was also the focus of attention on the other side of the continent, where in mid-February 1990, the New York Regents endorsed the recommendations of state Education Commissioner Thomas Sobol concerning the need to revise course content in the schools of the Empire State. They were responding to the report of a Task Force on Minorities that Sobol had empaneled in 1987.

That panel proclaimed that "African Americans, Asian Americans, Puerto Ricans/Latinos, and Native Americans have all been the victims of an intellectual and educational oppression," due in no small part to curricula with "a terribly damaging effect on the psyche of young people." If the group's wide-ranging recommendations were heeded, however, minority youngsters "[would] have higher self-esteem and self-respect, while children from European cultures [would] have a less arrogant perspective."[18]

Sobol used milder language than his task force but embraced its central psychodynamic premise. "We know," the commissioner told the regents, "that if children are to achieve they must trust their teachers and feel good about themselves." This happy state would be reached, he assured the board, through "curricula and teaching which represent children's backgrounds, which help them discover more about themselves and people like them."[19]

Self-esteem in California. Feeling good about oneself in New York. And more of the same across the land. The director of elementary schools in Fulton County, Georgia avers that "high self-esteem is a

prerequisite for high academic achievement and success in life."
Maryland governor William D. Schaefer has appointed a twenty-three-
member task force in his state. "Self-esteem citizen groups" are said
to be active in Missouri, New Mexico, and Florida. Michigan has a
"Teenage Council on Self-Esteem." The NEA tells its two million
members that schools "must structure esteem-building into the
curriculum."[20]

Since every education fad quickly spawns its own interest groups,
there now exist a National Council for Self-Esteem, a Center for
Self-Esteem, and a Foundation for Self-Esteem. It is rare to pick up
an education journal without encountering several articles on the
subject, and rarer still to attend any of the zillion professional conferences each year without finding rooms full of people solemnly discussing how best to foster self-esteem in children. Nor are such
notions confined to American shores. The First International Conference on Self-Esteem was held in Oslo in the summer of 1990.

Television culture has absorbed this mind-set without missing a
beat. Beneath the "underachiever and proud of it" tee shirt worn
by ten-year-old Bart Simpson on one of the most popular shows of
1990, beats a cartoon heart brimming with self-esteem. "Judging
from his behavior," writes author and former teacher Martha C.
Brown, "Bart really has learned to feel good about himself, regardless
of accomplishments, just as the education professors say he
should."[21]

"The main thing," Rita Kramer reports a student teacher saying
in an education college class she observed, "is for them to feel good
about themselves as readers"—this by way of explaining her decision
not to introduce her second-graders to any words that the children
did not already know. It is not surprising that her classmates and
professor beamed. "Teachers generally seem to accept the modern
dogma," Barbara Lerner has written, "that self-esteem is the critical
variable for intellectual development—the master key to learning."[22]

Unfortunately those educators may be quite wrong. Self-esteem
and its relationship to education (and to much else) has been the
subject of a vast body of research. It turns out to be as ambiguous
and inconclusive an array of social-science literature as one can
find, revealing self-esteem to be a more slippery and elusive item
than its promoters realize. Self-esteem levels are not easy to measure,
either, yet even when we obtain data they turn out to correlate
only slightly with the other desirable qualities that task forces and
teacher-training classes are hoping to foster. Many of the statistical
relationships are negative.

Summarizing the research literature for the California self-esteem task force, the distinguished Berkeley sociologist Neil J. Smelser had this glum comment:

> One of the disappointing aspects of every chapter in this volume . . . is how low the associations between self-esteem and its consequences are in research to date. . . . [T]o put the matter more simply, the scientific efforts to establish those connections that we are able to acknowledge and generate from an intuitive point of view do not reproduce those relations.[23]

This was a damning thing to say in a volume meant to provide scientific backing for the conclusions of a task force that was urging hugely increased society-wide attention to self-esteem.

Education *was* one of the areas where Smelser and his colleagues reported a positive association with self-esteem. Yet these correlations are quite low, accounting for less than 5 percent of variation in student achievement, and the causal link is obscure. It is as likely— many studies have come to this conclusion—that heightened self-esteem flows from academic achievement as that improved achievement is caused by self-esteem. It is also possible—again, from many studies—that the two attributes vary together, both affected similarly by independent influences such as innate ability, social class, and prior accomplishment.

Self-confidence is practically our national faith, of course, and has been since many of our ancestors forsook the deterministic religions and caste-paralyzed societies of the Old World for a land where social, economic, and physical mobility were all possible— provided one had enough ambition and drive. We read our children *The Little Engine That Could* not just because it has a happy ending but also because it attests to what Norman Vincent Peale called the power of positive thinking. Philanthropist Eugene Lang's "I Have a Dream" program, and its many clones around the country, do excellent work with disadvantaged youngsters not so much by encouraging them to dream as by assisting them to strive and to attain.[24]

Beyond the peaks of self-confidence, however, lies a treacherous canyon. It begins where what one thinks about oneself starts to diverge from reality, where dreams get confused with fact, where optimism about the future turns into delusions about the past. It is the disorder we know as narcissism, defined in psychopathology textbooks as "persistent and unrealistic overvaluation of one's own importance and achievements." Christopher Lasch has famously described the emergence in contemporary America of a "culture of narcissism," and nowhere did he find that culture more prominent than in our education system. "Under cover of enlightened ideologies," Lasch wrote:

> Teachers (like parents) have followed the line of least resistance, hoping to pacify their students and to sweeten the time they have to spend in school by making the experience as painless as possible. Hoping to avoid confrontations and quarrels, they leave the students without guidance, meanwhile treating them as if they were incapable of serious exertion.[25]

Remember those report cards, full of good news about Rusty and Kate. Recall those state testing programs that show most students achieving above the national average. Now inject the notion that all girls and boys need positive reinforcement and praise even if they haven't earned it through actual performance. Is it really to be wondered that American children (and their parents) have higher regard for their academic achievement than the facts warrant?

"Let us not confuse ourselves," psychologist Jerome Bruner has written, "by failing to recognize that there are two kinds of self confidence . . . one a trait of personality, and another that comes from knowledge of a subject. It is of no particular credit to the educator to help build the first without building the second. The objective of education is not the production of self-confident fools."[26]

BOUQUET OF WEEDS

Rejecting knowledge while embracing self-esteem typifies the ideas and attitudes that predominate in right-thinking education circles today. The array is untidy and it buzzes with factional quarrels and rival egos, yet we do not err in thinking of it as a new intellectual orthodoxy, an education establishment in the ideological sphere that parallels the one domiciled near the statehouse.

Like most orthodoxies, this one makes dissenting views none too welcome in its midst. Those who bring contrary ideas or embarrassing news find themselves treated like polecats at a garden club meeting. As in Hirsch's case, John J. Cannell, author of the "Lake Wobegon" report, has found it virtually impossible to raise funds from private or public sources with which to continue his valuable but unpopular mission of exposing misleading state and local test results. John Saxon, the creator of a math textbook series that emphasizes drill and practice, has had much success with children in those few school districts that let him inside the door. But the math-reform crowd, having decided that old-fashioned prowess in subtracting and multiplying must be superseded by estimating and problem solving, has wedged most portals firmly shut against him.[27]

Notwithstanding all the talk about valuing pluralism and appreciating differences, tolerance for philosophical heresy is not one of the more conspicuous attributes of this field. At the start of the ECS session recounted above, when the moderator introduced the panelists I was hissed (before I so much as opened my mouth) by a couple of people in the back of the hall. A friend remarked later that their name tags identified them as officials of the National Council of Teachers of English (NCTE), a group that from time to time has quarreled with my views on core curricula and student assessment. As for the state legislator who innocently asked our ECS panel whether teaching children to respect the flag and other symbols of nationhood might not be an important education goal in a democracy—well, nobody said anything rude to his face, but you could tell from the rustling, the body language, and the scowls that many in this audience found his query quaint but irrelevant, perhaps even slightly inappropriate.

Other traditional values and virtues get similar treatment. Competition, for example, is widely deemed to be bad for children and nations alike. Stanford's Elliot Eisner won plaudits from a throng of thousands at the 1990 ASCD conference when he wondered aloud "whether in fact a kinder and gentler America will be created by treating our schools as units in a race for educational supremacy."[28] Competition yields winners and losers, and nobody should have to lose, except perhaps those who have too much to start with (such as "arrogant" youngsters of European descent).

Those gifted with a powerful intellect pose a real quandary for modern education doctrine, which wants to respond to individual differences and disparate learning styles but which wants even more to avoid elitism. Hence many school districts are establishing ethnic quotas and affirmative-action schemes within their "gifted and talented" education programs, where these have not been scrapped altogether as a manifestation of the hated practice known as "tracking."

This is one of the touchiest issues in education policy today. The politically correct position is that children of widely differing levels of ability and prior attainment should be mixed in all schools and classrooms.[29] Just as handicapped children should be "mainstreamed" into regular classes, so, too, should high- and low-achieving youngsters. In a properly run school, this reasoning goes, there would be nothing but "regular" classes full of dissimilar youngsters. That vision has some appeal. Yet many parents disagree with it, and so do lots of teachers. An NEA staffer estimates that "about one-third of the teachers like academic tracking for one reason or another, one-third dislike it intensely, and the other third find it useful but don't like it."[30]

Placing children in separate groups for instructional purposes according to their prior achievement should be distinguished from the deeply-rooted practice of *curricular* tracking, which many people, myself included, regard as an abomination. That's the system by which some youngsters study algebra and literature in "college prep" classes while others are consigned to "consumer math," trivial readings, and dull workbooks in the vocational and general tracks.[31] The same rich content for all, in my view, is an educational necessity and a democratic imperative. But it's quite another matter to pretend that all children learn at the same speed or that all of them can master equal quantities of that content in the same time frames when taught under identical circumstances by ordinary teachers.

Practically everyone knows this isn't so. Even the staunchest advocates of "mixed ability grouping" recognize that teachers need retraining in order to have good results under the changed classroom conditions. And some teachers simply don't believe it's possible. "The needs of the college-prep students are not met," says a veteran Michigan high-school teacher. "The needs of the average and low students are not met; nobody's needs are met. . . . I know a lot of what I say flies in the face of a lot of Ph.D. researchers, but I'm a classroom teacher and I know what works."[32]

She is not alone. Many teachers report greater success with classes in which their pupils are at roughly the same level of attainment than they do with heterogeneous groups. And parents whose high-achieving progeny are, in the name of equity, denied entry to gifted programs, honors sections, Advanced Placement courses and other fast-moving instructional experiences are parents with perhaps the greatest propensity to search out a more accommodating private school. Meanwhile their children will learn less than they are capable of—a waste of human potential that the society can ill afford.

Contemporary education theorists try to shoot down both competition and tracking with a single bullet by promoting the strategy of "cooperative learning." Oversimplified, this means that the faster students help teach the slower and the mixed group, not the individual, is judged on its aggregate result. In human-relations terms, this is appealing, and it's well known that teaching somebody else strengthens one's own grasp of the content. The problem is that the tutors are not also learning the new material that their own intellects are ready to handle. Speaking for many parents, columnist Joan Beck argues that:

> Such proposals do irreparable injustice and harm to bright children, who are just as entitled as other youngsters to an education appropriate to their abilities. . . . They need the challenge of new ideas and new materials and opportunities to learn at the accelerated speed most comfortable for them. To expect them to sustain a love of learning while marking time waiting for slower students to catch up is like asking Michael Jordan to be challenged by playing basketball indefinitely at a local "Y."[33]

As Steve Allen points out: "It would be a very peculiar state of affairs if our society took the position that children who are found to possess remarkable musical aptitude were, nevertheless, not to be given any special consideration or instruction."[34] When it comes to intellectual talent, however, we do not need to wait for bright children's peers to brand them "nerds" or accuse them of "acting white." We can hear much the same message in the lecture halls of our schools of education, where we learn that it's fine to share your gifts with others but not to use them to learn as much as possible yourself.

Nobody should be made to strive, pressed hard, or allowed to become anxious and uncomfortable. Stress is out. Forget Browning's line about a person's reach exceeding his grasp "or what's a heaven for?" Its author was a Victorian romantic. Contemporary educators understand that to place emphasis on achieving more might induce worry, even unhappiness, and that is bad.

It's remarkable how the anti-stress mind-set has captured the profession, especially when it comes to minority students. No matter that Jaime Escalante terms these "misguided psychological precepts" the "kiss of death" for the youngsters he knows best.[35] Even Asian students, notable for their lofty academic-achievement levels, are being encouraged by some school officials to ease off instead of being held up as models to emulate. "I still deal with educators who tell me how great the Asian kids are," laments a New York high-school principal. "It puts an extra burden on the kid who just wants to be a normal kid."[36]

Asian immigrants constitute just a fragment of a far-larger concern. How to respond to minorities in general has become the single most vexed issue in education—as in so many other domains of social policy. I refer here not to the problems of "at risk" and low-income youngsters, many of whom are also minority group members, but to the cultural, curricular, and linguistic tensions embedded in the phrase *e pluribus unum.*"

Diane Ravitch has brilliantly illumined these, particularly in her magisterial essay "Multiculturalism."[37] She makes the essential distinction between *pluralism* and *particularism*. Applied to education, the former means that "We expect children to learn a broad and humane culture, to learn about the ideas and art and animating spirit of many cultures." Equal emphasis is placed on *unum* and *pluribus* and, especially, on helping students to see how the one emerges from and is enriched by the many. Cultural particularists, by contrast, "insist that children can learn only from the experiences of people from the same race." This is a "bad idea," Ravitch says, "whose time has come."

Explaining why it's a bad idea needs a whole book. Here I must settle for noting that, when we scan the globe for examples of multiethnic societies that have followed particularism to its all-but-inevitable conclusion, we find ourselves staring at places like Lebanon, Kashmir, and the Punjab, Azerbaijan and Armenia, Northern Ireland, Sri Lanka, and South Africa. The most conspicuous sentiment in such lands is intergroup hatred. The politics are those of subjugation and secession. Quite a lot of killing goes on, too, slaughters whose most prominent characteristic is that killer and victim belong to different groups.

Whether we will tear ourselves asunder in an American version of tribal conflict is, of course, a profound question, perhaps the most important one we face in the coming decades.[38] Schools will be the arena in which much of this struggle is waged, as we have seen since multiculturalism first swept off the college campuses and began to make its way into elementary-secondary classrooms. Examples can be found in bilingual education schemes that reject the goals of rapid English fluency and eventual assimilation and instead stress maintenance of children's native languages and cultures. The more dramatic evidence, however, is to be seen in the spread of "Afrocentric" curricula across the land. As described by the District of Columbia school system, its new curriculum is "an original program of learning experiences which at its core incorporates African and African-American traditions, culture and contributions to the immediate environment of the child and to the world." Even math and science will be included, if some proponents have their way. They are as zealous as the self-esteem builders, and as certain that they have a cure-all. Afrocentrism in the curriculum will even reduce the dropout rate. "I have talked to a lot of dropouts," says one Washington, D.C. curriculum reformer. "Many of them dropped out because they were not interested in learning how great white people are for the rest of their lives."[39]

Particularism is frequently encountered in our colleges of education, both in the "deconstructionist" readings of history and literature urged by Professor Banks and his colleagues and in articles in prominent journals suggesting that science and social science are themselves "Euro-American" knowledge systems that foster "hegemonic racial domination."[40] And gender is becoming as touchy a matter as ethnicity. Not long ago an eminent Harvard researcher announced that "Western culture" is the reason that adolescent girls in the United States doubt themselves and feel repressed.[41] This is the sort of statement so foolish that only an intellectual could believe it. Most others know that, for all its shortcomings, Western culture is the only major one the world has known that even regards gender blindness as a valid goal.

IN THE ACADEMY

Faculties of education are the brain and central nervous system of the school establishment. They are where ideas originate and get legitimated. They are also where beliefs are held—and transmitted to teachers and principals—that fly in the face of common sense, popular preference, and the express will of democratically elected policymakers. They are where the most absurd notions are promulgated, usually with an introductory phrase such as "research shows" or "we have learned."

Universities play an oppositional role in many realms of our national life, and in general this is healthy. It is why we respect the principle of academic freedom. I am not questioning the right of the professoriate to spout nonsense, even to enjoy a guaranteed income courtesy of the taxpayer while doing so. But we do not have to organize our other public policies to heed that counsel. And if we have reason to believe that teachers and principals are getting their heads stuffed full of it as they pass through colleges of education, we are within our rights to deter them from following that path into our children's schools.

It is not, I think, coincidental that these colleges are the most-despised institutions in the education universe, that alternatives to them are among the most popular reform policies being devised by governors and legislatures, and that limiting prospective educators' exposure to their teachings is one of the school renewal strategies with the greatest public appeal. The *New Republic* editors captured a widespread view when they asserted that "The real reform in teachers' training would be to abolish the undergraduate major altogether, and to make would-be educators learn at real four-year colleges the subjects they plan to teach."[42]

Teachers do not much like these institutions, either. By large margins, they favor radical alternatives to current university-based training programs.[43] And when principals and superintendents candidly appraise their university training in school administration, the language sometimes gets pretty earthy.

Complain though they do about what is dished up in the lecture hall, the in-service program, and the education research institutes, school practitioners can scarcely avoid its impact. Where, for example, did the teachers whose report card comments we examined in chapter 6 acquire the notion that they ought not give children any unfavorable feedback? From the intellectual leaders of their profession, naturally. Positive reinforcement of students was stressed in their college courses. And a federally financed school research center at Johns Hopkins recently urged that report cards become a "mechanism for rewarding all students." The teachers, one could say, are doing exactly what they're being admonished to do.[44]

Many such admonitions fly in the face of common sense. Do not, for example, use tests that lend themselves to absolute standards or invidious comparisons. Never hold a child back from passing with her age-mates to the next grade, no matter how ill-prepared she is for its intellectual challenges. Learning styles differ and intelligences are multiple, so we must not expect everyone to learn the same things, nor be taught in the same ways, nor attain the same standards. Never mind that they do not know when the Civil War occurred. That is a trivial and irrelevant fact.[45] Children need instead to learn about the dangers of nuclear proliferation and the importance of global understanding.

Most of these teachings have their roots in decent impulses, sometimes in solid research. Too many, however, get transformed into something else. Harvard's Howard Gardner, for example, is the father of the idea of multiple intelligences, based on his observations that several areas of intellectual competence (for example, "linguistic," "interpersonal," "musical," "spatial") are reasonably independent of one another and that many people are more adept in one than in others.[46] Well and good. But by the time this useful insight makes its way into the classroom, it has been transmuted into a ready-made justification for eliminating standards and excusing weak academic achievement, an excuse of the kind that blocks worry on the part of teacher or parent because, well, this child is gifted at "bodily-kinesthetic" learning, or whatever. Like Dewey's decades earlier, Gardner's scholarship, after filtering through the ideologies and preferences of the education profession, becomes a justification for the kind of shoddy schooling that placed us "at risk" in the first place. I do not mean to single out what happened to his work, though. Much the same could be said of a hundred other prominent figures in the field.

THE PROFESSIONAL JOURNALS

Of the nation's dozen or so heavyweight education schools, the two with the best-known and most august journals are the Harvard Graduate School of Education and Teachers College, which is affiliated with Columbia. I spent my own graduate student days at the former institution and my colleague Diane Ravitch is on the faculty of the latter. So it was natural that our Educational Excellence Network, which screens dozens of publications in order to share the best and most significant of what's being written in the field with some sixteen-hundred reform-minded members, would subscribe to both the *Harvard Educational Review* (*HER*) and the *Teachers College Record* (*TCR*). After nearly two years had passed, however, I noted that we were not actually including items from either journal in our monthly compilations. So I scooped up a pile of recent issues of both quarterlies and examined them more closely.

Despite modest circulations, these are arguably the two most prestigious periodicals in the field, education's counterparts of the *Harvard Business Review*, the *Yale Law Journal*, and the *New England Journal of Medicine*. They are also among the most ancient and both have published pathbreaking work in years past. If, over a span of eighteen months, neither contained anything worth passing along to Network members, there must at least be a gap between what today's editors and authors deem significant and what our network prizes. More important, insofar as these journals furnish a window onto the ideas and concerns that energize leading graduate schools in the field, by peering in we may better understand the mind of the modern education profession itself.

From the standpoint of ordinary Americans who lived through the 1980's, as we've seen, the central education drama of the decade was the onset of the "excellence movement." Yet if you resided on a remote island and depended on the *Harvard Educational Review* for your information, you would not know that anything of the sort was happening. Save for the odd book review, you would not even get a hint that the country has an acute problem with student achievement that many people are bent on solving.

Neither would you glimpse some of the remarkable changes that have swept over the schools as part of the excellence movement, changes such as the assumption of policy leadership by laymen, and the shift of the system's center of gravity from localities (and Washington) to the states.

By decade's end, as we saw in chapter 3, some once-taboo policy notions had also achieved a measure of legitimacy: parental choice among schools, alternative pathways into teaching, school-level accountability for pupil results, and so forth. Incomplete as they are, these qualify as developments with prodigious implications for the education system. Yet the close reader of those six issues of *HER* would encounter none of them.

The *TCR* subscriber was somewhat better served. Several articles, and the transcript of a campus symposium on national standards (recounted in chapter 8), dealt with some of the reform issues of the eighties. But our island dweller would find few inklings in *TCR* that these were promising, maybe even necessary alterations in the ground rules and operating assumptions of American education. For there was practically no suggestion in its pages that anything was seriously amiss with the existing arrangement, certainly nothing that could not be set right within the old structures and familiar relationships.

That's not to say either journal is well disposed toward the status quo. To the contrary. Both are full of criticism, sometimes brutal, about sundry aspects of American education and the surrounding society. But they list very different grievances than most citizens would name.

The villains in their pages include racism, homophobia, Eurocentrism, sexism and conservatism. Between their covers, the premier job of schooling is not to impart knowledge and skills, to transmit the culture, to empower individuals, or to produce competent, self-reliant adults. Rather, it is to reconstruct the society around it, a society that in its present form is too gravely flawed for conscientious educators to want to prepare youngsters to live in.

That conception of the mission of education traces back at least as far as the Great Depression when Teachers College Professor George S. Counts dared the schools to "build a new social order." The same strand has woven through college-of-education thinking ever since, finding perhaps its most notable contemporary voices in such disciples of Illich and Paulo Freire as Henry Giroux and Stanley Aronowitz.[47] In more modest terms, however, this view of the role of education leads us to expect schools to cure AIDS, end drug addiction, eliminate poverty, prevent teenage suicide and solve other pressing problems of the social order.

This orientation is clearest in *HER*, and never more so than in two recent "special issues." The August 1988 issue was devoted to "Race, Racism, and American Education."[48] The editors' stated purpose was to re-establish racism as the central explanation of the nation's ills and to squelch any suggestion that certain problems might better be attributed to social class, family structure or individual irresponsibility. They even challenged a cherished term of today's concerned educators, the "at risk" child, on grounds that this construction "serves to mask the concept of race."[49]

The other special issue of *HER* (November 1989) was devoted to "community-based education."[50] This sounds benign, even constructive, but it turns out to be a collage of radical grievances and enthusiasms. Here we find a lengthy interview in which Boston community activist Mel King discourses on differences between "the community of the preferred" and the "communities of the oppressed" and the malign role of the U.S. Constitution in maintaining the power of the former and the subjugation of the latter. We find a book review by former Weatherman (and present University of Illinois education professor) William Ayers that empathizes deeply with those "beaten down by racism, sexism, class exploitation, by the great White whale and the great White myth and the great White cultural emptiness." And we find an amazing piece on "The Palestinian Uprising and Education for the Future" that celebrates the *intifadeh* as an educationally and politically liberating experience, partly because the intermittent closing of conventional schools by Israeli authorities caused an outpouring of "popular education" and strengthened the resolve and solidarity of the Palestinians.

Reading these and other recent issues of *HER*, one recalls the jape about the 1960s still enduring on the campus. The earnestness, the sanctimony, the far-left politics, the distaste for dominant trends in society, the passion for particularistic multiculturalism and outré life-styles, the contempt for authority, and the sheer unreality of so much that appears here evoked in me faint memories of Joan Baez, sandal-shod stained-glass makers in Vermont, and upper-middle-class youths going "underground" after blowing up something for ideological reasons.

TCR is not so deeply rooted in romantic radicalism. Somewhat more attuned to the real education dilemmas of the day, the publication has its share of garden-variety essays, research reports, and analyses such as one expects in a "scholarly quarterly." The political leanings of its contributors are a bit more varied, even as their academic credentials are somewhat more conventional.

Yet *TCR* often engages in a subtler version of the same guerrilla warfare as its Cambridge-based counterpart. In its pages, too, the education system is seen as an instrument either of social change or of social repression, and contemporary school reformers who stress academic achievement usually emerge as wrongheaded reactionaries. The most-published author in the six issues of *TCR* that I examined was Michael W. Apple, a radical education professor at the University of Wisconsin. His lead article in the winter 1988 issue, an essay on "Redefining Equality," is a rousing summons to arms against the "authoritarian populism" of the New Right, with its "new hegemonic accord" combining "dominant economic and political elites intent on 'modernizing' the economy; white working-class and middle-class groups concerned with security, the family, and traditional knowledge and values; and economic conservatives." What is lost as this "accord" works its will, Apple asserts, is "the reality of the oppressive conditions that exist for so many of our fellow Americans."[51]

Other *TCR* authors are milder in print, some guilty of nothing more heinous than pedantry. But many of the reviews and essays display variations of Apple's distaste for education as cognitive learning, as the transmitter of western culture and values, or as the engine of economic growth. Because it is subtler, *TCR* is probably more effective than the more-strident *HER*. But it is also more inclined to enter into the jousts taking place in real education policy arenas, and on these occasions the subtlety may be suspended. Lest he escape with only one wound, E. D. Hirsch, for example, was blasted in *TCR*'s pages with a double-barrelled weapon: back-to-back critical reviews of *Cultural Literacy* by *two* senior members of the Teachers College faculty.

Peripheral as they seem to the great issues and large changes now shaking American education—and bizarre as they look alongside other professional journals edited on the same campuses—such publications as *TCR* and *HER* are far from irrelevant to the ideas and priorities of the education profession itself, the selfsame profession on whose millions of members we must rely for implementation of reforms in school policy, structure, and purpose. Though individual practitioners may be autonomous within their schools and classrooms, in the ideological sphere they tend eventually to echo the regnant orthodoxies of the field. The profession's intellectual irrigation system isn't very efficient, as we are about to see. Yet it goes on and on, ceaselessly dripping whatever ideas are in its tubing. The reservoirs from which it siphons many of these are the elite scholarly journals. To the extent that such publications ignore or rebuff the "excellence movement," the likelihood that it will be pursued with gusto in the nation's schools is diminished accordingly.

Colleges of education also transmit ideas by colonizing one another. Once they've obtained their doctorates, *HER*'s student editors will head off to become assistant professors at places like Murfreesboro State, California State, and Ohio University. There they will join faculty members who already contribute most of the essays and reviews that fill these journals.

Were American education in fine shape, this would not be cause for much concern. But if the sixties still strut their off-beat finery in the sheltered precincts of elite universities, the saga of American schools over the past quarter century has been one of ruinous decay. So the content of these pages cannot be dismissed as quaint or irrelevant. If our high-status colleges of education inhabit a world that is glimpsed with even partial accuracy through the prism of their journals, then it seems likely that what is occurring on their ivied campuses is exacerbating the problem rather than hastening its solution.

IMPERVIOUSNESS

So loosely coupled is the education system and so set in their ways are most of its participants that even purposeful efforts to place good information before them usually come to very little. This has been the incurable weakness of the education research enterprise for decades.

When I arrived at the U.S. Education Department in mid-1985, the first question Secretary Bennett asked was whether we could take some of the high-quality education research that had already been done and get it into the hands of practitioners. We agreed that the intellectual warehouses were bulging with solid findings that held practical implications for teachers, principals, and parents and that the performance level of American education would rise if those findings were put into general practice. Can't they be translated into plain language, Bennett asked, and widely distributed?

I wasn't sure about the translation part. In turning squirrelly social science formulations into standard English, we risked either doing violence to the research or failing to make it truly intelligible to principals and teachers. But I vowed to try, and an expert staff team swung into action, headed by the wise and talented Milton Goldberg. By burning much midnight oil and leaning hard on colleagues throughout the agency and the research world, the project took only nine months. In March 1986 Bennett and President Reagan released *What Works: Research About Teaching and Learning* at a ceremony in the East Room of the White House. "Armed with good information," Bennett confidently wrote in his foreword to the sixty-five-page volume, "the American people can be trusted to fix their own schools."[52]

That first edition contained forty-one findings, ranging from, "A good way to teach children simple arithmetic is to build on their informal knowledge," to, "Unexcused absences decrease when parents are promptly informed that their children are not attending school."[53] Most were commonsensical, even obvious, yet each also rested on a foundation of research whose robustness was a matter of fair scholarly consensus. Even the president of the AERA praised the volume's accuracy and soundness.

We had met the first part of Bennett's challenge. And the dissemination effort was unsurpassed, beginning with the White House hoopla, duly relayed to the nation on the evening network news. There was front-page attention in major daily papers and mass mailings to every professional organization and journal anyone could name, as well as to all school superintendents in the country. We exhausted the publication budget of the research office by printing a half million copies to be sent free to anyone who dialed an 800-number in Washington or mailed a postcard to Colorado. And in short order that enormous stack of booklets melted away.

Never before or since, so far as I know, have so much effort and money gone into making the fruits of education research comprehensible and accessible to practitioners—and to the general public.

Yet I came to see that we had failed with the second half of Bennett's assignment. About a year later, to take a single example, I was visiting a well-regarded western school system where the superintendent asked me to lunch with his high-school principals, perhaps eighteen of them in all. Invited to make some remarks, I sought to launch the conversation by holding up a copy of *What Works* and inquiring

how many of them were acquainted with the booklet, supposing
that by now most would have examined it and we could talk about
implementing some of the findings. It turned out, however, that
only four of them were even aware of its existence; two had actually
held copies in their hands; and one of these was enthusiastically
using it as a catalyst for faculty discussions in his school.

One out of eighteen, in a major metropolitan school system whose
superintendent is a strong leader and regular participant in national
education discussions. So much for our peerless dissemination effort.
If the combination of a quality product, national media attention,
maximum use of the "bully pulpits" of a high-profile cabinet secretary
and popular president, and free copies on request could not seize
the attention of these high-school principals in a year's time, it was
reasonably certain that few of their teachers were making use of
What Works and that its practical impact on their students was
nil.

Some people at least got hold of the book. St. Paul superintendent
David Bennett (no relation) had it reprinted and gave a copy to
every school system employee. A fifth-grader in Kenmore, New York,
asked for one to give his parents for Christmas. An Ohio mother
wrote that the "booklet has already given me ideas to help her [child]
learn more." At meetings I've attended in recent years, someone
occasionally cites *What Works* as a good example of the kind of
thing the federal government should do more of.

Still, I can't get those high-school principals out of my mind, nor
can I ignore Feistritzer's survey findings that fewer than one-quarter
of public school teachers read professional journals as often as once
a week, and that they are more apt to pore over *Good Housekeeping*
than *Instructor*, more likely to peruse *TV Guide* on a regular basis
than *Learning*.

How does one get fresh information before educators? With so
much foolishness circulating in the upper atmosphere of the field,
there is some virtue in inefficient distribution. Yet if educators are
impervious to new (or sound old) knowledge—and to changing their
ways on the basis of it—the prospects for fundamentally altering
what happens in our schools seem terribly dim.

ON THE RIGHT

The familiar "liberal" and "conservative" labels have lost their
meanings in contemporary education debates. Most people who

carry the latter sobriquet turn out to be mightily vexed with the status quo and to spend their time agitating for revolutionary changes in well-established assumptions, in the rules by which the system operates, and in its power relationships and governance arrangements. By contrast, those commonly dubbed liberals tend to be more satisfied with the basic formations that have evolved over time in public education and more resistant to strategies for nonincremental change.

Numerous exceptions can be seen in both directions. But we must recognize that what I once dubbed education's "liberal consensus" had dominated policy discussions in this field for so many decades before the dawn of the excellence movement as to earn a kind of intellectual tenure.[54] Conserving the precepts of that consensus, while blending in some of the newer orthodoxies of the profession, has become the goal of many liberals, whereas sharply altering the inherited priorities is the mission of most conservatives. The result is a curious inversion of the language.

Radical does not necessarily mean wise, of course. The ideas that drive "conservative" education reformers are as vulnerable to confusion, oversimplification, single-mindedness, and goofiness as those of the establishment they seek to overthrow.

Most conservatives, Lawrence Uzzell observed in 1985, can be sorted into "neo-centralists" and "neo-pluralists" according to their views on education.[55] The former construe schooling as a means of cultural transmission, societal integration, economic stimulation, and nation building. In pursuit of those desiderata they are prepared to impose rules, standards, obligations, and accountability on the system, as well as to install a sizable core curriculum for all. Neo-pluralists, by contrast, are devoted to the primacy of parents and family, to individual freedom and choice, and to boundless competition among schools, with accountability entrusted to the marketplace.

These views sometimes produce unexpected results. Neo-pluralists, for example, occasionally turn out to be allied with ethnic and minority separatists who are wary of any curricular core and reject the view that the United States has (or should have) a common culture that all children need to understand. When asked what they would do about schools devoted to witchcraft or cult worship, managed by the Klan, hostile to the English language, or patronized exclusively by members of a single ethnic group, they reaffirm their confidence in parents to make wise decisions and in the marketplace to root out charlatans. When I inquire how we're to know whether children are learning enough, the response is much the same. And when we ask what is going to jar children and parents out of their complacency so that they will be moved to change to better schools, we don't get much of an answer at all. Where families are content, perhaps we are supposed to conclude that the system is working satisfactorily.[56]

Neo-centralism comes with hazards, too. Along with such fine-sounding features as a rich core curriculum and uniform high standards, we risk the emergence of overregulated, cookie-cutter schools with achievement floors that turn into ceilings. We also have to contend with the tricky issue of *who decides* what will be in the core that everyone is to learn, and when to make exceptions for those who cannot or will not learn it. As observers of the ongoing New York State brouhaha over social studies will attest, we could find ourselves with a centrally designed and state-mandated curriculum so appalling that we would seek ways to shield our children from its distortions and untruths.

As abstractions neo-centralism and neo-pluralism are irreconcilable, rooted in different beliefs about the nature of man, the proper functioning of society and the role of government vis-à-vis the citizen. In practice, however, American education already accommodates elements of both philosophies and it is possible to design thoroughgoing reforms that contain some of the more attractive features of each—as I attempt to do in chapter 14. We need to understand, though, that such amalgams are conceptually untidy and will displease fervent followers on both sides.

In addition to this big philosophical schism, conservatives manifest certain blind spots and hang-ups when they turn to education. Some get highly agitated over the so-called "social" issues that make their way into the schools: things like prayer, sex education, the "creationist" interpretation of science, bizarre courses (like "death education") that turn up in classrooms from time to time, and books with dirty words (or unconventional relationships) in the school library.

These are matters that deserve careful deliberation, to be sure, but they deflect our attention from the center ring of cognitive learning. They also bring out the pluralist in me. Many concerns can be accommodated through the mechanisms of public policy, but some people harbor such strong enthusiasms and singular anxieties that they will probably never find satisfaction under the big tent of public education (or in most private schools) and should consider placing their children in equally specialized schools or even teaching them at home. I favor a core curriculum for all, but in a free society you ultimately cannot compel a minor to learn something his parents find grossly offensive to their morals and beliefs.[57]

When it comes to very young children, conservatives are properly wary of statist alternatives to privately arranged child care and duly skeptical of lofty expectations raised by promoters of school-based day care and early childhood education. But they may place too much faith in parents. For severely disadvantaged and "at risk" children growing up in sorely disorganized households, we must be ready with alternatives. Where families can be strengthened and parents helped, we should by all means do so. Where that strategy fails, the interests of the youngsters and of the society they will inhabit must be given precedence over our visceral, but sometimes naive, confidence in the family unit. As I see "crack babies" entering kindergarten, for example, their lives perhaps already ruined, I part company with those who would leave all important decisions in the hands of parents, some of them little more than hedonistic children themselves. Mom and Dad are swell—when they do a good job of looking after Junior and Sis. But there is no more reason for conservatives to place all parents on a pedestal than for liberals to put all professional educators there.

Many conservatives are overly enamored of capitalism and the private sector, too. They want to bring these perspectives into schooling and to empower business leaders to shape education policy decisions. I see impressive potential in ideas such as private contracting with schools for educational services, as well as for hot meals and security guards.[58] As for the involvement of businessmen (and women), we should welcome them to the conference room, particularly when they do not check their bottom-line orientation at the door. But the public that needs to take charge of important decisions about education priorities also includes bus drivers and dental hygienists, truck gardeners and viola players. In certain domains, such as the requisites of economic competitiveness, we may be especially receptive to the advice of business tycoons. But when considering curricular content, school organization, and countless other matters, the hog butcher in Sioux City has as much standing as the CEO in Manhattan.

That vision of broad-based participatory democracy as our central social and political value is itself offensive to a handful of conservatives, some of whom still yearn for a premodern society of aristocracies and priesthoods, highly traditional and infused with religious faith. I (and Allan Bloom and William Bennett and others) periodically get attacked in the pages of *Chronicles*, for example, a publication of the Rockford Institute, for clinging to the ideas of democracy, rationalism, and equality.[59]

Finally, many conservatives have a charming but antiquated devotion to "local control" of schools that bears scant relationship to contemporary reality. I've already noted handsome exceptions here and there but, in the general case, we must recognize that local control today is indistinguishable from maintenance of the status quo under the thumb of the education establishment. As for curriculum, standards, and pedagogy, while it is possible for a perspicacious (and well-to-do) family to locate itself in a neighborhood that boasts schools superior to those down the road, and while such a defensive strategy is fine for those able to pursue it, more local control is not going to produce many more such schools: If it could, it already would have. Although we may someday regret handing more of the big decisions to states (and to such national groupings as the assembled governors), if we want revolutionary changes in American education we have to overhaul its power structure and its ingrained practices.

Remind me again, please, just who is conservative?

III

⚜

Taking Charge:

Revolutionizing Education from the Outside In

If this bright future is to be realized, the educational standards that have been established in the nation's schools must be raised dramatically. Put simply, students must go to school longer, study more, and pass more difficult tests covering more advanced subject matter.

—William B. Johnston and Arnold H. Packer, *Workforce 2000*, 1987

Setting matters right in American education will be the hardest domestic challenge we face in the closing decade of this millennium. The changes that are called for will be as disruptive of familiar patterns as those that have been weaving into our foreign policy deliberations since the axioms of the Cold War began to unravel in one direction and the Middle East situation unraveled in another. We need to embrace ways of thinking about education that are as different from the past as our emerging ideas about international affairs. We require a new education policy as urgently as a new foreign policy.

Yet it isn't going to happen spontaneously. The general populace is not yet unhappy enough, worried enough, or angry enough, while those inside the enterprise have a great deal invested in its traditional modes and assumptions. Richard J. Barnet could have been describing American education instead of international affairs when he wrote:

There are strong emotional, political, and bureaucratic reasons for resisting any basic change in the story line of the post-Second World War years; the central struggle of those forty-five years has served so many powerful interests so well for so long in so many different ways. . . . Bureaucratic inertia and self-protection are playing their customary role in slowing the processes of change. Most of the technocrats drawing up plans for the next century have comfortable niches in the present security system. They see no reason to dismantle it.[1]

I do not know whether we will muster the will to rebuild our education system, especially since success in this endeavor also demands major renovations of durable structures outside the schools. But it is not difficult to imagine what a revamped system would look like and the principles by which it would operate. We may not complete the construction project, but with a little imagination we can visualize the result.

It is radically different from what we're used to. It abandons the incrementalism of the eighties. Its design could be said to involve a whole new aesthetic. And that may be why we will ultimately shrink from telling the contractor to go ahead and break ground. So many people involved with American education are so deeply implicated in the old aesthetic.

A nameless Democrat on Capitol Hill might have been reflecting on our education system in 1990 rather than the attitude of Congress toward campaign finance reform when he said: "The House doesn't want [it] to happen. The Senate doesn't want it to happen. They just want to get Common Cause and the editorial writers off their backs. These guys are paralyzed by the fear of change."[2]

American education isn't going to fix itself. These guys, too, are paralyzed by the fear of change. They will look properly grave about the problems, will slap on the Band-Aids, deliver the speeches, hold the conferences, and smilingly receive the money, but their enterprise will not ultimately disrupt itself in fundamental ways. No institution does. So far as I know, none can. Hence when the society's well-being depends on fundamental changes being made in major institutions, these have to be initiated and prosecuted from outside by those whose interest in change exceeds their fealty to the status quo—and who wield enough power to prevail.

The traditional proprietors of the education system won't like this very much, but they shouldn't take it personally. "The statement that 'war is too important to be left to the generals,' " business executive Earle C. Williams sagely observed during a Virginia education conference in April 1990, "is not a comment on generals but on the importance of war." Our view of education should be much the same.

In the next four chapters, I attempt to sketch the rules by which the education system ought to operate, the ideas that should impel it, and the changes outside the schoolhouse door that also need to be made if those undertaken within are going to have any chance of success.

13

❦

A New Constitution for American Education

The basis of our political system is the right of the people to make and to alter their constitutions of government.
—George Washington, Farewell Address, 1796

All revolutions are disruptive yet not all of them are violent. Big changes in fundamental arrangements entail organizational disarray and political strife but not necessarily military action. Consider the "velvet revolution" of 1989 and 1990 in Eastern Europe and the astonishing social, political, and economic changes that have followed. Incremental reform within the framework of a still-repressive regime could not jumpstart the economy or right the wrongs of the old order in Poland or Czechoslovakia any more than perestroika could succeed in the Soviet Union. Something far more sweeping was called for.

Consider the historic decision to replace the Articles of Confederation with the Constitution of 1787. That was a revolution, too, though not a bloody one. It needed, first, widespread apprehension that the existing scheme, new as it then was, was not working satisfactorily and, second, the ability of thoughtful people to design a better plan, followed by ratification of their efforts by the public's chosen representatives.

Yet there was no clamor in the streets during the 1780s on behalf of a new constitution. Many people had specific grievances and discontents, and these sometimes bubbled to the surface in episodes such as Shays' Rebellion. But the underlying structural defects were evident only to a small band with widely disparate ideas about how to resolve the situation. Moreover, even after their long, sweaty, and inspired summer's labor in Philadelphia, no one could be certain

239

that the country would buy their product. Powerful vested interests and determined spokesmen defended the prior arrangements, warned against radical change, argued for moderation and incrementalism, and vowed to make the Articles work. Just give them another chance, a bit more time. The words of Richard Henry Lee and Patrick Henry, declaiming against the new national constitution more than two centuries ago, would need only modest editing to be marched into rhetorical battle on behalf of today's education establishment.

"If we remain cool and temperate," Lee wrote in 1787, "we are in no immediate danger of any commotions. . . . It is natural for men, who wish to hasten the adoption of a measure, to tell us, now is the crisis—now is the critical moment which must be seized, or all will be lost. . . . This has been the custom of tyrants and their dependants in all ages."[1]

Neither side gave any quarter. "It must be by this time evident to all men of reflection," Hamilton wrote in *The Federalist* #22, "that it is a system so radically vicious and unsound as to admit not of amendment but by an entire change in its leading features and characters."[2] This, too, sounds familiar. The eighteenth-century prose is superior, but otherwise his characterization of the Articles of Confederation resembles some of the verdicts on American education reported at the beginning of chapter 4.

Stirring rhetoric throws issues into high relief, but words alone do not make a revolution, not even the bloodless kind. The words have to touch a nerve, spark a passion, resonate in the deeper levels of one's being. They need also to be accompanied by a vision, one grand enough to be worth struggling for, vivid enough to seem realizable, precise enough to suggest a path from here to there. Unhappiness with the present arrangement is not sufficient. Bread lines, bad schools, slack constitutional arrangements—all these could go on forever, until and unless those victimized by them both glimpse a bona fide alternative and conclude that the pain associated with making the change could not be worse than the suffering induced by the status quo.

THINKING BOLDLY ABOUT IMPORTANT MATTERS

To revolutionize American education in the 1990s, we must come to believe that it could be very different, that those differences are important, and that we possess the capacity to make the change. Madison, Hamilton, and Jefferson are not around to help. Gorbachev is preoccupied. Thatcher is deposed. We do not have philosopher-kings to make prudential but difficult decisions for us. We do not want dictators to bend us to their will. We expect "the government" somehow to solve problems like this, yet we hold government in low regard and pay it as little heed as possible.

For better and for worse, the education revolution is not wholly within the orbit of public policy anyway. Radical change in this domain is quite beyond the capacity of government to make. The tendency of government will be—always is—to amend the status quo just enough to ease an immediate crisis, to squirt a little oil on the parts that squeak. Government, when pressed, can produce perestroika, but only the will of the people can make a revolution.

Fortunately, we have never lost our faith in the capacity of ordinary people, presented with reliable information and clear alternatives, to make sound choices about weighty matters confronting them-selves, their children, and their communities. These include issues of government policy, to be sure, but sometimes they also involve individual behavior changes that are important over the long run to our public and private well-being. As Jay wrote in *The Federalist* #3, "The people of any country (if, like the Americans, intelligent and well-informed) seldom adopt and steadily persevere for many years in an erroneous opinion respecting their interests."[3] Even where we may be too lazy or timorous to act boldly on our own, the mounting weight of opinion of our fellow citizens often has the power to sway us. So does our capacity to learn from experience.

Consider all the men and women who have stopped smoking cigarettes, those who have altered their eating patterns to lower their cholesterol levels, who are getting more exercise than they once did, who are recycling newspapers and cans rather than dump-ing them in a landfill, who are driving smaller cars, and who are keeping their homes cooler in winter and warmer in summer. These are not easy changes to make, and not everyone has the self-discipline to make them, but many have persevered, notwithstanding the dis-comfort and inconvenience.

Individuals make such changes for complex motives, and no two of us arrive at these decisions in quite the same way. But it's likely that most people who put themselves through major reforms do so because they can visualize both the downside and the up: the danger to themselves, their loved ones, and the commonweal that is posed when a bad situation is allowed to persist, and the good life that is apt to follow if changes are made.

When the matter at hand is important to the general welfare (and sometimes even when it is not), we do not leave individuals to their own visions and their consciences. We also place warnings on cigarette packs and in liquor advertisements. We flood the land with information about the dangers of drug abuse, not driving after drinking, and how to avoid contracting AIDS. Public agencies and private organizations tell us which vacuum cleaner works best and what toys are dangerous for toddlers. Via the processes of democratic government, we also make policy decisions that oblige major institutions to alter their accustomed operating procedures. Thus automobiles have seat belts, car dealers display gas mileage figures, airlines bar smoking, medicine containers have "child-proof" caps, and packages of hot dogs report their fat content.

When the stakes are really high, and the society risks serious damage if many individuals make bad decisions, we intrude still further into personal freedom. That is why we have speed limits, stock-trading regulations, minimum drinking ages, and laws against incest. Indeed, that is why every state has enacted a statute spelling out the minimum amount of schooling that its children must undergo. All civilized peoples (and most primitive ones) levy certain requirements and expectations on their young that must be met before the adult society will welcome them as full members. Though these norms curb individual liberty in the short run, they are not incompatible with democracy. To the contrary, they include the means by which a democratic society sustains itself from one generation to the next, trying to ensure that its participants are capable of governing themselves and of sharing in the preservation and betterment of the commonweal. They are, in short, part of the basic constitutional arrangements of civil society. And when they do not work well, they must be repaired or replaced, daunting though that task may seem. The cost of sustained neglect is simply too heavy to bear.

APPORTIONING POWER

Any revolution begins with weighty decisions about where power is to be vested—decisions that should grow out of a sense of the purposes and beneficiaries of the enterprise.

Because education enriches the individual who receives it, because learning is a consensual act, and because the schooling of children is intimately associated with parents' raising of them, we recognize a sizable private interest in education, and we expect individuals to wield significant leverage on behalf of themselves and their progeny. For this they need power.

Yet society also has rights and expectations with respect to the education of its next generation. The nation is at risk of economic decline and civic deterioration on account of ignorant children and faltering schools. Prosperity, domestic tranquillity, and civic vitality hinge on reform and renewal in this realm. Accordingly, we also assign education a substantial public role, and we expect our governing structures and policymakers to exercise considerable power on our collective behalf.

Critics of education often select one of these two missions and conclude that virtually all power should be ceded either to the individual or to the state. That's conceptually neat and it's simpler than my approach, but it does violence to the mixed public-private nature of the enterprise. Here I part company with the partisans of a free market in education as well as with the devotees of a wholly centralized or top-down management system.

Inside the profession, meanwhile, a very different conversation has been going on. Here we find a tendency to downplay *both* the legitimate interests of the individual consumer and the proper demands of the larger society, and to contend instead that those working within schools should define their mission and wield most of the power.[4] Because insiders always have the most direct stake in those decisions (not to mention the best lobbyists), over time they will usually prevail within this—or any other—policy arena unless deliberate steps are taken to keep this from happening.

There is obvious appeal in the proposition that when we want a specialized service we should turn to those who specialize in providing it. We can surely benefit from their expertise, we welcome their commitment, and in any case we can't do the job without them. Yet we ought *never* to cede control to the professionals. For the same reasons that we do not put doctors in charge of health-care policy, social workers in charge of welfare policy, soldiers in charge of military policy or bankers in charge of monetary policy, we are ill-advised to place educators in charge of education policy. As for their many organizations, in making an education revolution we owe no greater deference to the NEA or the ASCD than we do to the AMA when we are overhauling the Medicare program or to the American Trial Lawyers' Association when revising liability laws. They, too, represent major segments of honored professions. They, too, possess technical expertise. They are in no sense enemies, but our dreams are not always the subject of their prayers.

Thus we find ourselves seeking a workable balance in education among three sets of interests: the private interests of the individual consumer, the public interests of a free society that wants to endure and thrive with the help of its education system, and the legitimate but necessarily self-serving interests of those who work within that system. All have large roles to play, but none should dominate the stage. We must devise an arrangement that fully engages all three in the performance yet does not confer stardom on any. Each will need some power, but none should have so much as to bend the others to its whim. "It will not be denied," Madison wrote in *The Federalist* #48, "that power is of an encroaching nature and that it ought to be effectually restrained from passing the limits assigned to it."[5] We need a structure consisting of separated but overlapping authority, divided but intersecting spheres of influence, and effective checks and balances. I do not mean to overstate the parallel with the situation in Philadelphia in 1787, but one could say that today we need a new constitution for American education.

TEN PRECEPTS

In the next chapter I suggest some specifics. To launch the process of constitution writing, however, we first need to get our principles straight, to select as navigational aids those stars that will enable us to steer a true course to our destination. As I scan the sky, ten are indispensable.

First, *let us always recall that we operate an education system for the benefit of its consumers, not its proprietors or employees.* This is an obvious maxim, but one from which much else follows—and one we too often disown in practice after affirming it in theory. I do not make light of the well-being of teachers, principals, and others who labor within the education system, but our interest in them is essentially instrumental: as important means to the ends we seek, not as the primary object of our attention. In retrospect, William Bennett's largest achievement at the Education Department was to redefine its clientele. Instead of continuing to function as the establishment's representative within the federal government, looking after the suppliers of education services much as the Agriculture Department looks after farmers, the agency instead came to see its constituency as the consumers of those services—ordinary citizens concerned about the education of their children, the condition of their nation, and the value received for their tax dollars.

To the great relief of establishment figures who feared this change might prove permanent, the department reverted to its previous role after Bennett left. But for all the feathers he ruffled, his instinct about this was sound. He understood—and we need to remember—the correct answer to the question *cui bono?*

This is why we should keep a sense of proportion in reading those recurrent polls of teacher satisfaction and surveys of educators that ask whether they feel sufficiently important, involved, appreciated and compensated. Of course it's swell if they're enthusiastic. One can, however, visualize an enterprise whose employees are contented but that produces very little. It is also possible to imagine a situation in which people who vehemently complain about their lot are actually producing good results. In education—we have to keep reminding ourselves—it's the results that matter. It is also well to bear in mind that the surest way to create a hypochondriac is continually to ask someone if he's sure he feels okay and is absolutely certain that nothing hurts even a little.

Second, *we must organize, manage, and judge the system in relation to the outcomes that we seek from it.* This, too, seems self-evident, yet fealty to this principle would reverse the established modus operandi of public education. Our attitude toward resources, precedents, plans, and activities needs to become flexible and experimental rather than dogmatic and controlling. Short of harming children, we'll try anything that may work. When it comes to results, however, our stance should be doctrinaire and unbending. We will insist on them; we will reward them; and, when we do not get them, we will change the arrangements that are failing to produce them. As President Kennedy said of liberty, we should be prepared to "pay any price, bear any burden, meet any hardship, support any friend, oppose any foe" on behalf of our children's education.[6] Out with the "compliance" mentality of yore, under which those in charge paid little heed to the product so long as procedures were meticulously followed and resources divided fairly. In with a "bottom line" fixation, one that brings few regulations or mandates but that keeps a spotlight constantly trained upon the quality of the product.

Third, while we stipulate that education has many results, just as it has multiple purposes, *in the United States in the 1990s the outcome we must concentrate on and gauge our success by is cognitive learning.* That's what we've been doing badly at, what has placed the nation at risk. We also applaud the work of schools in socializing children, making them physically fit, nurturing their artistic sensibilities, shielding them from hostile conditions, encouraging them to be law-abiding and sober, and so forth. But this is a time to set priorities and hew to them. Our premier goal in elementary-secondary education needs to be a sharp rise in the intellectual skills and knowledge of the average youngster emerging into adulthood from the average school.

This implies—and I intend it to—*a standard of intellectual attainment that we will oblige all our institutions to produce and all our young people to reach*, a standard based on what adults will need to know and be able to do in the United States at the dawn of the next millennium. I believe it is the proper function of grown-ups to determine what children must learn—and then to insist that they study it until they have achieved the requisite proficiency. Few boys and girls are autodidacts, at least with respect to academic learning. Adults were placed on earth to see that all children get satisfactorily educated, whether they like it or not.[7]

Fourth, *civilian control of education is meant to ensure that we don't let the first three precepts tarnish with time.* The proper roles of public policy are to spell out objectives, priorities, and the criteria by which performance will be judged; to furnish the necessary resources; and to construct and manage the accountability system.

Fifth, though the ends of education are the responsibility of society in general to prescribe through the familiar processes of democratic government, *the means by which we reach those ends are the province of expert professionals.* Managing the education delivery system as effectively as possible is the foremost duty of that profession, as operating the health-care-delivery system is the province of medical professionals. At first glance this may appear to leave the "experts" with only the details and logistics to handle. On closer inspection we see that working within an outcomes-based approach can be a liberating experience for those who control the means.

Sixth, we should *revitalize the delivery system by vesting management authority and responsibility in building-level educators*, even as we acknowledge that the problem is nationwide and that the primary locus of control and public financing is with the fifty states. The school is the vital delivery system, the state is the policy setter (and chief paymaster), and nothing in between is very important. This formulation turns on its head the traditional American assumption that every city, town, and county bears the chief responsibility for organizing and operating its own schools as a municipal function. That is what we once meant by "local control," but it has become an anachronism no longer justified by research, consistent with sound fiscal policy or organizational theory, suited to our mobility patterns, or important to the public.

Most decisions should instead flow upward to the state or downward to the individual school. We need not assume that the twenty-first century has to cling to education governance-and-management arrangements that we invented in the nineteenth century. The country has changed too much for that.[8]

Neither should we any longer suppose that a lively and efficient delivery system ought consist of only one school in each locale, or that all must operate under traditional auspices. Competition among providers is desirable, and schools could be organized and operated by teacher partnerships, universities, museums, a state or federal agency, a neighborhood association, even a corporation or a church. Nor need they be restricted as to the territory from which their students may come. They can compete for clients on the same turf.[9]

Seventh, education's individual consumers—children and parents—bear ultimate responsibility for meeting the system's norms and fulfilling its expectations, and *they must therefore have the right to choose how they will do this.* We can encourage and prod them with tempting incentives for success and distasteful consequences for failure. We can supply them with trustworthy information about their progress thus far, about the distance remaining to be traveled, and about the efficacy of rival providers of education services. We can surround them with attractive options, both for reaching society's standards of cognitive achievement and for obtaining as much further education as they may crave. But we must then trust people to make reasonable decisions about what will work best for themselves and their children.

Eighth, *it is time to put in place a rich, solid core of common learning for all young Americans and an effective means of determining how well it is being learned.* Let's reject those old bugaboos that a "national curriculum" is a prescription for catastrophe and national exams are a plot to turn us into a land of dutiful robots. Let's instead open our eyes to the fact that we're living amid a catastrophe that might be ameliorated by embracing a national curriculum and an examination system to accompany it. The public already understands this. The education system now must catch up—and our leaders need to come to grips with it as well. Note, however, that I do *not* mean a curriculum enacted by Congress and enforced by federal bureaucrats or judges. I visualize a *nationwide* core curriculum matched to the education goals set by the president and governors in 1990. Instead of construing Roseanne Barr, *People* magazine, and New Kids on the Block as the American core curriculum, let's fashion one from high quality history, geography, science, math, literature, and writing.[10]

Ninth, *because people differ in their educational and career aspira-*
tions, in their intellectual acuity and commitment, and in their cultural
values and religious beliefs, the education system needs to respond
accordingly. Just as the system's governance arrangements should
embody a constructive tension among three major forces, so its
mode of delivery ought to balance the solemn imperative of a core
curriculum against the recognition of individual differences, preferences, and capabilities. Multiple providers on the supply side and
choice among schools on the demand side will go a great distance
toward accommodating those realities of the human condition. But
just as important is a change in attitude. Historically, Harvard Education Dean Patricia A. Graham notes, we responded to differences
among individuals and groups by altering the *content* of the curriculum to which they were exposed while delivering it in essentially
the same way to all (as if we obliged everyone to wear shoes, but
because the leather ones came only in a single size a lot of people
had to be shod in rags or paper). The result was a good education
only for segments of the population that were comfortable in the
intersection between the academic curriculum and the unvarying
mode by which public schools were organized (that is, for those
whose feet fit into the leather shoes).

Today, Graham says, and I fervently concur, we should give everyone our very best curriculum but should offer it through enough
different pedagogical and organizational modes that we can reasonably expect everyone to learn it (real leather for all, but cut and
stitched to fit virtually any foot). Let us recognize, Graham writes:

> That there is a body of knowledge, skills, and values that needs
> to be acquired and that there may be various means to acquire
> it but that everyone needs it. This idea is in direct contradiction
> to current educational policy, which is based on the "good"
> students getting one curriculum and "poor" students getting a
> watered down version. Education is a vintage wine, one that is
> damaged by adulterations.[11]

Tenth, at every level of the education system (child, classroom,
school building, locality, state and nation) *we must demand a steady*
flow of reliable information about student achievement and other
important outcomes. The blockages and obstacles described in chapter 9 must finally be blasted away. Mr. and Mrs. Brady have to know
how Janet and Jerome are doing in school, how their school is
performing, and how their state is faring. This information needs
to include comparisons with national standards and international

performance levels that are clear and intelligible to laymen. Only an informed consumer can make well-considered education choices. Only an informed policymaker can make wise decisions. Only an informed professional can make accurate diagnoses and take the right corrective steps. Only with such information in hand can the principle of accountability be realized.

The precepts set forth in this chapter have great power to revitalize American education. They could even foment a bloodless revolution.

14

℣

Schools Where Learning Matters

A Guided Tour

*And the greater the proportion of minds in any community,
which are educated, and the more thorough and complete
the education which is given them, the more rapidly, through
these sublime stages of progress, will that community
advance in all the means of enjoyment and elevation; and
the more will it outstrip and outshine its less educated
neighbors.*

—Horace Mann, 1848

I present this chapter with rare diffidence. Confident as I am of
the principles laid out in the preceding pages, they can be
put into practice in different ways, and I cannot be sure that one
scheme will prove superior to another.

A fringe benefit of construing states as the main arenas of education
reform is that, as Brandeis suggested in the epigraph introducing
chapter 3, these hypotheses could be tested in fifty different laborato-
ries, no two of which would likely go about it in quite the same
way. Several of them could be ventured at the local level as well.

Some of that innovation is already happening. Here and there
around the land, changes are under way along these lines, not because I suggested them but because others have reached similar
conclusions. With the possible exception of Kentucky, however, no
large jurisdiction has yet built all these features into its basic educational arrangements.[1]

Though it may be true of education, as has been said of physics, that God is in the details, I believe that getting the essential principles of design straight and mustering the resolve to put them into practice are our foremost tasks. Hence the next several pages are more in the nature of an architect's rendering for the client to examine than a detailed blueprint for the contractor to follow. Note, too, that we are still primarily concerned here with the in-school education of the typical child. In the final two chapters, I offer some additional thoughts about "at risk" youngsters and the changes we must make outside the schools.

GOALS FIRST

"In this life," says Chet Atkins, as often quoted by Lamar Alexander, himself chosen in December 1990 as U.S. Secretary of Education, "you have to be mighty careful where you aim because you're likely to get there."

If we know what we want children to know and be able to do upon completion of their formal education, other decisions begin to fall into place. If we don't know, can't agree or won't say what the system would be producing if it were doing the job right, we will wander aimlessly through the policy wilderness for years to come.

We should set for ourselves the sublime but arduous task of equipping every one of our children with the intellectual skills, knowledge and understanding that constitute a sound liberal education. We cannot wait for college to do this; we dare not restrict the benefits of such an education to those who persevere all the way to a bachelor's degree.

What exactly do I mean by liberal education? The term has been defined on many occasions by clearer thinkers and more eloquent writers, and I plead *nolo contendere*. Among several excellent formulations already available, I offer Arthur Bestor's thoughtful 1955 statement that:

> [L]iberal education is the education worthy of a free man. More than that, it is the education by which a man achieves freedom.
> . . . To make himself truly free, a man must break the intellectual chains that keep him a serf by binding him to his parish, by binding him to his narrow workaday tasks, by binding him to accept the

authority of those placed over him in matters temporal and
spiritual. A liberal education frees a man by enlarging and
disciplining his powers. He is no longer bound to his parish,
because education makes him spiritually a citizen of all places
and all times. His workaday tasks no longer subdue his mind to
their narrow demands, for he is large enough to cope with them
and with the great intellectual tasks of a free man as well. He is
no longer obliged to accept blindly the authority of those above
him, for they are above him no longer. In the things of the mind
he is their peer, and he can decide for himself, on as good grounds
as they, the great human issues that confront him. Thereby he is
entitled to be the citizen of a free state, participating in its highest
decisions and obeying no political mandates save those that derive
their ultimate sanction from his own consent. The test of every
educational program is the extent to which it trains a man to
think for himself and at the same time to think painstakingly.
Originality and rigor, imagination and discipline—these are not
pairs of mutually exclusive qualities. They are qualities that must
be welded together in a liberal education.[2]

That is a considerable assignment and a worthy mission. It could
be the declaration that sparks a revolution in American education.
It does not, however, translate easily into a particular body of knowledge, skills, or school practices, and we should not force it to. Fortunately, the delineation of curricular content in most subjects has
already been done with much finesse by the state of California under
Bill Honig's leadership.[3] Bennett's "James Madison" curricula for
elementary and high school also rank with the best specific formulations of core content for a universal liberal education.[4] E. D. Hirsch
is developing an elementary school curriculum that strives to impart
cultural literacy to all children. And the College Board has produced
an exemplary summary of academic skills and knowledge that secondary students should acquire en route to higher education, a
nourishing menu that we could also proudly serve to those headed
for other post-high-school destinations.[5]

Though far less detailed, the most important recent initiative to
outline the results we seek from compulsory education comprises
the six national goals that the president and governors set for the
year 2000. One of these bears repeating. It says that all youngsters
will leave grades four, eight, and twelve "having demonstrated competency over challenging subject matter including English, mathematics, science, history and geography," and that every school in the

land will "ensure that all students learn to use their minds well, so they may be prepared for responsible citizenship, further learning and productive employment in our modern economy."[6]

I'd relish the chance to add some subjects to the governors' list, as would most educators. But we would not err as a country if we held our initial efforts to their five.[7]

Whether limited or comprehensive, the core of what is learned must be the same for all Americans. Never again should curricular tracking darken our schoolhouse doors.[8] Every young person deserves a full measure of what Matthew Arnold termed the "best which has been thought and said," as well as real math, authentic science, and engaging history.

That every child's curriculum needs an academic core does not, of course, mean everyone is aiming straight for higher education. Some teen-agers are bent on full-time employment as soon as they finish (or quit) school. For them, as has often been noted, American society has not made good arrangements to smooth the passage from education to work. Unlike Japan, we see few major firms with well-established employment ties to the schools. Unlike Germany, we have no elaborate system of vocational and technical apprenticeships. These transitions need more attention than we've given them, not in slavish emulation of other societies but in ways that fit our own distinctive contours. Still, there are several sound reasons why closer attention to the school to work transition should not distract us from also building a universal academic core.

First, a far larger proportion of Americans eventually find themselves in college, community college, or other postsecondary education than is the case in any other land. We have a more obliging and flexible system, and we want individuals to be able to change careers if they wish. We are not prepared, as a society, to tell anyone that his or her initial post-high-school choice must be permanent. That means everyone ought to be ready for further education and training, even if they don't immediately want to avail themselves of it. Hence everybody needs a broad, liberal education.

Second, in survey after survey and statement after statement, employers have declared their willingness to provide job-relevant skills to employees who possess good habits, sound character, solid basic skills, a fund of necessary background knowledge, and the capacity for further learning. If the formal education system will equip all its graduates with those qualities, employers will take on job-specific training.

Third, jobs and careers are not the only reasons we go to school.

Education also serves to prepare us as autonomous, self-controlled, and virtuous beings—as citizens, voters, parents, community members, participants in the good life of our society and culture. Beyond our customary utilitarianism, most Americans sense that there is more to education than getting ready to earn one's living. On the 1990 Gallup education survey, more than 67 percent of respondents insisted that math, English, history, and government also be part of the school curriculum for those *not* planning to attend college, and 58 percent favored science for them as well.[9]

Establishing a rich core curriculum for all our students does not mean that everyone will move through it in lockstep, however. Some learn faster than others. Some will go far beyond the required minimum—wherever that is set—while others struggle for a long time to reach that point. But universal mastery of a common core is what will hold us together as Americans, equalize our opportunities for happiness and prosperity, and revitalize the nation's civic, economic, and cultural life.

Though the core is fundamental, it ought not occupy the entire curriculum of our schools. We have understood since Aristotle's time that "there is no general agreement about what the young should learn either in relation to virtue or in relation to the best in life."[10] States and localities differ in their priorities and individual schools in their specialties and emphases. People have singular needs, interests, and passions of their own. All these differences need to be welcomed and accommodated, and one place to do so is in the portion of the curriculum lying outside the core. Reasonable people can debate how large that portion should be. My view is that about two-thirds of the high-school curriculum, perhaps 80 percent of the middle school program, and virtually all of the content of primary education should be the same for everybody, with the remainder given over to options, preferences, and specialties. But that's a debate worth having, and it won't come out the same everywhere in the country.

Moving from identifying the core subject categories to defining just what we mean by "competency over challenging subject matter" is the hardest part. We want standards lofty enough that, when our youngsters achieve them, we will no longer be a nation at risk. Minimum proficiencies of the sort that states have used as high-school exit standards will not suffice. Yet we also want our standards to be achievable by essentially all our young people, provided they work hard and long enough at it and that we give them enough instructional assistance.

How high these standards may need to be hit me recently when I saw the English translation of part of a national mathematics exam used in Japanese industrial high schools. Not academic high schools, mind you, but those attended by girls and boys pointed toward the work force. It was a multiple-choice test, the bane of trendy American assessment experts. But it consisted of complex, multistage, real-world problems, most of them at the intersection of math and science. And it was far more difficult—*every problem on it* was harder—than I could handle, three university degrees notwithstanding.

This is what the competition expects its ordinary students and future blue-collar workers to be able to do at the conclusion of secondary school. Yes, the country is Japan, and yes, the subject is math, perhaps the most daunting combination on the planet. But how much lower can we set our standards, even in math, and still expect to compete successfully?

Were we abruptly to impose such norms on young Americans attending today's schools, the vast majority would fail. Yet the purpose of setting standards is that they will be reached, not that people will fall by the wayside. Hence we must steel ourselves for major changes that go well beyond the establishment of achievement standards.

Who decides where to place our new norms? Whom do you trust to say what constitutes a satisfactory education for your child— and for the new employee in your office, and for the young person walking down the other side of the street late at night? I am reminded of William F. Buckley, Jr.'s celebrated quip that he would rather be governed by the first thousand people in the Boston phone book than by the Harvard faculty. It's obvious that the standard-setting process should include education experts of many kinds, but in this, as in all great political choices facing a free society, it seems to me fundamental that the pragmatism, the common sense, and the dreams of the "general public" should predominate. It is the public interest that we are seeking through this process to secure. After weighing all the evidence, listening to all the arguments from expert witnesses, interested parties, prosecutors and defense attorneys, and being advised by learned judges, this is a matter where we want life-and-death decisions made by a jury of our peers.

One such process is already under way, albeit tipped a bit too much toward the professionals. The NAEP Governing Board is currently striving to specify achievement levels that can be used in analyzing and reporting NAEP data. As a matter of policy, the board has determined that in every subject and each of the grades (four, eight, twelve) at which the national assessment tests are administered, there should be established a "proficient" level that reasonably embodies the governors' idea of curricular competency. In addition, there should be a higher ("advanced") level, representing world-class academic performance, and a lower ("basic") level as well.

What will these look like? A twelfth-grader judged proficient in math and science might, for example, be able to answer correctly the sample questions given in chapter 1—something fewer than one in ten of them can do today. An eighth-grader at the proficient level in history and English might be able to compose a short but cogent essay explaining why European settlers crossed the Atlantic. A fourth-grader at the advanced level might be able to read a story and then write several imaginative paragraphs outlining a different ending for it.

The board is using a labor-intensive, consensus-seeking process to derive these levels, involving educators, parents, business representatives and other laymen, college professors and subject-matter specialists, and state and local policymakers. The process entails much palaver. But as it evolves, we should find ourselves by mid-decade with a coherent definition of proficiency at each of these three grades in all five subjects identified by the governors and president.[11]

That is one way to derive a standard of achievement for the country as a whole and perhaps for the states. Due to statutory and structural limitations on NAEP, however, it cannot assist Mr. and Mrs. Rodriguez to determine how Consuela herself is faring, or to gauge the performance of her class, her school, or the local school system. If federal officials ever remove the shackles, the achievement levels by which we're gauging national and state performance could be used for these vital purposes as well. For the national exam outlined below to come into existence, something along these lines will eventually have to occur.

AS MUCH TIME AS NECESSARY

My gravest suggestion is likely also to prove the most contentious. Once we have identified the core skills and knowledge that we expect our young people to acquire before entering adult society, we must oblige them to engage in some sort of systematic study until they actually reach that standard, however long it may take.

Of course, we'll need a process for waiving or modifying that requirement in individual cases. Education is not punishment. Some volition is required for learning, and nobody relishes the image of a hulking twenty-four-year-old confined against his will among the tiny desks and chairs of a third-grade classroom.

The large point, however, is that outcome standards are pipe dreams if we lack any means of enforcing them with respect to individual students and schools. Of all existing U.S. education policies, surely the most foolish are compulsory attendance laws written in terms of birthdays. Today we allow a young person to drop out on reaching a certain chronological age (usually sixteen), whether he or she has learned anything or not. Those well-acquainted with adolescents may share my view that sixteen- and seventeen-year-olds are perhaps the worst-qualified people in the entire society to decide what is in their own long-term best interests, especially when the "correct" decision entails waking up early, day after day, to study chemistry and literature. And of course the young people most apt to drop out are those who have had the least success in school, those farthest from meeting any reasonable standard of intellectual competency.

I do not suggest that everyone must sit under the roof of a conventional school building until they meet the exit standard. Study can take place in a thousand places, including work sites, neighborhood centers, and one's own home. Learning can happen in high-technology research centers as well as on Georgian campuses. Instruction can occur on the shop floor, in the lab and library, even on television, not only from lectures and books. It can come about in July as well as March, on Saturday as well as Tuesday, and at 9 P.M. as well as 9 A.M. It need not always be overseen by a teacher, either; the hundreds of thousands of Americans earning high-school-equivalency certificates each year attest to the feasibility of organizing one's own program of study. The important point is that every young person would be obliged to engage in some program of systematic study until he or she can meet the core learning standard for entry into adult society. Individualizing such a program is not beyond our capacity.

Perhaps the best way to enforce this standard is to confer valuable benefits and privileges on people who meet it, and to withhold them from those who do not. Work permits, good jobs, and college admission are the most obvious, but there is ample scope here for imagination in devising carrots and sticks. Drivers' licenses could be deferred. So could eligibility for professional athletic teams. The minimum wage paid to those who earn their certificates might be a dollar an hour higher. We'll return to such possibilities in chapter 16.

I'm not suggesting prison for those who haven't learned. Still, I know this approach sounds awfully severe. Civil libertarians will proclaim Everyman's right to remain ignorant and unskilled. Many educators will balk at the idea of learning that is coerced by external incentives and disincentives. I agree that we should make the subject matter as enticing as we can, the instruction as stimulating, the classroom as supportive. Our preference should always be for kindling that inner flame that, once lit, makes learning a self-motivated pursuit. But when it will not kindle, or when it lights for some subjects but not for others, we should be ready with external motivators. Similar reasoning brought the Commission on the Skills of the American Workforce, chaired by two former secretaries of labor, to its ambitious 1990 recommendation that the United States institute an assessment-based "Certificate of Initial Mastery" and make this a precondition for higher education and for employment.[12] My view is essentially the same.

Wherever such a standard is pegged, if it is uniform we must expect some people to take longer than others to reach it. Incorporating that reality into our educational arrangements is, therefore, another of the fundamental changes we must make. The purpose of an exit standard, I repeat, is to have something that practically everyone eventually meets, not something that large numbers fail to attain.

Along with replacing our familiar age-bound conception of compulsory attendance, therefore, we need to erase the unrealistic (though widely held) assumption that all youngsters can learn the same amount during a 180-day school year. We need to break the age-grade link. That means doing away with the traditional twelve grades of school. Instead we should array the skills and knowledge that young people need to acquire into three broad "bands" of learning—primary, intermediate, secondary—and give each person as much time as necessary to pass through one band and into the next.

This may sound far-out, but the National Governors' Association has also recommended moving away from age grading, especially in the early years of school. Kentucky's comprehensive school reform plan does away with age-grading below fourth grade, and several other states, including Mississippi and Florida, are experimenting with this approach.

The average student may take four years to move through each band, twelve years in all. But some will tarry longer and others will proceed faster. Passing through a band is not just a matter of putting in an arbitrary amount of time. It means acquiring and demonstrating—on exams and other measures—the skills and knowledge that are needed before starting the next band, with these standards cumulating across the bands to become the level of learning that we expect of all new adults.

Parents accustomed to judging how their child is progressing in school by grade-to-grade promotion will of course need different kinds of feedback. Accurate, regular reports on how the youngster is doing vis-à-vis the outcome goals for his present band should be an acceptable substitute.[13]

In order to ensure that children can succeed in the primary band, they need to be prepared to learn when they enter it. Significantly, President Bush and the governors made readiness for learning the first of their six national education goals. Achieving this means paying careful attention to preschoolers. I believe we should also develop a pre-primary band, the exit point from which is readiness for academic learning of the kind traditionally begun in first grade. Attendance in the pre-primary band could begin, at the parent's option, anytime after the age of three, and would be voluntary—but if a child does not meet the school-readiness standard before entering the primary band, the parent must expect a relatively slow start for the youngster and probably longer than four years in that band.[14]

This is *not* the same thing as extending Head Start (or any other existing program) to everyone who wants it. Unless we also change what happens *after* preschool, we won't get the overall cognitive gains we need.

An important asset of learning bands instead of grades is that they repeal the no-win alternatives of "grade retention" and "social promotion." Making a child repeat the same experience in which he has failed—while his classmates move on to the next grade—is not very constructive. But promoting him willy-nilly into a grade for which he is academically unready does him no kindness either. If we had no grades, and did not pretend that all nine-year olds should have reached identical levels of academic proficiency, schools could be far more effective with both slow and fast youngsters.

If our exit standard is as ambitious as it ought to be, virtually every student will need to spend substantially more than 9 percent of his or her first eighteen years learning all that is needed to reach it. We tend to learn only that which we study and the amount we learn is roughly proportionate to the time we spend studying. So long as young people in other nations devote far larger shares of their lives to academic learning, our standards will perforce be lower than theirs and our children will never equal theirs in cognitive accomplishment. Hence our new-found flexibility with respect to learning time must also extend to the school day, week and year, as well as to homework and other out-of-school education.

We might, for example, imagine schools open for business as many as three hundred days a year but with some students present for more of those days than others. Each year would have, say, seven instructional modules of seven weeks each, of which five or six would be required, the others available as options for those who want or need them. Similarly, while five days may continue to be the usual school week, a sixth day should be provided, too. And the school should routinely be open from 7 A.M. to 7 P.M., both as a safe harbor from the hazards of the street and as a place where teachers, tutors, and counselors are ready to advance the learning process. If we are serious about equipping all children to meet our high expectations, many will need that extra time and help.[15]

The flexible calendar further eases the pressure to make a "pass-fail" decision in June. For some youngsters an additional module or two will be all they need to catch up. For others the sixth day of school or a regular late-afternoon tutorial session may do the trick. The added availability of school will also assist modern families with their day- and summer-care problems, while making possible year-round jobs—and commensurate salaries—for teachers and other educators. And the all-day, all-year use of the school building is a more efficient way to operate this valuable facility, as well as a more satisfactory arrangement for auxiliary social services that are efficiently supplied under the school roof but must not detract from teaching and learning time.

My goal is not to oblige children to sit in class longer. It is, however, to set a standard of achievement much loftier than the ones most American youngsters are reaching today, recognizing that if such a norm is actually to be met, many of them *will* need to devote substantially more time to study and learning. Some of this increase, perhaps a great deal of it, could take place outside the school. But we need to be ready to supply as much of it on the school's premises as the children require.

The foregoing plainly presages fundamental changes in the educational expectations of our society and in the lifestyles of our children and their families. This will not be popular, but it is part of the revolution that we need.

INSTITUTIONAL ACCOUNTABILITY, TOO

Thus far I have placed the primary burden of accomplishment on the individual receiving the education. We must also construct a system in which its providers are accountable for the quality and effectiveness of what they are supplying.

"Outcomes-based accreditation" is an idea that several states (among them Maryland, Indiana, North Carolina, Alabama, Missouri, and Louisiana) are developing and others are considering. In theory, this means that a school will be allowed to operate only so long as its results are satisfactory. If they aren't, then like a college whose accreditation is threatened, the school is placed on probation and, if insufficiently improved within a reasonable period of time, it is closed down.

It's an attractive idea. Unfortunately, at the college level accreditation has worked abysmally as a form of educational quality control. Because postsecondary outcome measures are weak-to-nonexistent, the process has concentrated on inputs and resources and, even then, because it is primarily a peer-review process, it has depended on the willingness of college officials to get tough with one another, something they are notoriously loath to do. Behind the attractive face we find no teeth.

The pitfalls of accreditation may be even deeper at the elementary-secondary level. In higher education, 3,400 institutions compete and no geographic boundaries separate their markets. If a college closes, plentiful alternatives exist for present and future students. As our public school system is presently organized, however, we ordinarily find a single school serving a particular area. How likely are the managers of the accreditation system actually to close the only school in the neighborhood, no matter how ineffectual it may be? What if it is in a region of particular ethnic sensitivities and political volatility? What if its principal is just a couple of years from retirement?

Yet when the possibility of being shut down is not perceived as real, all the warnings and probations in the world will have little effect. A state takeover and possible loss of jobs makes the risk more vivid. I suspect, however, that so long as essentially all schooling is provided by a public monopoly, so long as there is no bona fide competition among suppliers, and so long as quality control is handled exclusively by the same agencies that are responsible for service delivery, we are not going to get very far with this kind of institutional accountability.

We know that bad schools *should* be vulnerable to closure and those responsible for their failure should be obliged to seek other work. We also know that good schools deserve rewards, accolades, and privileges, as do their professional staff and other employees. Once we have clear outcome goals for all schools, once performance standards are specified and a good information feedback system is installed, accountability becomes possible through several means. What is needed for it actually to occur is to install *both* a top-down mechanism, operated by the state, and a marketplace mechanism driven by the consumers.

The marketplace is achieved by encouraging multiple suppliers to compete with each other in the delivery of education services, and by according to every child and family the right to choose the provider they favor. The state's indispensable role in this is to manage the examination-and-information-feedback system by which consumers get reliable information about alternative suppliers (and about their own child's progress at the hands of the present provider).

Educational choice is desirable for many reasons.[16] Moreover, its absence is unjustifiable. To me, it is a public policy sin to force a child against her will to attend a dismal school that she and her parents would flee were it not for the coercive power of the state. It is a public policy sin to deny poor people the same kinds of educational options for their children that we routinely accord to the wealthy. It is also a public policy sin to oblige a child gifted in art and music to attend a school that specializes in science and math—or to attend an "all-purpose" school that doesn't respond to anybody's special needs, talents, or enthusiasms. The rigidities of today's sole-provider education system keep driving people out of it. Every few months, another friend with school-age children reports that they've opted for private schooling after discovering that the local public authorities are inflexible and smug. The 1990 Christmas cards, for example, brought word from old friends in Colorado that their neighborhood junior high school principal refused to provide any sort of program for gifted students, on the grounds that young adolescents should be shielded from competition and comparison. My friends agonized only long enough to conclude that their fealty to the *concept* of public education must not get in the way of doing right by their own child.

Start with those sobering considerations. Then add the salutary effects on quality, efficiency and accountability that come from the workings of the marketplace; the fact that choice among providers is a standard feature of almost every social policy domain *except* elementary-secondary education; the American people's keen enthusiasm for choice, rivaling in intensity their unhappiness with the current education system; and then remind yourself again that we run this system for the benefit of its consumers, not its suppliers. Weigh those thoughts, and then see whether you agree with me that we should put the burden of proof on those who oppose choice.

But oppose it they do, especially when it is suggested that multiple providers be encouraged to compete within the same territory and that legitimate schools may be operated under nongovernment auspices, too.

Choice confined to public education is better than no choice at all, and the fact that nine states have already embraced interdistrict choice, while many localities are operating magnet and alternative schools or open-enrollment plans, signals that the political environment is no longer hostile to this philosophy. Yet we still treat such arrangements as exceptional, and most of the education establishment continues to protest them.[17] As for withdrawing the exclusive franchise of the public school system, as suggested in chapter 13, after years of being shunned completely this is again beginning to be seriously talked about. Discontent with existing school reforms, openness to more radical alternatives, the persuasive pens of Ted Kolderie, Joe Nathan, Sy Fliegel, John Chubb, and Terry Moe, and the remarkable political coup that Polly Williams pulled off in Milwaukee have combined to make this idea a thinkable option. I think it needs to become a fundamental operating assumption.

NATIONAL EXAMS

The reader is by now aware of my frustration at the wretched state of our consumer information system. Most of the data we need, we cannot get. Much of what we get, we cannot trust. Of that which we can trust, far too much is obsolete, unintelligible to laymen, or unsuited to crucial analyses and comparisons.

So long as this situation endures, we will continue to inhabit a fools' paradise, bereft of the data about individual children and schools that would make possible true choice and accountability, never sure how our daughters and sons are doing, uncertain whether the country is making progress.

The present arrangement is unacceptable. It can be set right, however, provided we are willing to make some fundamental changes. Here is what I think these are:

- We should scrap all current tests and testing programs except those that teachers give for purposes of monitoring and diagnosing

their students and those that private organizations such as the
College Board give for purposes of college admission.[18]

• In their place we should institute a comprehensive new national
examination program, similar to the "external exams" used in
other countries—and to the Advanced Placement, International
Baccalaureate, and New York Regents exams already in operation
here. These exams would be developed outside the schools and
administered under secure conditions by an independent public
authority, paid for by (but not under the thumb of) the federal
government.[19] Unlike its overseas counterparts, which typically
click in at the end of secondary school, the new U.S. exams would
be given at three stages in the typical student's school experience.
Under the current grade structure, pupils would take suitable
versions of them in grades four, eight, and twelve, as the governors
suggested, in at least the five subjects they identified. If we replace
grades with "learning bands," as I have urged, the national exams
would be administered to students preparing to move from one
band to the next.

• The new exams will differ from today's National Assessment
program in that every child will take them and obtain a personal
score. This is *not* a sample-based program that yields results only
for institutions and political units.[20] And the exams will differ
from today's familiar standardized testing programs, too, in that
teachers and schools will be encouraged to "teach to" them; indeed,
preparing students for these exams will comprise a sizable portion
of what schools do. Though the actual questions will be secure,
the exam syllabus will track the curriculum. Thus the core curriculum will consist of the content and skills the exams probe, and
vice versa. Working in league with the curriculum, these exams
are meant to *alter* behavior in millions of individual instances.

• They will be high-quality exams with essay, free-response, and
open-ended questions, not just multiple-choice items. As techniques of assessment and measurement improve, so will the exams.
As it becomes possible to incorporate simulations, performances,
portfolios, computer adaptations, and other innovative methods,
this should be done, too.

• At each stage, the exam will be scored (as Advanced Placement
tests now are) from one to five, with three representing "competency over challenging subject matter" and five representing a
level of performance equivalent to that of strong students in other
advanced countries.[21] To score a three on the twelfth-grade version

is to meet the national standard for entry into adult society. To score a five is to be ready to compete as an equal with the best that Germany or Korea can offer. (To permit such comparison, the new exams will have to be administered to a sample of children in other countries, too, or else equated to exams already given in those lands.)

• Because these will be exams worth studying for, we can be relaxed about the appearance of commercial tutoring centers, American counterparts to Japanese *juku*. Since doing well on these exams means mastering the content of the syllabus, not acquiring clever test-taking techniques, the more different settings in which people can prepare for them the better. Clubs and organizations might help their members (or their members' children) to learn. An industry of supplementary audio, video, and print material is bound to spring up. The more the merrier.[22]

• The exams will appraise individual achievement but will be designed so that their results can be aggregated, analyzed, and compared at all the other levels we care about: the classroom, the school, the local system, the state, and the nation as a whole.[23] Because they will be given annually, changes over time at each of these levels can be detected as well.

• Those designing, administering, and underwriting the national exams will control nothing but testing program. As external examiners, they will give you your results but will not mete out consequences. At the national level, therefore, these will be no-stakes exams. Others, however, can be expected to use the results for a variety of high-stakes purposes of their own. They may base students' progress from one grade or learning band to the next on their exam performance. They may make high-school graduation or college entry contingent on achieving a certain score. Parents may choose schools on the basis of the school's—or their child's— performance. Officials may confer bonuses on the staff in some schools and terminate the contracts of those in others, according to how well their students do. Public agencies may grant or withhold work permits and drivers' licenses from individuals. Employers may pay more—or less—depending on exam results. The possibilities are many. But because the exam itself has no consequences, others are also free to ignore its results or to augment them with other data they deem germane. As noted earlier, my own view is that important decisions about individuals ought not hinge exclusively on test scores.

• Because exam results can be aggregated and analyzed at each level from the individual child to the entire state and nation, and because they can also be monitored over time, many jurisdictions will need no other formal indicators of cognitive achievement. But because the new exams will be tailored to the core curriculum, some states, localities and schools will want to supplement them with assessments of student performance in domains outside that core.

• Most important, Mr. and Mrs. Brady will receive Janet's results in a form they can understand: five subjects, five possible grades on each. They will also see results from her classroom and school, their community and their state, other states, and the country as a whole. They will be able to compare these results with student performance levels in other lands as well. If they aren't sure how Janet or her school is doing and would rather not wait years between results, they can select a school that administers the national exam (or a clone of it) more often. Or they can go to a walk-in test center and there, for a small fee, Janet can take a grade-appropriate version of the exam, whose results are mailed to the Bradys within three weeks. If we can get our blood-pressure and cholesterol levels checked whenever we like, why not our children's cognitive-achievement levels?[24]

SCHOOL-LEVEL DECISIONS

Much has been said and written about school-site management and school restructuring, two popular but perilously fuzzy terms. In line with the reapportionment of power outlined in chapter 13, we should transfer practically all decisions about the *means* of education to the school team—so long as the ends to be attained have been specified, the information and accountability systems are in place, and the customers can choose among suppliers. Under those circumstances, it is reasonable and educationally sound to liberate the experts to make choices of their own and to run their schools as they think best.

The issues that they will handle are numerous and weighty. Essentially all organizational, pedagogical, and management decisions belong with the school team, beginning with, Where to locate the school? Which months, days, and hours will it operate? What will it specialize in, and how will it distinguish itself from others? How to organize the instructional process so that students learn what they're supposed to and more? Who will work in the school and on what terms? How to allocate resources between, say, the gym and the library, computer-aided instruction and instrumental music, fourth grade science and sixth grade history? How to tailor instructional strategies to the capabilities and preferences of the staff as well as the values of parents? How to reward outstanding teachers and what to do about weak ones? How to engage parents and community? How to link the school's efforts with those of other agencies, from police to child-welfare authorities? What auxiliary services to provide on the school premises? Which textbooks to use, how heavily to use them, and what instructional materials to develop on site? Which controversial novels to allow on the shelves? What extracurricular activities to organize? How best to structure tutorial services for children needing extra help?

And that's only the beginning. Few operational or instructional decisions should be withheld from the school site, provided its staff is capable of making them and of producing satisfactory results. I believe that individual schools should even have the authority to contract with private vendors for everything from janitorial services and hot lunches to advanced instruction in German and specialized math assistance for dyslexic youngsters.

How many school teams are presently up to handling all these decisions and responsibilities is an open question. How many really want all those burdens is unknown. Their numbers are surely not as great today as we would like, though if this modus operandi became the norm they will surely increase. But all should be given as much leeway as they want and prove able to handle. When results are satisfactory, more slack should be placed on the line. When they are not, the tension should be increased. Parents retain the right to exit. The information system will yield to them—and everyone else—ample data about the school's performance. For their parts, state and local authorities retain the power to intervene, in extreme cases even to take over the management of the school, replace its staff, withdraw its accreditation, or close it down as the health authorities shut a pestiferous luncheonette.

In that sense, the cession of authority to the building level is provisional on both sides. The school team, too, must determine how much authority it wants. In England, where individual schools can "opt out" from control of local public authorities if they wish, only a few dozen chose to do this in the first year. I believe that is the soundest approach for American schools, too, enabling only those that want to and can handle it to free themselves from central-management shackles. I wish we could be more sweeping, installing site management across the board tomorrow in all 83,000 public schools as well as in the others that will spring up.[25] But some would be paralyzed by the abrupt acquisition of greater decision-making power, and there are others where all that stands between passable school performance and educational meltdown is the obligation to follow standard rules and procedures. We cannot sacrifice children to the theory of school restructuring, attractive as it is.

EXPERT PERSONNEL FOR THE SCHOOLS

Who will work in these reconstituted schools? Who will lead them? Who will teach our children so well that they not only pass the national exam but also become credits to their schools, communities, and families?

I have four suggestions for increasing the numbers of outstanding teachers and would make parallel recommendations for principals and other key professionals.

First, we should hugely enlarge the pool of *prospective* teachers and thereby enhance our ability to choose and retain individuals on the basis of their knowledge, ability, character, and instructional effectiveness. In the past, we limited ourselves to recent graduates of state-approved training programs who can obtain a teaching certificate by matching their college transcript to a course list maintained by a clerk in the state education department. Where we have not been able to find enough people who are qualified in those terms, we have resorted to waivers, "emergency" credentials, and sometimes alternative certification. The alternative-certification strategy was meant to redefine the pool itself but, as we saw in chapter 11, that has actually occurred in just a few jurisdictions. It's time to complete the process.

My rule of thumb is simple: Any well-educated adult of sound character, who knows a subject and is willing to try teaching it to children, should be considered a candidate for entry into the classroom.[26]

We can readily determine whether someone is well-educated, knows a subject, and what his character references think. His willingness to try teaching is demonstrated by interest in the job. All that remains is to ascertain whether what he knows can be successfully taught to pupils—and pique their interest in acquiring more.

As yet we have no sure way of checking this without placing the prospective teacher in a classroom and seeing what ensues. So that is what we ought to do, accompanying the trial with plenty of supervision and advice from veterans, and with such training in the arts of pedagogy as the neophyte teacher may want. That choice is the teacher's, but ample opportunities should be available throughout one's classroom career.

At the end of a year or two on the job, we either will or won't have a novice beginning to turn into a journeyman. If we do, he should be given a regular job. If we don't, he should be encouraged to seek (or return to) another line of work.

It's not quite that simple, but it's really not very complicated. It is how good private schools have always hired their faculty. And if we find ourselves with a competent instructor who wants to spend only a few years in the classroom, before or after embarking on a different career path, we should be grateful for the time we have rather than fretting that something has gone awry.

Second, we should compensate teachers in accord with the dictates of the marketplace. That means paying good ones more than bad ones; those in shortage subjects (such as science, math, and special education) more than those in overstocked fields; those who assume extra duties (such as developing materials and mentoring novice teachers) more than those who do only the minimum; and those willing to take on uncommonly challenging or hazardous situations more than those in comfortable surroundings. It means year-round work for those who want it. And it means retaining a person only so long as he is effective on the job. Long contracts for teachers are fine. But tenure has no place—none—in an education system run for the benefit of students.

Third, the decision to hire, promote, and retain a teacher, as well as the agreement about how much to pay, should be made at the building level. The team already in place in that school should decide who can join it. The principle of school choice must operate among the professional staff, too. The school and teacher then enter into an agreement with each other, either a formal contractual agreement or an individual side agreement envisioned in a master contract. The principal, too, should be picked by the school team so long as that school has won and retained its management autonomy by demonstrating good results.

Fourth, we should provide teachers with working conditions befitting their status as professionals. I have been struck, when visiting Asian schools, by the fact that teachers rarely have corridor duty, lunchroom duty, playground duty, and the like. They work long days and full calendar years and they handle large classes, but they are only "on duty" when actually teaching. At other times, they go to a pleasant room where each has a desk (and access to a phone), there to work on lesson plans, correct homework and exams, develop the curriculum for the next unit, work with individual students in need of help, and so forth. Teachers also meet with parents—usually by visiting the home of each pupil—and run interference in other aspects of students' lives. Most of them appear to do a great deal more than their job descriptions call for, and it's rare to see them bolt for the door when the bell rings. But just about everything they do is consistent with the belief that teaching is an honored calling.

Transferring this conception of the teacher's job into American schools is compatible with school site management and professional decision making, but the effort required goes well beyond that. It requires us also to begin to conceive of teacher and principal as independent contractors who enter into voluntary associations with a particular school on the basis of mutual respect and benefit. This is no conventional employer-employee affiliation, much less an industrial model labor-management relationship. It is more akin to the bond between a lawyer and his partners, a minister and his congregation, a professor and his university department.[27] To complete this changed relationship, we also need to differentiate roles and duties within schools in ways that we seldom see in American public education, to introduce clerical and paraprofessional help with noninstructional duties, and to seek heightened community regard for what teachers do. I believe (but cannot prove—until we try it) that the status and esteem we crave for good teachers will follow from school outcomes we are proud rather than ashamed of.

PARENTS, TOO

We will return to parents in both the remaining chapters, first as influential (if sometimes unreliable) forces in the lives of "at risk" children, then in relation to changes in the zeitgeist without which our best-conceived school-based reforms will come to little.

Here I want only to note the role of parents in those reforms. It has two essential elements, the first of which we have already begun to explore under the heading of school choice. A well-ordered education system will present parents with options for their children, as well as the data by which to make informed selections. The more that schools come to differ from each other, the more important it is to choose wisely among them. Selecting the best possible school for one's child has long been deemed a right by the well-to-do and the elite. Extending it to the entire population is not only a matter of social justice; it is also an indispensable element of educational accountability and improvement. Once people have that right, however, it withers if not regularly exercised. Advising and assisting parents unaccustomed to selecting schools for their children may even turn out to be a lively new cottage industry. We are used to sharing our financial decisions with agents, brokers, accountants, retirement planners and the like, chiefly because that world is too complex and treacherous for most of us to explore alone. In selecting colleges (and private schools), one can also find knowledgeable advisors. Why should we not look for expert help in choosing among school alternatives? What could be more important, after all, than making sure the decision is a sound one?

Selecting the school is only the first stage, however. The second is to become the school's partner in educating one's children. For some parents, participation in governance of the school itself is a feasible and rewarding activity, one that gives them substantial influence over what happens to their (and other people's) daughters and sons. Others will eagerly plunge into more traditional parent activities: chaperoning school trips, joining in school events, conferring with their own child's teacher, and attending PTA meetings. What's most important for all parents is to *share* responsibility with schools for how well their children learn.

Most schools would do well to make greater demands on parents to function as education partners. I have sometimes suggested to teachers and principals that a corner of the child's report card be used to grade Mom and Dad on their performance in that role. My audience usually chuckles appreciatively, but so far as I know nobody has tried marking the parents. In many situations it would make no difference, but some parents, seeing that they had received a C− from their child's teacher, might be moved to spend more time volunteering in the classroom, helping with the homework assignment, or reading to the heir apparent before bedtime.

So drastic a move would, of course, require courage on the part of the school staff, and this is sometimes in short supply when it comes to parents. Kindergarten teacher Mike Rutter, who has made exceptional use of parent volunteers in his classroom, candidly admits that he began with trepidations. "Too often," he writes, "we teachers are in mortal fear of parents—because they might criticize what we do, because we might look foolish in front of them, or because we might say something to a child we don't want parents to hear."[28]

Pulling parents into the educational process isn't just a help to the school. It also assists them to become more responsible parents. Too many are falling down on the job these days. They go about their own business, travel and socialize, watch television and read the paper, attend ball games and tennis matches and aerobics classes. Often they cart their children along on these activities, as well as buying them toys, fancy duds, and too much bubble gum. They think they are being good parents, and in some respects they probably are. But they and their children are suffering from a case of what educators call "affluenza," and that isn't good for anyone. In the cognitive-learning domain in particular, parents often have little idea what the school is trying to teach their child or how well their child is learning it. "The parents most driven professionally can be the least helpful at school," notes John McCormick in a perceptive *Newsweek* article. "Many behave as though the school exists for their child alone; a particularly annoying subspecies of the self-absorbed pulls kids out of class for family vacations *and* asks teachers to prepare a week's lessons, presumably to be administered by the ski patrol."[29]

Instead of getting tough with parents, many educators settle for trying to "improve communications." Yet the only forms that most attempt are meetings and conferences at school, and the occasional open house or parents' night. These are often stilted, rushed, and frustrating affairs, especially if the parent is aggressive or defensive or too out of touch with school matters to understand what is being said. Moreover, a lot of parents can't make it to school very often, especially during hours when the teacher is customarily present.

Like many other aspects of contemporary education, although technology cannot supply the gumption or the ideas, it can greatly facilitate teacher-parent communication without Mom or Dad even setting foot in the school building. Most parents have easy access to telephones. As noted in chapter 5, some teachers now use an answering machine to leave a brief message each evening that parents can dial and listen to for an update on classroom plans and homework expectations. During the same call, parents with questions or concerns can record them for the teacher. Audio- and videocassettes also have immense promise for two-way communication. Imagine an end-of-week (or -month or -marking-period) tape that comes home from the teacher, perhaps fifteen minutes summarizing what has been happening to the class as a whole and then five minutes about

Jason or Abby. The parent could listen and, if inclined, reply. The same could be done in more elaborate form on videocassettes. Electronic bulletin boards, already used by some students and teachers to converse, could become means of home-school communications. A few school systems have established their own cable television channels, suitable both for (one way) communication and for delivering additional instruction to adults as well as children.

I mention the gadgetry only to stimulate the imagination. We need not confine our notions of parent involvement to traditional face-to-face teacher conferences. But even the snazziest contemporary hardware cannot furnish commitment or conscience. For better or worse, the parent is the child's first and most important teacher. No school-reform scheme will succeed unless parents scrupulously play this role. No teacher can turn an unwilling parent into a responsible partner. Adults who want their child to get a good education will realize—as good parents have always realized—that this is at least as demanding as whatever jobs they work at by day. It's the functional equivalent of a second full-time career. And if they don't take it that seriously, not even an excellent school can accomplish all that it should with their child.[30]

15

✿

All the Children
Ten Tentative Truths

The best education for the best is the best education for all.

—Robert Maynard Hutchins

To this point, we have focused on the meager cognitive attainments of the average child emerging from the typical school, and on how to strengthen, deepen, and broaden them. This is a grave problem but if we fail to solve it the reason is not because we don't know what to do.

There is also a second crisis, however, overlapping yet not identical to the first, and far less tractable. It is the plight of what we used to term deprived or disadvantaged youngsters, those today known as the children of the underclass or, more generically, children "at risk." These girls and boys are in danger of a great deal more than not learning enough math, science, history, and geography, although those lacunae are part of their problem, too. They are also at risk of life and limb, of body and soul, of spirit and morality, of abandonment and abuse, of drugs and poverty, of neglect and crime and prison. And of reproducing under circumstances that make it likely their progeny, too, will face similar dangers, only perhaps worse.

This, clearly, is not just an education problem, nor is it a condition that schools alone can reverse, especially so long as their leverage is limited to 9 percent of a youngster's first eighteen years on earth. Here we must assume that the other 91 percent is not benign or neutral, as it so often is for children of the middle classes. Assume it is dysfunctional and destructive. Assume that this child lives in poverty, with mother and siblings but no father on the scene, in a tenement or housing project in a neighborhood infested with drugs, crime, and random violence, with little by way of Camp Fire Girls, Boy Scouts, safe parks, and supervised recreation opportunities. Suppose that Mom—a school dropout, perhaps a teenage mother, an unemployed welfare recipient—is also an alcoholic or addict who will not get up in the morning to dress and feed the youngster and get him properly off to school, much less check on last night's homework. Grimmer still, suppose she was addicted while this child was in the womb, and that the tyke we see wandering toward school is part of the first generation of "crack babies" now entering kindergarten and first grade with things messed up inside their heads in ways we do not yet fully understand.

To be sure, I'm depicting a worst-case scenario, but it's no fantasy. These situations exist in tens of thousands of cases and millions more contain elements of the same pathology.[1] "Sam should be in kindergarten now," related a March 1990 story in USA Today about a Florida nursery school for the children of cocaine users, but "he won't be ready for at least two years. The 6-year-old, whose mother smoked crack while pregnant, is developmentally just 1½. He is unable to pick up a small button, knows no alphabet and can't identify the colors pink, purple, green, orange and white. 'Repetition doesn't work with him,' " noted his preschool teacher. His classmate Tom "has a constant cold. Recurrent ear infections have thrown off his equilibrium, making him clumsy. The whites of his eyes are yellowed. Staffers say his mother's alcohol and cocaine use weakened Tom's immune system."[2]

FROM LEFT AND RIGHT

There's a strong possibility, I fear, that Sam and Tom will never be entirely okay, no matter what is done for them. But when asked how to deal with situations such as these, neither "left" nor "right" is hesitant to recite its familiar position.

From liberals, we hear an earnest plea for ever-more-comprehensive social services of many sorts, from income maintenance to prenatal health care to family counseling to homeless shelters to drug treatment. These and innumerable other benefits and services are to be provided through public agencies by trained and licensed

professionals using approved procedures that conform to government regulations. Lots of time and energy must be devoted to coordination among all these services. The government making the regulations and the taxpayer footing the bill should be as distant as possible—that is, federal is better than state is better than local. Private
social agencies may be involved in limited ways if they conform to
government standards and procedures. Private funds are welcome
so long as they do not displace public resources. It is best if they
are used for pilot and demonstration purposes—trip advancers, so
to speak, for future journeys by government. To the extent that benefits and services are not universal, eligibility should be income-related.
The poorer you are, the more assistance you receive. Sometimes
you also get more if you belong to a designated ethnic group. In
no case will any moral judgments be rendered. Your misfortunes
result from forces outside yourself and are therefore wholly beyond
your control.

The conservative version has certain ritualized features, too. Government should stay out of people's lives as much as possible. If
the family is deteriorating, it is at least partly the fault of unwise
public policies that reward sloth and foster indolence. Irresponsibility
and dependency flow from overgenerous social programs, and the
more the government does with, to, and for children, the more it
undermines the authority of parents. Families are supreme, and
wise policy will help them to make important decisions for their
own children, including choosing among various providers of any
services they require. Instead of routinely putting the kids under
the care and supervision of others, economic strategies—preferably
via the tax code rather than handout programs—should strengthen
the family's ability to fend for itself, including having a parent stay
home to look after young children directly. The alternatives to fending
for oneself should be as unattractive as possible. And social policy
should carry a heavy load of moralizing and messages of abstinence
and self-discipline. Society didn't mess up your life, except perhaps
by trying too hard to help. You mostly brought these tribulations
upon yourself.

Most of our social policy debates are framed by these opposing
views. We need to bear in mind, however, that these aren't just
debates about government programs. The visible parts of these ice-
bergs comprise mere fractions of their mass. Under the surface float
huge issues involving our most profound beliefs about human nature,
the essential elements of organized society, the nature of our polity,
and the shape of our culture.

These are weighty matters. They need periodic reexamination, and there is no reason to suppose that a diverse population of a quarter billion will agree on all of them.

TEN PROPOSITIONS

I do not expect to resolve these disputes, to forge consensus about the proper role of society with respect to crumbling families or to craft optimal policies for government vis-à-vis endangered children. But before returning to more specific issues of schooling, it's desirable to outline some general propositions that may guide us in the quest for broad policies. These are in addition to, not in lieu of, the education reform precepts of chapter 13. This second crisis is *not* going to be resolved within the boundaries of public education and it would be dishonest to veil the dimensions of the larger task before us. These ten propositions, meant to help us think constructively about the second crisis even as we are wrestling with the first, are anchored in my own understanding of human nature, the good society and the capabilities and frailties of government.

First, in this domain we should not expect to treat everyone alike. The norms of uniformity and universality do not work here. For policy purposes, the crack baby of the slums is simply not the same as the healthy infant of the middle class. The child pedaling his tricycle through a safe and tranquil neighborhood is not the same as the toddler trying to nap while gunfire crackles down the street. I disagree completely with observers such as the UCLA sociologist who recently wrote that policies and programs for children should be blind to differing circumstances because acceptance of the principle of differentiation would result in lower standards for programs that serve the needy, segregation of children from one another, and stigmatizing of both services and those receiving them.[3]

I respond that any policy or program designed to apply to all fifty million American youngsters is going to be unimaginably clumsy, unacceptably costly and probably ineffectual, far too intrusive for some children's needs yet not nearly bold enough for others. To pretend otherwise does none of them a favor. It is also contrary to common sense.

Yet to agree that we need tailored policies and differentiated programs is to adopt a standard that democratic government can seldom meet. We've sadly jumbled the meaning of equality, turning a principle of governance into a concept of programmatic entitlement that leaves us all but helpless in the presence of dissimilar conditions. We can usually get away with differentiating by income—though even this sometimes has perverse consequences.[4] I am talking about something harder: differentiating by what James Coleman calls the "social capital" that has accumulated in the lives of individual children and families.[5] Because we find that so difficult to do in our public policies, be warned that my first precept portends a great deal of nongovernment involvement in society's response to children's varying circumstances.

Second, we must steel ourselves to speak the truth in public places about social norms that we know to be good for children and about the malign consequences of deviating from those norms. This, too, is something government—and those in elective office—find nearly impossible to do. When public officials utter unwelcome truths, we tend to criticize them, make them apologize, and then not reelect them. For this kind of honesty, we may need to turn instead to religious and business leaders, educators, columnists, even sports figures and television personalities.

They should, for example, say what everyone knows to be the truth about families and parenting, politically ticklish though this has become. With rare exceptions, two parent families are good for children, one parent families are not half as good, zero parent families are horrible. This is not something to be ashamed of. It is the product of our species' experience in billions of instances spanning the millenia.[6] Nor is this the only wisdom we've acquired. We know, too, that with rare exceptions, a couple that has children must remain a couple if the children are to be well served. We know that people who are not married—or joined in some other stable fashion—should not have children. When they do, we know that it is to their children's disadvantage.

We know that a well-functioning society must condemn behavior that results in children being born to people who are not prepared to be good parents. I find it astonishing, in the face of that knowledge, that today we seem to attach greater opprobrium to blowing cigarette smoke in someone's face, experimenting on a cat, or uttering nasty remarks on campus than we do to giving birth to what, not so many years ago, were called "illegitimate" children. This has to do with morality, of course, but the larger point is about honesty: children fare better in some circumstances than others, and no decent society will remain silent about which circumstances are which. We do this not because we enjoy sermonizing, but because if we really care about "at risk" children we need to help people understand—

and internalize—the behavioral norms that make for environments in which children thrive.

Third, really a corollary of the second, we need to understand, and to teach our fellow citizens, that once the normal arrangements for child rearing are ruptured—using "normal" here in the sense of conforming to the norms I've just alluded to—all the alternatives will be worse. There are individual exceptions, such as the happy adoption that takes a child from bad circumstances into a loving family. Basically, however, we must acknowledge that all child-rearing arrangements not rooted in a decently functioning family are inferior to arrangements that *are* based on such a family. It's like a heart transplant. You may live for a while with one, and you may be better off than when your own heart was failing, but you are always worse off than are people in possession of healthy hearts that entered the world with them.

To acknowledge this is not enough. We need to teach it, to preach it, to persuade people of it. It's a whole lot more important to the society's future than saving obscure owls, ingesting more fiber, or finding alternatives to landfills.

Fourth, we are not talking mainly, or even primarily, about poverty of the sort that is measured in dollars and dealt with via income strategies or employment programs. Poverty is certainly present in many cases of deteriorating (or unformed) families and endangered children, but it is seldom the dominant factor today. What we are chiefly concerned with here is what Senator Daniel P. Moynihan terms "the importance of behavior." In an important essay in *The Public Interest*, Moynihan had this to say of antipoverty endeavors of the past:

> [The effort] was most successful—was hugely successful—where we simply transferred income and services to a stable, settled group like the elderly. It had little success—if you like, it failed—where poverty stemmed from social behavior. Indeed, it could not have succeeded there because of a massive denial that a problem really existed. . . .
>
> It is obvious that American society rewards traditional family patterns, and punishes those that in the past would have been called deviant. What is less obvious is why this fact is so obscure to so many. The disjunction between our norms and our behavior is dysfunctional in the extreme.[7]

Family structure is not the sole variable. "Substance abuse," Moynihan points out, "is equally dysfunctional." We could say the same of gang warfare, attacks on innocent joggers and cyclists, and the proliferation of automatic weapons in city streets. All are examples of antisocial behavior that bespeaks impoverishment of the soul more than the pocketbook, desolation of the value structure of civil society, erosion around the edges of the singular characteristics that led our kind to be called "human."

Fifth, economic measures may deal with dollar poverty, but dollars cannot be counted upon to alter anti-social behavior. Income transfer programs will not win the war on behavioral poverty. "A tough-minded approach to post-industrial social issues," Moynihan concludes his essay, "may lead to the coming of age of American social policy."[8]

Here, it seems to me, is where conservative commentators on family policy sometimes verge on naive utopianism. I just don't see expansion of the earned-income tax credit or other indirect economic incentives as making people significantly less apt to shoot one another with assault rifles. We also have evidence that classic welfare strategies leave a residue of unwanted consequences. Recalling two of the "laws of social programs" from Charles Murray's seminal book, *Losing Ground,* the "law of unintended rewards" holds: "Any social transfer increases the net value of being in the condition that prompted the transfer." The "law of net harm" asserts that "the less likely it is that the unwanted behavior will change voluntarily, the more likely it is that a program to induce change will cause net harm."[9]

The crucial realization here, however, is that just as we cannot count on schools successfully to carry out all the noncognitive missions they have been assigned, so we cannot rely on conventional welfare-type programs, grounded in an economic conception of poverty, to set matters right when the underlying disorders are essentially behavioral. Hence I believe we need to promulgate—and then enforce—a doctrine of accountability for parents as well as for their children and their schools.

In earlier chapters, we examined accountability in the realm of public services. I suggest that we also need to devise systems of private accountability. "Parents," Karl Zinsmeister writes, "are responsible for their children. They need to be *held* responsible."[10] Here, as in our public institutions, such systems must incorporate consequences, both the warm, fuzzy kinds and the kinds one would as soon avoid. Without accountability there is no real pressure for change, and without that pressure being felt by parents there is not likely to be much change in the behavior of their offspring. We ought therefore be ready to impose palpable consequences on adults when they *or their children* deviate from reasonable behavioral norms.

There are not many situations in which a child is well served by clapping his parent into jail. But the principle of "parent liability" must include the willingness of the larger society to inconvenience people in ways they do not welcome. Florida punishes parents whose guns wind up in the hands of their children. California has a law under which parents can be arrested if their children engage in outrageous gang activity or where the parents contribute to such behavior. In Los Angeles, Zinsmeister reports:

> Thirty to forty cases are being processed every month. These include instances where parents have openly tolerated guns and gang insignia in the home, where friends of the parents have tried to recruit their children into prostitution, where drug-addicted parents have simply stopped caring for their children.[11]

Wisconsin and Hawaii oblige parents to support the illegitimate issue of their unmarried teenage sons and daughters. (Wisconsin also cuts the parent's welfare benefits when the child is truant from school.) A local ordinance in Arkansas provides for a fine of up to five hundred dollars (and jail for up to thirty days) for parents whose children violate the town's curfew. Twenty-nine states have received federal waivers enabling them to evict families from public housing if their children sell (or use) drugs. Prosecutors in at least five states have started to charge women who take drugs while pregnant with child abuse, drug pushing, even assault with a deadly weapon.

I won't here try to evaluate the merits of individual measures of this kind. I merely assert that the doctrine of parental accountability for their own and their children's behavior means we must be prepared to think along these lines, even though civil libertarians will object and professors of social work will rend their clothes. Our purpose, it will be recalled, is to *alter* dysfunctional behavior, not to reward or condone it. In the words of a Michigan judge who ordered a pregnant crack smoker to stand trial, "I feel sympathetic toward the defendant, but her behavior is proscribed criminal behavior. And you don't excuse it by saying she's disadvantaged or a mother."[12]

Sixth, we should embrace as a guiding principle of social policy Urie Bronfenbrenner's proposition that "In order to develop, a child needs the enduring, irrational involvement of one or more adults

in care and joint activity with the child." When asked to restate
what he meant by "irrational involvement," he said "Somebody has
got to be crazy about that kid!"[13]

This I believe we know to be true. But do we also understand
that public policy cannot vouchsafe love? The most it can usually
manage is to meet the child's corporeal and cognitive needs. Seldom
can government fill spiritual and emotional voids. Once in a while,
it can create conditions in which something nice happens. But we
dare not count on it.

Seventh, if government cannot furnish suitable shepherds for our
lambs, we must ask through what other mechanisms society may
be able to. Social policy should not be equated to public policy. As
we look beyond government, we turn—in addition to extended families, kindly neighbors, and individual benefactors—to what have been
termed mediating structures, voluntary associations, small platoons,
even "points of light." The United States has many of these; it's
one of our abiding strengths as a society. But they haven't always
had a happy marriage to our public norms. We get nervous when
private providers of social services have religious ties, for example,
when they give priority to people of their own race or creed, when
they impose entrance requirements or fees or make people wear
uniforms or affirm moral codes. We tease people about being "Boy
Scouts" even though the scout virtues—trustworthy, loyal, obedient,
and so on—are reasonable summaries of the kind of behavior we
need many more people to display. We also worry about unevenness
in the services such organizations render and inconsistency in the
treatments they provide.

But let me say it again: If we are serious about guiding the moral,
behavioral, spiritual, and emotional development of all our children,
we cannot limit ourselves to government. We need uncles and neighbors, Big Brothers and Sisters, college fraternity members who tutor
fourth-graders, athletic teams that "adopt" classrooms, businessmen
who spend their Saturdays with junior-high-school students, retirees
and foster grandparents, and right on through a thousand thousand
points of light. Nor can our schools and other institutions confine
their actions to what has commonly been thought fitting for their
professional staffs to do. As we saw in chapter 2, when a group of
Chicago businessmen opened a free private school as a model of
effective education for disadvantaged children, one of the first decisions they and the new principal made was that teachers would
routinely conduct home visits. (Teachers in Japan do this as a matter

of course. Teachers in the "restructured" schools of Rochester, New York, are supposed to.) The *Washington Post* recently reported on an elementary school in Prince William County where an eighth-grade teacher, having concluded that some of her students needed a strong, black male role model, brought her own husband to school— more than once—to work with them. This, I suspect, was not covered in the employment contract for teachers in that school system. The teacher received no extra pay. She may even have broken a rule or two. But she understood the problem and was not abashed to do what was necessary to try to solve it. "Somebody's got to be there for these kids," insisted teacher Madre Mack, unconsciously echoing Bronfenbrenner.[14]

Eighth, we should always try first to improve the situation within a child's own family, to buttress the natural parents in whatever ways we can, from parent-education programs to church-basement support groups to job-training programs. Experienced organizations, such as Dorothy Rich's Washington-based Home and School Institute, are skilled at devising such strategies. But sometimes the family is too far gone, or never really formed. "I am not sure," writes child abuse expert Douglas Besharov of the American Enterprise Institute, that "crack addicts who give birth to a child constitute anything approaching a family. . . . In such a situation, the child comes first and has to be protected."[15] Reluctantly, I conclude that we must prepare more frequently to remove "at risk" children from their homes—to remove them before great harm is done them—and to send them into other settings where someone will be crazy about them. Our priority must never waver from the children. Parents do not always know best, and their interest is not always paramount. Here I disagree with many conservatives. But where I dispute many liberals is that I have little faith in temporary, "foster care" settings where the child stays for a time until—maybe—his family gets straightened out. Too many such situations turn out to be unsatisfactory for too many years for too many children. Adoption is in many cases to be preferred. So are the terrific residential schools and orphanages such as Boys Town in Nebraska and the Milton S. Hershey School and Glen Mills Schools, both in Pennsylvania.

These are light years from the grim Dickensian institutions we associate with the term orphanage. They are environments vastly more salubrious than those in the child's own home, school and neighborhood, whether one is judging their physical safety, moral climate, the presence of reliable and caring adults, or the effectiveness

of their education and training. At the Hershey school, it may be
noted, most of the 1,150 youngsters in residence today are not real
orphans. They have at least one living parent. They are, in the phrase
of a *Wall Street Journal* reporter who profiled the school, the "products of a different sort of calamity."[16] Their parents cannot or will
not take care of them.

No, I do not want to let parents off the hook. Yes, part of me
balks at taking children from their parents—or letting parents transfer
their child-rearing responsibilities to the paid staff of schools like
this. It's hugely expensive, too, in the vicinity of thirty thousand
dollars per child per year, five or six times our average public school
outlay. But it's worth it if we end up with someone who is "crazy
about" those boys and girls.

Ninth, as one of our foremost policy objectives, we should be
devising means to generate and accumulate more social capital everywhere it is in short supply. This means, above all, trying to build it
up within the family and between parent and child. Social capital
is a new and elusive concept. Here is James Coleman's own explanation:

> While physical or financial capital exists wholly in tangible
> resources, and human capital is a property of individual persons,
> social capital exists in the relations between persons.
>
> Social capital can be of several sorts, serving different purposes.
> If a child trusts an adult, whether a parent or a member of the
> community, and the adult is trustworthy, this relation is a resource
> on which the child can draw when in difficulties. . . . If the relations
> in a community are strong enough to establish norms about the
> behavior of children and youth and to impose effective sanctions
> toward their observance, this constitutes a resource for children,
> protecting them from the predations of peers, and a resource for
> parents to aid in shaping the habits of their children. These are
> two forms of social capital; more generally, social capital held by
> a person lies in the strength of social relations that make available
> to the person the resources of others.[17]

How can social capital be generated where it does not naturally
occur? That ought to be one of our premier policy questions of
the 1990s. Coleman offers some clues. He suggests, for example,
steps that schools can take to help parents learn how to assist their
children in the pursuit of education, actions that parents in a neighborhood or workplace can take in collaboration with each other to

increase the net social capital available to their children, and mutually reinforcing relationships among the important adults in a child's life.

A stable friendship between one's uncle, say, and a policeman gives one access to understanding and acceptance of the norms of lawful behavior and law enforcement that may otherwise be absent. A mother who has a clergyman she can count on gives her child a "drawing account" in the spiritual domain that he may not readily acquire on his own. A Big Brother, Big Sister, or other mentor program serves much the same purpose, as do the projects of the "I Have a Dream" foundation (which provide more tangible forms of capital as well!) When black Annapolis midshipmen tutor black Maryland junior-high-school pupils, more is being stockpiled in their young lives than the improved math skills that are the explicit purpose of the program. The point is clear: we have purposeful policy strategies for boosting physical, investment, and human capital. We need them for social capital, too.

Tenth, and finally, we should treat these matters as we would a national defense crisis, not just as problems that plague individuals. We are dealing with threats to the commonweal, to the society itself. When five-year-olds enter school with their neural circuits miswired, when law-abiding people fear walking down the street or riding the subway, when babes in their cribs and youngsters on the playground may be struck down by random gunfire, and when packs of marauding teenagers go "wilding" in the park, it is no exaggeration to say we are facing a national emergency, different in kind but not, perhaps, in degree from threats posed by hostile nations. If, to recall the 1983 words of the National Commission on Excellence in Education, an unfriendly foreign power had done this to us, we would have deemed it an act of war.

We should, therefore, think about mobilizing to deal with it as we would a major menace to our national security. The threat is a lot closer to home, and at least as grave, as a crisis in the Middle East. We should expect to submit ourselves to the organizational arrangements, the disruption of familiar assumptions and practices, the expense, the inconvenience and perhaps the inhibitions that we associate with grave threats to the nation's well-being. My purpose is not to be melodramatic or to advocate harsh measures. I am convinced, though, that if we have any serious expectation of winning this new war on behavioral poverty, we're going to need not only the imagination to devise strategies suited to victory but also the resolve to see them through.

IN THE SCHOOLS

Nothing we are doing today in the education domain is commensurate with these guidelines; short of building thousands of year-round residential schools, it's unlikely that anything could be. We need a revolution here, too, one that leaps the bounds of conventional education policy.

We dare not assume that the institutions we know as schools can solve massive noncognitive problems, and we mustn't let anyone get away with claiming otherwise. Yet we *can* define some school-based strategies that meet the cognitive learning needs of "at risk" children and that may also help a little with the other kind.

The basic guidelines sketched in the previous two chapters apply here, too, beginning with clear goals and lofty expectations. The biggest disservice one can render disadvantaged children is to suggest that they should not be expected to learn as much as youngsters from more favored circumstances, that they ought to learn something different, or that in their case the standards can be set aside. Jaime Escalante is acid in his denunciation of the "psychological approach," citing, among many examples, a note from a school counselor explaining that "Johnny did not do his homework because he had a bad dream" and that the famed math teacher should therefore be understanding. "I told the kid, in no uncertain terms," Escalante recounts, " 'You do the homework or else you get an F. Period.' Miraculously, the kid and the homework appeared the next day and that student went through the program, not with a residue of resentment but with a sense of accomplishment."[18]

Patricia Graham's maxim holds: "There may be various means to acquire it but . . . everyone needs it." California's Bill Honig is even more outspoken:

It is racist, by definition, to say that most black or Hispanic children aren't smart enough to cope with an academic course load with which most white children can cope. It is also grossly untrue. And look at the insidious consequences of this patronizing doctrine. Under the guise of compassion (since they can't learn the academic curriculum, we should spare them the misery of trying), this doctrine gives all parties an easy excuse for loafing. Teachers shrug: my students can't do any better, so why should I push them? . . . An education that prepares children to hang out on neighborhood street corners for the rest of their lives, that isolates them from, rather than ushers them into, the larger worlds of business, science, and government, isn't worthy of the name. This is true for the whole spectrum of "at-risk" kids.[19]

Yet a number of educators do not believe that all students can succeed. On Emily Feistritzer's 1990 survey, though 80 percent of teachers concurred that "students, regardless of their socioeconomic backgrounds, can perform at the highest levels of achievement"— two teachers in ten *disagreed*. On a Carnegie Foundation teacher survey conducted the same year, 39 percent affirmed that "public schools cannot really expect to graduate more than about 75 percent of all students."[20] I do not doubt that these glum judgments are faithful to the teachers' own experience—but what message gets communicated to students by teachers who don't think they can learn very much, and to what extent do these become self-fulfilling prophesies?

Let us nevertheless assume—as I believe—that Graham and Honig are right, and that we have general agreement that curricular content and outcome standards for disadvantaged youngsters should be the same as for everyone else. By what means can this ambitious result be achieved?

We can cite successful examples and adduce some lessons from them. What we don't have are patented processes or foolproof recipes. We cannot be confident that the characteristics of today's effective schools and programs can be transplanted into every setting.

Consider the widely hailed approach of Dr. James P. Comer, a Yale psychiatrist who has had considerable success with a method that melds home life, school life, and other social services, seeking concurrently to meet children's social, psychological, emotional, behavioral, and cognitive needs—and reaching deep into the 91 percent to do so. This is a multidimensional strategy, centered on, but by no means confined to, the classroom. In the two New Haven schools where Comer began (in 1968), it is evident from test scores, other objective measures, and the testimony of countless visitors that improvement has occurred. New Haven has accordingly extended the "Comer process" to all its schools, a dozen other systems have adopted it, and the Rockefeller Foundation decided in early 1990 to spend fifteen million dollars to transport it to other communities.

Will it prove portable? How well will it work in settings that do not have the constant attention of James Comer himself? As with so many other successful schools and programs, it's easy to be wowed by the original. It's harder to say with confidence that the magic can be franchised, particularly in the bureaucratic mazes of dilapidated urban school systems where so many "at risk" youngsters are found.

It's not magic, of course. Comer insists that it's all "common sense," and he's probably right. But that does not mean everyone is inclined to embrace his version of common sense, much less to alter their time-worn procedures. Like Sizer's Coalition of Essential Schools, the Paedeia plan, the Copernican project, the Beethoven project and a hundred other laudable efforts at education renewal, the "Comer Process" depends on people wanting to do things in a new way rather than their accustomed way. "If you looked at it generically as a school improvement plan, used all the components, followed the guidelines, it's almost foolproof," reports a school official in Benton Harbor, Michigan. "But you generally have not had a strong commitment on the part of the principals. For a lot of people, it's a pain."[21]

Other approaches also demonstrate considerable promise in the places where they began. The "Success for All" project, developed by Robert E. Slavin and his associates at Johns Hopkins University, concentrates on basic academic skills in the preschool years and early grades, using a mixture of parent involvement and family support, intensive tutoring, individualized learning plans, and frequent assessment. Judging from early returns in the handful of Baltimore schools where the project has operated, it works. Test scores rose on most measures, even among severely disadvantaged youngsters (though not to the point that the project's brash title came true, at least in the first year). But we do not know how many other schools will be willing to change their ways to incorporate this approach, nor how many will be able to obtain the additional resources (roughly one thousand dollars per child per year) that it costs, nor how it will work if the Hopkins team isn't around.[22]

Superintendent John Murphy of Prince George's County, Maryland, one of the nation's most impressive education executives, demonstrates strong results with "at risk" children in troubled neighborhoods through school-based strategies that carry smaller price tags. The extra services he has installed in these schools—computer labs, full-time reading specialists, guidance counselors, and the like—add 10 to 15 percent to the typical school budget.[23]

Murphy's approach is not magic either. It's commonsensical. It ought therefore to be portable. Yet it may not be. Thus arises the great frustration of finding a foolproof solution to the education problems of "at risk" children: Replicating success is not just a matter of tracking down the right scheme to copy. It is not just a matter of obtaining the funds. The features that the most promising strategies appear to have in common include levels of energy, commitment and role definition that exceed the usual requirements of public schooling (and school employees) in the United States. To put the matter more sharply: What seems to succeed with disadvantaged children draws on qualities not found in the formal job descriptions of those who manifest them and not easy to write into the job descriptions of others, precisely because these qualities elude the bureaucratic paradigm we noted in chapter 9 and partake instead of abnormal energy, a deep love for children and a raging passion for results.

So far as I can tell, the schools and programs that are uncommonly effective in educating at risk children begin with the "maverick" school characteristics described in chapter 2, and then emphasize four qualities, none of which will surprise readers who have persevered to this point:

First, they not only hold high standards and expectations for their students; they also work assiduously with every child to ensure that he has all the instruction (and counseling, tutoring, and so on) necessary to *meet* those standards. Instead of softening their norms and diluting their efforts, they intensify and concentrate them. These are outcome-oriented institutions with highly individualized yet relentless strategies.

Second, they are "crazy about" their pupils. Relentlessness is coated with kindness. Hugs are as common as workbooks. Ears to listen and shoulders to cry on are readily available. Staff members often dig into their own pockets to help children who need school supplies, food, or medicine. They install washers and dryers in the school so that their pupils can have the experience of wearing clean clothes. They arrive as early and stay as late as there are students to be looked after. Someone in the school—often the principal or teacher, but sometimes a reading specialist, the attendance officer, even a security guard—establishes a personal relationship with practically every youngster. In other words, they generate, invest, and—as necessary—expend great reservoirs of social capital. And when people on the school staff are spread too thin or don't have the necessary qualities, these schools recruit mentors from the community, from businesses that have "adopted" them, and from wherever else they can be found.

Third, they push well past the 9 percent limit. Many different approaches are possible here, from early childhood and preschool programs that inaugurate the learning-readiness process before the age of six, to parent education programs that enlist mothers and fathers as educational partners, to after-school and summer programs that expand learning time into more of the year, to the purposeful engagement of other social agencies in meeting children's non-cognitive needs so that they will be better able to concentrate on academic pursuits in the classroom.

Such expeditions beyond the traditional roles and bounds of school occasionally raise hackles and anxieties. Some teachers are uncomfortable, others frightened. Some rise up and declare that it's not part of their jobs, not professional, not something they were trained for, not something they are paid for, not this or not that.[24] Other agencies complain that their turf is being invaded. Conservative organizations rue the intrusion by schools into domains once entrusted to families and churches. And seldom is the school system budget designed to underwrite all the costs of such extra activities.

Yet those who are most effective with "at risk" children refuse to budge. Madeline Cartwright, former principal of Blaine Elementary School in sorely depressed North Philadelphia, routinely goes far beyond the provisions of her job description. "My children are less abused," she says, "because the parents around here know if they send that child to school dirty, that's neglect. I'm going to clean that child up. And I'm going to ask that mother, 'Why is this child dirty?' I'm not going to let it go. They know these kids tell me everything. And when these children tell me they've been hurt, I talk to the parents, call them in."[25]

Jaime Escalante has a similar approach to his calculus students:

Students who enter the Escalante Math Program must sign a contract which binds them to participation in the summer programs . . . strict completion of daily homework, and attendance at Saturday morning and after-school study sessions. The students' parents are also required to sign the contract. . . . To succeed, a program as intense as mine must have 100 percent support from the parents. While most parents are thrilled to have a teacher show so much interest and welcome the opportunity to do anything for their children, sometimes my efforts to help my students succeed take me beyond the usual parent-teacher relationship. One time I even scolded a parent who was drinking too much and harassing his child. "You cannot do that," I told him. "It is interfering with your daughter's math class . . . so you will have to stop drinking." More than once, this startling communication of priorities has had a salutary effect.[26]

Escalante, it may be noted, also checks his students' cafeteria trays to make sure they are eating wholesome food. Yet how can we incorporate that sensible and caring impulse into a "job description"? The mind boggles at the prospect of a bargaining table session devoted to how many minutes of the teacher's work-day will be spent inspecting carrots and enumerating yogurt containers.

Fourth, successful educators use proven instructional strategies in (and out of) class. They understand that homework helps when it is graded or commented on, for example, not just assigned and collected; that students need to be coached in what educators call "metacognitive" skills, whereby they learn how to attack a problem, to size up a situation, even to reflect on their own thought processes; that "mastery learning," in which something is taught and retaught, studied and restudied, until it has actually been learned, is infinitely more potent than sticking willy-nilly to a predetermined schedule; that analytic and reasoning skills need to be learned at the same time as basic skills and knowledge, not as if they were distinct mental processes.[27]

That's not the whole tool kit, to be sure. Much good research has been done on which instructional strategies are most effective. This, alas, is not to say that all school practitioners are acquainted with that research, much less that they have adjusted their own methods in response. A great many educators, as we have seen, go through their careers teaching pretty much as they were taught and living off the ideas they originally imbibed in the college of education.

Nor should we think that every scheme emanating from a scholar or expert *deserves* to be implemented. Some are fads, others mere notions or earnest hopes. Some are intimately linked to the reputation—and perhaps the living standard—of their chief promoter.[28] The experts sometimes disagree with one another.[29] "I only use those ideas which have been proven worthwhile by demonstration," Escalante wisely notes, "and which I have tested. I test everything that comes to me before using it, no matter how vaunted the authority who invented it."[30]

The field of education, as we saw in chapter 12, is full of dubious notions, but in no branch of it are these more often encountered than in the schooling of "at risk" children. Ideas and practices that no middle-class family or suburban community would tolerate for their own children are solemnly accepted in this domain. Here we defer to the proposition that students must be taught by members of their own race. (If said of white or even Asian youngsters, this would instantly—and correctly—be denounced as racism, possibly apartheid.) That social studies curricula should be rewritten to accord with the image one or another group would like to have of its ancestors. (Rather than honoring the facts, this imposes quotas on history.) That disadvantaged youngsters should not be expected to acquire the same knowledge, language, and norms as others learn, on the grounds that some sort of cultural imperialism is thereby encouraged, even though mastery of those things is the surest path to upward mobility within American society. (This restricts rather than enlarges opportunities and in an earlier era would have been called "keeping them in their place.") That new immigrants should be steered into linguistic- and cultural-maintenance classes instead of being taught English and socialized into American ways as quickly as possible. (Often deceptively labeled "transitional" classes, these reveal the influence of organized ethnic pressure groups more than they do the wishes of immigrant families.) That low-income and minority parents ought not be looked to for conscientious choices about the education of their children. (Though some need assistance when making such decisions, the implication that they do not care or will not bother is patronizing and paternalistic.)

Many educators also fly into a pother over what the professional literature habitually refers to as the "changing demographics" of the schools. Innumerable conferences and "in-service" teacher education days begin with slides displaying uncertain forecasts based on unprovable assumptions about future fertility rates and immigration and behavior patterns.[31] Much is made of the appearance of so-called "majority minority" schools, even though this is not a new or particularly worrisome development in American society.[32] But it's all strangely inconclusive, with a Chicken Little quality that warns us the environment is undergoing abrupt changes but never quite says what should be done in response. The implication is that somehow we should reorder the entire curriculum and pedagogy of the schools, as if children with different income levels or skin colors need to learn different things in wholly different ways.

Fortunately our best practitioners know better. "Yes," concludes Escalante, who strives to give his Hispanic students pride in their heritage but is far too wise to allow a double standard to take root in their minds, "the barriers disadvantaged or minority students face are substantial, but it is the very possibility of their remaining trapped by them for an entire lifetime which requires that such students be urged to succeed in their academic studies. It may be their only way out."[33]

16

A Four-Front War

*Everything beyond this must be left to the prudence and
the firmness of the people.*

—Alexander Hamilton, *The Federalist*

As the 1990–91 school year opened, three new reports emerged
within a few days. The College Board announced that the average
score on the verbal portion of the SAT had declined for the fourth
straight year, regressing to its all-time low of 424, a level last seen
in 1981 before the excellence movement gathered steam.[1]

In its annual "back-to-school" forecast, the Education Department
estimated that spending by U.S. public schools during the new academic year would reach the unprecedented sum of $5,638 per pupil,
amounting to a 33 percent increase across the previous decade *after*
adjusting for inflation.

And the Gallup Organization, in conjunction with Phi Delta Kappa,
disclosed the 1990 results of its yearly survey of public opinion about
education, revealing that only 21 percent of the American people
now give honor grades to the nation's schools and just 22 percent
believe that the schools in their communities have improved during
the past five years, while 30 percent think they've deteriorated and
36 percent judge them to be "about the same."

Scores down again. Spending steadily up. Widespread popular
disapproval. Little sense that things are getting better.

WHY, THEN, AREN'T WE ANGRIER?

Is it that we're numb from the ceaseless barrage of bleak data?
That we feel helpless to do anything about so knotty and intractable

a problem? That we have faith in those who claim to be solving it? That we think this national affliction, grave though it may be, is mostly someone else's worry? Or have we forgotten that the good life we seek for ourselves and our children depends on the education they acquire, on what enters their minds and hearts, not just what diverts, decorates, cossets and excites them?

Our passivity seemed especially ironic in late 1990 as the American people, speedily and with a rare semblance of unity, rallied behind President Bush's bold decisions to send a vast military force to the Persian Gulf, to impose an embargo on Iraq, and to rouse virtually the entire planet—even the lethargic United Nations—to respond stoutly to Saddam Hussein's seizure of Kuwait and his menacing gestures toward other Arab states and the world's oil supply.

We remain capable of outrage, it appears, and of spirited action to counter threats to our well-being. We'll endure inconvenience, expense and potential sacrifice if such are required to safeguard our interests and do what is right. We're still vulnerable to being influenced, even inspired, by leaders who speak plainly of crises, communicate their priorities, offer explanations, and brook no nonsense.

All this even though many Americans never heard of Kuwait, few can find Iraq on a map, servicemen disembarking on the Saudi sands had not known the country existed, and a platoon of pundits somehow encountered difficulty detecting any threat to vital U.S. interests. How remarkable, then, that we were so susceptible to forceful leadership in reacting to these distant developments. And how tragic that we have not been whipped into a furious froth these past few years over the clear and present danger to our individual and collective well-being that is posed by the wretched state of our very own education system.

To be sure, Americans do tend to rally round the flag in the face of foreign perils while turning an apathetic countenance toward most domestic woes. We did not, it's fair to note, get exercised about the S & L disaster, either, costly and destructive though that is. Villains with names, scoundrels with faces, and tyrants with hostages get our adrenaline flowing in ways that systemic breakdowns, institutional failures, and policy debacles rarely manage to do.

Yet that's too glib an explanation for the lack of outrage about education in a society with matchless capacity to work itself into a lather almost at will. The United States virtually invented advertising, public relations, image making, and the art of waging semipermanent campaigns for and against countless issues and causes. We've allowed ourselves to be convinced that hair mousse and body sculpting are among life's necessities. We voluntarily send millions of hard-earned dollars to organizations and movements about which we know no more than is contained in the direct-mail envelopes the postman brings. We create new appetites for oat bran, canola oil, and Alar-free apples. We made a best-seller of a mawkish book called *Everything I Need to Know I Learned in Kindergarten.* (Consider the message *that* sends about the importance of education?) We are converted to new faiths by television evangelists and exercise fanatics, wooed by loss-leader sales at the local appliance store, inveigled to subscribe to magazines we won't read, and lured by "bargain" tickets aboard planes to places we have no need to go. We seemingly cannot survive nowadays without VCRs, personal computers, exotic bottled waters, camcorders, liposuction, balsamic vinegar, compact disks, Nintendo, Federal Express, extra-virgin olive oil, modems and faxes, fresh cilantro, minivans, Rollerblades, *U.S.A. Today,* frozen yogurt, and a thousand other goods and services, many of which did not even exist a few years back. We pay more attention to the impressions conveyed by political candidates' television and radio spots than to their voting records and position statements. We swore off Perrier when we thought it was contaminated, we swore off butter and eggs when advised that they would clog our arteries, and many of us swore off Detroit when we found its cars shoddy and inefficient. We bought junk bonds and took out "balloon" mortgages. We wear narrow neckties, then wide, then narrow again. Skirt lengths rise and fall, as do network news anchormen. We go wild over athletes, singers, and actors who six months earlier were admired mainly by their mothers.

We are, in a word, impressionable. We are open to suggestion. We are sometimes gullible and occasionally fickle. (Though we refused to abandon the old version of Coca-Cola, a great many of us have turned away from our old wives and husbands.) We ceaselessly rearrange our environments, redefine our needs and priorities, and recategorize our manias and phobias in ways that puzzle residents of more staid societies.

Amid this hubbub, the "education issue," as pollsters call it, has already enjoyed a longer run than most such. Eight years after *A Nation at Risk* and more than a decade after we headed "back to the basics," a veritable school-reform industry has arisen, complete with personalities, issues, terminology, and a bevy of conferences and publications of its own; hundreds of pilot projects, studies, and experiments; and tens of millions of grant dollars. It's still a pretty good issue for politicians, too, a high priority concern of voters, and a rewarding topic for the media. The *idea* of education reform has won tenure. It has caused the demise of forests. It has given us something to fret about. The only thing it hasn't done is palpably improve the skills and knowledge of the average child. Which, of course, is the only important thing it was asked to do.

Could we not now take our huge talent for marketing, our voracious appetite for being persuaded, our amazing receptivity to public relations, our zeal for self-improvement, and our worship of celebrity, and marshal all these to work ourselves into a towering rage? To purge our minds of tolerance for excuses, patience with "more of the same," leniency for mediocrity, and forbearance toward promises that never come true? To abandon perestroika and make a revolution?

Of course we could. They did it in Chicago. They did in Chelsea. They did it in England.

But first, I think, we have to remind ourselves why it matters, and that means recalling that there is more to life than taut thighs, a nice smile, Monday Night Football, a fax in the den, and a pizza about to be delivered.

Once upon a time, tradition, family, religious faith, and a concern with the hereafter gave people a focus for their lives that transcended immediate gratification. The insightful Tocqueville observed as early as 1830, however, that "in skeptical ages the vision of the life to come is lost, a problem that is exacerbated in democracies, where people are set free to compete with each other to improve their situations." To compensate for what had been lost in the modern era, and to infuse people's lives with something nobler than their appetites, he urged the leaders of democracies to "strive to set a distant aim as the object of human efforts; that is their most important business."[2]

Of what might that "distant aim" consist today? "In a secular age," John Silber suggests, "it is unlikely that such a vision can be grounded in anything other than free pursuit of truth for the sake of human betterment."[3]

That's pretty lofty stuff for a pragmatic people, quite a distance from "skills training for economic competitiveness" and the other mundane rationales we usually muster on behalf of education reform.

In fact, however, these two ways of thinking are complementary. Just as education serves both private and public purposes, so also is it our entrée to the "good life" in *both* senses of the phrase: to the prosperity and material well-being, on the one hand, that we can have only when the economy is strong and our own job prospects bright; and, on the other hand, to the virtues, enchantments, and inner peace that we can have only when our freedom is secure, our communities are civil, and our minds have been opened to possibilities beyond wealth and pleasure.

That's not easy to market. It's hard to come up with a slogan or jingle. But that's exactly why it's worth the effort. Selling heaters to people who already know they're chilly is no challenge. The great accomplishment is to persuade millions of Buddy Hacketts that there really is such a thing as not having heartburn—and that life is far better when one achieves that condition.

REWRITING THE HISTORY OF THE NEXT GENERATION

Those who study the past are apt to conclude that things turn out the way they do for reasons that are understandable but seldom alterable. Historicism shades into determinism in the writings of even so fine a scholar as the late Lawrence A. Cremin, who insisted that we oversimplified the tale (and needlessly alarmed ourselves) during the 1980s when we decried the population's lack of learning and knocked the schools for allowing this to happen. Instead, Cremin said, we should realize that education always has critics, that we're never content with it, that recent commentators hold too narrow a view, and that we should be more appreciative of having accomplished so much.[4]

Diane Ravitch, also a distinguished historian, is far less serene. "We get the schools we deserve," she writes, because we haven't clearly and systematically demanded otherwise:

The problem is that we lack consensus about whether there should be a common curriculum, and whether there are knowledge and skills that everyone should have. If we believed that it was important to have a highly literate public, to have a public capable of understanding history and politics and economics, to have citizens who are knowledgeable about science and technology, to have a society in which the powers of verbal communication are developed systematically and intentionally, then we would know what we wanted of our schools.[5]

We could turn this around, in other words, if we really made up our minds to do so, pressed ourselves to agree on some fundamental precepts, and embarked on the mission with a sense of confidence akin to the self-esteem we've been trying to instill in our children. Remember the little engine that could?

But shared beliefs, structured consensus, and coherent strategies do not come easily to a big, diverse society that is full of freedom-loving individualists accustomed—even while they grouse about the results—to leaving education to the educators, ever less confident that government can get us out of the messes it creates, and unsure whether the kid with the good grades is really a hero or a nerd. We are perfectly capable of voting for the Kantian philosopher John Silber—and then going home and chilling out with Bart Simpson and a Bud. If we have to applaud the youngster with the high test scores, please don't let it be one who rubs our noses in how hard he works. Let him be like the National Merit semifinalist who told a newspaper reporter, "My study habits are nonexistent," or the one down the road who boasted about regularly "tak[ing] the weekend to relax and wind down."[6]

It's not just the kids who strive to persuade us (and themselves) that they don't take education very seriously. We also need to break through their parents' extraordinary capacity for denial, com-pounded partly of complacency, partly of misinformation, partly of wishful thinking, and partly of a tendency to view societal disasters as living in someone else's house, usually on the other side of town. The "urban problem" isn't terribly upsetting to those in the suburbs. Prison overcrowding doesn't ring the chimes of people who don't know anyone in jail. Even serious drug abuse, perhaps our most acute domestic inflammation, though way up on the lists of problems we all think should be solved, is pretty remote from most of our lives.

This isn't apathy or selfishness so much as lack of immediacy, the absence of direct harm to oneself and one's family, and the serene confidence that, whatever the state of the nation, our own lives are in tolerable shape.

The education problem is a little different. As the high-blood-pressure alerts say, it's a secret killer. We have turned our backs on it not because it doesn't exist in our neighborhood, but because we haven't realized the degree to which it's stealthily harmed *our* children and their schools, too.

Making ourselves understand this more clearly must be the first stage of any real education revolution. Our beliefs, attitudes, and values vis-à-vis education need as much attention as our school policies. So do the rewards and incentives we create for success and the consequences we attach to mediocrity. Launching such a revolution, therefore, is going to require heavy-duty leadership well beyond the schools themselves. By comparison, it's easier to launch 40,000 air sorties over Iraq. Mobilizing us to do battle with "dumbth" isn't half so dramatic, and it won't be nearly so rewarding politically, but it will demand almost as much courage and lots more tenacity. Its success will depend in no small measure on the ability of our leaders to get us angry—at this hijacking of our children's future, this colossal waste of resources, this shameless and unnecessary weakening of our economy, our culture, and our civic life. Ignorance needs to become our domestic Saddam Hussein.

Get us angry, keep us angry, move us to demand redress, point the way to specific alternatives, revive us when we tire, reassure us when we falter, conspire with us on strategies, and swallow no nonsense from the keepers of the status quo, neither the Panglosses who say that all is well nor the Cassandras who say that all is lost.

Are these not the defining qualities of leadership in any era? Was this not the genius of Lincoln during the Civil War, of Roosevelt during the Great Depression, of Churchill during World War II? Is this not roughly the role played by Walesa in contemporary Poland, by Thatcher in Britain, and, as I've suggested, by Bush in the Middle East? It's visible in moral, cultural, scientific, and religious revolutions, too, not just the political and military kinds. Consider the role of Martin Luther King, Jr., in the civil rights movement or of his namesake in the Protestant reformation four and a half centuries earlier. Consider, for that matter, the role of Horace Mann and his contemporaries in the establishment of American public education itself.

In any real revolution, only the treetops are visible. The roots, trunks, and branches that support them are concealed in the minds and hearts of the populace. That is why revolutions only succeed when a revolutionary spirit invades people's attitudes and actions, and when the consequences of failure are judged to be more ominous than the costs of persevering to victory.

The revolution against ignorance, therefore, has to be waged simultaneously on four fronts. The first and best mapped of these consists of schooling itself. Most of this book has been given over to what's wrong in that domain and what should be done differently. Chapters 13 and 14, in particular, set forth principles by which the elementary-secondary system ought to function and a number of ambitious changes that we should make in its actual operations. Necessary as these are, however, they are not sufficient. Taking charge of our future means prosecuting the education revolution on fronts two, three, and four as well.

ALARMING—AND ARMING—OURSELVES

The second front is almost infinitely wider. It consists of the signals we send to the young about what the culture prizes, the examples we set for them, the messages we deliver, and the values we transmit.

It is not difficult, as we have seen, to induce disgruntlements, expectations, and cravings in the American people. Some of these are healthy, some not, but we certainly aren't immune to them. The problem is that while we have had messages about educational mediocrity dinning in our ears, we do not yet have them gnawing at our vitals.

What will be entailed in piercing our private complacency, in making superior educational outcomes a good we crave more than Cuisinarts, Walkmen, and World Series tickets, in alarming us about our own kids' schools and their intellectual development, in turning education into what famed community organizer Saul Alinsky called a "real issue," the kind that people talk about in the beauty parlor, between halves of the hockey game, in the coffee shop, and around the kitchen table? Taxes have made it to our dens and breakfast rooms. So have the issues of abortion, euthanasia, capital punishment, civil rights, the Vietnam War, and Oliver North's innocence or guilt. How do we get the shoddy education of the average child onto that short and changeable but immensely consequential list?

Accurate outcomes data that we can understand and compare, a recurrent theme of this book, would be a big help. Knowing just how our child and his school are doing in relation to clear goals and standards is more apt to move us, at least those of us who are parents, than anything else that can be said or done.

But we need help in understanding the standards, evaluating the data, and recognizing that the problem lives in our neighborhood, too. That means we need a different message than we've been getting from our leaders and opinion shapers. We need for them to look us in the eye and say: "When I'm talking about weak educational results, Mr. and Mrs. McIntire, I'm talking about the school down the street, the one your kids attend. And when I warn of youngsters whose futures are in jeopardy, I'm referring to your George and Janet, to Carlos and Tamako, to Kareem and Maneka and Emily. You need to get a whole lot more serious, Mom and Dad, this evening and tomorrow and the next day, in your own living room and around the dining table, in the voting booth, and in the teacher conference."

These aren't easy things for politicians to say in a democracy. We seldom thank people who drench us with cold water, who remove our pacifier, or tell us to get more exercise. Once in a while, we reward politicians who promise to throw the rascals out, but how often do we reward them for giving us bad news about ourselves? We're not sure we trust politicians, anyway. Nor are we certain that how we're raising our children is any of their business. That, in any case, has been the conventional wisdom. Perhaps we are ready for it to change, too, much as we say we're ripe for radical revision of other time-worn assumptions about education.

Here is where national leadership has its most important role to play in the reform drama, where an "education president" and education secretary willing to occupy the bully pulpit with eloquence, passion, and stamina might make a difference. The White House has unrivaled access to our attention. Nobody has more influence with the national zeitgeist. But it's not only the executive branch of the government to which we should look, much less a parade of garrulous senators. Federal officials are not the only leaders we have, and certainly not the sole shapers of opinion. This is also where business moguls, entertainment figures, governors, ministers and rabbis, coaches, doctors, shopkeepers, civil rights leaders, university presidents, trade union chiefs, television personalities, sports stars, community activists, editorial writers, and radio hosts can make a difference. We already owe deep gratitude to Bill Cosby and syndicated columnist William Raspberry for keeping us focused on education and child rearing and for speaking the truth about them. Suppose they were joined by Oprah Winfrey and Phil Donahue, Johnny Carson and Arsenio Hall, fifty or a hundred professional athletes, the editors of the *Reader's Digest* and *People* magazine, the producers of Hollywood and the wizards of Madison Avenue? This would make a bigger dent in the public consciousness than a dozen State of the Union messages or a hundred solemn commission reports.

We can't compel people to value good education, or to work hard to obtain it, yet we need to do our utmost to persuade our fellow citizens that their well-being depends on it—and that the kind of education most people are receiving today should worry them as much as the discovery that their house oozes radon or their water supply contains industrial effluents. We should muster all the ingenuity we've got to convince youngsters that they need excellent educations more than they need inflatable sneakers, and that the society

admires well-developed brains at least as much as it prizes flat stom-
achs, clear complexions, and winning personalities.

That's a hard sell, even for American advertisers. We have to begin
by convincing the grown-ups that exhortation alone won't do the
trick and that they must therefore provide visible rewards for successful youngsters, rewards denominated in status, celebrity, and acclaim
as well as money and goods. Pleasant as it would be to inhabit a
society in which boys and girls learn in return for the pure joy of
exercising their minds, in the real world we need to make it worth
their while. Exercising their bodies yields obvious rewards: health,
beauty, varsity status, celebrity, perhaps success in romantic pursuits.
How can we also cement their self-interest and self-concept to their
academic performance?

Spelling bees, geography contests, and math olympiads ought to
be on television as often as basketball games and beauty pageants—
and not just during a week of back-to-school education specials in
early September. Outstanding students should lead the Fourth of
July parade, get their names in the papers, be lionized on the radio
stations, clapped on the shoulder by the mayor, and profiled in
Life magazine.

We can turn some youthful appetites to constructive ends, too.
With characteristic insight, and as shrewd a merger of both meanings
of the "good life" as I've seen, William Raspberry suggests:

> identifying the young people who "present" themselves as
> exemplars of the behavior we urge and then giving them rewards
> consonant with their good behavior. The behavior could be
> anything from perfect school attendance and good grades to
> volunteer work, good citizenship and general academic and social
> improvement; the rewards could range from status-symbol
> sneakers and spending cash to guarantees of scholarships and
> career-oriented jobs. The point is that the rewards must confer
> status within the children's own environment.[7]

The same strategies, a bit more refined, are appropriate for adults,
too. We want to elicit the very best from them, after all. Successful
teachers should address the Rotary Club, deliver guest sermons at
church, and hold visiting lectureships at the local university. They
should be given keys to the city and receive lush trips and new
cars and guest memberships as well as cash bonuses. The principals
of outstanding schools ought to be elected to the board of the United
Way, the symphony orchestra, the local electronics firm, or whatever
else confers status and prosperity in the community. They should

also receive new contracts containing juicy raises for themselves and added autonomy for their schools.

We cannot cultivate roses without occasionally feeling the thorns. Though I don't think we should set out to humiliate unsuccessful students, we should call as much attention to bad schools as to unsanitary restaurants, failing banks, shaky bridges, hospitals with staph infections, factories that emit noxious chemicals, and unsafe autos that are being recalled. We should call attention to hazardous educators, too. When public officials accept bribes, financiers break the trading rules, the mayor smokes dope, parents abuse their children, and doctors take improper advantage of their patients, we expect to read about them in the paper, watch them squirm before the cameras, and more often than not see them disciplined, prosecuted, or barred from the activities in which they betrayed their trust. Why should we not expect the same for those who engage in educational malpractice?

CARROTS AND STICKS

The third front in this war involves colleges and employers, the major institutions whose policies and expectations shape the most important of the tangible rewards and sanctions by which young people (and their parents) gauge how much and how well they need to learn.

The single most potent boost that could be given to student learning in the United States in the 1990s would be for all our colleges and universities to stand in a phalanx and inform the schools that they intend to go out of the business of remedial secondary (and primary) education and therefore that, beginning on a specific future date, none will enroll any applicant who does not possess at least "the following skills and knowledge." Perhaps they would use student scores on the new national exams described in chapter 14 as prima facie evidence of preparedness. Maybe they would employ other indicators of competency and performance. And yes, they should give plenty of advance notice, so that nobody could claim surprise or lack of opportunity to prepare. But then they would stick to their guns.

This would have an instantaneous, catalytic effect on virtually every school in the land and on at least half the students. The remainder would be reached if the nation's major public and private employers were to behave similarly: deliver themselves of a solemn and sincere pledge not to hire anyone who cannot demonstrate certain skills and knowledge.

Such announcements would reverberate through every high school in the land, and from them into the middle and primary schools. Inasmuch as entry requirements for colleges and jobs constitute the de facto exit requirements of the elementary-secondary system, these policies would penetrate deep. Every fifteen-year-old would quickly hear of them and so would the parents of every seven-year-old.

We can anticipate the arguments, principled and practical, why such a thing cannot and should not happen. Many will be cloaked in language of fairness, full employment, and equal opportunity. When stripped bare, however, most will have to do with the insatiable appetite of colleges for millions of warm bodies and the anxiety of employers that too high an entry standard would leave them strapped for personnel or vulnerable to competitors in Pakistan.

But pause a moment. When employers cannot hire adequately skilled and knowledgeable workers, either they must invest heavily in remedial education for those they do hire or, just as likely, they move the work to another state or country where they can find the work force they need. How much more efficient and economical it would be, from almost every standpoint, if the people they first sought to employ were capable of doing the work.

As for colleges, when their applicants do not meet their standards, they nearly always lower the latter. Then they spend heavily to provide their ill-prepared matriculants with the education they should have had in high school. The same students end up with less college-level work, or they take more years to get the same amount, or they fall by the wayside in frustration. And their eventual employers, uncertain whether the bachelor's degree signifies a "real" higher education, look for evidence of a graduate or professional degree. This may be good for student-hungry universities, but for the society as a whole it, too, is immensely inefficient, wasteful, and cruel.

I don't expect employers or colleges to take the risks associated with doing the right thing. The period of adjustment would be too difficult for them. They lack the gumption of Eastern European countries now putting themselves through enormous hardship during the painful transition from planned to free economies. But what about less draconian versions of the same ideas? Could colleges give tuition discounts to well-qualified students and send a bill for extra instructional services to schools that send them underprepared matriculants? We're accustomed to differential net pricing of higher education on the basis of income. We've even kept alive, though barely, a tradition of "merit" scholarships—tuition discounts by another name—for a handful of extraordinarily able students. Why not institute an across-the-board lower fee structure for all who enter with the skills and knowledge necessary for college-level work? Far from reducing opportunities, this approach would increase them. Everyone would understand that the surest way for a school (or parent) to make college affordable for youngsters would be to educate them thoroughly in advance. It's rational for the colleges, too, inasmuch as ill-prepared students need costly extra instruction.

What about denying "degree credit" for remedial courses, so that young adults with a weak secondary education may physically be attending class on campus but are not accumulating college credit until they are ready for college-level work?[8] Or how about not permitting federal or state student-aid funds to be used to pay for remedial courses? If enough people find themselves spending extra semesters and more of their own money on what amounts to a belated secondary education—one that would have been completely free if completed while in school—the word would quickly reach schools, parents, and younger siblings.

On the job front, if employers will not declare an absolute minimum education standard (and, for that matter, even if they do), they should treat their new hires differentially according to their educational preparedness. The prospect of an additional dollar an hour for the first five years for employees who were on the high-school honor roll, or who got superior scores on the national exam, or who distinguish themselves on the company's own placement test, would fire extra spark plugs in the motivational engines of a great many young people. So would word that those with strong transcripts and scores get *better* jobs and working conditions than those whose diploma is chiefly a symbol of time served. The military could start good students at a higher rank or give them preference for more attractive specialties. The civil service could start them at higher grades. Those for whom meritocratic principles are repugnant will recoil in horror from all such notions. Those who sincerely want to revitalize American education will be well advised to let their minds roam these paths.[9]

Much could be done to smooth the way. Missouri, for example, is experimenting with wallet-size high-school transcripts that young graduates can carry with them to show prospective employers.[10] School records might be placed on electronic data bases that employers and admissions offices could easily access—and young people who earn additional credentials outside of school could have them posted to their files. The ETS, in conjunction with the American Business Conference and the National Alliance of Business, is developing a job skills readiness exam that young people can take in order to generate a score meant to serve as a noncollegiate analogue to the SAT. A commission organized by former Labor Secretary Elizabeth Dole is pursuing a similar concept.[11] Several blue-ribbon panels and study groups have recently outlined other strategies for easing school-to-work and school-to-college transitions.[12]

Carrots and sticks are not the exclusive property of employers and postsecondary institutions, however. Privately funded scholarship programs for disadvantaged youngsters, such as those organized by Eugene Lang's "I Have a Dream" Foundation, hold out tangible rewards for persistence and success in school, and in most cases they provide additional counselling, mentoring, trouble-shooting, and similar help along the way. Driver's licenses have been withheld by some states from school dropouts; why should they not be withheld from those who haven't learned enough in school? Theater owners give discounts to the elderly; they could do the same for "A" students. Airlines hand free tickets to frequent flyers. Why not to class valedictorians?

There is plenty of scope for imagination, private generosity, and gutsy public policy. The general point is clear: Instead of pretending that we didn't notice, thus signaling that we don't much care, we should set out to create tangible rewards and incentives for solid academic performance, and real costs (but no surprises) for those who fail or who only slide by. Let us look to the day when "rational" self-interested decisions by our young people will be decisions to learn as much as possible—and thus to contribute to a better society whether they mean to or not.

OUTSIDE THE SCHOOLS

The huge territory that awaits the opening of the fourth and final front in our education revolution is inhabited by the individuals, agencies, organizations, and services that dominate the 91 percent of youngsters' lives spent outside school. The responsibility for educating the next generation does not belong only to teachers and principals.[13]

What happens at home is much the most consequential. With characteristic keenness, Martin Luther King, Jr., termed the family the "main educational agency of mankind."[14] Nothing else is so powerful. The family's influence goes way beyond parents communicating with teachers, checking on homework, and turning off the television to make quiet hours for study. Even more important are the values and attitudes that parents convey to their daughters and sons. Taking charge of education doesn't mean just getting last night's French assignment discussed at the kitchen table. It means sending the right signals across the dinner table, too. Boston University's Edwin J. Delattre is particularly eloquent on this matter:

> If children learn at home that classrooms are not part of the real world, schooling will seldom be able to do them much good intellectually. If they learn from their parents that the sole purpose of education is to make money, they will treat everything in their schooling not obviously connected to this end as superfluous. If at home they learn indifference to informed judgment as citizens, their courses in civics, history and political theory will be taught at a disastrous disadvantage. If they learn to look out only for the proverbial Number One, emphasis in formal education on justice and liberty will accomplish little. If they learn at home that subjects they don't like are a waste of time, no core curriculum will have a fair chance to cultivate fully their natural talents. Education can be undermined at home as surely as it can be encouraged.[15]

Immigrant parents illustrate these basic truths with rare clarity. Explaining the recurrent pattern of superior academic performance he (and many others) have found among the children of Asian American families, Stanford Professor Sanford Dornbusch says that "Most American parents are willing to accept a child's weak areas and emphasize the strengths. But for Asians, the attitude is that if you're not doing well, the answer is to study later at night, and if you still don't do well, to get up and study earlier in the morning. They believe that anyone can do well in school with the right effort."[16]

Parents make a huge difference in how much and how well their children learn. We're coming to understand this—and starting to lose patience with those who shirk their duties. On the 1990 Gallup education survey, Americans were more critical of contemporary parents than of schools. Only one respondent in four gave honor grades to "the parents of students in the local public schools for bringing up their children."[17]

Yet we've paid greater attention to strategies for reforming the schools than to those for improving parents and home lives. The education revolution needs to focus on them, too, not just to note dispassionately that the family is changing. Like training a vine, we can shape the direction of some of that change.

In chapter 14, I noted two crucial roles that parents play in school reform, and in chapter 15 I suggested a "doctrine of accountability" for parents, with consequences for those who mess up badly. Parents can be *strengthened*, too. Thoughtful books and self-help manuals are available for those seeking to improve their parenting skills or effectiveness as education partners.[18] A number of states and localities have also mounted systematic education programs for young and inexperienced parents, most often low-income mothers with pre-school children. Many of these are modeled on the Home Instruction Program for Preschool Youngsters pioneered in Israel.[19] Missouri's "Parents as Teachers" plan, already replicated in half a dozen other jurisdictions, makes available in-home training (and group sessions) for parents of babies and toddlers. "Our assumption, going into any home," says a program administrator in St. Louis, "is that here are parents who love their children, want the best for their children and want to get information that can make parenting less stressful and more fun."[20] There is also some evidence that these youngsters acquire stronger cognitive and social skills, at least in their early years.[21]

Though the voluntary nature of such efforts inevitably means that participation will be spotty, and many of these projects await rigorous evaluation, the large point to be derived from proliferating activity of this kind is that we need not accept parents as we find them.

Middle-class families can improve, too. "Parenting classes," some of them conducted by school systems, some by churches and other agencies, assist inexperienced, frustrated, or confused parents in puzzling out matters as basic as getting their children to clean their rooms or eat dinner without tantrums, do their homework, or get along better with their siblings. This doesn't have to be formal; far more parent education probably occurs over the back fence or by chatting with battle-scarred veterans than sitting in class. But the American zest for self-improvement, the same antideterministic impulse that gets people to sign up with Weight Watchers, do low-impact aerobics at the health club, or buy a book on growing better azaleas can be channeled into the systematic improvement of parenting.

Parents aren't the only custodians of the 91 percent, of course. Hundreds of other organizations own shares of it: libraries, churches, Scout troops, summer camps, health and welfare organizations, Little

League teams, community and neighborhood groups, extended families, law-enforcement agencies, and so on through a long and variegated list. Here we find still more adults who are "crazy about" kids and able to provide tangible services and benefits to them.

The fragmentation of such services can become a problem in its own right, especially for children whose parents do not run interference for them. A number of youngsters have pressing noncognitive difficulties that sprawl across the jurisdictions of a dozen or more agencies. And some problems—such as ensuring order and safety in the lives of children—cut across many institutional, policy and geographic boundaries. "Physical safety and psychological security," writes Karl Zinsmeister in a powerful essay, "are the foundations—the essential preconditions—for a child's health, education and overall development. . . . In failing to insulate our children from criminal activity, we are jeopardizing the future of millions of American youngsters."[22]

To the extent that we can get children's other needs met, they will learn more in school. Insofar as we can free schools from direct responsibility for dealing with those difficulties during their precious 9 percent, we will be more successful in teaching algebra and civics. And to the extent that we can get the most debilitating of the noncognitive woes—especially the modern plagues of pregnancy, drugs, alcohol, and violence—assigned to people who know something about how to meet those challenges, rather than dumped on principals and teachers whose forte is literature or chemistry, we are likely to fare better on all fronts.

That does not mean isolating the schools. They should be part of a coordinated effort on behalf of children. But in few cases should schools be the primary coordinators, and in none ought they be expected to solve these other problems on their own.

Fitting schools into the bigger puzzle is beneficial for education reform, too. There is considerable evidence that the communities with the brightest prospects for turning around their schools are places that have mustered broad support and widespread participation in these efforts.[23]

We return, inevitably, to individual responsibility and institutional accountability. Good things should happen to those who meet society's expectations, support its standards, fulfill its hopes. Bad things ought to befall those who don't do what they should. That's not to say that we deny the possibility of redemption or forget the thousands of successful adults walking around who were cutups or sluggards when young. One of the handsomest features of American society is its abiding faith in the capacity of individuals to mend their ways, start afresh, or make a midcourse correction.

Yet we've slipped too far toward letting people of all ages slough off responsibility for the consequences of their own actions. We're too ready to let young and old plead victim status, blame forces beyond their control, cite the evils of society and shortcomings of "the system."

Taking charge of education means, first and foremost, taking charge of ourselves and our ideas. I've made frequent mention of the value of strong societal leadership, and heaven knows we would benefit from more of that. But the president must occasionally fight other wars. Governors don't last forever, and sometimes they owe too many chits to the school establishment. Business leaders have to spend a little time running their businesses. Most of the surrogate organizations and structures we have counted on to look after education for us have grown soft, lost faith, or "gone native." We shouldn't let them off the hook, and we most certainly ought not to be taken in by them. In the final analysis, however, the education revolution is not something that somebody else is going to fight for us.

Waging this revolution is not the same as having a "program." It is not a single reform or even a package of them. Passing a law or bond issue won't do the job. It does not lend itself to glib talk-show explanations. It won't be achieved by incremental renovation undertaken by the establishment itself or by perestroika-type changes. It is more like a populist revolt or mass movement and, in order to prevail over the huge inertia of the status quo, we may need to create new organizations to exert sustained pressure on all four fronts. In other vexed domains we already have huge, powerful organizations on every side of the issue: gun owners, elderly people, tobacco growers, truck drivers, bankers, and hundreds of others. In education we already have every imaginable sort of organization looking after the interests and defending the doctrines of the system's employees and managers. Where are the education consumer groups, though, to look after the people?

We have the capacity to organize marches on the Capitol to protest tax increases, abortion laws, and countless civil rights and foreign-policy issues. Where are the marches for good education? The organized protests against "dumbth"? Where are the organizations to foment them? Where is the revolution to take the place of the perestroika that isn't working? Who will lead the revolutionaries? We have seen a thousand meetings and conferences among education's so-called stakeholders. Our children are the stakeholders who matter most, yet no group speaks for them.[24]

The American people say they are discontented with the education system they have. They endorse radical changes. By huge margins, they assign high priority to the governors' and president's six great goals. It's time for them to take charge of education—in truth it's well *past* time—so that they can obtain the education they say they want, rather than the one that today perhaps they deserve. But the American people are us. We have been part of this problem. If there's to be a solution, it will come from us.

This book has been gloomy, sometimes irascible. Contemporary education is a subject that invites anger, exasperation, even dismay. The good news is that our society remains strong in so many ways. That too many of our children are ignorant does not keep us from caring for them, or them from caring for their country. The marine in the desert may never have heard of Saudi Arabia but that has not prevented him from serving his nation in faraway places.

Our test scores are rotten, yet we have deep underlying virtues, ample good sense, great reserves of talent and energy, wealth aplenty, high ideals, and an unwavering belief in progress. We may go lazy and slack when we think all is well, but over the years we have shown ourselves able to get it together when the danger is great and the stakes are high. This is one of those times. "Human history," H. G. Wells wrote in 1920, "becomes more and more a race between education and catastrophe." Three-quarters of a century later, we may finally be grasping his meaning. To take charge of our education is not only to avert catastrophe—it is also to create a more auspicious prospect for the history that our children and grandchildren will make. Could any legacy we leave them be more valuable?

Notes

Introduction Reform Is Not Enough

1. "Japan, Weary of Barbs on Trade, Tells Americans Why They Trail," *New York Times*, 20 November 1989, pp. A1, A7.

Part I A Nation Still at Risk

1. David Maraniss and Bill Peterson, "U.S. Students Left Flat by Sweep of History," *Washington Post*, 2 December 1989, pp. A1, A23.
2. This transformation is explained more fully in Chester E. Finn, Jr., "The Biggest Reform of All," *Phi Delta Kappan* 71, no. 5 (January 1990): 345–57.

Chapter 1 Asleep at the Wheel

1. Chester E. Finn, Jr., "The Future of Education's Liberal Consensus," *Change* 12 (September 1980): 25–30.
2. Arthur Eugene Bestor, *Educational Wastelands: The Retreat from Learning in Our Public Schools* (Urbana: University of Illinois Press, 1953), p. 4.
3. Francis Keppel, *The Necessary Revolution in American Education* (New York: Harper & Row, 1966), pp. 108–9.
4. James S. Coleman, *Equality of Educational Opportunity* (Washington, D.C.: U.S. Government Printing Office, 1966). These findings pertained to public schools. Using other data bases, Coleman later produced provocative evidence that private schools are more effective than public in terms of student learning, though not because of additional resources. See James S. Coleman, Thomas Hoffer, and Sally Kilgore, *High School Achievement: Public, Catholic, and Private Schools Compared* (New York: Basic Books, 1982).
5. Chester E. Finn, Jr., "The Biggest Reform of All," *Phi Delta Kappan* 71 (April 1990): 584–92.

6. Lawrence A. Cremin, *Popular Education and Its Discontents* (New York: Harper and Row, 1989), p. 25.

7. Diane Ravitch, *The Troubled Crusade: American Education 1945–1980* (New York: Basic Books, 1983), p. 311.

8. Ibid., p. 312.

9. Cremin, p. 32.

10. Chester E. Finn, Jr., "The Future of Education's Liberal Consensus," *Change* 12 (September 1980): 26.

11. A decade later, the network is going strong, with 1,500 members, a monthly journal, and a dozen major projects, books, and other products to its credit.

12. Steve Allen, *Dumbth: And 81 Ways to Make Americans Smarter* (Buffalo, N.Y.: Prometheus Books, 1990), pp. 15–16.

13. Arthur N. Applebee, Judith A. Langer, et al., *The Writing Report Card, 1984–1988* (Princeton, N.J.: National Assessment of Educational Progress, Educational Testing Service, January 1990), p. 10.

14. John A. Dossey, Ina V. S. Mullis, et al., *The Mathematics Report Card: Are We Measuring Up?* (Princeton, N.J.: National Assessment of Educational Progress, Educational Testing Service, June 1988), p. 43.

15. Ina V. S. Mullis, Lynn B. Jenkins, et al., *The Science Report Card: Elements of Risk and Recovery* (Princeton, N.J.: National Assessment of Educational Progress, Educational Testing Service, September 1988), p. 52.

16. Diane Ravitch and Chester E. Finn, Jr., *What Do Our 17-Year-Olds Know?* (New York: Harper & Row, 1987), pp. 74–78.

17. David C. Hammack, Michael Hartoonian, et al., *The U.S. History Report Card* (Princeton, N.J.: National Assessment of Educational Progress, Educational Testing Service, April 1990), p. 65.

18. Lee Anderson, Lynn B. Jenkins, et al., *The Civics Report Card* (Princeton, N.J.: National Assessment of Educational Progress, April 1990), p. 60.

19. Deirdre Carmody, "Many Students Fail Quiz on Basic Economics," *New York Times*, 29 December 1988, p. A1, A12.

20. Gallup Organization, Inc., *Geography: An International Gallup Survey: Summary of Findings.* Study conducted for the National Geographic Society, Princeton, N.J., July 1988, p. 45.

21. U.S. Department of Education, *Digest of Education Statistics 1989* (Washington, D.C.: U.S. Government Printing Office, 1989), table 117, p. 128. This course package, termed the "new basics" by the commission, consists of four years of English, three years each of math, science, and social studies, two years of a foreign language, and half a year of computer study. Even lopping off the last two items, the proportion of 1987 graduates taking the remainder rises only to 29 percent.

22. Carol Innerst, "Schools 'Really Bad' says AFT Leader," *Washington Times*, 5 July 1990, p. A4.

23. The Carnegie Foundation for the Advancement of Teaching, *The Condition of the Professoriate: Attitudes and Trends, 1989* (Lawrenceville, N.J.: Princeton University Press, 1989), pp. 19–20.

24. Ernest L. Boyer, *Campus Life: In Search of Community*. Prepared for the Carnegie Foundation for the Advancement of Teaching (Lawrenceville, N.J.: Princeton University Press, 1990), p. 10.

25. *Digest of Education Statistics 1989*, p. 276.

26. Ansley A. Abraham, Jr., *A Report on College-Level Remedial/Developmental Programs in SREB States* (Atlanta, Ga.: Southern Regional Education Board, 1987), p. i.

27. *New Jersey College Basic Skills Placement Testing: Fall 1989* (Trenton, N.J.: New Jersey Basic Skills Council, Department of Higher Education, Fall 1989), p. 19, table 1.

28. Audrey Pendleton, "Young Adult Literacy and Schooling," (Washington, D.C.: National Center for Education Statistics, U.S. Department of Education, October 1988), p. 18.

29. Lynne V. Cheney, *50 Hours: A Core Curriculum for College Students* (Washington, D.C.: National Endowment for the Humanities, 1989), p. 11.

30. Gallup Organization, Inc., p. 61.

31. *Education and European Competence* (Brussels: ERT Study on Education and Training in Europe, European Roundtable of Industrialists, 1989).

32. Julie Amprano Lopez, "System Failure: Businesses Say Schools Are Producing Graduates Unqualified to Hold Jobs," *Wall Street Journal*, 31 March 1989, pp. R12, R14. Mollie Rorner, " 'Education Gap' Scares U.S. Chamber's Chief," *Richmond Times-Dispatch*, 20 October 1989, p. A14.

33. Edward B. Fiske, "Impending U.S. Jobs 'Disaster': Work Force Unqualified to Work," *New York Times*, 25 September 1989, p. A1, B6.

34. Seth Mydans, "For Skilled Foreigners, Lower Hurdles to US," *New York Times*, 5 November, 1990, p. A12.

35. Fiske, 25 September, 1989.

Chapter 2 Schooling in a No-Fault Culture

1. Jay Mathews, *Escalante: The Best Teacher in America* (New York: Henry Holt and Company, 1988).

2. Ellen Graham, "Bottom-Line Education: A Business-Run School in Chicago Seeks to Improve Learning Without a Big Rise in Costs," *Wall Street Journal*, 9 February 1990, pp. R24, R26–27.

3. U.S. Department of Education, *Schools That Work: Educating Disadvantaged Children.* (Washington, D.C.: U.S. Government Printing Office, 1987), p. v.

4. A number of other successful inner-city schools are profiled and analyzed in *Making Schools Work* by Robert Benjamin (New York: Continuum Publishing Co., 1980).

5. Gerald Grant, *The World We Created at Hamilton High* (Cambridge, Mass.: Harvard University Press, 1988), p. 174.

6. The heroic principal of one such school was profiled in Richard Low, "Hope in Hell's Classroom," *The New York Times Magazine,* 25 November 1990, pp. 30–32, 63–67, 74–75.

7. Lawrence A. Cremin, *The Transformation of the School* (New York: Alfred A. Knopf, 1961), p. 227.

8. Judith A. Langer et al, *Learning to Read in Our Nation's Schools* (Princeton, NJ: Educational Testing Service, 1990), p. 25.

9. Office of Educational Research and Improvement, U.S. Department of Education, *Youth Indicators 1988: Trends in the Well-Being of American Youth* (Washington, D.C.: U.S. Government Printing Office, August 1988), p. 70. Archie E. Lapointe, Nancy A. Mead, and Gary W. Phillips, *A World of Differences: An International Assessment of Mathematics and Science* (Princeton, N.J.: Educational Testing Service, January 1989), p. 55.

10. More American thirteen-year-olds spent upward of two hours a day on homework, however, than in several Canadian provinces. Lapointe et al., p. 57.

11. Langer et al., pp. 16, 25.

12. Bureau of Labor Statistics, *Handbook of Labor Statistics 1990* (Washington, DC: U.S. Government Printing Office, 1989), p. 257. Ellen Greenberger and Lawrence Steinberg, *When Teenagers Work* (New York: Basic Books, Inc., 1986), p. 17.

13. Bureau of Labor Statistics, *Employment and Earnings* 37, no. 3 (March 1990): 34.

14. Institute for Social Research, *Monitoring the Future: A Continuing Study of the Lifestyles and Values of Youth.* Ann Arbor, Mich., 1989, p. 257.

15. Bruce D. Butterfield, "Long Hours, Late Nights, Low Grades," *Boston Globe,* 24 April 1990, pp. A1, A12.

16. Ibid.

17. Annetta Miller, "Work and What It's Worth," *Newsweek* (Summer/Fall 1990 special issue): 30.

18. Deborah Fallows, "Turning Out Japanese: Back to School in Yokohama," *Washington Post,* 4 September 1990, p. D4.

19. In *The Underachieving Curriculum,* Curtis C. McKnight and colleagues suggest that at least in mathematics, time spent on the subject is

not a "sole, sufficient explanation" for international differences in achievement levels. Curtis C. McKnight, et al., *The Underachieving Curriculum: Assessing U.S. School Mathematics from An International Perspective* (Champaign, Ill.: Stipes Publishing Company, January 1987), p. 55.

20. Lester C. Thurow, "America Adrift," *Washington Post*, 11 February 1990, pp. C1-C2.

21. National Commission on Excellence in Education, *A Nation at Risk: The Imperative for Educational Reform.* (Washington, D.C.: U.S. Government Printing Office, April 1983), p. 29.

22. This is not something most employers yet seem to have realized. The Commission on the Skills of the American Workforce was deeply critical of them for not being more "concerned about growing educational skill needs," and suggested that they are lagging behind their counterparts in other lands. The Commission on the Skills of the American Workforce, *America's Choice: High Skills or Low Wages* (Rochester, N.Y.: The National Center on Education and the Economy, June 1990).

23. Stanley M. Elam and Alec M. Gallup, "The 21st Annual Gallup Poll of the Public's Attitudes Toward the Public Schools," *Phi Delta Kappan* 71, no. 1 (September 1989): 41–56.

24. Kenneth J. Cooper, "Lengthening the School Year: A 'Reform' Widely Resisted," *The Washington Post*, 9 May 1990, pp. A1, A16.

25. William Schneider, "The Trivializing of American Politics," *National Journal* 14 (7 April 1990): 872.

26. Roberto Suro, "Education Secretary Criticizes the Values of Hispanic Parents," *New York Times*, 11 April 1990, p. B8.

27. Roberto Suro, "Hispanic Criticism of Education Chief," *New York Times*, 15 April 1990, p. A13.

28. "Cavazos's Comments Touch Off Controversy at First Public Hearing on Hispanic Education," *Education Reports*, 23 April 1990, p. 2.

29. Credit is due Lauro Cavazos for sticking to his guns. Far from being cowed, he kept repeating the point in speech after speech, interview after interview. The media, predictably, kept paying greater attention to the angry reaction than to his message.

30. Dale Mezzacappa, "City's High Hispanic Dropout Rate Is Failure of System, Group Argues," *Philadelphia Inquirer*, 23 March 1990, sect. A.

31. "Murderous Consequences of Missed Lunches," *Times Educational Supplement*, 24 August 1990, p. A7.

32. Richard Cohen, "Johnny's Miserable SAT's," *Washington Post*, 4 September 1990, p. A19.

33. Meg Greenfield, "Playing the Blame Game," *Newsweek* (28 May 1990): 82.

Chapter 3 Band-Aids for Battle Wounds: Reforms of the 1980s

1. U.S. Department of Education, *Digest of Education Statistics 1989*, (Washington, D.C.: U.S. Government Printing Office, 1989), p. 156. U.S. Department of Education, "1990 Back-to-School Forecast," 23 August 1990, table 5.

2. U.S. Department of Education, *Digest of Education Statistics*, p. 10. A substantial enrollment decline set in around 1976. It had attenuated by 1980, as the first effects of the "baby-boom echo" began to be felt in the early grades, offsetting most of the continuing erosion of secondary enrollments. But a small net shrinkage persisted through 1984, when it "bottomed out." Total enrollments began to rise slowly the next year, returning by 1990 almost—but not quite—to the 1980 level.

3. Vance Grant, Office of Educational Research and Improvement, telephone conversation, 3 July 1990. Figures do not include fringe benefits.

4. U.S. Department of Education, *Digest of Education Statistics*, p. 78, and "1989 Back-to-School Forecast," p. 2.

5. Thomas H. Kean, *The Politics of Inclusion* (New York: Free Press, 1988), p. 216.

6. *Digest of Education Statistics*, p. 34.

7. Kean, p. 217.

8. John Silber, *Straight Shooting: What's Wrong With America and How to Fix It* (New York: Harper & Row, 1989), p. 19.

9. A 1984 study of teacher-training programs concluded that most of them had no serious entrance standards and only formalistic exit requirements. C. Emily Feistritzer, *The Making of a Teacher: A Report on Teacher Education and Certification* (Washington, D.C.: National Center for Education Information, 1984).

10. C. Emily Feistritzer, *Alternative Teacher Certification: A State-By-State Analysis 1990* (Washington, D.C.: National Center for Education Information, 1990). American Association of Colleges for Teacher Education (AACTE), *Teacher Education Policy in the States* (Washington, D.C.: AACTE, 1990).

11. National Governors' Association, *Time for Results: The Governors' 1991 Report on Education*. (Washington, D.C.: National Governors' Association, 1986), p. 3.

12. Sheila Heaviside and Elizabeth Farris, *Education Partnerships in Public Elementary and Secondary Schools* (Washington, D.C.: U.S. Department of Education, 1989).

13. For example, see the special section "Corporate Influence on Schools," in *Educational Leadership* 47, no. 4 (December 1989/January 1990): 68–86.

14. There are a couple of notable exceptions, such as Chicago and Chelsea, which involve radical restructuring of the schools at the behest—and with the participation—of the lay community. See chapter 4.

15. This conversion process began with *Time for Results: The Governors' 1991 Report on Education* (Washington, D.C.: National Governors' Association, 1986) and evolved in several stages, signified in successor reports of the next three years: *Results in Education 1987* (Washington, D.C.: National Governors' Association, 1987); *Results in Education 1988* (Washington, D.C.: National Governors' Association, 1988); *Results in Education 1989* (Washington, D.C.: National Governors' Association, 1989); and, especially, in the NGA's July 1990 Education Task Force report, *Educating America: State Strategies for Achieving the National Education Goals* (Washington, D.C.: National Governors' Association, 1990). See also Jane I. David et al., *State Actions to Restructure Schools: First Steps* (Washington, D.C.: National Governors' Association, 1990).

16. The "effective schools" research has been widely reported in the professional literature. For one good summary, see Stewart C. Purkey and Marshall S. Smith, "Effective Schools: A Review," *Elementary School Journal* 83 (March 1983): 427–52.

17. I led one such institute on the Vanderbilt campus in the summer of 1984, underwritten by the National Endowment for the Humanities and attended by about thirty high-school principals from around the country. It was perhaps the greatest single teaching experience I've had.

18. For years the Gallup education survey has shown strong public support for educational choice. In 1990 the notion of "allowing students and their parents to choose which public schools in this community the students attend, regardless of where they live" was favored by 62 percent of all respondents, by 65 percent of public school parents, and by 72 percent of minority-group members. Stanley M. Elam, "The 22nd Annual Gallup Poll of the Public's Attitudes Toward the Public Schools," *Phi Delta Kappan* 72, no. 1 (September 1990): 44.

19. John E. Chubb and Terry M. Moe, *Politics, Markets and America's Schools* (Washington, D.C.: The Brookings Institution, 1990).

20. For further discussion, see Chester E. Finn, Jr., "Why We Need Choice," in William Lowe Boyd & Herbert J. Walberg, eds., *Choice in Education* (Berkeley, Calif.: McCutchan Publishing Corp., 1990), pp. 3–19.

21. Center for Educational Innovation, *Education Policy Paper Number 1—Model for Choice: A Report on Manhattan's District 4* (New York: Manhattan Institute for Policy Research, June 1989).

Chapter 4 Educational Perestroika

1. National Governors' Association, "National Education Goals," February 25, 1990, p. 1.

2. Gary Putka, "Lacking Good Results, Corporations Rethink Aid to Public Schools," *Wall Street Journal,* 27 June 1989, pp. A1, A9.

3. National Alliance of Business, *Education: The Next Battleground for Corporate Survival,* 1983, p. 1.

4. Jean Merl, "Corporations Find No Easy Cure for Education Ills," *Los Angeles Times*, 28 March 1990, sect. A.

5. Putka, "Lacking Good Results."

6. "Restructure Schools to Aid All Students, Shanker Says," *Ed-Line*, 6 March 1990.

7. William A. Firestone, Susan H. Fuhrman, and Michael W. Kirst, *The Progress of Reform: An Appraisal of State Education Initiatives* (New Brunswick, N.J.: Center for Policy Research in Education, October 1989), p. v.

8. "More Good News—California Students Better Prepared for College," California State Department of Education News Release, 29 May 1990.

9. Bill Honig, " 'Comprehensive' Strategy Can Improve Schools," *Education Week*, 28 February 1990, p. A56.

10. Bill Honig, *Last Chance for Our Children: How You Can Help Save Our Schools* (Reading, Mass.: Addison-Wesley Publishing Co., 1985), pp. 4–5.

11. California Business Roundtable Education Survey, conducted by Booz, Allen & Hamilton, in press.

12. Jean Merl, "Writing Scores of State's 8th Graders Fall Back Slightly," *Los Angeles Times*, 22 February 1990, p. 4.

13. Specifically, the so-called "a–f requirements" for admission to the University of California have included four years of English, three years of math, U.S. history, a laboratory science, two years of foreign language, and elective courses. In 1990, the University Regents stiffened these: Beginning in 1994, entering students will also have to display a second year of laboratory science and a year of world history. It may be recalled that the National Commission on Excellence in Education had urged that all high-school students take at least four years of English, three years each of math, science, and social studies, two years of foreign language, and a half year of computer science.

14. James Guthrie, Michael Kirst, and Allan Odden, *Conditions of Education in California 1989* (Berkeley, Calif.: PACE, 1989), p. 100.

15. Robert Rothman, "State and Testing Officials Dispute Gloomy View of Pupil Achievement," *Education Week*, 16 May 1990, p. 1.

16. New Jersey State Department of Education, *Turning the Tide: A Progress Report on Public Education*, 1989, p. 49.

17. Florio has shelved several of his predecessor's accountability schemes and has opted instead for a massive redistribution of school funds—more than the State Supreme Court required—from rich to poor districts. Those who still believe that money buys learning will naturally have a more optimistic forecast than mine. See Peter Kerr, "Florio Shifts Policy From School Testing to More Aid to Poor," *New York Times*, 14 May 1990, sect. A.

Sometimes Republican governors behave similarly. In 1990 California Governor George Deukmejian administered a line-item veto to the $11 million appropriation to operate Bill Honig's highly regarded California Assessment Program during the 1990–91 school year. Ruth Mitchell, "Deukmejian Gets Dunce Cap for Spiking Innovative School Assessment Program," *Los Angeles Times*, 19 August 1990, pp. M5, M8.

18. South Carolina Business-Education Subcommittee, *An Evaluation of the Educational Progress from South Carolina's Education Improvement Efforts*, Columbia, S.C., Winter 1989–90, p. 7.

19. Students are permitted three tries; the state estimates that the "cumulative" pass rate for the high-school class of 1989 was about 86 percent.

20. South Carolina Department of Education, *What Is the Penny Buying for South Carolina: Assessment of the Fifth Year of the South Carolina Education Improvement Act of 1984*, Columbia, S.C., December 1989, p. 57.

21. Marcia Belcher, *Who's Prepared for College?* (Miami, Fla.: Miami-Dade Community College, Office of Institutional Research, 1990). Betsy White, "Many Teens Unprepared for College," *Atlanta Journal and Constitution*, 11 April 1990, sect. 4.

22. U.S. Department of Education, Office of Educational Research & Improvement, *Dropout Rates in the United States: 1988* (Washington, D.C.: U.S. Government Printing Office, September 1989), p. x.

23. Ibid., p. 53. Note, however, that the Hispanic dropout rate remains much higher.

24. National Assessment of Educational Progress, *The Reading Report Card 1971–88*, (Princeton, N.J.: Educational Testing Service, 1989), p. 65.

25. College Entrance Examination Board, *College-Bound Seniors: 1989 Profile of SAT and Achievement Test Takers*, New York, 1989, p. iv. It should be noted that a small portion of the "gap closing" resulted from declines in average white SAT scores between 1976 and 1989.

26. Nabeel Alsalam and Laurence T. Ogle, eds., *The Condition of Education 1990*. National Center for Education Statistics, U.S. Department of Education (Washington, D.C.: U.S. Government Printing Office, 1990).

27. Peter Brimelow, "American Perestroika?" *Forbes* (14 May 1990): 86.

28. G. Alfred Hess, Jr., Executive Director, *Chicago School Reform: What It Is and How It Came to Be* (Chicago, Ill.: Chicago Panel on Public School Policy and Finance, March 1990), p. 15.

29. Ibid.

30. Chester E. Finn, Jr., and Stephen K. Clements, "Complacency Could Blow 'Grand Opportunity,' " *Catalyst* (May 1990): 2–6; and Stephen K. Clements and Chester E. Finn, Jr., "Chicago School Reform: A First

Year Retrospective and Political Analysis, *Network News & Views* 9, no. 8 (August 1990): 32–39.

31. Karen Thomas, "Chicago Schools Are Set For Year 2 of Reform," *Chicago Tribune*, 2 September 1990, pp. B1-B2.

32. Jeffrey Mirel, "What History Can Teach Us About School Decentralization," *Network News & Views* 9, no. 8 (August 1990): 40–47.

33. Robert Rothman, "A Town and Gown Reform: Boston University Plan Brings 'Hope' to Chelsea," *Education Week*, 7 September 1988, pp. 1, 16.

34. Peter Greer, "The Boston University–Chelsea Public Schools First Annual Report" (Boston, Mass.: Boston University School of Education, 1990); and David Hill, "Chelsea at the Crossroads," *Teacher Magazine* (September 1990): 55–61. See also Mark Starr, "Not a 'Miracle' Cure," *Newsweek* (17 September 1990): 60–63.

35. Patrick Howington and Michael Jennings, "Emotional Plea Sends Reforms to Governor," *Louisville Courier-Journal*, 30 March 1990, p. A1; and Regan Walker, "Lawmakers in KY Approve Landmark School Reform Bill," *Education Week*, April 4, 1990, p. 1.

36. "Milwaukee Voucher Plan Evokes Fear of School Privatization," *Education USA*, 20 August 1990, p. 1.

37. Whereas a voucher gives a parent a claim to a fixed amount of public funds for a stated purpose—much like Food Stamps or a college student's Pell grant—a tax credit serves to reduce the taxes the parent owes, in this case to the state of Oregon. In order to gain the benefit of a tax credit (unless it is "refundable"), one must have income and tax liability.

38. Beginning in 1947, with a case known as *Everson v. Board of Education*, the Supreme Court has handed down a long series of decisions pertaining to the "establishment clause" that are distinguished neither for logic nor for soundness. To take but a single example, it's acceptable in the eyes of the Supreme Court to provide a publicly financed scholarship to an eighteen-year-old attending Georgetown University (a Jesuit institution), but it is strictly forbidden to provide such aid to his seventeen-year-old sibling attending Georgetown Prep, a Catholic secondary school a few miles away.

39. The differences in measurable cognitive achievement are not so great as one might suppose, especially when private school pupils are matched against those public school students enrolled in the "academic" or "college preparatory" curriculum. I have pointed this out to private school audiences with the suggestion that they have little basis for complacency, especially in a time of public school reform. My own view is that most private school students do not learn nearly enough either, and that few of these schools take proper advantage of their freedom to be different. Of course, vouchers or tax credits would greatly improve their competitive situation, particularly given

all the noncognitive advantages that parents also see in private schools, beginning with physical safety and character formation. See Chester E. Finn, Jr., "Are Public and Private Schools Converging," *Independent School* 48, no. 2 (Winter 1989): 45–55; James Coleman, Thomas Hoffer, and Sally Kilgore, *High School Achievement: Public, Catholic and Private Schools Compared* (New York: Basic Books, 1982); Andrew M. Greeley, *Catholic High Schools and Minority Students* (New Brunswick, N.J.: Transaction Books, 1982); John Chubb and Terry Moe, *Politics, Markets, and America's Schools* (Washington, D.C.: The Brookings Institution, 1990).

40. Three works particularly relevant here are: Myron Lieberman's *Public School Choice: Current Issues/Future Prospects* (Lancaster, PA: Technomic Publishing, 1990); Chubb and Moe's *Politics, Markets, and America's Schools;* and a study by Abigail Thernstrom, *Educational Choice in Massachusetts: A Modest Proposal* (Boston, Mass.: Pioneer Institute, 1991).

41. Albert Shanker, "The End of the Traditional Model of Schooling-and a Proposal for Using Incentives to Restructure Our Public Schools," *Phi Delta Kappan* 71, no. 5 (January 1990): 27.

42. Kenneth H. Bacon, "Use of Free-Enterprise Philosophy Is Urged for Reform of Public Schools," *Wall Street Journal,* 5 June 1990, p. A26.

43. Stanley M. Elam and Alec M. Gallup, "The 20th Annual Gallup Poll of the Public's Attitudes Toward the Public Schools," *Phi Delta Kappan* 70, no. 1 (September 1988): 33–46 and "The 21st Annual Gallup Poll of the Public's Attitudes Toward the Public Schools," *Phi Delta Kappan* 71, no. 1 (September 1989): 41–56.

44. "Schools Face a Variety of Challenges," *Dallas Morning News,* 8 April 1990, p. J8.

45. Stanley M. Elam, "The 22nd Annual Gallup Poll of the Public's Attitudes Toward the Public Schools," *Phi Delta Kappan* 72, no. 1 (September 1990): 42–43.

46. For more information on the British school reform act, see Stuart Maclure, *Education Reformed: Guide to the Education Reform Act* (Toronto: Hodder & Stoughton, 1988).

47. I attribute much to the Thatcher government in this analysis, and much tribute is due, but in fact there is evidence that the opposition Labour party also now embraces both central principles, while disagreeing on a number of important specifics. See "The Non-Politics of Education," *The Economist* (10 March 1990): 59–60.

Part II American Education Is to Education What the Soviet Economy Is to Economy

1. David Lawrence, "His Letter to the Editor Ran 221 Pages," *Miami Herald,* 24 June 1990, sect. C.

2. Uri Afanasyev, "Lost in a Fog," *The New Republic* (10 and 17 September 1990): 17.

Chapter 5 "How about a Marshall Plan for the Schools?" And Other Talk-Show Explanations of Educational Meltdown

1. For an excellent synthesis of this research, see Eric A. Hanushek, "The Impact of Differential Expenditures on School Performance," *Educational Researcher* (May 1989): 45–62.

2. Bruce S. Cooper, Robert Sarrel, and Toby Tetenbaum, "Choice, Funding, and Pupil Achievement: How Urban School Finance Affects Students—Particularly Those at Risk." Paper prepared for the American Educational Research Association Annual Meeting, Boston, Mass., 18 April 1990, p. 11. See also Dana Wechsler, "Parkinson's Law 101," *Forbes* (25 June 1990), and Bruce Cooper, "Ax Bureaucrats, Not Teachers," *New York Newsday*, 31 August 1990, p. A62.

3. C. Emily Feistritzer, *Teacher Crisis: Myth or Reality?* (Washington, D.C.: National Center for Education Information, 1986), pp. 65–66.

4. C. Emily Feistritzer, *Profile of Teachers in the U.S.* (Washington, D.C.: National Center for Education Information, 1986), p. 26, and Bureau of the Census, *Statistical Abstract of the United States, 1988* (Washington, D.C.: U.S. Government Printing Office, 1988), p. 428.

5. Mary Rollefson, U.S. Department of Education, "Teacher Turnover: Patterns of Entry to and Exit From Teaching." Paper presented to 1990 Annual Meeting of the American Educational Research Association, Boston, MA, 18 April 1990.

6. This is a topic on which controversy rages among the "experts." See, for example, Lynn Olson, "Teacher Attrition Rate Much Lower Than Assumed, New Surveys Find," *Education Week*, 25 April 1990, p. 1.

7. C. Emily Feistritzer, *Profile of Teachers in the U.S., 1990* (Washington, D.C.: National Center for Education Information, 1990), p. 48.

8. U.S. Department of Education, "1990 Back to School Forecast," Washington, D.C., 23 August 1990, table 5.

9. Tommy M. Tomlinson, "Class Size and Public Policy: Politics and Panaceas," *Educational Policy* (September 1989): 262–63.

10. Ibid., pp. 263–64.

11. Ibid., p. 268.

12. Ibid., p. 265.

13. Glen E. Robinson, "Synthesis of Research on Class Size," *Educational Leadership* (April 1990): 90. Allan Odden, "Class Size and Student Achievement: Research-Based Policy Alternatives," *Educational Evaluation and Policy Analysis* 12, no. 2 (Summer 1990): 224. Classes run

much larger in some other countries, notably including Japan and Korea, whose students continually outscore the United States. They are also larger in Catholic private schools. This is one reason the per pupil costs of those schools are low but are not, evidently, a source of acute quality problems or customer dissatisfaction.

14. "America to Spend $213 Billion on Public Schools This Year," *Ed-Line*, 23 August 1990.

15. Ruth Hubbell McKay et al., *The Impact of Head Start on Children, Families and Communities*. Final Report of the Head Start Evaluation, Synthesis and Utilization Project, Executive Summary, prepared for the Department of Health and Human Services (Washington, D.C.: U.S. Government Printing Office, June 1985), p. 1.

16. Ron Haskins, "Beyond Metaphor: The Efficacy of Early Childhood Education," *American Psychologist* (February 1989): 274–82.

17. Gary Natriello, Edward L. McDill, and Aaron M. Pallas, *Schooling Disadvantaged Children: Racing Against Catastrophe* (New York: Teachers College Press, 1990), p. 68.

18. David Elkind of Tufts University cautions against the "hurried child" syndrome. See David Elkind, *The Hurried Child* (Reading, Mass.: Addison-Wesley, 1981); and "Formal Education and Early Childhood Education: An Essential Difference," *Phi Delta Kappan* 67, no. 9 (May 1986): 631–36.

19. William B. Johnston and Arnold E. Packer, *Workforce 2000: Work and Workers for the Twenty-First Century* (Indianapolis, Ind.: Hudson Institute, 1987), p. 58, table 2.3.

20. A lot of eleventh-graders—and occasionally other students—also sit for AP tests, so the total number of exams taken by a given individual in the course of his/her entire education is apt to be greater than the number taken during the senior year. Still, the 104,000 eleventh-grade AP test takers in 1989 represented barely 3 percent of all high-school juniors.

21. Maurice Wolfthal, "Johnny Couldn't Read in 1905, Either," *New York Times*, 24 February 1990, p. L25.

22. Carl F. Kaestle, "The Public Schools and the Public Mood," *American Heritage* 41 (February 1990): 70.

23. Avis Carlson, *Small World . . . Long Gone: A Family Record of an Era* (Evanston, Ill.: Schorri Press, 1975), pp. 83–84.

24. Stephen R. Graubard, "Alarmist Critics Who Cry Beowulf," *New York Times*, 1 October 1987, p. A27.

25. Benjamin Barber, "Our Teen-agers are Learning Well What We're Teaching Them," *Reno Gazette-Journal*, 27 December 1987, p. 2C.

26. For thoughtful accounts of Japanese education, see *Japanese Education Today*, directed by Robert Leestma (Washington, D.C.: GPO, Janu-

ary 1987), and Merry White, *The Japanese Educational Challenge: A Commitment to Children* (New York: Free Press, 1987). Particularly noteworthy is William J. Bennett's "afterword" to *Japanese Education Today,* in which the then secretary of education spells out the implications for American education.

27. In his evocative book, *Small Victories,* Samuel Freedman describes the difficulties New York City school teacher Jessica Siegel encountered in providing her class with photocopies: "The handful of copying machines at Seward Park (High School) labored for the central administration, and a teacher could use them only with special permission. . . . Without regular access to this standard piece of modern office equipment, a teacher had only three choices in developing curriculum—relying on texts already in stock, typing materials on rexos, or paying for high-quality duplication out of pocket. . . . Every time Jessica taught her lesson on Equiano, for instance, she had to type two 8½-by-14-inch stencils and print seventy copies of each on the rexo machine. And it was a blessed day when the contraption could do seventy copies of passing legibility." *Small Victories* (New York: Harper and Row, 1990), p. 195.

28. Lawrence A. Cremin, *Popular Education and Its Discontents* (New York: Harper & Row, 1989), p. 124.

29. See the 1990–91 Resolutions of the National Education Association, particularly Resolutions A-2, A-12, D-3, D-19, printed in *NEA Today,* September 1990, pp. 15–24.

30. For further discussion of this issue, see Chester E. Finn, Jr., "Teacher Politics," *Commentary* 75, no. 3 (February 1983): 29–41; "A New Age Lobby Unrepentant," *The American Spectator* (October 1987): 33–34, and "Teacher Unions and School Quality: Potential Allies or Inevitable Foes?" in John H. Bunzel, ed., *Challenges to American Schools: The Case for Standards and Values* (New York: Oxford University Press, 1985).

31. Ms. Holdridge, it is worth noting, had come to teaching after five years in the private sector. "Because of recent salary gains for teachers," explained the *New York Times* reporter who sat in her class on the first day of school, "suburbs are getting a glut of well-qualified applicants. There were 1,700 for 20 jobs here" in Mineola. Michael Winerip, "It's September: Miss Who? I Bet She's Mean!" *The New York Times,* 7 September 1990, p. B1.

Chapter 6 The Lake Wobegon Effect: Ignorance Is Somebody Else's Problem

1. Archie E. Lapointe, Nancy A. Mead, and Gary W. Phillips, *A World of Differences: An International Assessment of Mathematics and Science* (Princeton, N.J.: Educational Testing Service, 1989), pp. 13, 24–25.

2. Harold W. Stevenson, "America's Math Problems," *Educational Leadership* 45, no. 2 (October 1987): 5–6.

3. Mayor's Taskforce on Children and Youth, *A Strategic Plan for Addressing the Issues of Children and Youth* (St. Paul, Minn.: Office of the Mayor, April 1990).

4. Stanley M. Elam, "The 22nd Annual Gallup Poll of the Public's Attitudes Toward the Public Schools," *Phi Delta Kappan* 72, no. 1 (September 1990): 51–52.

5. Harold W. Stevenson, "The Asian Advantage: The Case of Mathematics," *American Educator* 11 (Summer 1987): 30.

6. Louis Harris and Associates, Inc., *The Metropolitan Life Survey of the American Teacher 1989: Preparing Schools for the 1990's* (New York, 1989), tables 1–1 through 1–4.

7. Robert Ritchie and Wendy E. Abbott, et al., *Reactions to the American Public Education System*. Study prepared for the American Association of School Administrators and Allstate Insurance Company, January 1989, p. 5.

8. C. Emily Feistritzer, *Profile of School Administrators in the U.S.* (Washington, D.C.: National Center for Education Information, 1988), p. 34.

9. C. Emily Feistritzer, *Profile of School Board Presidents in the U.S.* (Washington, D.C., National Center for Education Information, 1989), p. 36.

10. Seymour Martin Lipset and William Schneider, *The Confidence Gap: Business, Labor, and Government in the Public Mind* (New York: Free Press, 1985), p. 159.

11. There are limits, of course, to our love of incumbents. Consider the political fates of, say, Richard Nixon, Jimmy Carter, and House Speaker Jim Wright. But only when there is substantial and undeniable evidence of nonfeasance or wrong-doing are we apt to bestir ourselves to make a change. And while we have plenty of such evidence about the education system in general, the point of this chapter is that, with respect to the parts of it that we can most reasonably contemplate changing—an individual school, a local school system, perhaps a set of state policies—most people have received little troubling evidence to date.

12. Lipset and Schneider, p. 159.

13. Ibid., p. 155.

14. Ibid., p. 159.

15. Stanley Elam, ed., *The Gallup/Phi Delta Kappa Polls of Attitudes Toward the Public Schools, 1969–88: A 20-Year Compilation and Educational History* (Bloomington, Ind.: Phi Delta Kappa Educational Foundation, 1989), p. 5.

16. John Jacob Cannell, *Nationally Normed Elementary Achievement Testing in America's Public Schools: How All Fifty States Are Above the*

National Average (Daniels, W. Va.: Friends for Education, 1987), pp. 1–2.

17. Daniel Koretz, "Arriving in Lake Wobegon: Are Standardized Tests Exaggerating Achievement and Distorting Instruction?" *American Educator* 12 (Summer 1988): 11.

18. Robert L. Linn, M. Elizabeth Graue, and Nancy M. Sanders, "Comparing State and District Test Results to National Norms: Interpretations of Scoring "Above the National Average." Performed pursuant to a grant for the Office of Educational Research and Improvement, U.S. Department of Education (Boulder, Colo.: Center for Research on Evaluation, Standards, and Student Testing, University of Colorado, October 1989), p. 28.

19. John Bartlett, *Familiar Quotations* (New York: Little, Brown, 1980), p. 111.

20. The preponderance of research evidence appears to show that children who are made to repeat grades are more likely to drop out of school. The summary of this research that is most commonly cited by educators, however, has also been criticized for overzealousness in the service of ideology. See Lorrie A. Shepard & Mary Lee Smith, *Flunking Grades: Research and Policies on Retention* (Philadelphia: Falmer Press, 1989), and also Mark Wilson's review of Shepard and Smith in *Educational Evaluation and Policy Analysis* 12, no. 2 (Summer 1990), pp. 228–30.

21. U.S. Department of Education, Office of Educational Research and Improvement, *A Profile of the American Eighth Grader* (Washington, D.C.: U.S. Government Printing Office, June 1990), p. iii.

22. The school system requested anonymity. Before giving me copies of the report cards, it deleted the children's—and in most cases the teachers'—names. Where a first name slipped through in the text, I've changed it in the excerpts quoted here.

23. Rita Kramer, personal correspondence to the author, February 27, 1990.

24. Mary Faber, "Low Self-Esteem Often Leads to Student Failure," *NEA Today*, February 1989, p. 6.

25. Lauro F. Cavazos, "Six Dreams and a Deadline for Improving American Education, Says Secretary Cavazos," *Roll Call* (May 1990): 1.

26. John A. Murphy, "Improving the Achievement of Minority Students," *Educational Leadership* 46 (October 1988): 41.

27. Jaime Escalante, "Hold to a Dream," *Network News & Views* 9 (February 1990): 15.

28. Harold W. Stevenson, Chuansheng Chen, and David H. Uttal, "Beliefs and Achievement: A Study of Black, White, and Hispanic Children," *Child Development* 61 (1990): 508–23.

29. Henry M. Levin, *Toward Accelerated Schools*. Prepared for the Center for Policy Research in Education of Rutgers University, The Rand Corporation, and the University of Wisconsin (Stanford, Calif.: Stanford University, June 1987), pp. 22–23.

30. Theodore R. Sizer, *Horace's Compromise: The Dilemma of the American High School* (Boston: Houghton Mifflin Company, 1984), p. 156.

31. "An Exhausting Trip for the Pilots," *Times Educational Supplement*, 25 May 1990, p. A12.

32. David Gergen, "Lake Wobegon's Schools," *U.S. News & World Report* (5 March 1990): 74.

Chapter 7 Rational Fools: What's In It for Me?

1. Mihaly Csikszentmihalyi, "Literacy and Intrinsic Motivation," *Daedalus* 119, no. 2 (Spring 1990): 123. Professor Csikszentmihalyi's name is pronounced Chick-sent-me-hi.

2. John H. Bishop, "Is the Test Score Decline Responsible for the Productivity Growth Decline?" *The American Economic Review* 79 (March 1989): 178–97.

3. Csikszentmihalyi, "Literacy and Intrinsic Motivation," p. 123.

4. There is no absolutely reliable source of data on college selectivity. "Probably fewer than fifty" is how Ernest L. Boyer, citing College Board data, estimates the number of "highly selective" institutions. Ernest L. Boyer, *College: The Undergraduate Experience in America* (New York: Harper & Row, 1987), p. 26. In preparing this book we also spoke with experts at the College Board, the U.S. Department of Education, the American Council on Education, and the National Association of College Admissions Counselors. All agreed that "about fifty" is in the right ball park.

5. These institutions endeavor in various ways to verify that an individual is adequately prepared to handle their academic work. Standards vary, of course, depending on the nature of the college. At elite institutions (where admission without a high-school diploma is uncommon) the main point of this policy is to be able to enroll the occasional audodidact, the person who was taught at home, or the brilliant but eccentric dropout.

6. Kim R. Kaye, ed., *National College Databank* (Princeton, N.J.: Peterson's Guides, 1987), pp. 198–200.

7. U.S. Department of Education, *Projections of Education Statistics to 2000* (Washington, D.C.: U.S. Department of Education, 1989), p. 54.

8. I intentionally oversimplify. Higher education enrollments are running about 13 million. Approximately 2.7 million high-school diplomas are awarded annually. I ignored "equivalency" certificates. I disregarded graduate students, who nearly always spend more than a

total of four years at it. On the other hand, I also disregarded the fact that enrollees in community colleges are usually participating in two-year (or shorter) programs of study.

9. John Bishop, "Motivating Students to Study: Expectations, Rewards, and Achievement," *NASSP Bulletin* 73, no. 520 (November 1989): 30.

10. John Bishop, Cornell University, "Incentives for Learning: Why American High School Students Compare so Poorly to their Counterparts Overseas." Prepared for the Secretary of Labor's Commission on Work Force Quality (Ithaca, N.Y.: Center for Advanced Human Resource Studies, 1989), p. 12.

11. Robin Wilson, "Colleges Scramble to Fill Openings in Freshman Classes," *Chronicle of Higher Education*, 20 June 1990, pp. A1, A34.

12. Ibid.

13. John Bishop, Cornell University, "The Productivity Consequences of What is Learned in High School." Paper presented at the Allied Social Sciences Meeting in New York, on December 28, 1988 (Ithaca, N.Y.: Center for Advanced Human Resources Studies), pp. 29–30.

14. Commission on the Skills of the American Workforce, *America's Choice: High Skills or Low Wages* (Rochester, NY: National Center on Education & the Economy, 1990), p. 45.

15. William T. Grant Foundation Commission on Work, Family and Citizenship, *The Forgotten Half* (Washington, D.C.: William T. Grant Foundation, 1988), chap. 1.

16. Quoted in Robert J. Samuelson, "The College Charade," *Washington Post*, 13 June 1990, sect. A.

17. Another possible explanation for the scant attention that employers pay to school records is that differentiating among new hires on the basis of past academic performance invites allegations of discrimination or prejudice. It is probably less costly—in both dollars and aggravation—to treat everyone uniformly, even though this erodes the incentive for young people to do well in school.

18. Louis Uchitelle, "Surplus of College Graduates Dims Job Outlook for Others," *New York Times*, June 18, 1990, p. B9.

19. *America's Choice*, p. 45.

20. Uchitelle, "Surplus of College Graduates."

21. See Roman Cujko and David Bernstein, *Who Takes Science: A Report on Student Coursework in High School Science and Mathematics* (New York: American Institute of Physics, 1989).

22. Csikszentmihalyi, "Literacy," p. 123.

23. U.S. Department of Education, "Study of 8th Graders Shows High Aspirations, Many at Risk," News Release, 6 April 1990, p. 2.

24. Catherine A. George, *Course Enrollment Practices of High School Students in California*. Prepared for Program Evaluation and Research

Division, California State Department of Education (Sacramento, CA: California State Department of Education, 1990), p. v.

25. Paul Regnier, "On 'Disparity' in the Goals and Actions of 8th Graders" (letter to the editor) *Education Week*, 16 May 1990, p. 24.

26. Judith K. Ide, JoAnn Parkerson, Geneva D. Haertel, and Herbert J. Walberg, "Peer Group Influence on Educational Outcomes: A Quantitative Synthesis," *Journal of Educational Psychology* 73, no. 4 (1981): 483.

27. Patrick Welsh, "Why Our Students Keep Snoozing through Science," *Washington Post*, 20 May 1990, p. B1.

28. Signithia Fordham and John U. Ogbu, "Black Students' School Success: Coping with the Burden of 'Acting White,'" *The Urban Review* 18, no. 3 (1986): 176–205.

29. John H. Bishop, "Why the Apathy in American High Schools?" *Educational Researcher* (January-February 1989): 9.

30. Ferdinand Protzman, "A Worry in West Germany: Indolence in East Germany," *New York Times*, 4 April 1990, p. A1.

31. Jane Kramer, "Letter from Germany," *The New Yorker* 18 (June 1990): 37.

32. Bishop, *Incentives for Learning*, pp. 14–15 and Exhibits 1 and 2.

33. Csikszentmihalyi, "Literacy," p. 124.

34. Ibid., p. 131.

35. Ibid., pp. 136–37.

Chapter 8 Journey Without a Destination

1. Quoted in Chester E. Finn, Jr., "Norms for the Nation's Schools," *Washington Post*, 16 July 1989, p. B7.

2. Diane Ravitch, *The Troubled Crusade* (New York: Basic Books, Inc., 1983), p. 48.

3. Diane Ravitch, *The Schools We Deserve: Reflections on the Educational Crises of Our Time* (New York: Basic Books, Inc., 1985), p. 147.

4. Adolphe E. Meyer, *An Educational History of the American People* (New York: McGraw-Hill Book Company, 1967), p. 395.

5. Ibid., p. 192.

6. Alan Rosenthal, ed., *Governing Education: A Reader on Politics, Power, and Public School Policy* (Garden City, N.Y.: Anchor Books, 1969), p. xiii.

7. Ibid., p. 4n.

8. Eugene Eidenberg and Roy D. Morey, *An Act of Congress: The Legislative Process and the Making of Education Policy* (New York: W. W. Norton & Co., 1969), p. 11.

9. National Commission on Excellence in Education, *A Nation at Risk: The Imperative for Educational Reform* (Washington, D.C.: U.S. Government Printing Office, 1983), p. 9.

10. Ibid., p. 24.

11. Ibid.

12. Ernest L. Boyer, *High School: A Report on Secondary Education in America* (New York: Harper & Row, 1983), p. 61.

13. Ibid., pp. 60–61.

14. Ibid., p. 61.

15. Ibid., p. 63.

16. Ibid., pp. 66–67.

17. National Governors' Association Center for Policy Research and Analysis, *Time for Results: The Governors' 1991 Report on Education* (Washington, D.C.: National Governors' Association, August 1986), p. 4.

18. Thomas H. Kean, *The Politics of Inclusion* (New York: Free Press, 1988), p. 230.

19. Illinois Revised Statutes, 1981, chap. 122, para. 27–12ff; "Standards for Accreditation of Teachers and Secondary Schools," *Mississippi State Department of Education Bulletin*, no. 17111, July 1981, p. 2; California State Board of Education, Curriculum Development and Supplemental Materials Commission, History-Social Science Framework Committee, *History, Social Science Framework for California Public Schools, Kindergarten through Grade 12* (Sacramento: California State Department of Education, 1981), pp. 38–39; Maine Revised Statues Annotated, Title 20, SS 1221, 1980. Taken from Ernest L. Boyer, *High School* (New York: Harper & Row, 1983), pp. 58–59.

20. Carnegie Forum on Education and the Economy, Task Force on Teaching as a Profession, *A Nation Prepared: Teachers for the 21st Century* (New York: Carnegie Forum on Education and the Economy, May 1986), pp. 66–68.

21. American Association for the Advancement of Science, *Science for All Americans* (Washington, D.C.: American Association for the Advancement of Science, 1989). Working Groups of the Commission on Standards for School Mathematics, *Curriculum and Evaluation Standards for School Mathematics* (Reston, Va.: National Council of Teachers of Mathematics, March 1989). The Bradley Commission on History in Schools, *Building a History Curriculum: Guidelines for Teaching History in Schools* (Washington, D.C.: Educational Excellence Network, 1988).

22. William J. Bennett, *James Madison Elementary School: A Curriculum for American Students* (Washington, D.C.: U.S. Government Printing Office, 1988), p. 7. See also William J. Bennett, *James Madison High School* (Washington, D.C.: U.S. Government Printing Office, 1987).

23. "Teacher Programs Urged to Shift Emphasis from Research to Training," *Education Week,* 25 April 1990, p. 10.

24. I had served as one of the survey advisers that year, and will take some credit for the fact that this series of questions was asked. I was as startled as anyone, however, by the public's answers.

25. National Governors' Association, *National Education Goals,* February 25, 1990, pp. 3–4.

26. Quoted in Chester E. Finn, Jr., "Kidnapping the Education Goals," *Network News & Views* 9, no. 4 (April 1990): 7.

27. Ibid.

28. National Governors' Association, *Educating America: State Strategies for Achieving the National Education Goals* (Washington, D.C.: National Governors' Association, 1990).

29. The Council of the Great City Schools is engaged in a conscientious effort to tailor the goals to the circumstances of large urban districts and will soon issue its own strategy for achieving the goals.

30. Lynn Olson and Julie A. Miller, "Congress Set to Fight Over Panel Overseeing Goals," *Education Week,* 5 September 1990, pp. 34, 39.

31. "National Curriculum May Make Teachers More Accountable," *Ed-Line,* 18 April 1990.

32. "National Standards for American Education: A Symposium," *Teachers College Record* 91 (Fall 1989): 3–30.

Chapter 9 A System Without Accountability

1. Obviously it's possible to define accountability in terms *other* than outcomes and results; building on the work of Henry Levin, Michael Kirst has laid out six approaches to accountability in education. Michael W. Kirst, *Accountability: Implications for State and Local Policymakers* (Washington, D.C.: GPO, 1990) and Henry Levin, "A Conceptual Framework for Accountability," *School Review* 82, no. 3 (May 1974): 363–91.

2. Robert Bolt, *A Man for All Seasons* (New York: Samuel French, Inc., 1960), p. 12.

3. Steven Kelman, "The Renewal of the Public Sector," *The American Prospect,* no. 2 (Summer 1990): pp. 51–57.

4. See also Chester E. Finn, Jr., "Policy, Interest Groups, and the 'Gang of 237'," *Education Week,* 10 May 1990, p. 32.

5. Cognitive learning is not, however, the only domain in which schools are doing poorly and should be held to account for doing better. Karl Zinsmeister powerfully and correctly argues, for example, that guaranteeing physical safety in the school is a precondition for any real learning, and one that today is not being met in far too many

situations. Carl Zinsmeister, "Growing Up Scared," *Atlantic Monthly* (June 1990): 49.

6. Outcomes accountability in education actually has a long history and has come in several waves, including a mid-nineteenth-century British school-incentive scheme called "payment by results." Kirst tracks the modern revival of this idea to Leon Lessinger's 1970 book, *Every Kid a Winner.* I'm more inclined to trace it to the "old fashioned horse-trading" that the National Governors' Association proposed in 1986. Leon Lessinger, *Every Kid a Winner* (Palo Alto, Calif.: Science Research Associates, 1970). National Governors' Association, *Time for Results: The Governors' 1990 Report on Education* (Washington, D.C.: National Governors' Association, 1986).

7. Quoted in Thomas H. Kean, *The Politics of Inclusion* (New York: Free Press, 1988), p. 225. William J. Bennett, *Our Children and Our Country* (New York: Simon & Schuster, 1988), p. 224.

8. Diego Ribadeneria, "State Warns Boston of a School Takeover," *Boston Globe*, 29 August 1990, p. A1.

9. Philip Hilts, "U.S. Forming a Central Data Bank to Identify Incompetent Doctors," *New York Times*, 30 August 1990, p. B8. Under this plan, hospitals, insurance companies, medical boards, and medical societies are required to report any disciplinary actions against doctors to the data base, and settlements in medical malpractice suits will also be recorded.

10. James Simpson, *Simpson's Contemporary Quotations* (Boston: Houghton Mifflin Company, 1988), p. 110.

11. John E. Chubb and Terry M. Moe, *Politics, Markets and America's Schools* (Washington, D.C.: The Brookings Institution, 1990).

12. Sam Ginn, letter to California State Senator Gary Hart, 4 June 1990.

13. Joseph Garcia, "Iowa Test Results Meaning is Debatable, Educators Say," *The Dallas Morning News*, 24 July 1990, sect. A.

14. *The Governors' 1991 Report on Education: Results in Education 1989* (Washington, D.C.: National Governors' Association, 1989), p. 80.

15. Council of Chief State School Officers, prepared by Todd Landfried, *State Education Indicators, 1989.* (Washington, D.C.: Council of Chief State School Officers, 1990), p. 67.

16. Joseph D. Creech, *Educational Benchmarks, 1990.* Prepared for the Southern Regional Education Board (Atlanta, Georgia: SREB, 1990), p. 2.

17. Susan T. Fuhrman, "Legislatures and Educational Policy." Paper presented at the Eagleton Institute of Politics Symposium on the Legislature in the Twenty-First Century, Williamsburg, Virginia, 27–29 April 1990, p. 26.

Chapter 10 The War on Testing: A Dead Messenger Brings No Bad News

1. See for example, National Commission on Testing and Public Policy, *From Gatekeeper to Gateway: Transforming Testing in America* (Chestnut Hill, Mass.: National Commission on Testing and Public Policy, 1990); D. Monty Neill and Noe J. Medina, "Standardized Testing: Harmful to Educational Health," *Phi Delta Kappan* 70, no. 9 (May 1989): 688–97; Grant Wiggins, "A True Test: Toward More Authentic and Equitable Assessment," *Phi Delta Kappan* 70, no. 9 (May 1989): 703–13; James Fallows, "What's Wrong With Testing," *Washington Monthly* (May 1989): 12–24; Lorrie Shepard, "Why We Need Better Assessments," *Educational Leadership* 46, no. 7 (April 1989): 4–9.

2. Ernest Boyer, "What to Teach, How to Teach It, and to Whom," in Samuel B. Bacharach, ed., *Education Reform: Making Sense of It All* (Boston, Mass.: Allyn and Bacon, 1990), p. 35.

3. Robert J. Braun, "Testing Takes a Beating for the Wrong Reasons," *Newark Star-Ledger*, 3 June 1990, p. A53.

4. This is a double-edged sword. One reason for the "Lake Wobegon" effect described in chapter 6 is that test directors tend to select the commercial test that *is* most closely aligned with their own curriculum, partly in order to present their students' results in the most favorable light.

5. For a good illustration of this attitude, see George F. Madaus, "The Distortion of Teaching and Testing: High Stakes Testing and Instruction," *Peabody Journal of Education* 65, no. 3 (Spring 1988): 29–46.

6. Not everyone would praise such teachers. One school of thought within the field construes education as a liberating act; to them, any foreordained objectives involving specific skills or knowledge are links in an enslaving chain. The chief intellectual heroes of this school are Ivan Illich and Paulo Freire.

7. Practicing teachers customarily play leading roles in developing the exam questions and evaluating students' answers. But only by rare coincidence is one's *own* teacher involved.

8. In the compulsory domain, all I can spot are state "minimum competency" tests, which are an extremely primitive form of external exam. New York's Regents Examinations are somewhat more sophisticated but not, strictly speaking, mandatory, since one can earn a high-school diploma in the Empire State without taking them.

9. Barbara Lerner, "Rethinking Education's Cinderella Reform," Paper presented at Annual Convention of the American Psychological Association, Boston, Mass., 11 August, 1990.

10. Amy Goldstein, "The Secret Behind the Scores: At District Heights Elementary School, Preparation is Key," *The Washington Post*, 20 May 1990, p. A1.

11. Amy Goldstein, "Finding a New Gauge of Knowledge," *The Washington Post*, 20 May 1990, p. A20.

12. Kenneth H. Bacon, "Connecticut Grades Its Schools and Holds Officials Responsible," *Wall Street Journal*, 24 April 1990, p. A1.

13. Wiggins, p. 704.

14. No good deed goes unpunished, however. The tentative decision to incorporate an essay segment into the SAT, something many educators believe is long overdue, was immediately criticized by some minority leaders and spokesmen for immigrant groups for tying children's fate even more tightly to fluency in standard written English. The College Board eventually backed off and left it optional. Larry Gordon, "Biggest Overhaul of SAT Test in 50 Years Planned," *Los Angeles Times*, 24 August 1990, p. A1.

15. Barbara Lerner, "A Consumer's Guide to a National Census of Educational Quality," *Peabody Journal of Education* 63, no. 2 (Winter 1986): 203.

16. Virginia Department of Education, *Virginia International Mathematics Assessment Project: Mathematics Counts in Virginia* (Richmond, Va.: Virginia Department of Education, 1990).

17. "Trend Away From Standardized Testing Gaining Momentum," *Education Reporter* 24 (May/June 1990), p. 1.

18. "Transforming the Test," *ASCD Update*, September 1990, p. 4. For another excellent summary of the utility—and limitations—of multiple choice tests, see Lawrence Feinberg, "Multiple Choice and Its Critics," *The College Board Review*, No. 157 (Fall 1990): 13–17, 30–31.

19. H. Dickson Corbett and Bruce L. Wilson, "Unintended and Unwelcome: The Local Impact of State Testing," (Philadelphia, Pa.: Research for Better Schools, April 1990), p. 6–7.

20. Test security also becomes somewhat less of an issue when we switch to a syllabus-and-exam system in which we encourage teachers to "teach to" what is expected on the upcoming exam. We still have to ensure that nobody has premature access to the exact questions, or postexam opportunities to alter their answers. But we would no longer condemn pretest review and coaching as a lamentable "narrowing of the curriculum."

21. An eloquent indictment of testing for bungling the sorting-out process among individuals is James Fallows's "What's Wrong With Testing," *The Washington Monthly*, May 1989, pp. 12–24.

22. National Commission on Testing and Public Policy, p. 30.

23. Another solution is to match the same teacher or teaching team with the same group of students for several years, as is commonly done in the private Waldorf Schools, in Germany's much acclaimed Holweide School, and in the one room schools now practically vanished from rural America. See Albert Shanker, "Restructuring Our

Schools," *Peabody Journal of Education* 65, no. 3 (Spring 1988): 88–100.

24. Shepard, p. 4.
25. Braun, June 3, 1990.
26. NAEP is a federal project, administered by grant or contract with private testing organizations. Though there are specific constraints on what can be done with federal NAEP funds, the contractor or grantee has some flexibility in undertaking related work for other clients.
27. Lamar Alexander and H. Thomas James, *The Nation's Report Card: Improving the Assessment of Student Learning* (Washington, D.C.: U.S. Department of Education, 1987).
28. The sums for assessment (and other statistics programs) are paltry, however, alongside the massive direct aid programs. The Alexander-James panel projected an annual federal cost of about $26 million *if* all its recommendations were taken, this in an Education Department budget now nearing $29 *billion.*
29. Commission on the Skills of the American Workplace, *America's Choice: High Skills or Low Wages* (Rochester, N.Y.: National Center for Education and the Economy, 1990), pp. 69–70.
30. Tom Morganthau, "The Future Is Now," *Newsweek* (Fall/Winter 1990 special issue): 76.

Chapter 11 Paralyzed by Design?

1. For perhaps the most erudite and insightful of these "traditional" accounts, see Michael W. Kirst, *Who Controls Our Schools?* (Stanford, Calif.: Stanford Alumni Association, 1984), especially chapters 4, 6, and 7.
2. John E. Chubb and Eric A. Hanushek, "Reforming Educational Reform," in Henry J. Aaron, ed., *Setting National Priorities: Policy for the Nineties* (Washington, D.C.: The Brookings Institution, 1990), p. 223.
3. American Federation of Teachers president Albert Shanker is an important exception to this statement. He, his Washington staff, and the heads of three or four AFT locals display an ardor for education improvement that goes beyond shrewd tactics and organizational interests. The problem is that when dozens of other AFT locals sit down at the bargaining table, they, too, are almost exclusively concerned with number one. The same is generally true of state affiliates lobbying the legislature. This leads me to view the AFT as a positive force at the national level, but still essentially a preserver of the status quo in most states and localities, which of course are where most important decisions get made.

4. Why this is so warrants a book itself. I believe the primary explanation is that a more-or-less permanent professional staff, comprising people just like those who work for the other organizations, shapes and executes most of the PTA's policy stances.

5. National School Boards Association, *Resolutions, Beliefs and Policies, Constitution and Bylaws 1990–91* (Alexandria, Va.: NSBA, 1990), p. 9.

6. Janette Turner Hospital, "India Air Pass: Waiting for Enlightenment," *New York Times*, 2 September 1990, p. E1.

7. Lynne V. Cheney, *Tyrannical Machines* (Washington, D.C.: National Endowment for the Humanities, 1990), p. 1.

8. Chubb and Hanushek, p. 223.

9. Lynn Olson, "Unexpectedly Little Interest Found in State Offers to Waive Key Rules," *Education Week*, 11 April 1990. For a diplomatically-phrased but similarly disappointing account of a sixteen district de-regulation-and-innovation initiative launched by the U.S. Department of Education in the mid-eighties, see Nancy Paulu, *Experiences in School Improvement: The Story of 16 American Districts* (Washington, D.C.: U.S. Government Printing Office, 1988).

10. Ibid.

11. Joseph Berger, "80 Schools Chosen for New York Test of Power Sharing," *New York Times*, 19 July 1990, p. A1.

12. Charisse L. Grant, "School Chief Earns an Incomplete," *Miami Herald*, 1 January 1990, sect. B.

13. Lynn Olson, "Missouri School Reform: Getting Better or 'Messing Around with a Good Thing'?," *Education Week*, 13 June 1990, p. 1.

14. Chester E. Finn, Jr., and Stephen K. Clements, "Complacency Could Blow 'Grand Opportunity,' " *Catalyst* (May 1990): 2–6.

15. Carol Innerst, "Dean Hired to Fix Schools Fears Activist Power Grab," *Washington Times*, 17 July 1990, p. A3.

16. Not every district operates its own schools, and some superintendents serve more than one district. That is why there are about two thousand more districts than superintendents nowadays.

17. Karin E. Kock, Susan B. Martin, and Annette Novallo, eds., *Encyclopedia of Associations* (Detroit, Mich.: Gale Research Inc., 1989), pp. 641–769.

18. In December 1990, for example, ten of the forum's member organizations issued a strident denunciation of vouchers and other forms of aid to students in private schools. See Forum of Education Organization Leaders, "Education Vouchers Masquerading as Choice," Washington, D.C., December 1990.

19. You can do the same, of course, in Atlanta, Austin, Albany, or St. Paul. But it's harder to spot them without the exterior nameplates. You have to walk into big office buildings and scrutinize the tenant rosters.

20. Quoted in Lamar Alexander, *Steps Along the Way* (Nashville, Tenn.: Thomas Nelson Publications, 1986), p. 120.

21. Ivan Gluckman, *Legal Memorandum.* Prepared for the National Association of Secondary School Principals with the substantial research assistance of Thomas Koerner (Reston, Va.: National Association of Secondary School Principals, March 1990).

22. Joseph Berger, "School Opens and Teacher and Students Find Rapport," *The New York Times*, 11 September 1990, p. B1.

23. Quoted in Chester E. Finn, Jr. "Teacher Politics," *Commentary* 75 (February 1983): 29.

24. Lynnell Hancock, "The Chancellor Express: A Man with a Plan and a Two-by-Four," *Village Voice*, 3 July 1990.

25. See also Chester E. Finn, Jr., "Education As Funny Business," *National Review* 41 (24 February 1989): 34–37.

26. American Association of Colleges for Teacher Education, *Teacher Education Policy in the States: A 50-State Survey of Legislative and Administrative Actions*, Washington, D.C., June 1990). Note, though, that their definition includes "emergency" as well as "alternative" certification, the former being the ancient and unfortunate practice, when a "qualified" teacher is unavailable, of hiring a warm body without respect to competency *or* credentials.

27. C. Emily Feistritzer, "Break the Teaching Monopoly," *Wall Street Journal*, 29 June 1990, p. A12.

28. C. Emily Feistritzer, *Alternative Teacher Certification: A State-by-State Analysis 1990* (Washington, D.C.: National Center for Education Information, 1990).

29. Feistritzer, "Break the Teaching Monopoly."

30. "Channel One Television Continues to Draw Fire," *Ed-Line*, 25 April 1989.

31. "Major School Groups Blast Plan for Commercial TV in Classes," *Education Week*, 8 March 1989, p. 5.

32. "Channel One Television," *Ed-Line*.

33. "California Schools Penalized for Using TV Ads in Class," *Ed-Line*, 30 May 1989.

34. Report of the Task Force on Teaching as a Profession, Carnegie Forum on Education and the Economy, *A Nation Prepared: Teaching for the 21st Century* (New York: Carnegie Forum on Education and the Economy, 1986), p. 66.

35. Student results are inadmissible on grounds that they will wrongly penalize teachers of difficult pupils and unfairly advantage those whose classes are full of honors students.

36. See also Chester E. Finn, Jr., "A Teacher's Pet That's a Porker," *Wall Street Journal*, 16 November 1988, p. 418, and testimony in Senate

Committee on Labor and Human Resources, *National Board for Professional Teaching Standards: Hearing Before the Subcommittee on Education, Arts and Humanities*, 100th Cong., 2nd sess., 1988, pp. 73–81.

37. These freedoms are especially important to private school teachers, few of whom have completed a conventional teacher education program or obtained a state license. But they will also matter to teachers who entered via "alternative routes," or whose prior teaching has been in the college classroom or industrial training center.

38. Dorothy Wright, "School Leaders Question Costs, Competition of Nationally Certified Teachers," *School Administrator* 47 (January 1990): 22–25.

39. Ann Bradley, "N.E.A. Assails Board's Policy on Prerequisites for Certification," *Education Week*, 17 January 1990, p. 1.

Chapter 12 Bad Ideas Whose Time Has Come

1. William Raspberry, " 'Reform' or Good Traditional Education?" *Washington Post*, 23 March 1990, p. A23.

2. C. Emily Feistritzer, *Profile of Teachers in the U.S.* (Washington, D.C.: National Center for Education Information, 1986), p. 60. Also see *Profile of School Administrators in the U.S.* (Washington, D.C.: National Center for Education Information, 1988), p. 18 and Carnegie Foundation for the Advancement of Teaching, *The Condition of Teaching, 1990* (Princeton, N.J.: Carnegie Foundation).

3. Audiotape of "Teaching and Learning For a Democracy" session at 1990 Education Commission of the States National Forum and Annual Meeting, Seattle, Wash., July 12, 1990.

4. Ibid.

5. Ibid.

6. Ibid.

7. Ibid.

8. Siobhan Morrissey, "A Cartoonist Can't Worry About the Good of the Country," *Washington Post*, 14 July 1985, p. B3.

9. "Babbitt: 'Shared Culture' is Vital," *Education Week*, 25 January 1989, p. 27.

10. Richard Barbieri, "The Old Order: Hirsch & Bloom," *Independent School* 47. no. 1 (Winter 1988): 72.

11. Decker F. Walker, "Back to the Future: The New Conservatism in Education," *Educational Researcher* 19, no. 3 (April 1990): 37 and Leon Botstein, "Education Reform in the Reagan Era: False Paths, Broken Promises," *Social Policy* 18, no. 4 (Spring 1988): 8.

12. Bill Honig, *Last Chance for Our Children: How You Can Help Save Our Schools*, (Reading, Mass.: Addison-Wesley Publishing Co., 1985), pp. 56–58.

13. William J. Bennett, *Our Children and Our Country: Improving America's Schools and Affirming the Common Culture* (New York: Simon & Schuster, 1988), pp. 16–17.

14. Lawrence A. Cremin, interview with Richard D. Heffner on radio program, "Open Mind," New York, 17 March 1990.

15. James Atlas, *Book Wars: What It Takes to Be Educated in America* (Knoxville, Tenn.: Whittle Direct Books, 1990), p. 89.

16. California Task Force to Promote Self-Esteem and Personal and Social Responsibility, *Toward a State of Self-Esteem* (Sacramento: California Department of Education, 1990), p. 4.

17. Quoted in Chester E. Finn, Jr., "Narcissus Goes to School," *Commentary* 89, no. 6 (June 1990): 40.

18. Taskforce on Minorities, *Equity and Excellence: A Curriculum of Inclusion* (Albany, N.Y.: New York State Department of Education, 1989), pp. iii–iv. It may be noted that the task force cited not a single example to buttress its allegations. New York's social studies curriculum had been rewritten just a few years earlier and was already so fervently multicultural that in explaining the "foundation" of the U.S. Constitution to eleventh-graders, for example, it assigned as much significance to the "Haudenosaunee political system"—the Iroquois confederation—as to "17th and 18th century Enlightenment thought." For further discussion of the task force report in particular and multiculturalism in general see Diane Ravitch, "Multiculturalism," *The American Scholar* 59, no. 3 (Summer 1990): 337–56; "Diversity and Democracy," *American Educator* 14, no. 1 (Spring 1990): 16–20, 46–48; and "A Phony Case of Classroom Bias," *New York Daily News*, 23 January 1990, p. A41.

19. Thomas Sobol, New York State Commissioner of Education, Memo to Members of State Board of Regents, January 16, 1990 (Albany, N.Y.: New York Department of Education, 1990), p. 9.

20. Mary Faber, "Low Self-Esteem Often Leads to Student Failure," *NEA Today*, February 1989, p. 6.

21. Martha C. Brown, "How Bart Became a 'Super Kid'," *Atlanta Journal and Constitution*, 8 July 1990, p. 67.

22. Barbara Lerner, "Self-Esteem and Excellence: The Choice and the Paradox," *American Educator* 9, no. 4 (Winter 1985): 10.

23. Andrew Mecca, Neil Smelser, and John Vasconcellos, eds., *The Social Importance of Self-Esteem* (Berkeley, Calif.: University of California Press, 1989), p. 15.

24. General Accounting Office, *Promising Practice: Private Programs Guaranteeing Student Aid for Higher Education* (Washington, DC: GAO, 1990).

25. Christopher Lasch, *The Culture of Narcissism* (New York: Warner Books, 1980), p. 140.

26. Jerome Bruner, *The Process of Education* (Cambridge, Mass.: Harvard University Press, 1963), p. 65.

27. The math reformers may turn out to be correct. If they happen to be wrong, however, it will be a larger disaster for the country than the "New Math" of twenty years earlier. Until we can be certain, cutting out alternative approaches is like burning the old grain stocks before knowing whether the new seed will yield a crop. That the new seed is sterile is argued by, among others, Caleb Nelson, "Bring Back the Old Math," *American Spectator* (November 1989): 36–37; "Math Education," *Philanthropy*, (July–August 1990): 8–9; and Edward G. Effros, "Perhaps Nobody Will Count," *Education Week*, 12 April 1989, p. 36.

28. "Winning 'Race' Not a Valid Goal, ASCD Told," *ASCD Update*, (May 1990): 1.

29. See, for example, Jeannie Oakes, *Keeping Track: How Schools Structure Inequality* (New Haven, Conn.: Yale University Press, 1985).

30. Daniel Gursky, "On the Wrong Track?" *Teacher Magazine* 1, no. 8 (May 1990): 50.

31. For an extended discussion of curricular tracking, see Diane Ravitch and Chester E. Finn, Jr., *What Do Our 17-Year-Olds Know?* (New York: Harper & Row, 1987), pp. 168–72.

32. Gursky, p. 50.

33. Joan Beck, "Let Bright Pupils Move Ahead, Even If It Seems Unfair," *Chicago Tribune*, 4 June 1990, p. A13.

34. Steve Allen, *Dumbth: And 81 Ways to Make Americans Smarter* (Buffalo, N.Y.: Prometheus Books, 1990), p. 118.

35. Jaime Escalante, "Hold to a Dream," *Network News & Views* 9, no. 2 (February 1990): p. 15.

36. Felicia R. Lee, " 'Model Minority' Label Taxes Asian Youth," *New York Times*, 20 March 1990, p. B1.

37. Ravitch, "Multiculturalism."

38. See Charles Krauthammer, "The Tribalization of America," *Washington Post*, 6 August 1990, p. A11.

39. Jonetta Rose Barras, "Schools' 'Afro' Plan Gets Impetus, *Washington Times*, 17 August 1990, p. B1.

40. John Stanfield, "The Ethnocentric Basis of Social Science Knowledge," in Edmund Gordon, ed., *Review of Research in Education* 12 (Washington, D.C.: American Educational Research Association, 1985), pp. 387–415, and Edmund Gordon et al., "Coping With Communicentric Bias in Knowledge Production in the Social Sciences," *Educational Researcher* 19, no. 3 (April 1990): 14–19.

41. Karen J. Winkler, "Scholar Whose Ideas of Female Psychology Stir Debate Modifies Theories, Extends Studies to Young Girls," *Chronicle of Higher Education*, 23 May 1990, pp. A6–8.

42. "Notebook," *The New Republic* (13 August 1990): 10.

43. Metropolitan Life Insurance Co., *The American Teacher 1989* (New York: Metropolitan Life), p. 71.

44. Center for Research on Elementary and Middle Schools, "Implementation and Effects of Middle Grades Practices," *CREMS Report*, March 1990, p. 5.

45. See Catherine Stimpson, "Is There a Core in This Curriculum?" *Change* 20, no. 2 (March/April 1988): 26–31.

46. Howard Gardner, *Frames of Mind: The Theory of Multiple Intelligences* (New York: Basic Books, 1983).

47. See, for example, Stanley Aronowitz and Henry Giroux, *Education Under Siege* (South Hadley, Mass.: Burgin & Garvey, 1985). Also Henry Giroux, *Ideology, Culture and the Process of Schooling* (Philadelphia: Temple University Press, 1981); Henry Giroux, *Teachers as Intellectuals: Toward a Critical Pedagogy* (Granby, Mass.: Bergin & Garvey, 1988) and Henry Giroux et al, ed., *Critical Pedagogy, the State and Cultural Struggle* (Albany, N.Y.: State University of New York Press, 1989).

48. *Harvard Educational Review* 58, no. 3 (August 1988).

49. Ibid., p. v.

50. *Harvard Educational Review* 59, no. 4 (November 1989).

51. Michael Apple, "Redefining Equality: Authoritarian Populism and the Conservative Restoration," *Teachers College Record* 90, no. 2 (Winter 1988): 167–184.

52. U.S. Department of Education, *What Works: Research About Teaching and Learning* (Washington, D.C.: U.S. Government Printing Office, 1986), p. vi.

53. Ibid., p. 13, 49.

54. Chester E. Finn, Jr., "The Future of Education's Liberal Consensus," *Change* 12, no. 6 (September 1980): 25–30.

55. Lawrence A. Uzzell, "Contradictions of Centralized Education," *Wall Street Journal*, 4 January 1985 p. A14. Also see Chester E. Finn, Jr., "Our Schizophrenic Educational System," *Wall Street Journal*, 23 October 1984, p. A28.

56. This is my main disagreement with John Chubb and Terry Moe, as well as with such veteran voucher advocates as John Coons and Stephen Sugarman. John E. Chubb and Terry M. Moe, *Politics, Markets, and America's Schools* (Washington, D.C.: The Brookings Institution, 1990). John E. Coons and Stephen D. Sugarman, *Education By Choice: The Case for Family Control* (Berkeley, Calif.: University of California Press, 1978). In describing their reform plan, Chubb and Moe, for example, say that "The state will not . . . hold the schools accountable for student achievement or other dimensions that call for assessments of the quality of school performance." In light of the unwarranted

but endemic complacency that we saw in Chapter 6, I regard this prohibition as equivalent to tying one hand behind the education reform fighter before sending him into the ring to battle the status quo.

57. As we shall see in chapter 15, there are some "melt-down" families and grossly negligent parents where sound public policy dictates removing the child from the home and placing him in a more salubrious setting. I include among those situations a parent who denied his child access to all reasonable education, much as I would not let parents deny their child badly needed medical care.

58. Myron Lieberman, *Privatization and Educational Choice* (New York: St. Martin's Press, 1989) and *Public School Choice: Current Issues, Future Prospects* (Lancaster, Pa.: Technomic Publishers, 1990).

59. See, for example, Paul Gottfried, "Academics, Therapists, and the German Connection," *Chronicles* 14, no. 9 (September 1990): 21–23. See also Thomas Fleming, "Revolution and Tradition in the Humanities," and Thomas Molnar, "The Teaching of Humanities and Other Trivia," in the same issue.

Part III Taking Charge

1. Richard J. Barnet, "Reflections," *The New Yorker*, 16 July 1990: 48.

2. Tom Kenworthy, "Campaign Bill Causes Revolt By Democrats," *Washington Post*, 2 August 1990, p. A18.

Chapter 13 A New Constitution for American Education

1. Richard Henry Lee, "Letters from a Federal Farmer," in Herbert J. Storing, ed., *The Complete Anti-Federalist* (Chicago: University of Chicago Press, 1981), p. 225.

2. Alexander Hamilton, "Federalist Paper #22," in Clinton Rossiter, ed., *The Federalist Papers* (New York: NAL Penguin, 1961), p. 151.

3. John Jay, "Federalist Paper #3," in Rossiter, p. 41.

4. For a good account by a thoughtful educator of the theory and practice of education reform beginning within the school, see Roland Barth's *Improving Schools From Within* (San Francisco, CA: Jossey-Bass, 1990).

5. James Madison, "Federalist Paper #48," in Rossiter, p. 308.

6. Theodore Sorensen, *Let the Word Go Forth: The Speeches, Statements, and Writings of John F. Kennedy* (New York: Delacorte Press, 1988), p. 12.

7. Here and elsewhere I refer to "uniform standards" or expectations for "all." That is the right goal. I understand that we must be prepared to make exceptions for severely handicapped individuals and people

whose disabilities make it impossible for them to reach high levels of cognitive performance. A decent society will accommodate such circumstances. But it is still a far better thing to have uniform standards to which we make exceptions than to have no norms at all.

8. I don't expect this to happen overnight. So long as local taxes supply significant fractions of school revenues, municipal authorities will remain involved in education decisions. He who pays the piper will continue to call the tunes. Nor are school boards and superintendents going to disappear of their own volition. But we are heading toward a fiscal arrangement in which states either provide all the money directly or equitably gather and disburse local revenues for this purpose. In terms of education policy, we are heading into an arrangement—in many places have already reached it—in which essential decisions about important matters come from the state as well. Sooner or later, the organization chart needs to catch up with the reality.

   This does not mean we will have no structures between the state capital and the individual school. With 1160 public schools in the average state today, many jurisdictions will continue to need intermediate service centers of some kind, if only to monitor school performance, provide customers with information and manage the flow of people and resources.

9. For the idea of "diversification," I am indebted to Ted Kolderie of the Center for Policy Studies in Minneapolis. See Ted Kolderie, "The States Will Have to Withdraw the Exclusive," (Minneapolis, Minn.: Center for Policy Studies, 1990).

10. It would be a fairly simple matter to empanel a blue-ribbon commission—consisting of laymen, please—to draft a core curriculum, put it out for comment, and then revise it from time to time. I believe this should be done under the aegis of the governors and president. Because it will be voluntary, its success depends on how well it embodies a reasonable consensus about what Americans think their children should learn in school, and it will have impact only to the extent that it elicits respect, enthusiasm and voluntary compliance. Hence the core, especially at the outset, may be more limited than I personally would like. Note, too, that in speaking of a "core curriculum" I do *not* mean uniform lesson plans, homework assignments, textbooks and lists of subskills to be covered in a particular sequence. I *do* mean that we should strive for agreement on, and then broadly promulgate, a general description of the knowledge and cognitive capabilities that we want our young people to possess upon completion of their formal education and entry into adulthood.

11. Patricia A. Graham, "Revolution in Pedagogy," in Metropolitan Life, ed., *Preparing Schools for the 1990s: An Essay Collection* (New York: Metropolitan Life, 1989), p. 17. See also Dean Graham's luminous 1984 essay in *Daedalus* on the importance of liberating disadvantaged

children from their circumstances by inducting them into the same curriculum as their advantaged classmates: "Schools: Cacophony About Practice, Silence about Purpose," *Daedalus* 113, no. 4 (Fall 1984): 59–74.

Chapter 14 Schools Where Learning Matters

1. I say "possible exception" because, while the architects of the Kentucky reform plan appear to have followed organizational and political principles very similar to those outlined in chapter 13, they left some crucial details—such as the desired learning outcomes—to be worked out later.

2. Arthur Bestor, *The Restoration of Learning* (New York: Alfred A. Knopf, 1955), p. 38.

3. See the following California state curriculum frameworks: *History and Social Science* (1988), *English-Language Arts* (1987), *Foreign Language* (1989), *Mathematics* (1985), *Science* (1990), *Visual and Performing Arts* (1989). In addition, the California Department of Education has published *Handbook for Planning an Effective Literature Program* (1987) and *Handbook for Planning an Effective Writing Program*. All are available from Bureau of Publications, California State Department of Education, P.O. Box 271, Sacramento, CA 95802-0271.

4. William J. Bennett, *James Madison High School* (Washington, D.C.: U.S. Government Printing Office, 1987), and *James Madison Elementary School* (Washington, D.C.: U.S. Government Printing Office, 1988).

5. The College Board's "green book," as it is known, titled *Academic Preparation for College: What Students Need to Know and Be Able to Do* (New York: College Board, 1983) is accompanied by separate volumes setting out the particulars of the six subjects deemed to be central to the academic curriculum: English, math, science, foreign language, social studies, and the arts.

6. National Governors' Association, "The National Education Goals," (Washington, D.C.: National Governors' Association, February 25, 1990), p. 4.

7. The new national core curriculum in England spans ten subjects: mathematics, English, science, history, geography, technology, music, art, physical education, and modern language. Religious education is expected in school, too. There is a powerful case to be made for each, but the totality has turned out to be a heavy load for schools and students alike and the government is having second thoughts about defining it so comprehensively.

8. If we cannot manage to agree on a core for the entire country, then states should at least undertake this for themselves. I have little doubt that their products will be similar to one another and, to the extent

that this proves true, the nascent national core curriculum will gradually emerge.

9. Stanley M. Elam, "22nd Annual Gallup Poll of the Public's Attitudes Toward the Public Schools," *Phi Delta Kappan* 72, no. 1 (September 1990): 58.

10. Aristotle, *The Politics*, translated by T. A. Sinclair (Baltimore, Md.: Penguin Books, 1974), p. 300.

11. The *content* of the NAEP tests was developed through an earlier and separate—but very similar—"consensus" process. The effort outlined here involves determining "how good is good enough" on these tests, and displaying the results accordingly.

12. Commission on the Skills of the American Workforce, *America's Choice: High Skills or Low Wages* (Rochester, N.Y.: National Center on Education and the Economy, 1990).

13. While I've suggested that children move through each band at their own speed, parents also need to be involved in these decisions, particularly in situations where an intellectually quick youngster may not be socially mature enough to hurry into a band of mostly older students.

14. Some people would make pre-primary education compulsory. Others feel this is an inappropriate role for the state—and damaging to families. I believe that institution-based education prior to the age of six should be available (and free) but must be optional, though for disadvantaged children in particular I believe we should take considerable pains to explain its benefits to parents. As will be noted below, I also favor multiple providers of education at every level, so we need not confine our pre-primary possibilities to those offered by traditional public schools.

15. Some public school systems, notably Houston and San Francisco, are already experimenting with after-school and weekend sessions for youngsters who need them. The mayor of Boston recently recommended lengthening the day and year for all students. The Maryland state board of education also came within a whisker of adding twenty days to the school year.

16. For additional reading on the theory and practice of school choice see: William L. Boyd and Herbert J. Walberg, *Choice in Education: Potential and Problems* (Berkeley, Calif.: McCutchan, 1990), pp. 3–19; John E. Chubb and Terry M. Moe, *Politics, Markets, and America's Schools* (Washington, D.C.: The Brookings Institution, 1990); John E. Coons and Stephen D. Sugarman, *Education by Choice* (Berkeley, Calif.: University of California Press, 1978); Denis P. Doyle and Chester E. Finn, Jr., "American Schools and the Future of Local Control," *The Public Interest*, no. 77 (Fall 1984): 77–95; Joe Nathan, ed., "Progress, Problems, and Prospects of State Educational Choice Plans," (Washing-

ton, D.C.: U.S. Department of Education, July 1989); Joe Nathan, ed., *Public Schools by Choice* (St. Paul, Minn.: The Institute for Learning and Teaching, 1989), pp. 13–40; Charles L. Glenn, *Choice of Schools in Six Nations* (Washington, D.C.: U.S. Government Printing Office, 1989).

17. Here is another instance of the profession being ill-served by its own leaders. The 1989 Metropolitan Life poll of public school teachers shows a majority of them saying that allowing parents and children to choose their schools would improve the quality of education, and 69 percent agreeing that competition for students would lead individual schools to improve. This is not something one would deduce from the utterances of the leaders of most professional associations.

18. I am not referring to tests originating outside the schools themselves, such as the SAT and ACT exams used for purposes of college admissions. But if my plan were followed, we would no longer be tempted to use these as institutional accountability measures.

19. I suggested earlier that the existing National Assessment program could do the trick if it were greatly elaborated. So encumbered is it with its own legislative strictures, rituals, assumptions, interest groups and critics, however, that we might get further faster by starting afresh, perhaps embedding enough old NAEP test items in the new test to permit comparisons of future and past performance for the country as a whole. A more complex but technically feasible variant, which may prove politically more palatable, is to encourage multiple authorities to develop their own forms of the "national exam," with a federally sponsored agency evaluating and approving those that are in fact equivalent in difficulty and that track the national core curriculum. A city or state, a regional compact, a university, a private testing company—any of these could become an examining board, and could add feature of its own choosing to the exam, including curricular additions important to one or another jurisdiction. England has had multiple examining bodies for many years but also has a coordinating mechanism by which equivalency is pursued among the various exams. This will be particularly attractive to states that opt not to embrace a national core curriculum but that want their young people to be able to demonstrate equivalent intellectual attainment.

20. A fringe benefit is that youngsters will be motivated to do their best. When they receive no individual score and the results don't "count," we can never be sure whether the results represent maximum effort.

21. For this to be psychometrically possible, either the American test must be administered to samples of students in other countries, or it must be equated to an international assessment program.

22. The extended school day, week, and year will also mean that most youngsters will have access to plenty of supplementary help from teachers and others on the school staff.

23. See R. Darrell Bock and Michele F. Zimowski, *Duplex Design: Giving Students a Stake in Educational Assessment* (Chicago: National Opinion Research Center, 1989).

24. These "walk-in" centers will also serve individuals whose study plan is not school based, and may be of use to adult literacy programs and other nonschool education activities that have reason to want to know how their participants are faring.

25. Those that do "opt out" should find themselves with substantial added revenues for instructional purposes if, as in Britain, they also receive their "share" of the huge sums previously absorbed by central administrative budgets. See David Brooks, "British Schools Declare Independence," *Wall Street Journal,* July 26, 1990, p. A16.

26. The counterpart rule for principals is that any first-rate executive, regardless of background or experience, who is prepared to try leading a school, should be considered a candidate for that position.

27. Among the possibilities that come into focus once we start thinking about the job in this way is that a teacher, rather than signing on as a full-time employee, instead contracts to provide certain professional services to a particular school, much as some school doctors, psychologists, and other specialists do today.

28. This assumes, of course, that the teacher and principal have the gumption to give honest grades. As we've seen, they already tend to sugar-coat the news they send home about the child's performance. Will they be more candid about parents? Mike Rutter, "Parents Are True Education Partners in This Kindergarten Class," *Executive Educator* 12, no. 9 (September 1990): 30.

29. John McCormick, "Where Are the Parents?" *Newsweek* (Fall/Winter 1990 special issue): 54–58.

30. A number of books have been written on how parents can help their children succeed in school, among them: Gene I. Maeroff, *The School-Smart Parent* (New York: Times Books, 1989); Dorothy Rich, *Megaskills: How Families Can Help Children Succeed in School* (Boston: Houghton Mifflin Company, 1988); Martha C. Brown, *Schoolwise: A Parent's Guide to Getting the Best Education for Your Children* (New York: St. Martin's Press, 1985); Sherry Ferguson and Lawrence E. Magin, *Parent Power: A Guide to Your Child's Success in School* (Florence, Ariz.: Pinal County Schools, 1986); and American Association of Publishers, *Helping Your Child Succeed in School* (Chicago: Sandra Conn Associates, 1989).

Chapter 15 All the Children: Ten Tentative Truths

1. Natriello, McDill, and Pallas estimate that "at least 40%" of American children are "educationally disadvantaged." By my lights, this is a wild exaggeration since, for example, they assume that every black or Hispanic child in America is automatically disadvantaged at birth

on the basis of ethnicity alone. I think that's fallacious and offensive. Still, we are looking at nontrivial numbers. Gary Natriello, Edward L. McDill, and Aaron M. Pallas, *Schooling Disadvantaged Children: Racing Against Catastrophe* (New York: Teachers College Press, 1990), pp. 30–31.

2. Andrea Stone, "First Wave of Crack Kids Hits Schools," *USA Today*, March 9, 1990, p. 41.

3. Julia Wrigley, "Different Care for Different Kids: Social Class and Child Care Policy," *Educational Policy* 3, no. 4 (December 1989): 421–39.

4. A well-known example is the "notch effect" in welfare programs, whereby a family whose income rises by a small amount passes an arbitrary threshold and loses some other benefit, such as Medicaid eligibility, the value of which surpasses the extra income.

5. James Coleman, *Foundations of Social Theory* (Cambridge, Mass.: Harvard University Press, 1990), pp. 300–320 and "Social Capital in the Creation of Human Capital," *American Journal of Sociology* 94 (1988): S95–S120.

6. See, among many examples, Emmy E. Werner, *Against the Odds* (Ithaca, N.Y.: Cornell University Press, in press). See also Spencer Rich, "Troubled Children Assessed: Two-Parent Family Key to Stabilization," *Washington Post*, 17 April 1990, p. A22.

7. Daniel Patrick Moynihan, "Towards a Post-Industrial Social Policy," *The Public Interest*, no. 96 (Summer 1989): 16–27.

8. Ibid., p. 27.

9. Charles Murray, *Losing Ground* (New York: Basic Books, 1984), p. 212.

10. Carl Zinsmeister, "Growing Up Scared," *Atlantic Monthly* (June 1990): 56.

11. Ibid.

12. Jan Hoffman, "Pregnant, Addicted, and Guilty?" *New York Times Magazine* (19 August 1990): 44.

13. Urie Bronfenbrenner, "Who Needs Parent Education?" *Teachers College Record* 79, no. 4 (May 1978): 773–74.

14. Alice Digilio, " 'Somebody's Got to Be There for These Kids,' " *Washington Post*, 19 February 1990, p. A1.

15. Douglas J. Besharov, "Crack and Kids," *Society* 27, no. 5 (July/August 1990): 26.

16. Thomas F. O'Boyle, "These Days, Parents of Many 'Orphans' Are Still Very Much Alive," *Wall Street Journal*, 11 January, 1990, sect. A.

17. James S. Coleman, *Parental Involvement in Education* (Washington, D.C.: U.S. Department of Education, in press).

18. Jaime Escalante and Jack Dirmann, "The Jaime Escalante Math Program," *The Journal of Negro Education* 59, no. 3 (Summer 1990): 407–23.

19. Bill Honig, *Last Chance for Our Children* (Reading, Mass.: Addison-Wesley, 1985), pp. 76–77.

20. C. Emily Feistritzer, *Profile of Teachers in the U.S.—1990* (Washington, D.C.: National Center for Education Information, 1990) and Carnegie Foundation for the Advancement of Teaching, *The Condition of Teaching 1990* (Princeton, N.J.: Carnegie Foundation, 1990).

21. Karen Tumulty, "Educator's Methods Now Getting Straight A's," *Los Angeles Times*, 19 May 1990, p. A23.

22. Robert E. Slavin, "Success for All: Policy Implications of Zero Reading Failures." Paper presented at "Raising Children for the 21st Century: A Seminar for Senior Government Executives," Williamsburg, Va., 4 May 1990; Nancy Madden, et al., "Restructuring the Urban Elementary School," *Educational Leadership* 46, no. 5 (February 1989): 14–18; and Robert E. Slavin et al., "Success for All: First Year Outcomes of a Comprehensive Plan for Reforming Urban Education," *American Educational Research Journal* 27, no. 2 (Summer 1990): 255–78.

23. "In Suburban Maryland County, Schools Can Defeat Poverty," *Education Daily*, 7 February 1990. Murphy has instituted many other important reforms in racially mixed Prince George's County since he arrived in 1984, including one of the nation's most extensive magnet school programs. Like most other "change agents" in this often-thankless profession, however, the more he has initiated, the more local critics, backbiters, naysayers, and political troublemakers he has encountered. Had he made no waves, he would undoubtedly be better liked. But the children of Prince George's County would be worse off.

24. Lisa W. Foderaro, "Teachers as Social Workers: Experiment Finds Resistance," *New York Times*, 14 April 1989, p. A1.

25. Richard Louv, "Hope in Hell's Classroom," *The New York Times Magazine*, 25 November, 1990, p. 67.

26. Escalante and Dirmann, pp. 415, 418.

27. See Natriello et al.; Herbert J. Walberg, "Studies Show How Curricular Efficiency Can Be Attained," *NAASP Bulletin* 71, no. 498 (April 1987): 15–21; Michael S. Knapp, Brenda J. Turnbull, and Patrick Shields, "New Directions for Educating the Children of Poverty," *Educational Leadership* 48, no. 1 (September 1990): 4–9; Lorin W. Anderson and Leonard O. Pellicer, "Synthesis of Research on Compensatory and Remedial Education," *Educational Leadership* 48, no. 1 (September 1990): 10–16; U.S. Department of Education, *What Works: Research About Teaching and Learning* (Washington, D.C.: U.S. Government Printing Office, 1986).

28. See for example David L. Kirp, "The Classroom According to Hunter," *Los Angeles Times Magazine* (12 August 1990): 16–18, 22–23, 37–39.

29. They bicker and snipe, too, not an uncommon occurrence among intellectuals with strong views and large egos. Robert Slavin, for exam-

ple, roundly criticizes "mastery learning," a program chiefly associated with Benjamin Bloom, even though the lay observer would spot many similarities between mastery learning and Slavin's "success for all" scheme. See Robert E. Slavin, "Mastery Learning Re-Reconsidered," *Review of Educational Research* 60, no. 2 (Summer 1990): 300–302; and James A. Kulik et al, "Is There Better Evidence on Mastery Learning? A Response to Slavin," *Review of Educational Research* 60, no. 2 (Summer 1990): 303–307.

30. Escalante and Dirmann, p. 413.
31. Stephan Thernstrom, "The Minority Majority Will Never Come," *Wall Street Journal*, 26 July 1990, p. A16.
32. The segregated school systems of the pre-1954 south obviously included "majority minority" schools, as have many inner cities for many years. Depending on how one defines "minority," we've also had mostly minority schools all over the country, from the Lower East Side in New York City to the small towns of rural Minnesota. What's especially offensive in the current discussion is the implication that only certain minorities qualify as such today.
33. Escalante and Dirmann, p. 422.

Chapter 16 A Four-Front War

1. The SAT math score was flat—at 476—for the fourth year in a row, ten points above its 1980–81 nadir but seventeen points below its 1969 peak.
2. Quoted in John Silber, *Straight Shooting: What's Wrong With America and How to Fix It* (New York: Harper & Row, 1989), p. 66.
3. Ibid., p. 67.
4. Lawrence A. Cremin, *Popular Education and Its Discontents* (New York: Harper & Row, 1989), pp. vii–x, 1–50.
5. Diane Ravitch, *The Schools We Deserve* (New York: Basic Books, 1985), p. 57.
6. Lynne K. Varner, "Cream of the Academic Crop Defies the Egghead Image," *Washington Post*, 20 September 1990, p. MD1.
7. William Raspberry, "Rescue the Children of the Underclass," *The Washington Post*, 20 August 1990, p. A13.
8. A 1986 study by the U.S. Department of Education found that only 16 percent of colleges awarded no credit for remedial coursework. Margaret Cahalan and Elizabeth Farris, *College Level Remediation* (Washington, D.C.: U.S. Department of Education, 1986), p. 5. In recent years, however, several states have imposed this policy on their public institutions.
9. For additional suggestions of tangible incentives and rewards for students who apply themselves and do well in school see John Bishop,

"A System Wherein Students Become Active Learners," in Samuel B. Bacharach, ed., *Education Reform: Making Sense of It All* (Needham Heights, Mass.: Allyn and Bacon, 1990), pp. 234–58.

10. "Missouri Aims to Connect Students' Records to Jobs," *Ed-Line*, 27 April 1990. Having seen a few false Missouri driver's licenses used as identification by under-age drinkers, I'm sensitive to forgeries. But it's better to have evidence of school attainment, and take that risk, than to request no evidence at all. It's actually refreshing to contemplate the possibility that young people might come to prize academic achievement enough to want to prove it to others. In any case, the point is not limited to Missouri.

11. It is officially called the Secretary's Commission on Achieving Necessary Skills and is chaired by former Labor Secretary William Brock.

12. Among them, Commission on the Skills of the American Workforce, *America's Choice: High Skills or Low Wages* (Rochester, N.Y.: National Center on Education and the Economy, 1990); Commission on Workforce Quality and Labor Market Efficiency, *Investing in People: A Strategy to Address America's Workforce Crisis* (Washington, D.C.: U.S. Department of Labor, 1989); U.S. Departments of Education, Labor, and Commerce, *Building A Quality Workforce* (Washington, D.C.: U.S. Department of Labor, 1988); Educational Testing Service, *From School to Work* (Princeton, N.J.: Educational Testing Service, 1990).

13. I assume that even if we succeed in obliging the average child to spend a significantly larger portion of his young life attending school or otherwise acquiring academic skills and knowledge, the out-of-school part is unlikely to fall below 85 percent.

14. Quoted in Paul Weyrich, "Conservatism for the People," *National Review* 42, no. 17 (3 September 1990): 26.

15. Edwin J. Delattre, *Education and the Public Trust* (Washington, D.C.: Ethics and Public Policy Center, 1988), pp. 196–97.

16. Daniel Goleman, "Probing School Success of Asian-Americans," *New York Times*, 11 September 1990, p. C1.

17. Stanley M. Elam, "22nd Annual Gallup Poll of the Public's Attitudes Toward the Public Schools," *Phi Delta Kappan* 72, no. 1 (September 1990): 52.

18. See note 30, chapter 14. In addition, for information about state parent-education programs, see Council of Chief State School Officers, *Family Support, Education and Involvement: A Guide for State Action* (Washington, D.C.: Council of Chief State School Officers, 1989).

19. Nina Darnton, "A Mother's Touch," *Newsweek* (Fall/Winter 1990 special issue): 60–61.

20. Thomas C. Hayes, "The Home Front," *New York Times*, 5 August 1990, p. A33.

21. Judy Pfannensteil, "New Parents as Teachers Project: A Follow-Up Investigation," (Jefferson City, Mo.: Missouri Department of Elementary and Secondary Education, 1989).

22. Carl Zinsmeister, "Growing Up Scared," *Atlantic Monthly* (June 1990): 49.

23. Paul T. Hill, Arthur E. Wise, and Leslie Shapiro, *Educational Progress: Cities Mobilize to Improve Their Schools* (Santa Monica, Calif.: Rand Corp., 1989).

24. Organizations such as the Children's Defense Fund have devoted themself to the special needs of "at risk" youngsters. They have not made the cognitive learning of the average child their focus. Indeed, their primary intersection with the field of education is at the pre-school level.

Index